The
Continuity
of
Peirce's
Thought

Other recently published titles in the series include

Rorty and Pragmatism: The Philosopher Responds to His Critics
edited by Herman J. Saatkamp, Jr.

The Relevance of Philosophy to Life
John Lachs

The Philosophy of Loyalty
new paperback edition
Josiah Royce

The Thought and Character of William James
new paperback edition
Ralph Barton Perry

Genuine Individuals and Genuine Communities: A Roycean Public Philosophy
Jacquelyn Ann K. Kegley

The Loyal Physician: Roycean Ethics and the Practice of Medicine
Griffin Trotter

Elements of Knowledge: Pragmatism, Logic, and Inquiry
Revised and Expanded Edition
Arthur Franklin Stewart

Intensity: An Essay in Whiteheadian Ontology
Judith A. Jones

The Continuity of Peirce's Thought

KELLY A. PARKER

Vanderbilt University Press
Nashville and London

Copyright © 1998 by Vanderbilt University Press
All rights reserved
First edition 1998
98 99 00 01 / 4 3 2 1

This publication is made from recycled paper
and meets the minimum requirements of
American National Standard for Information Sciences
—Permanence of Paper for Printed Library Materials. ∞

Library of Congress Cataloging-in-Publication Data

Parker, Kelly A., 1963-
    The continuity of Peirce's thought / by Kelly A. Parker. -- 1st ed.
        p.   cm. -- (The Vanderbilt library of American philosophy)
    Includes bibliographical references and index.
    ISBN 0-8265-1296-8
    1. Peirce, Charles S. (Charles Sanders), 1839-1914.   I. Title.
II. Series.
B945.P44P37 1997
191--dc21   97-21191
                                                            CIP

Manufactured in the United States of America

To Sandy and Drake

Yes, Callicles, wise men claim that partnership and friendship, orderliness, self-control, and justice hold together heaven and earth, and gods and men, and that is why they call this universe a world order, *my friend, and not an undisciplined world-disorder. I believe that you don't pay attention to these facts, even though you're a wise man in these matters. . . . That's because you neglect geometry.*

Plato, Gorgias

For me, on the contrary, on the first assault of the enemy, when pressed for the explanation of any fact, I lock myself up in my castle of impregnable logic and squirt melted continuity out upon the heads of my beseigers below. . . . This is a damned easy way of explaining things, my critics will say (I mean the really noumenal *ones will say this) but how is this to be verified by observation? Good! I applaud this objection; and if I do not answer it satisfactorily set me down as a failure if not a humbug.*

Peirce, The Charles S. Peirce Papers, 949

Contents

Figures

Tables

Acknowledgments

This book is the result of research that began at Vanderbilt University under the guidance of John Lachs. I offer my thanks to him for his generous assistance, both during that time and since. I also wish to thank John J. McDermott, whose remarkable teaching at Texas A&M University sparked my interest in American philosophy as an undergraduate.

Numerous others have helped with preparation of this book. The idea for such a work came to me virtually on the site of Peirce's childhood home, during the Charles S. Peirce Sesquicentennial International Congress held at Harvard in 1989. The Graduate School of Vanderbilt University generously enabled me to attend this conference, and later to carry out necessary research in Cambridge and Indianapolis. Grand Valley State University and my colleagues in the Philosophy Department have supported more recent work on the project, both materially and otherwise.

The staffs of the Houghton Library (Harvard University) and of the Peirce Edition Project (Indiana University-Purdue University at Indianapolis) have been extremely helpful in identifying and obtaining materials from the Peirce Papers. The Peirce Papers are quoted with permission of the Department of Philosophy, Harvard University. The editors of the *Transactions of the Charles S. Peirce Society* granted permission to use material in chapter 8 from "Peirce's Semeiotic and Ontology" (vol. 30, Winter, 1994).

Two members of the Peirce Edition Project deserve special mention. André De Tienne has gone beyond the call of duty to settle several questions about the Peirce Papers. In his extensive critical comments on a draft of this manuscript, and in numerous conversations, Nathan Houser has provided a much needed and welcomed element of secondness for my efforts to interpret Peirce's work. It is only after careful deliberation, and with some unresolved second thoughts, that I have decided to differ from him on a few points.

I would also like to thank the wider community of Peirce scholars, without whom one works in isolation. The annual meetings of the Charles S. Peirce Society and of the Society for the Advancement of American Philosophy are invaluable events for scholars working in American philosophy. The participants in the Peirce-L electronic discussion list and the Peirce Telecommunity project have also been the source of stimulating ideas, conversation, and criticism.

As Peirce insisted, the task of interpretation is not only communal, but open-ended. As I submit this study to the public, I am acutely aware of the pragmatic significance of these principles of inquiry. First, I regret that I cannot possibly name or properly thank everyone who directly or indirectly helped with the project. Here I only hope that no one will take offense at being omitted. Second, I know that this book is the product of a finite inquiry and is neither complete nor completely correct. On this point, I only hope that my interpretation of Peirce's philosophy is on the right track throughout. Another Peircean principle: time will tell if it is not. In any case all omissions or errors that may come to light are my own.

Kelly A. Parker
Grand Rapids, Michigan

Abbreviations

CP   *Collected Papers of Charles Sanders Peirce*, ed. C. Hartshorne, P. Weiss, and A. Burks. References indicate volume and paragraph number: (CP 1.1).

NEM   *The New Elements of Mathematics,* ed. C. Eisele. References indicate volume and page number: (NEM 1:1).

MS   The Charles S. Peirce Papers, Houghton Library, Harvard University. References indicate item number assigned in R. S. Robin, *Annotated Catalogue of the Papers of Charles S. Peirce* and R. S. Robin, "The Peirce Papers: A Supplementary Catalogue." Page number and date are also included where appropriate, for instance, (MS 1, p. 1, ca.1903).

SS   *Semiotic and Significs: The Correspondence between Charles S. Peirce and Victoria Lady Welby,* ed. C. Hardwick. References indicate page number: (SS 1).

W   *Writings of Charles S. Peirce: A Chronological Edition*, ed. E. Moore, C. J. W. Kloesel, et al. References indicate volume and page number: (W 1:1).

A number of sources cited in this study are published in the journal *Transactions of the Charles S. Peirce Society.* This title is abbreviated *Transactions* in all references.

Introduction

In a chapter on philosophical method, Immanuel Kant defined *architectonic* as "the art of constructing systems."[1] Though this chapter of Kant's is easily overlooked, appearing as it does at the end of his monumental first *Critique*, it had a definitive effect on the thought of Charles Sanders Santiago Peirce (1839–1914).[2] Peirce read Kant as a young man, and embraced the ideal of architectonic philosophy as his own. He made it his life's work to construct a scientifically sophisticated and logically rigorous philosophical system—not merely a system to rival those of Plato, Aristotle, Kant, and Hegel, but one intended to correct and supplant such preceding systems as theirs. The present study is an attempt to reconstruct and explore the results of Peirce's philosophical artistry.

Except for a brief but very fruitful period as part-time lecturer in logic at The Johns Hopkins University (1879–1884), Peirce pursued his philosophical work in relative isolation and obscurity. After retiring to Arisbe (his home near Milford, Pennsylvania) in 1887, Peirce set about working on the details of the various parts of the system, in anticipation of the day when he would be able to synthesize these parts into an organic whole. Though he published numerous essays and gave an overview of his philosophy in several series of lectures, circumstances kept Peirce from writing the definitive series of books that would have been required to express his philosophy in all its richness. The upshot is that the grand philosophical system Peirce envisioned lies before us only in fragmented form. His literary remains consist of over eight hundred published works and some eighty thousand manuscript sheets.[3]

One who wishes to know Kant's thought may turn to the three *Critiques* and a few other writings. One who wishes to know Hegel's thought, likewise, can find it presented in a few definitive works. In both these cases there is the additional advantage of being able to consult several generations of scholarship concerning points of difficulty or obscurity in the originals. Although the student of Plato's thought must work with a limited portion of his original writings, and the student of Aristotle must make do with fragmentary and second-hand presentations of his philosophy, here, too, there is help. One may take advantage of centuries of editing, commentary, and interpretation to gain initial access to these thinkers' systems.

The student of Peirce has neither the advantage of a definitive expression of the system from the philosopher's own hand nor the assistance of a body of scholarship that has developed over a number of generations. Peirce's philosophy became available to the general public only with the publication of six volumes of the *Collected Papers* in 1931–1935; two additional volumes appeared in 1958. Much important material was left out of this collection, and many works were broken up and scattered across several volumes. The system that was left in fragments by its creator was thus further fragmented by his first editors, and there is still no consensus among Peirce scholars about which works provide the most accurate and definitive statement of his mature thought. Getting acquainted with Peirce is, therefore, difficult. One who wants to discover Peirce must stumble in by whatever doorway happens to stand open, and then sift through a vast quantity of material in hopes of separating the gems of his thought from its mere germs.

The scholarly community is still in the early stages of understanding Peirce's thought. Much good work has been done on isolated areas, but there is relatively little consideration of the system as a whole. Early commentators often saw Peirce as an interesting failure, and one even concluded that he must have suffered from a kind of philosophical split personality.[4] Serious students of Peirce today agree, however, that to a great extent the systematic unity Peirce sought can be found in his work. There are inconsistencies, to be sure, but these are not the deep, systematic contradictions suspected by some. Most of Peirce's alleged contradictions arise when writings from different periods in the evolution of his thought are juxtaposed, or when the context-dependent qualifications to particular assertions are ignored. Some excellent studies have appeared that provide a perspective on the whole system, but subsequent developments—especially the understanding and appreciation of Peirce's semeiotic that has emerged over the last two decades— have exposed gaps in the earlier studies.[5]

With the publication of new collections of Peirce's writings (such as the microfilm edition of the Harvard Peirce manuscripts, *New Elements of Mathematics,* and the first volumes of the chronological edition of the *Writings of Charles S. Peirce*), and with the establishment of the Peirce Edition Project in Indianapolis, Indiana, and of the Institute for Studies in Pragmaticism in Lubbock, Texas, the resources are now available for specialists and other interested persons to get a broad and accurate picture of Peirce's work. This study is an attempt to present just such an overview of his philosophy, and, in the course of doing so, to propose that a particular concept of continuity be recognized as the main unifying thread in Peirce's system.

The Quest for a System

In his draft introduction for a proposed work entitled "A Guess at the Riddle," written in 1887–1888, Peirce says:

> The undertaking which this volume inaugurates is to make a philosophy like that of Aristotle, that is to say, to outline a theory so comprehensive that, for a long time to come, the entire

work of human reason, in philosophy of every school and kind, in mathematics, in psychology, in physical science, in history, in sociology, and in whatever other department there may be, shall appear as the filling up of its details. The first step toward this is to find simple concepts applicable to every subject. (CP 1.1)

Like many nineteenth-century thinkers, Peirce was troubled by the influence of positivism. In his view, the positivistic effort to avoid empty metaphysical speculation embodied both good and bad advice. On the one hand, we should reject the kind of empty and dogmatic speculation that all too often passes for metaphysics. But on the other hand, to think or act at all betrays some metaphysical assumptions, and anyone who attempts to avoid metaphysical speculation altogether is merely condemned to embracing a superficial and uncritical metaphysics. In Peirce's view, the modern age reached a low point in metaphysics when it embraced the mechanistic conception of the world. Being well-versed in medieval logic, he saw this mechanistic philosophy, or physicalism, as a revival of nominalism. He hoped that his projected system of ideas would lead scientific and popular thought away from this tendency, which he considered to be both deeply entrenched and debilitating in all areas of thought.

Peirce held that metaphysics is the basis for the special sciences. The last of his "simple concepts applicable to every subject," the category of Thirdness, recognizes an idealistic element in the very structure of things, a purposive element that cannot be reduced to mere mechanism. As we shall see, however, Thirdness presupposes the two other concepts of Firstness and Secondness. Secondness correlates with mechanical action and reaction: Peirce is not abandoning physicalism, but is rather looking beyond it. Firstness recognizes a degree of genuine spontaneity in things. This element sets Peirce's metaphysics against all forms of determinism, including both the mechanistic and theological varieties. If his philosophy were adopted, then, we would recognize not only matter but also mind and pure possibility as irreducible constituents of reality.

In his mature thought, Thirdness is identified with a novel concept of continuity which arose from his work in set theory. *Synectics* is a word Peirce uses to name the mathematical study of continua.[6] Although there is an obvious verbal affinity between *synectics* and *synechism,* the name he gives to his metaphysics, and while mathematics is indeed the original source of Peirce's metaphysical concepts, the path linking the two disciplines is rather long. The present study is especially concerned to show how the principle of continuity functions in phenomenology and semeiotic, the two most novel and important of Peirce's "philosophical sciences" mediating between mathematics and metaphysics.

The passage from one of the philosophical sciences to the next in Peirce's system is always risky. It involves taking the results of a previous science as explanatory hypotheses in the next. The hard-won conclusions of any science are always subjected to criticism, refinement, and revision as they are put to use in another. The movement of thought through the system cannot, then, be simply linear. The process of active inquiry involves attaining ever higher grades of clearness about the meaning of our basic concepts, and each new discovery resonates throughout the whole system.[7]

Yet Peirce was confident that with a good plan and a well-chosen set of key concepts we could find safe passage among the sciences, and the whole edifice of philosophy could gradually be furnished in detail. The hypothesis that guides the following interpretation of Peirce's philosophy is suggested by him in a late manuscript:

> In consequence of being fed upon mathematical conceptions from my tenderest years, it is no wonder that I was led at the very outset to think that one great desideratum in all theorizing was to make fuller use of the principle of continuity. My attention was from the beginning drawn to the need of looking at matters in the light of that conception: but I did not, at first, suppose that it was, as I gradually came to find it, the master-key of philosophy. (MS 949, p.1)

As Peirce worked with his system over the course of almost five decades, his basic concepts and his view of their significance for the various sciences continually evolved. The present study is based on the idea, suggested in the preceding passage, that Peirce's mature philosophy is best understood as an extended exploration and application of his novel concept of the mathematical continuum.

Plan of the Work

Peirce wrote the following in a letter to Victoria Lady Welby on 11 October 1909, less than five years before his death:

> The truth is that there are great obstacles to my writing. In the first place I am 70 years old and can perceive that my powers of mind are beginning to fail, and I feel that it is my most sacred of all duties to write that book which shall show that many powerful minds have held views apparently the most antipodal upon the subjects of highest concern to all men, merely because they have all alike missed that point of view

which would have reconciled them all in one truth. . . . I feel
that I am in possession of truth which must be put into writing
before my powers quite fail. (SS 133–34)

The "truth" to which he here refers, I am certain, was that of synechism, the
philosophy of continuity. Peirce's powers did fail before he gave his truth an
organic, systematic expression, and his mature philosophy never made its
way intact out of the universe of ideas and onto paper.

I once heard it said that Peirce wanted only two things in life. One was
to have his name pronounced correctly (it is pronounced *pûrs*); the other
was to teach logic at Harvard University. The former is probably true; the
latter is certainly true, to judge from his letter to William James dated 30
May 1897.[8] One suspects that Peirce's excitement at the prospect of a regular
university position was less that he would be teaching logic to young men,
as he claims in the letter, than that he would be in a position to write the
books which would definitively express his philosophy. The letters he wrote
to Lady Welby reveal that in the last years of his life Peirce still aimed to
write something like the whole series of memoirs he proposed in his 1902
application for aid from the Carnegie Institution.[9] He was also beginning to
see the wisdom in writing a short introduction to the system, a roadmap of
his thought that could serve as an introduction to the longer work if that
work were completed, or as a guide through his manuscripts if it were not.
Unfortunately, it appears that not even this introduction was ever written.

The Continuity of Peirce's Thought is intended to provide an in-depth
introduction to Peirce's philosophy. The book as a whole provides a convenient overview of his philosophical system, situating Peirce's philosophy
within the history of ideas and mapping interconnections among the diverse
areas of his work. Individual chapters introduce his major contributions in
such areas as mathematics, logic, phenomenology, value theory, semeiotic,
philosophy of mind, philosophy of science, metaphysics, and cosmology.
The reconstruction and interpretation of Peirce's philosophy presented here
is deliberately sympathetic. Peirce himself was the first to insist on close
criticism of his work, but he also insisted that all meaningful criticism
requires faithful comprehension of the work in question. Those who are
interested in any aspect of Peirce's work can only benefit by seeing the
whole system through his eyes, as a developing continuum of profound
thought.

Part One of this study, "Peirce's Architectonic," sketches the background
to Peirce's mature philosophy and presents an outline of his classification of
the sciences. Chapter 1 discusses Peirce's debt to Kant both for the idea of
architectonic philosophy and for the problems he saw in Kant's philosophy
that prompted him to try to do better. Some of the particular mathematical
and logical resources that Peirce brought to the task of constructing his

philosophy are also introduced. Chapter 2 presents the blueprint for Peirce's system: his conception of *science* and his classification of the sciences.

Part Two, "Mathematical Hypotheses," explores the mathematical basis of the system. Chapter 3 presents the theory of the three "cenopythagorean categories" in their formal aspect, as modes of relation. The notion of three-valued logic that the categories suggested to Peirce is also discussed. Chapter 4 explores Peirce's conceptions of continuity and of the infinitesimal, showing their origins in his revision of Georg Cantor's theory of transfinite sets.

Part Three, "The Categories in Experience," examines the role of the continuity principle in the sciences that bridge the gap between mathematics and metaphysics in Peirce's system. Chapter 5 presents Peirce's phenomenological investigation of the three categories as they are manifest in experience. Chapter 6 presents Peirce's theories of esthetics (where he develops the crucial notion of the summum bonum) and ethics, and also presents the basic elements of his semeiotic, the philosophy of representation. Chapter 7 presents Peirce's semeiotic theory of mind, and discusses the aspects of semeiotic that constitute "normative logic": the evaluation of arguments and the description of the nature and proper procedures of scientific investigation.

Part Four, "The Categories of Being" (chapter 8) sketches the main features of Peirce's metaphysics and cosmology, and specifically addresses the problem of the ontological status of extra-semeiotic existence in Peirce's metaphysics. The chapter and the study conclude with a consideration of Peirce's requirement that metaphysical hypotheses, and especially the hypothesis of synechism based on the principle of continuity, be subject to conditions of verification.

Part One

Peirce's Architectonic

CHAPTER 1

Architectonic Philosophy and the Principle of Continuity

Kant's Influence

Peirce described his thought as "the attempt of a physicist to make such conjecture as to the constitution of the universe as the methods of science may permit, with the aid of all that has been done by previous philosophers" (CP 1.7). Kant is clearly foremost among these previous philosophers. Peirce says that as a young man he "had come upon the threshing-floor of philosophy through the doorway of Kant" (CP 5.12), and had "devoted two hours a day to the study of Kant's *Critic of the Pure Reason* for more than three years, until I almost knew the whole book by heart, and had critically examined every section of it" (CP 1.4). Above all, Peirce shared Kant's view that there are a small number of fundamental categories of thought. These are a priori concepts applicable to, and necessary for, all possible objects of knowledge. Where Kant had found twelve categories, however, Peirce found three, which he came to call Firstness, Secondness and Thirdness.[1] Whatever their number, the definition of such concepts is the first step in erecting an architectonic philosophy.

ARCHITECTONIC AND LOGIC

In a draft for his 1867 paper "On a New List of Categories," Peirce writes:

> The categories of Kant are derived from the logical analysis of judgments, and those of Aristotle (framed before the separation of syntax and logic) are derived from a half-logical half-grammatical analysis of propositions. Now upon the table [of] categories philosophy is erected, . . . To form a table of the categories is, therefore, the great end of logic.[2]

It is the belief that the categories are "objectifications of logical forms" that gives Aristotle's and Kant's philosophies "such preeminent vitality," according to Peirce.[3] Peirce's long study of Kant left him with the conviction that the categories' dependence upon formal logic "really did and must exist" (CP 1.561).

Why the articulation of the categories ought to be based on logic is by no means obvious. A brief review of Kant's reasons for holding this belief will pave the way for understanding Peirce's own view on the matter. Kant holds that all knowledge rests on *intuitions*—representations immediately related to an object, and on *concepts*—representations of another concept or of an intuition. Concepts are mediate representations of an object.[4] Intuitions arise from affections of the sensibility, while concepts arise from spontaneous acts of the understanding. The function of a concept is "the unity of the act of bringing various representations under one common representation."[5] It is this bringing together of several representations in the understanding that makes knowledge of an object possible.

With respect to a given object, there are *empirical* intuitions and concepts, which arise from the peculiar nature of the object before us, *pure forms of intuition* (space and time) that apply to any possible object of experience whatever, and *pure concepts of the understanding*, which apply to all representations of a possible object of experience. The latter are the categories, "concepts which prescribe laws *a priori* to appearances, and therefore to nature, the sum of all appearances."[6]

We can now see why Kant bases his account of the categories on logic. The table of categories must, above all, be complete (i.e., comprehensive). Completeness cannot be guaranteed if the categories are merely discovered and catalogued empirically. There must be some principle that tells us what to expect when we do confront empirical phenomena. The principle must afford the idea of a *totality* of a priori knowledge of the understanding: "such an idea can furnish an exact classification of the concepts which compose that totality, exhibiting their *interconnection in a system*."[7] Kant claims to find such a principle in the absolute unity of the understanding. "These [a priori] concepts spring, pure and unmixed, out of the understanding which is an absolute unity; and must therefore be connected with each other according to one concept or idea."[8]

All acts of the understanding can be reduced to *judgments,* "functions of unity among our representations."[9] Concepts, then, are predicates of possible judgments (or, since Kant relies on Aristotelian logic, are predicates of possible propositions). All Kant needs in order to construct an exhaustive list of the categories is an exhaustive list of the formal functions of unity in propositions. This he readily obtains from the canon of traditional logic. Once laid out, it is easy to describe the forms of understanding that correspond to each of the twelve "moments" of judgment.[10] The possible forms of the understanding, abstracted from any particular representations to which they might apply, are thus rooted in the soil of logic. The resulting table of categories should be both correct (because logicians had analyzed and cataloged all the possible forms of judgment) and complete (because no other forms of understanding can exist).

Peirce learned from Kant that if there are any fundamental concepts that can give unity to all knowledge, they will be derived from logic. As we shall see in chapter 2, Peirce came to see the mathematics of logic as an a priori science that discovers all possible forms of *relation,* without regard to whether such forms are manifest in phenomena. This "first science" provides an a priori shopping list of possible categories that the philosopher then looks for in phenomena. Whether they will all be encountered in phenomena is, from the side of the mathematics of logic, unknown. It is known, however, that no *other* forms could be encountered. As early as 1866 Peirce appeals to "several great thinkers," undoubtedly Kant and Aristotle, when urging the view that metaphysics must be based on logic (W 1:490). The following statement from 1894 shows the mature application of this insight: "The *list of categories* . . . is a table of conceptions drawn from the logical analysis of thought and regarded as applicable to being" (CP 1.300).

Almost from the beginning, however, Peirce disagrees with his master on two fundamental points. He rejects first the traditional logic that Kant relied upon and second Kant's doctrine of the transcendental object. Each of these departures leads him to affirm the fundamental importance of the continuity principle. In the first case, Peirce's criticism of Kant's logic leads him to define *reality* as the object of a coherent and complete representation of all possible experience. This introduces the notion of an infinite community of inquiry—the only form of subjectivity capable of cognizing such a representation. This concept requires that there be continuity among ideas in the present, and that there be continuity among the past, the present, and an infinitely distant possible future. In the second case, his rejection of the transcendental object leads him to view cognition as a series of real, infinitesimally brief events, which commence with a continuous semeiotic process rather than with direct intuition of a nonsemeiotic transcendental object.

CRITICISMS OF KANT'S LOGIC

Kant derives his categories from the table of judgments. This table is adapted from Aristotelian logic, which appeared to Kant as "a closed and completed body of doctrine," and hence as eminently trustworthy.[11] Peirce notes the potential problem with this approach: "The correspondences between the functions of judgment and the categories are obvious and certain. So far the method is perfect. Its defect is that it affords no warrant for the correctness of the preliminary table [of functions of judgment]."[12] If the table of judgments is flawed, then the categories will reflect that flaw. It is a testament to the perverse nature of intellectual history that, before Kant's first *Critique* was a century old, logic underwent revisions that left the table of judgments looking rather archaic.[13]

Peirce tells us that he came away from the first *Critique* "with the demonstrative certitude that there was something wrong about Kant's formal logic" (CP 4.2). Kant held that all the syllogistic figures are reducible to *Barbara,* and hence believed that the fundamental subject matter of formal logic concerns only the analysis of propositional forms. The table of judgments reflects the findings of such a logic. One of Peirce's earliest logical discoveries, however, is that the second and third figures each involve a logical principle *not* found in *Barbara*.[14]

Peirce's Logic and the Categories: Early Approaches

Peirce noted that every argument contains three essential parts: premises, conclusion, and a principle of inference. "Every inference involves the judgment that, if *such* propositions as the premises are true, then a proposition related to them, as the conclusion is, must be, or is likely to be, true. The principle implied in this judgment, respecting a genus of argument, is termed the *leading principle* of the argument" (W 2:23). Peirce set out to describe the leading principles in the various figures of the syllogism. He thereby shifted from analyzing forms of propositions to analyzing types of inference.

Retaining Kant's terminology, Peirce began his 1867 "On a New List of Categories" with the statement that "the function of conceptions is to reduce the manifold of impressions to unity" (W 2:49). He also maintained Kant's doctrine that all phenomena are representations.[15] The function of the mind, then, is to bring diverse *representations* together. If there were fundamental conceptions underlying the unity of the mind, they would manifest themselves as rules that govern the combination of representations, and they would give rise to various kinds of thought. Peirce later recounted the implications of this insight:

> I came to see that Kant ought not to have confined himself to divisions of propositions, or "judgments," as the Germans confuse the subject by calling them, but ought to have taken account of all elementary and significant differences of form *among signs of all sorts,* and that, above all, he ought not to have left out of account fundamental forms of reasonings. (CP 1.561, emphasis added)

This passage indicates that the categories, being applicable to *any* sign relations, would potentially have broader application than merely to the species of human reasoning, which always follow the forms of inference.[16]

THE FORMS OF INFERENCE

Peirce argued that all forms of valid inference share a "minimum leading principle," and that, in addition, each form has its own unique leading principle. The minimum leading principle that grounds any inference whatever is that "if two facts are related as reason and consequent and the reason be true the consequent is [either necessarily or probably] true" (W 2:295). Note that this statement does not strictly concern relations among existent *objects* to which terms or propositions may refer. It concerns the relations among facts, which can themselves be terms or propositions. In 1865 he had seen that there must be general principles of representation that give rise to the forms of valid inference, since inference is a type of representation (called symbolization) (W 1:280). But first he had to demonstrate that there *are* three distinct forms of inference.

Peirce identifies deduction, induction (or adduction), and retroduction (also called abduction or hypothesis) as the elementary forms of inference.[17] Deduction may be expressed in the following form.[18]

DEDUCTION

RULE:	M is P;
CASE:	S is M;
RESULT:	S is P

For example: all bears are dangerous; Ursula is a bear; therefore, Ursula is dangerous. The leading principle of deduction may be stated, "if a Rule is true, and a Case comes under it, the predicate of the Rule is true of the subject of the Case" (W 1:441).

We can give similar accounts of induction and retroduction:

INDUCTION

CASE:	S, S', S'', etc. are (classified as) M;
RESULT:	S, S', S'', etc. are P;
RULE:	Any M is (probably) P

An example would be: Ursula and numerous others are classified as bears; Ursula and the others are dangerous; therefore, any bear is probably dangerous. The leading principle can be stated briefly: "as is the sample, so is the whole" (W 1:431).

RETRODUCTION

RULE:	M is P, P', P'', etc.;
RESULT:	S is P, P', P'', etc.;
CASE:	S is (probably) M

Bears are thick-furred, clawed, and lumbering; the object in the path ahead is thick-furred, clawed, and lumbering; therefore, the object in the path ahead is probably a bear. The leading principle of retroduction is that if it is true that all members of a class exhibit some characteristic(s), and a given subject exhibits the same characteristic(s), then we may guess that the subject belongs to that class.

As we move from deductive to inductive and retroductive inferences, the force of the conclusions becomes weaker, while their informative value increases. Peirce observes that the only reason we allow so weak an inference as retroduction is that we *must* trust it "if we are ever to learn anything or to understand phenomena at all" (CP 5.171). Deduction merely allows substitution in a proposition among equivalent representations of an object, and this accounts for the relative certainty of its conclusions (W 1:458). Substitution also figures in the forms of probable inference, but these differ from deduction because they introduce a middle term that brings a manifold to unity:

> The function of induction is to substitute for a series of many subjects, a single one which embraces them and an indefinite number of others. . . . The function of hypothesis is to substitute for a great series of predicates forming no unity in themselves, a single one (or small number) which involves them all, together (perhaps) with an indefinite number of others. (W 2:217–18)

The discovery of the three distinct forms of inference allowed Peirce to take his first steps away from Kant's table. Thought conforms not to the functions of judgment, but to the forms of valid inference, which express law-like regularity in the relation of premises to conclusions.

THE PRINCIPLES OF REPRESENTATION

Grounding the categories on the forms of inference would have brought Peirce uncomfortably near to psychologism, but he maintained that something deeper than mere psychological association underlies the relations among representations. He noted similarities between the forms of propositions and the forms of arguments: "the relation between subject and predicate, or antecedent and consequent, is essentially the same as that between premiss and conclusion" (CP 4.3). His explanation for this striking similarity is that the forms of inference themselves derive from the more general principles of representation, which apply to all associations of signs. The forms of inference, it turns out, depend on one general and three particular principles of representation.[19] In order to get at the principles of representation, we may work backward from a description of *kinds* of representation.[20]

One of Peirce's earliest classifications of signs identifies the three basic kinds as copy, sign, and symbol:

> A term has comprehension in virtue of having a meaning and has extension in virtue of being applicable to objects. The meaning of a term is called its *connotation;* its applicability to things its *denotation.* Every symbol *denotes* by *connoting.* A representation which *denotes* without connoting is a mere *sign.* If it *connotes* without thereby *denoting,* it is a mere *copy.* (W 1:272)

In the "New List" he described *signs* as *indices* (representations corresponding to their objects "in fact"), and *copies* as *likenesses* (which merely share a common quality with their objects). He later adopted the name *icon* for the latter kind of sign. The third kind, the symbol or *general sign,* represents its object via an "imputed character" (W 2:56). This is more precisely described in terms of the *information* a symbol carries. The combined denoting and connoting of a symbol constitutes a "process of information" which "disturbs the relations of extension and comprehension for a moment" (W 1:276). The information of a symbol is "its reference to all the synthetical propositions in which its objects in common are subject or predicate" (W 2:59).

Some examples may help make these distinctions more clear.

1. An unmanned spacecraft recently sent back a photo of a Martian landscape, showing a rock formation very much resembling a human face. The photo was printed in tabloids with captions like "SCIEN-TISTS FIND SCULPTURE OF ANCIENT MARTIAN GOD." If we skeptically assume that the object before the camera was a mere rock formation, then as long as the photo *appears* to show a face, it is an example of a term that has meaning (connotations of sculpted eyes, nose, forehead, and so on) but does not denote any sculpture. The term lacks extension because there is no sculpture left by an ancient Martian race. The photo (the term) is a mere icon, a likeness of a merely possible photo of a sculpture.

2. Suppose there is somewhere a board, taken from a house now fallen into ruins, which bears a bullet-hole. The hole connotes nothing, because (by hypothesis) nobody has ever taken it as a sign of any sort. Because it does bear an existential (causal) relationship to a particular gun and the person who fired it, however, the hole is an index. It in fact indicates something, but has no meaning.

3. A young child hears the word "football" spoken. This symbol connotes the Super Bowl, the Chicago Bears, a favorite quarterback, heavily padded uniforms, an oblong leather or rubber ball. These are the term's meaning for the child. Through these connotations the symbol denotes a number of actual sporting events. These are the symbol's extension. The information of the symbol consists of all the conversations, sportscasts, newspaper articles, and so forth in which the symbol serves, or could serve, as subject or predicate. It is applicable to the sport of football *in general.* As things progress, the child discovers that there is another cluster of connotations associated with the word "football": the local YMCA is sponsoring a youth league in which children can participate. This process of information restructures the comprehension of the term, and hence its extension as well: "football" now also denotes organized games played by children rather than professionals. The information of the term has increased for the child, as it now symbolizes a number of possible games of a very different sort than those originally envisioned.

Peirce initially focused on the study of symbols, whose nature *requires* that they occur in mind of some sort. Peirce posited that symbolization and inference are the same thing: "Inference in general obviously supposes symbolization; and all symbolization is inference. For every symbol as we have seen contains information. And . . . all kinds of information involve inference" (W 1:280). Thus "the objects of the understanding, considered as representations, are symbols" (W 2:56), and the search for the categories is ultimately a search for the principles grounding symbolic representation. Peirce later recognized that symbolization also involves iconic and indexical representation. This approach to the categories thus ultimately involves the study of all forms of representation.

The general principle of symbolization posits "the possibility of representations acquiring a nature, that is to say an immediate representative power" (W 1:280). This possibility informs the simplest definition of a representation: "A representation is an object which stands for another, so that an experience of the former affords us a knowledge of the latter" (W 3:62). The general principle is primitive. To deny it, for Peirce, would be to deny the possibility of thought.

Because there are three distinct forms of inference, there must also be three particular principles of representation that explain how these forms can be valid. The principle underlying retroduction is that all *forms* are symbolizable; underlying induction, that all *things* are symbolizable; and underlying deduction, that all *symbols* are symbolizable (W 1:282). Retroduction is the process by which various experiences are classified together on the basis of similarities in form. Induction is the process by which new experiences are included under established classes. Deduction allows explication of the meaning of the terms used in classifying our experiences. "Hypothesis [retroduction] gives us our facts. Induction extends our knowledge. Deduction makes it distinct" (W 1:283).

PEIRCE'S EARLY CONCEPTION OF THE CATEGORIES

Peirce identified a total of five categories in the "New List."[21] Substance (It, or the present in general) and Being (what is) are the beginning and end of thought, respectively. These are later dropped from the list of categories because they prove to be *incognizable limits* of cognition, and hence are not part of cognition proper (W 2:238–39). Peirce refers to the three categories "intermediate between the manifold of substance and the unity of being" as *accidents*. These are Quality (Reference to a Ground), Relation (Reference to a Correlate), and Representation (Reference to an Interpretant). A quality is a "pure species or abstraction," and is indispensable for thought "because we cannot apprehend an agreement of two things, except as an agreement in some *respect*." Reference to a ground, then, is reference to some abstract character or quality: it is reference to a *form* (not entirely un-Platonic). As for relation, a quality cannot be recognized as distinct without an act of comparison, and "the occasion of the introduction of the conception of reference to a ground is the reference to a correlate." Qualities are distinct, but for this to be the case, they must be correlated; qualities must bear some differentiating relations to one another, and must bear the relation of identity to themselves. This requires that qualities have duration, which is the peculiar feature of *things*. Finally, in order for us to know either the relations among things or the identity of a thing over a duration, the correlates must be represented *as* related. This requires a mediating representation, or *interpretant*.

The interpretant of a sign has several interesting properties. First, the interpretant is itself a sign. Second, it does not arise arbitrarily; rather, it is determined both by the sign that it "translates" and the laws that govern the association of signs. Finally, no actual interpretant is ever complete. The interpretant's function is to make its predecessor "more determinate, to place it in a context of other signs so as to yield more information about its represented object, to develop or enhance any meaning it might have."[22] The process of information occurs when an interpretant is produced in a mind.

The essential function of a sign is to address itself to and determine some other sign (W 2:207). An icon may in principle give rise to another icon (abstract quality succeeding abstract quality), to an index (an enduring instance of an abstract quality), or to a representation (a quality interpreted by a mind, as when a red flag is taken as a danger signal).[23] An index may give rise to another index (a thing determining another thing, as when a finger leaves its print on a pane of glass) or to a representation (a thing taken as a sign by a mind, as when the fingerprint incriminates a burglar in a jury's consideration). A symbol, however, can only give rise to another symbol: it thus *essentially* involves an interpretant. A symbol is a moment in an endless sequence of cognitions which by its very nature extends indefinitely into the future (W 2:224).[24]

Recalling that a symbol is an inference, "We here see, thoughts determining and causing other thoughts, and a chain of reasoning or of association is produced. But the beginning and the end of this chain, are not distinctly perceived" (W 3:29). This is Peirce's early description of the three elemental categories: quality, relation, and representation. He later realized that, because all cognition is symbolization, no cognition is a pure quality or a pure relation. Further, because all representations essentially involve an interpretant, no cognition is a static representation. Thus, looking back on the "New List" around 1905, Peirce modified his original descriptions somewhat, so that they would accord with this insight:

> there are but three elementary forms of predication or signification, which as I originally named them (but with bracketed additions now made to render the terms more intelligible) were *qualities* (of feeling), (dyadic) *relations,* and (predications of) *representations.* (CP 1.561)

Reality and Continuity: The Infinite Community

Peirce's study of Aristotle and the Scholastics influenced his revision of Kant's logic. Indeed, Duns Scotus probably led Peirce to see propositional forms as deriving from forms of inference—the reverse of Kant's position.[25] While he was studying Duns Scotus's logic, though, he also discovered a form of realism to his liking. Duns Scotus sought a way out of nominalism that did not commit him to Platonism. He thus affirmed that universals exist outside the mind, but did not locate them in an ontological realm of pure forms.[26]

Peirce, too, wanted to escape nominalism without going all the way into Plato's world. His approach to such a position involves the novel combination of two ideas, each intriguing in its own right. First, as we have seen, he retained and adapted Kant's view that phenomena are representations. Peirce added that phenomena are signs, and all thought occurs in signs. This view is defended in "Questions Concerning Certain Faculties Claimed for Man":

> QUESTION 5. *Whether we can think without signs.*
> This is a familiar question, but there is, to this day, no better argument in the affirmative than that thought must precede every sign. This assumes the impossibility of an infinite series. But Achilles, as a fact, will overtake the tortoise. *How* this happens, is a question not necessary to be answered at present, as long as it certainly does happen. (W 2:207)

How this happens involves the reality of infinitesimals, and is discussed in chapter 4. That it does happen indicated to Peirce that his form of semeiotic phenomenalism can be defended against the most serious argument against it. If all thought is in the media of signs, then no thought in the sequence of cognition is not itself a sign. The obvious objection is that this implies an infinite regress, with no initial nonsemeiotic thought. Peirce was confident that there is nothing objectionable about this, though, and held to this form of phenomenalism throughout his life.

The second part of Peirce's approach to the nominalist-realist controversy involves an adaptation of Duns Scotus. In logic, universality can be defined as general predicability, "a relation of a predicate to the subjects of which it is predicated" (W 2:472). The universal, accordingly, is a term like "horse" that can be applied to a number of individuals. As Peirce notes, "In such a sense it is plain universals are real," because there really is a horse (W 2:472). The metaphysical controversy centers on the question whether such a term corresponds to anything independent of its application to individuals. Nominalism contends that the universal is only a word, arbitrarily applied to a collection of things that exhibit similarities. Realism, on the other hand, insists that separate things would not share properties unless there were some ontologically real universal (such as a Platonic Form) that caused them to do so. Duns Scotus suggested that *universality* is a mode of

11

things that is independent of the mind that apprehends it, but which is none the less distinguishable from the things' common nature.[27]

In Peirce's view, universality is not a matter of a term's reference to any character (ground) or thinghood (relations), but of reference to a future ultimate interpretant, where its complete information would be exhibited. This is a departure from Duns Scotus: "Even Duns Scotus is too nominalistic when he says that universals are contracted to the mode of individuality in singulars, meaning, as he does, by singulars, ordinary existing things" (CP 8.208). Like Duns Scotus, however, he saw the reality of universals as a metaphysical fact influencing the logical fact that the same property can be predicated of many subjects.

In the 1868 "Some Consequences of Four Incapacities," Peirce adopted the view that the beginning and end of thought are not *in* consciousness. He wrote of the manifold of substance that originates thought: "the ideal first . . . is quite singular, and quite out of consciousness. This ideal first is the particular thing-in-itself. It does not exist *as such*" (W 2:238). In a footnote he wrote, "[b]y an ideal, I mean the limit which the possible cannot attain." The end of a stream of cognition, the final interpretant, is likewise an ideal limit.

The interpretant is most readily conceived as a thought that arises in a mind when it encounters a sign, but Peircean *mind* is not the Cartesian *individual* mind. Insofar as they fulfill their function, signs may be interpreted by individuals or by communities of various kinds. The mind that performs the last inference, attains complete information, and cognizes reality in its fullness is an ideal community of mind.[28] In "Some Consequences" Peirce offered his best-known definition of the *real*: "that which, sooner or later, information and reasoning would finally result in, and which is therefore independent of the vagaries of me and you."[29] He continued: "this conception essentially involves the notion of a COMMUNITY, without definite limits, and capable of an indefinite increase of knowledge" (W 2:239).

Any stream of cognition ultimately would lead to one of two ends. Reality is defined with reference to these possible results:

> those two series of cognitions—the real and the unreal—consist of those which, at a time sufficiently future, the community will always continue to reaffirm; and of those which, under the same conditions, will ever after be denied. Now, a proposition whose falsity can never be discovered, and the error of which therefore is absolutely incognizable, contains, upon our principle, absolutely no error. Consequently, that which is thought in these cognitions is the real, as it really is. (W 2:239)

The real, in other words, is what is represented in the *consistent* semeiotic stream, whose interpretants need never be revised or rendered more precise. This is a statement of Peirce's pragmatic theory of reality.[30] The finite community, of course, has no such series of cognitions that it *knows* to be entirely correct. This fact led Peirce to balance his pragmatism with the epistemological principle he called *fallibilism*: No knowledge supported by finite cognition can ever be supposed to be absolutely true. It must, however, be supposed that *some* series of finite cognitions do approximately represent reality. Such streams tend toward an indefinite increase in information, and to an increasingly determinate knowledge of the objects of the signs (themselves signs) represented in those streams.

Individual mind is not then the best paradigm of mind. The notion of an individual mind belonging to a self only arises when one discovers that a stream of cognitions does *not* accord with reality as then represented by the community: "All human thought and opinion contains an arbitrary, accidental element, dependent on the limitations in circumstances, power, and bent of the individual; an element of error, in short" (W 2:468). It would be better to think of mind as the shared thoughts of the infinite community, perhaps extending beyond the human realm, which constitutes the universe of semeiotic activity. "Mind is a sign developing according to the laws of inference" (W 2:240), and these laws actively guide the course of thought. "Let any human being have enough information and exert enough thought upon any question, and the result will be that he will arrive at a certain definite conclusion, which is the same that any other mind will reach under sufficiently favorable circumstances" (W 2:468). In fact, we note that it is not unusual for groups of scientists, working separately, to arrive at similar discoveries at about the same time. It may correctly be said that such groups share thoughts.[31] They are together in the semeiotic stream, and the laws of inference guide them to quite similar interpretations of the signs which serve as their "raw data."

This notion of community is implicit in his version of Duns Scotus's realism: "what anything really is, is what it may finally come to be known to be in the ideal state of complete information, so that reality depends on the ultimate decision of the community" (W 2:241). This position is elaborated later in a review of Berkeley. The nature of the real lies to be determined in future interpretants, and its reality consists precisely in its potentiality for being so determined. There is yet an element of nominalism in this "objective idealism," since it links reality to cognition. But because cognition is governed by laws and is carried out over the long run by the community of interpreters, it avoids the objectionable features of nominalism. "This final opinion . . . is independent, not indeed of thought in general, but of all that is arbitrary and individual in thought; is quite independent of how you, I, or any number of men think" (W 2:469).

We are now prepared to see how Peirce dealt with the problem of universals. All thought occurs in the media of signs, and conforms to the principles of representation and the three forms of inference. Mind is the community of thought, the universe of semeiotic operation. *Whenever* appropriate antecedent signs have been cognized, the laws of inference ensure that a true symbol may be generated. These symbols are not much restricted by temporal and spatial factors: We may have one of Peirce's thoughts here and now, for example, if we apprehend a series of signs similar to those which led Peirce to that thought. Thought may thus be continuous across time and space, so Peirce can speak of a community of mind spread throughout infinite time and even infinite space.

We come now to his argument for the reality of universals. First he defines an *absolutely true* proposition: "if a proposition is logically inferable—by deduction, induction, or hypothesis—from the sum of all possible information, past, present, and to come, then it is absolutely true, for it is true in the whole of its meaning" (W 2:175). The *real* is nothing other than the object of such a proposition. A universal is a proposition that relates a quality to an indefinite number of subjects. Because it is entirely possible that a universal proposition may prove to be inferable from the sum of all possible information, "there is nothing to prevent the universal propositions from being absolutely true, and therefore universals may be as real as singulars" (W 2:175).

Peirce thus establishes a theory that liberates the universality of a proposition from the denotative and connotative reference of its terms. Universality is dependent on the outcome of all possible cognition concerning the proposition. In other words, universality is a matter of what would be the case if the symbol acquired a state of complete information. Universals are real, but their reality depends on the fact that the future interpretants of the symbols in which they occur would come to be seen as true. This is certainly independent of any individual's opinion on the matter, and because Peirce does not claim that anyone actually *possesses* the idea of the universal that would come with complete information, there is no need to appeal to any antecedently existing forms to which the universals correspond.

The theory of the infinite community that he introduces instead, though, may at this point appear no more plausible than the theory of forms. Peirce is aware that his reliance on the concept of infinity is bound to make his theory problematic. In the "Grounds of Validity," he leaves us with an exhortation that we *must* assent to this conception, because it is the only thing that can justify the presupposition of reality that he finds at the basis of all thought:

> [H]e who recognizes the logical necessity of complete self-identification of one's own interests with those of the community, and its potential existence in man . . . will perceive that only the inferences of that man who has it are logical, and so views his own inferences as being valid only so far as they would be accepted by that man. But so far as he has this belief, he

becomes identified with that man. And that ideal perfection of knowledge by which we have seen that reality is constituted must thus belong to a community in which this identification is complete. (W 2:271)

Peirce does not here offer positive reasons to think that such a conception of the community is plausible: "the assumption that man or the community (which may be wider than man) shall ever arrive at a state of information greater than some definite finite information, is entirely unsupported by reasons"; it can only be supported by an "infinite hope" that this is the case (W 2:271–72).

Peirce's conception of the infinite community of inquiry represents a synthesis of two ideas that commanded his interest from early on. The first is the notion of evolution, which came to prominence with Darwin's publication of *The Origin of Species by Means of Natural Selection* in 1859. What is of decisive importance in evolutionary theory, for Peirce, is not the particular explanation it offers for certain biological occurrences. Rather, it is "the Idea of Evolution," the notion that there is a principle directing the course of natural events, and that this principle can itself be characterized in naturalistic (but not merely mechanistic) terms. In 1903, Peirce recalled the "immense sensation" that the theory created among his circle (and especially upon Chauncey Wright, the mentor of a number of young Harvard intellectuals including Peirce and William James) (CP 5.64). Peirce saw in the evolutionary theories ideas of development that compel us to recognize "that there is a mode of influence upon external facts which cannot be resolved into mere mechanical action" (CP 5.64).

The theory of evolution provided a new paradigm for scientific thinking in the nineteenth century, and was soon applied beyond the biological sphere. Perhaps the most notorious of these applications were the theories of "social Darwinism," which made the concepts of natural selection and survival of the fittest the basis for a naturalistic understanding of human society. Peirce, however, took the idea of evolution in a very different direction from that of the social Darwinists. Rather than emphasizing the brutal "naturalistic" aspects of evolutionary theory, he saw the positive idea "that chance begets order" as the truly important insight in the new paradigm (CP 6.297). Because for Peirce "all matter is really mind," the evolutionary theory of development could be applied to ideas as well as organisms (CP 6.301). Chaotic and irrational ideas tend, over time, to become more determinate and ordered under the influence of an evolutionary teleology. In his surveys of various evolutionary theories, he consistently rejected those *anancastic* theories, such as Herbert Spencer's, which offer a purely mechanistic account of evolution (CP 6.14, 6.303).

He considered Darwinian theory to be somewhat better, as it bases development on the effects of fortuitous variation (CP 6.302). Peirce found this *tychastic* theory inadequate as well, however, because it fails to recognize the positive value of the harmonious and ordered arrangement toward which development may tend. He argued for an *agapastic* theory of evolution, in which "advance takes place by virtue of a positive sympathy among the created springing from the continuity of mind" (CP 6.304). Peirce saw some truth in tychasm and anancasm, but only so far as they are degenerate or imperfect forms of agapasm (CP 6.303). Peirce proposed a theory of evolution of ideas that regards their development as an evolution *toward* a harmonious state of rational order, of reality. Peirce summed up the importance of evolution for his thought in the following terms:

> Almost everybody will now agree that the ultimate good lies in the evolutionary process in some way. If so, it is not in individual reactions in their segregation, but in something general or continuous. Synechism is founded on the notion that the coalescence, the becoming continuous, the becoming governed by laws, the becoming instinct with general ideas, are but phases of one and the same process of the growth of reasonableness. (CP 5.4)

The second commanding idea that influenced Peirce's conception of the infinite community of inquiry was that of the medieval community of scholars. Ideas are not private things; persons in different times and places can share the same idea. Thus the evolution of ideas is best conceived as a social phenomenon, and mind is a general entity not confined within a Cartesian consciousness or shut up within the human skull. The community, not the individual, is the primary thinking thing and seeker of truth. He compares the work of medieval scholars, such as Duns Scotus, to the work of their contemporaries who built the great cathedrals:

> Nothing is more striking in either of the great intellectual products of that age, than the complete absence of self-conceit on the part of the artist or philosopher. That anything of value can be added to his sacred and catholic work by its having the smack of individuality about it, is what he has never conceived. His work is not designed to embody *his* ideas, but the universal truth. (W 2:465–66)

A historian familiar with life in a medieval abbey would detect more than a tinge of romanticism in Peirce's account; nonetheless, it does provide a fine image of the "complete self-identification of one's own interests with those of the community, and its potential existence in man," the faith in which Peirce saw as a necessary condition for apprehending truth (W 2:271).

The evolution of ideas in the infinite community of inquiry is a powerful concept. It is problematic, however, in the importance it places upon the interrelated concepts of (1) a state of information greater than any specifiable state, (2) a community wider than any specifiable size, and (3) an inquiry carried on longer than any specifiable time. These concepts must be made more clear, and must be shown to be at least plausible. On the face of it, they all appear self-contradictory. In attempting to clarify these concepts, Peirce found himself looking directly into the principle of continuity and the theory of transfinite numbers developed by Georg Cantor in the 1880s. These investigations began to bear fruit with the 1892 article "The Law of Mind." This article contains Peirce's first public attempt to defend his principle of continuity. These attempts lay the mathematical groundwork for Peirce's mature philosophy, and will be taken up in Part Two.

Anti-transcendentalism

In what has become known as the first published statement of the *pragmatic maxim*, Peirce writes: "Consider what effects, which might conceivably have practical bearings, we conceive the object of our conception to have. Then, our conception of these effects is the whole of our conception of the object" (W 3:266).[32] As this statement indicates, Peirce's philosophy is decidedly anti-transcendentalist. All that can be said to *be* has its being in the effects it could have on some mind: "*cognizability* (in its widest sense) and *being* are not merely metaphysically the same, but are synonymous terms" (W 2:208). Here it is worth noting what this principle implies for the list of categories and the objects of cognition.

There are two sides to Peirce's anti-transcendentalist coin. First, he maintained that a transcendental deduction of his list of categories is neither possible nor wanted to sanction the validity of that list. The reality of the categories is like any other reality: the real categories are those that would be affirmed by the community at the end of continuous, infinite inquiry. Second, he insists that we need not introduce an incognizable or transcendental object to stand at the ultimate beginning of a stream of cognition. The beginning of cognition is only intelligible as a continuous process: there is no "first cognition," and hence no *object* of the first cognition. In both cases Peirce relies on the principle of continuity to fill the explanatory gap left when transcendentals depart from philosophy.

CATEGORIES WITHOUT A TRANSCENDENTAL DEDUCTION

As we have seen, Peirce develops his list of three categories by identifying the forms of inference, stating the principles of representation that explain the possibility of these forms, and finally identifying the categories as the simple elements these principles themselves presuppose. All thought is inference, and all inference is representation in symbols. Qualities of feeling, dyadic relations of things, and interpretants or predications of representations are the three simple elements that must be introduced to explain the possibility of symbolization. These, then, are the categories discovered by metaphysical deduction in the "New List."

The question of how to ensure the correctness of such a list inevitably arises. Peirce found early in his career that no principle of representation can be shown to be valid without employing that principle in the demonstration (W 1:280). Thus a circularity problem arises if we try to demonstrate the correctness of the three categories, because the demonstration obviously would have to utilize some form of inference. Peirce could not satisfy those who demand a demonstrative justification, or transcendental deduction, of his categories.

He would insist, however, that although no transcendental deduction is possible, neither is it needed. The reason is that the list of categories is not itself a secure deductive result, but is rather a hypothesis.[33] The categories are concepts that unite a large number of phenomena (all the actual inferences and representations one might encounter) under a small number of classes. No hypothesis is in itself demonstrably certain. Its appeal depends, rather, on its explanatory power. All that is required of the list of categories, as a hypothesis, is that the categories hold some promise of being approximately true. Peirce disparaged transcendentalism as "the system of investigation which thinks [it] necessary to prove that the normal representations of truth within us are really correct" (W 1:72). He put great effort into discovering the categories, and he retained them because they appeared to be the most likely representation of the truth on this matter. The Peircean rejoinder to the persistent skeptic on this matter is that all that ought to concern us is the resolution of actual doubt, not the mere *possibility* of a doubt: "Let us not pretend to doubt in philosophy what we do not doubt in our hearts" (W 2:212). If after examining the list of categories we are satisfied that it suits our present needs, and contains no apparent faults that could be remedied, then we ought to accept the list as provisionally correct.

This is not to say that Peirce's list of the categories and the logic from which it is derived can be only instrumentally true. All that he says of reality and truth applies to these conceptions as well. "The opinion which is fated to be agreed to by all who investigate, is what we mean by the truth, and the object represented in this opinion is the real" (W 3:273). The correctness of Peirce's statement of the three forms of inference, the principles of representation, and the categories is approximate—as is every other truth. Fallibilism applies here as in every finite inquiry. Fallibilism does not prohibit the possibility of genuine truth, however, and *if* Peirce's list of categories should turn out to be true, then it is true *now.*

A good hypothesis should be testable in the course of further inquiry, though there are some hypotheses that can never be tested (CP 6.524). The test of a hypothesis comes when its conclusion is successfully employed in a series of inductions (which expand the sphere of the hypothesis) and deductions (which make its implications distinct) (CP 6.526–27).[34] A hypothesis such as the list of categories admits of innumerable opportunities for testing and revision, since in principle it ought to apply to absolutely everything anyone could ever possibly experience. The only *conclusive* proof of the categories' truth is that they would continue to be affirmed in the final opinion. In the meantime (the only *real* time), the truth of the categories is a matter of their presently conceivable effects, as satisfactory or unsatisfactory explanations of phenomena.

THE PHENOMENON WITHOUT A TRANSCENDENTAL OBJECT

Kant's phenomenalism admits two types of representation: intuitions, which are immediately related to their objects, and concepts, which represent an intuition or another concept. Common sense seems to insist that if all our thoughts are representations, there must be something "really there" behind at least some of the representations. The features of a photograph, for example, are determined by the real thing that reflected light into the camera. Although some photographs are actually photos of photos, it seems ill-advised to suppose that *all* of them are. If we follow tradition and think of cognitions as mental pictures of the world, then a concept is like a photo of a photo, while an intuition is like a photo of the thing itself, which lies outside the series of cognitions.

> [An intuition is] a cognition not determined by a previous cognition of the same object, and therefore so determined by something out of the consciousness. . . . *Intuition* here will be nearly the same as "premise not itself a conclusion"; the only difference being that premises and conclusions are judgments, whereas an intuition may, as far as its definition states, be any kind of cognition whatever. But just as a conclusion (good or bad) is determined in the mind of the reasoner by its premise, so cognitions not judgements may be determined by previous cognitions; and a cognition not so determined, and therefore determined directly by the transcendental object, is to be termed an *intuition*. (W 2:193–94)

The object of an intuition, unlike the object of a photograph, *cannot* be apprehended without the intervening representative mechanism. Thus the thing-in-itself cannot be thought without being subjected to the structures of the mind. It is absolutely incognizable.

Peirce agreed with Kant that all phenomena are representations, but denied that we have any intuitions. This apparently conflicts with common sense, but common sense is perhaps too heavily influenced by the visual model. All thought occurs in the media of symbols, which by definition

19

relate an object to an interpretant. We tend to think of the object of a representation as a thing, but there are no pure things or qualities in mind. Only when things or qualities are represented, in icons or indices, can they be the objects of a symbol. Any possible object of a cognition must, then, itself be of a semeiotic nature. Peirce, therefore, denies that the notion of a transcendental object, the absolutely incognizable thing-in-itself, is a coherent notion. "The representationists tell us that we can have no knowledge of things-in-themselves. But we go further and deny that we can so much as attach any meaning to the 'absolutely incognizable.' Hence if we mean anything by the very things themselves, they are cognizable" (W 2:191). Thus the object of a first cognition is not a transcendental object, and "incognizable object of thought" cannot be what is meant when we discuss these objects (W 2:208). There must be *some* beginning to cognition, though, and the question of what it is must be addressed.

FIRST IMPRESSIONS

I have already noted that Peirce is an empiricist, even to the point of insisting that a priori knowledge is ultimately based on a kind of experience. Although he rejects the Kantian account of the ultimate origin of thought because it posits an incognizable entity, neither does he accept the doctrine of British empiricism that all thought derives from impressions imprinted on a passive mind. Hume is the worthy opponent against whom much of Peirce's early work on cognition is directed.[35] Hume defined *impressions* so as to include not only the deliverances of the senses (which would be the position of a naive empiricism), but also passions, emotions, and volitions.[36] Peirce's objection is not against the point that these are the "raw material" of thought, but is rather that the empiricists neglect the constitutive role of the mind in perception.

In his 1866 Lowell Lectures, Peirce makes the following assertion in an attempt to walk the line between Kantianism and empiricism: "The first impressions upon our senses are not representations of certain unknown things in themselves but are themselves those very unknown things in themselves" (W 1:471). Unlike a transcendental object, a first impression is *cognizable*—because it has being. Unlike a Humean impression, though, it is *unknown*—because it is the originary limit of the series of inferences that constitutes thought. The first impression is not experienced, but may be inferred to exist because we have cognitions that *are* known. The first cognitions that *can* be known are "nothing else than predicates which the mind affixes by virtue of a hypothetical inference in order to understand the data presented to it" (W 1:471). These are sensations, "a sort of mental name," arbitrarily assigned to a group of "data" (W 1:472). The name is given

> on account of a logical necessity; namely the necessity of reducing the manifold of the predicates given to unity. We give the name *man* because it is needed to convey at once rationality,

animality, being two-legged, being mortal, &c. To give a name is therefore to make a hypothesis. Such a hypothesis, however, differs from what we usually comprehend under that term in a very important respect; namely, that while the data require *some* name they do not require any name in particular. . . . So that a sensation is like a name—the data demand it but do not demand that it shall be of any particular sort so long as it is consistent. (W 1:472)

The mind encounters *something,* in other words, and performs an abduction which represents that something (and "so long as it is consistent," all other similar somethings) in a coherent symbol—a sensation, or "a constitutional nominal hypothesis."[37] The sensation can then be contrasted and associated with other unified sensations and cognition can occur. The first impression is in effect an unconscious premise that initiates a series of cognitions leading to a conscious representation (CP 2.27).[38]

It is clear that Peirce's first impression and Kant's transcendental object fill precisely the same role in the theory of knowledge. The only difference between them, and a significant difference indeed, is that the notion of a first impression is not inherently contradictory. Hence, it is at least possible that a meaningful account can be given of it. Peirce's account brought him once again to the principle of continuity:

It is true, that since some judgment precedes every judgment inferred, either the first premises were not inferred, or there have been no first premises. But it does not follow that because there has been no first in a series, therefore that series has had no beginning in time; for the series may be *continuous,* and may have begun gradually. (W 2:247)

Thought and Continuity: Infinitesimal Cognitions

Peirce's assertion that there is no definite beginning point to a stream of cognition, although there is indeed a beginning, is certainly paradoxical. It implies that an infinite series of cognitions takes place between a time when some particular idea is *not* present in mind, and a later time when that idea *is* present. As definite dates can be assigned to mark each of these times, the interval of time involved is finite. Recall the passage quoted earlier in which Peirce likens this to Zeno's paradox of Achilles and the tortoise (W 2:207). Though he can easily halve the tortoise's lead at any time, Achilles apparently cannot overtake the tortoise, indeed cannot catch up to the tortoise, because he would have to cover an infinite number of finite distances in a finite time. If the distance between the two racers is d, and the time between starting and catching up to the tortoise is t, Achilles must cover ($\frac{1}{2}d + \frac{1}{4}d + \frac{1}{8}d + \ldots$) in the finite time t. If the distance series were expanded to infinity, its limit would approach *d*, but Achilles clearly does not have until infinity to win the race.

The parallel to cognition is that an infinite series of cognitions must occur before we get from the first impression of sense to the first cognition, or representation, of that impression. The series intervening between the two times must be infinite because cognitions are inferences, and there is no premise of an inference not itself the conclusion of some previous inference (W 2:163). There is no beginning *point* to cognition. Rather, "cognition arises by a *process* of beginning, as any other change comes to pass" (W 2:211).

The originary limit of cognition, then, is the unknown first impression. This gives rise to a series of more and more distinct representations, until the first conscious representation arises.

> There is nothing absolutely out of the mind, but the first impression of sense is the most external thing in existence. It may . . . be said to be so far out of the mind, that it is as much external as internal. Our experience of any object is developed by a process continuous from the very first, of change of the cognition and increase in the liveliness of consciousness. At the very first of this process, there is no consciousness but only the beginning of becoming conscious. It is also not a real state of mind because it instantaneously passes away.
>
> There is a paradox here. But so there is in respect to any beginning or other limit of anything continuous. (W 2:191)

As long as Achilles *does* overtake the tortoise, we can rest assured that the mistaken conception is somewhere in Zeno's argument, and not in the notion of an infinite series occupying a finite time.

Peirce's solution to Zeno's paradox involves treating space as a *continuum* not made up of the kind of discrete parts represented in the distance series. "All the arguments of Zeno depend on supposing that a *continuum* has ultimate parts. But a *continuum* is precisely that, every part of which has parts, in the same sense" (W 2:256). To resolve the paradox of cognition, Peirce asserts that thought, likewise, is a continuum not composed of discrete parts. Thus to say that thought conforms to the three kinds of inference is one thing, but to say that it follows distinct syllogistic steps from premises to conclusion is probably incorrect. The syllogistic structure is merely a coarse representation of the mind's process which is of great use to the logician, just as a topographical map is merely a coarse representation of the land which is of great use to the surveyor (W 2:249–50).

Cognitions are not syllogisms, then, because a thought does not have distinct parts. A completely accurate description of a cognition is difficult to give, of course, but Peirce does identify two properties it would have to include. First, a cognition cannot occupy any definite duration of time, however small. Otherwise the infinite series problem arises in full force. Second, a cognition must occupy some positive duration of time, because it is obvious that time elapses while cognitions take place.

Peirce was familiar with entities having these properties. They are described in the theory of infinitesimals, one of whose staunchest defenders in nineteenth-century America was Benjamin Peirce, Harvard's leading mathematician and Charles's father.[39] An infinitesimal is a nonzero positive quantity, which is smaller than any specifiable positive quantity. A continuum, as Peirce indicates in his objection to Zeno, has no ultimate parts. It is infinitely divisible. That is, no matter how small an interval of a continuum we consider, that interval can again be divided into two parts that are qualitatively the same as the original interval, each of these may be likewise divided, and so on forever. The same holds true even if our original interval is an infinitesimal. An infinitesimal is an indefinite quantity, *defined* by the parameters "positive nonzero quantity" and "smaller than any finite quantity." Thus if we divide an infinitesimal, we get an infinitesimal. Every part has parts, in the same sense. Peirce's definition of the continuum went through several revisions, but it always involved the notion that there are no ultimate parts to a true continuum, and that infinitesimals are real.[40]

Thought is a continuum, and cognitions are its smallest parts. These occupy time, but only an infinitesimal duration of time: an endless series of cognitions can occur before the first conscious cognition. And as they are themselves infinitely divisible, we can trace the originary process of cognition back indefinitely without ever reaching *the* beginning, the unknown first impression. Just as Peirce's theory of reality introduces continuity in the community that extends into the infinite future, his theory of cognition introduces continuity at the beginning of cognition.[41] In both cases, the principle of continuity replaces transcendentalism. The transcendental is by definition inexplicable; continuity is at least explicable in principle. Before the 1880s, however, Peirce lacked the tools to attempt a rigorous account of continuity.

Subsequent Developments

By 1870, a decade and a half after his earliest study of Kant, Peirce had identified the major problems to be dealt with in his architectonic system and had developed a general idea of what concepts would be required to resolve those problems. But he still lacked three things. First, he needed assurance that these ideas were logically tenable. Above all, he needed to develop an account of infinity that was both mathematically rigorous and adequate to his needs. It would have to allow for the reality of continua and of infinitesimals. Second, he needed an architectonic blueprint showing the place and interrelation of all areas of knowledge, from the most abstract mathematics to metaphysics, the special sciences, and the practical arts. Third, he needed a clearer understanding of how the various concepts he had already developed would complement one another. He was in the position of a builder who looks at a pile of stones and sees that all the important pieces are present, but does not know whether the stones are sound, has no clear image of the final structure, and is not sure how to fit the stones together. The concluding sections of this chapter briefly note the major developments that allowed Peirce to refine his thought concerning logic, continua, and the categories, and so to set about building his system of knowledge.

DEVELOPMENTS IN LOGIC

Between publication of the "New List" and the period of Peirce's mature philosophy, two developments in logic occurred that influenced his conception of the categories. The first was the development of the logic of relatives, which laid the groundwork for modern symbolic methods and the calculus for deductive logic. The second was the development of quantification theory. Some of the earliest explorations of the latter were carried out by Peirce and his students (notably O. H. Mitchell and Christine Ladd-Franklin) at The Johns Hopkins University, and were published in the 1883 *Studies in Logic* edited by Peirce.[42] These discoveries bore fruit in a revision of the categories in 1885, which found its way into several papers written that year.[43]

Peirce had arrived at his list of three categories with a modification of traditional logic, and he retained the subject-predicate propositional form in the "New List." By 1868 he had read Augustus De Morgan's paper "On the Syllogism, No. IV, and on the Logic of Relations."[44] In 1870 he communicated a paper to the American Academy of Arts and Sciences that extended George Boole's system of logical notation to the logic of relatives.[45] The new logic introduces propositions that are not reducible to simple subject-predicate form, such as 'A gives B to C'. The net result is that the categories themselves become kinds of predicates, rather than the elementary conceptions that join subject and predicate *in* a proposition.[46]

> The great difference between the logic of relatives and ordinary logic is that the former regards the form of relation in all its generality and in its different possible species while the latter is tied down to the matter of the single special relation of similarity. The result is that every doctrine and conception of logic is wonderfully generalized, enriched, beautified, and completed in the logic of relatives.
>
> Thus, the ordinary logic has a great deal to say about *genera* and *species,* or . . . about *classes.* Now, a *class* is a set of objects comprising all that stand to one another in a special relation of similarity. But where ordinary logic talks of classes the logic of relatives talks of *systems.* A *system* is a set of objects comprising all that stand to one another in a group of connected relations. (CP 4.5)

Rather than confining itself to a universe where things are represented merely as having similar or dissimilar characteristics, logic could now treat of a universe in which properties, things, and the relations among them all bear various relations to one another. There will be level upon level of possible representations in such a universe, and Peirce was forced to revise his conception of the categories in light of this.

Take three assertions as examples: "A is Red," "A is to the north of B," and "A is B." Under the traditional subject-predicate theory of propositions, these are interpreted as meaning, respectively, "A is a member of the class of Red things," "A is a member of the class of things north of B," and "A is a member of the class of B's." Under the new logic of relations, however, each of these assertions is interpreted to say different things about a system of qualities, things, and relations: "A is (or has) the quality Red," "A is (existentially) to the north of B," and "A is represented as B to an observer or interpreter." The most interesting consequence of the move to a logic of relations is that Peirce reinterprets the third of his categories, representation, as *mediation* between relate and correlate (CP 1.561). It is not now identified as the only category which unites relate and correlate, as in the "New List," but as the kind of relation that *essentially* involves the transfer of information about such a unification to a third party, another symbol. Thirdness is the kind of relation that implies infinite semeiosis, as we shall see, and this led Peirce to assert that "Continuity represents Thirdness almost to perfection" (CP 1.337).[47]

The insight is corroborated, and was perhaps inspired, by Bernhard Riemann in a paper published in English in 1873. In it he raises the question whether the hypotheses of geometry hold good when applied to infinitely small space. The question leads Riemann to propose two possibilities: either the ground of metric relations derives from what is measured, or it is imposed from outside.

> [I]n a discrete manifoldness, the ground of its metric relations is given in the notion of it, while in a continuous manifoldness, this ground must come from outside. Either therefore the reality which underlies space must form a discrete manifoldness, or we must seek the ground of its metric relations outside it, in binding forces which act upon it.[48]

The ground for the relations described in geometry, then, is either given in the nature of the things related or it derives from some mediating "binding force." This must have rung a bell for Peirce, who already had a conception of such a binding force in his account of reality. The real is independent of what anyone thinks it to be, but is not entirely independent of mind: Thought is the mediating binding force on reality. The real is in a process of evolutionary development, from the indeterminate to the absolutely determinate, where determination consists in the establishment of more and more settled relations via the influence of mind.

We see, dimly, an image of cosmic evolution emerging. The absolute first is a mere wash of ideas, of possibilities that do not even constitute a proper continuum yet because they are transitory abstract qualities, completely unordered. Next comes the force of existence, "thisness," which serves as the ground of relations. Qualities, things, and relations begin to persist, and an ordered system begins to emerge. The end is a true continuum of relations, "a set of objects comprising all that stand to one another in a group of connected relations," where all possible relations are realized and rendered determinate in a final (ideal and unrealizable) representation. In this ideal end, Thirdness would indeed represent perfect continuity—the system of continuous relations.

If the logic of relatives led Peirce to redefine Thirdness, it suggested a revision in the category of Secondness as well. I noted earlier that the new logic allowed for the expression of existential relations among things. The development of the theory of quantification in the early 1880s was icing on the cake. Though nothing in this theory strictly requires the revision of Secondness that Peirce instituted,[49] the ability to designate individuals in the logical calculus made it easy for him to distinguish a separate kind of sign relation, that of *mere* dyadic relation. This is an existential association between two individual things, an association that need not be represented to a third to exist as relation. A tree falling in the philosophical solitude of a forest bears a relation of Secondness to the ground it hits, because the crash, *in fact*, occurs. But the tree's fallen state does not necessarily bear a relation to any third that is its interpretant. With the logical tools of quantification, the new logic can be used to represent a relation (such as "is north of" or "falls on") between an individual A and an individual B, without reference to classes at all.

DEVELOPMENTS IN SET THEORY: TRANSFINITE COLLECTIONS

Georg Cantor laid the groundwork for modern set theory in a series of works beginning in 1872.[50] In them he introduced definitions for *collection* and *cardinality* (size) of a collection, and the rules for rigorous demonstration of results concerning the theory of sets. The most important aspect of Cantor's work is that it provides a means for reasoning about the properties of infinite sets. Cantor's theory of transfinite sets was of decisive importance for Peirce's philosophy in two respects.[51] First, it supplies a rigorous mathematical theory that resolves many of the paradoxes of the infinite. Second, Cantor's specific claims about the mathematical continuum motivated Peirce to develop his own theories concerning the nature of infinity and continuity.

Cantor's "continuum hypothesis" is a conjecture implying that the cardinality of the set of real numbers equals two raised to the power of the cardinality of the first infinite multitude (what is naively known as "infinity").[52]

Cantor asserts that a collection of this multitude has all the mathematical properties requisite for a continuum, even though he had shown, in the result known as Cantor's Theorem, that it is possible to describe an infinite number of other, greater transfinite multitudes. Peirce embraced this result as providing exactly what his philosophy needed: The continuum Cantor describes has the peculiar property of being larger than any infinite series. In 1892, in "The Law of Mind," he put this result to work. He confidently set out to develop his ideas involving the apparently paradoxical assertions about a state of information greater than any specifiable state, a community wider than any specifiable size, and an inquiry carried on longer than any specifiable time. With the new set theory in hand, he felt sure that the paradoxes were *only* apparent.

In the course of working out the details of his philosophy of continuity, however, he came to see the implications of Cantor's hypothesis for continuity as arbitrarily restrictive. Although Cantor's continuum may well serve the needs of mathematics, Peirce left room in his theory of the transfinite for a fundamentally different notion of the continuum, based on the conception of continuity that his philosophy requires. This conception of continuity (which he called "true continuity") is the notion that he identified as "the master-key of philosophy." Its influence is manifest in every corner of his architectonic system, the structure of which is the subject of the next chapter.

The Classification of the Sciences

In 1887 and 1888 Peirce wrote parts of a book to be entitled "A Guess at the Riddle."[1] These notes represent an attempt to arrange his architectonic philosophy, which still stood in disarray. Peirce proposed to analyze almost every area of inquiry in terms of his three categories. He warned that the work would be organized as a game of "'follow-my-leader' from one field of thought into another," but there is a logical progression in his outline (CP 1.364). The first section treats of the categories themselves. The next considers "the triad in reasoning": It would apply the categories to a theory of signs and to logic proper. Subsequent sections would apply the three categories to metaphysics, psychology, physiology, biology, physics, sociology, and, finally, theology (CP 1.354).

Two things are especially notable about this project. First, Peirce proposed to take up metaphysics immediately after a detailed discussion of logic. This accords with his view that metaphysics ought to be based on logic. Second, he proposed to discuss the categories themselves *before* he takes up logic. Because he maintained that the categories are in some sense derived from logic, it seems paradoxical that he would undertake to do things in this order, treating the categories independently.

If Peirce meant in his earlier work that the categories are "derived" from logic in the order of discovery, but are nonetheless more fundamental to thought than logic, then there would be no problem with his treating the categories first in the proposed work. He would merely be omitting the discussion of how they were discovered and getting right to their exposition and application. On the other hand, if Peirce meant that the categories are "derived" from logic in the sense that logical forms somehow determine the nature of the categories, then the order of treatment would mark a significant change in his thinking. I suspect that in his early work, Peirce was undecided about the relation of the categories to logic. He set out to settle the issue in "A Guess at the Riddle," but this problem would not be resolved satisfactorily until he divided the *mathematics of logic* from *logic proper,* a separation that appears in the "Minute Logic" manuscripts (ca. 1902).

We have already seen that Peirce commended Kant for basing metaphysics on logic, and he often cited Kant as an authority for doing likewise. Kant held that the categories and the logical forms of judgment both arise from the nature of the understanding, and that the table of categories is *discovered* through the study of logic. The table of judgments is merely a "clue" to the table of categories. The logic from which the table of judgments arises is the pure work of the understanding, and is the most fundamental science.

The science of logic can provide a clue to the structure of the categories, because its fundamental concepts arise from the same source as the categories and, presumably, have a corresponding structure. Given his close scrutiny of the first *Critique,* it seems unlikely that Peirce misread Kant on this point.

Nonetheless, when Peirce asserted that the categories are derived from logic he apparently meant more than that they are discovered via the clue of logical forms. The categories, for Peirce, are necessary a priori forms, *and* they are logical forms. That Peirce differs from Kant on this point is rendered more likely when we recall that he denied the possibility of a transcendental deduction of the categories. All that he has is a "metaphysical deduction," so he *must* hold that the categories are logical forms in some sense. Peirce's categories are the fundamental conceptions of all thought. They are fundamental logical conceptions, and arise with the possibility of thought itself. They are *discovered* via the study of the foundations of logic, as Kant claims, but, moreover, their *genesis* is part and parcel of the genesis of thought, and therefore of logic. The categories are a priori, elemental concepts in the mathematics of logic.

The Role of a Classification of the Sciences

By the late 1880s Peirce began to see a problem with founding the categories on logic. As Murphey notes:

> it is one of the most significant results of the doubt-belief theory [of inquiry] that the legitimacy of the architectonic principle itself is called into question. For if inquiry is relative to a particular state of evolution, then logic is itself merely a means to the attaining of an end which may not be desirable in a further evolutionary stage. To found a cosmology upon categories derived from a logic which that cosmology shows to be of temporary value only is not likely to advance the cause of knowledge.[2]

Peirce chided Kant for depending on an outmoded logic in formulating the table of categories; he now found himself potentially falling into the same error. For although his own logic was state of the art in the late nineteenth century, Peirce himself insisted that *any* body of scientific knowledge, logic included, must in principle be considered incomplete and potentially incorrect. To identify the fundamental concepts of a historically contingent logic as *the* universal categories could not be legitimate.

Peirce offered no principle to explain his arrangement of topics in "A Guess at the Riddle." This could be expected if he were at that time aware of the difficulty just noted, but was unsure how to resolve it. His game of "follow-my-leader" simply commences with what *must* come first—an independent discussion of the categories. It then proceeds to what had always appeared to him the most basic science, logic, and only then to the other sciences. The completed parts of this work give a nice survey of how useful the three categories would be, if only there were some rational account of how we *get* them in the first place. Peirce could not have been fully satisfied with his project while it lacked such a derivation. This may well be one reason "A Guess at the Riddle" was never completed: there was still work to be done on the architectonic.

The problem he faced in this regard is a tough one. On the one hand, the categories are a priori universal concepts, applicable to all sciences. On the other hand, he maintained that the categories somehow derive from logic, itself a developing science. The derivation of the categories must show, therefore, that the categories are both derived from and prior to logic. If this situation *could* be straightened out, it would at least require a clearer account of the interrelations of the sciences than that in "A Guess at the Riddle." Peirce wrestled with the problem of deriving the categories until 1902, when he finally produced his mature classification of the sciences.[3] This classification provided the needed architectonic blueprint.

Peirce stressed the importance of attending to the features of various sciences in "The Architecture of Theories," published in 1891:

> What I would recommend is that every person who wishes to form an opinion concerning fundamental problems should first of all make a complete survey of human knowledge, should take note of all the valuable ideas in each branch of science, should observe in just what respect each has been successful and where it has failed, in order that, in the light of the thorough acquaintance so attained of the available materials for a philosophical theory and of the nature and strength of each, he may proceed to the study of what the problem of philosophy consists in, and of the proper way of solving it. (CP 6.9)

Surely no one person could be expected to fulfill this requirement! The classification of sciences is a labor-saving device in the search for fundamental categories of thought. A classification would exhibit the philosophically important features of the sciences, which are almost entirely a matter of their interrelations. On the one hand, any science introduces ideas not found in others. On the other hand, any science must presuppose certain ideas. The ideas presupposed by one science are justified by the findings of some other, more basic science. The hierarchical chain could be traced back to the most basic science, the source of the fundamental conceptions Peirce sought. This discipline would not concern itself with any matter of empirical fact, but only the necessary consequences of abstract speculation. Mathematics, absent from the outline of "A Guess at the Riddle," turned out to be the most basic science in Peirce's classification.

Peirce's approach to the categories through a classification of sciences, and his belief that the categories can be discovered in the abstract reasonings of mathematics, illustrates how rationalism and empiricism operate together in his philosophy. Because these two outlooks are traditionally considered antithetical, a few words about Peirce's position are in order. Peirce espouses an empiricism that, like the "radical empiricism" of William James, finds rational patterns evolving in the midst of chaotic experience (CP 4.86). There is a priori knowledge, which comes to us through a certain kind of observation rather than in a singular intuition:

> if there are really any . . . necessary characteristics of mathematical hypotheses . . . this necessity must spring from some truth so broad as to hold not only for the universe we know but for every world that poet could create. And this truth like every truth must come to us by way of experience. No apriorist ever denied that. (CP 1.417)

Here Peirce stressed empiricism, identifying it as the source even of necessary universal truths which would apply in every possible world.

In other passages, though, he emphasized rationalism. One typical passage starts by asserting that "Experience is our only teacher," but goes on to qualify the statement:

> Far be it from me to enunciate any doctrine of *tabula rasa*. For . . . there manifestly is not one drop of principle in the whole vast reservoir of established scientific theory that has sprung from any other source than the power of the human mind to *originate* ideas that are true. But this power, for all it has accomplished, is so feeble that as ideas flow from their springs in the soul, the truths are almost drowned in a flood of false notions; and that which experience does is gradually, and by a sort of fractionation, to precipitate and filter off the false ideas, eliminating them and letting the truth pour on in its mighty current. (CP 5.50)

The mind is credited with originating ideas, indeed in such profusion that experience is needed to sort them out. Experience is the reagent that separates false from true ideas in the stream of thought. Confusion is bound to arise unless we realize that Peirce was neither an empiricist who considered the mind a passive receptacle for ideas, nor a rationalist who saw it as the active creator of ideas. He was a pragmatist, and refused to identify "the mind" as something separate from "the world." There can *be* no mind that merely "receives ideas from" or "imposes ideas on" the world if mind and world are fundamentally continuous, as he claimed.

31

The real *source* of our ideas is nothing other than our previous ideas or cognitions—some of which are classed together as "the external world."[4] An idea arises from a process of inference, or else from a process of perception very much resembling abductive inference except that it cannot be controlled.[5] The human mind is thus neither a passive receptor nor an autonomous creator of ideas. In cognitive processes, whether perceptive or inferential, the mind actively makes and tests relations among various components of thought. In the course of further experience, some relations the mind originates prove to be successful, others unsuccessful. According to the pragmatic view, these are the marks of true and false ideas, respectively. The "rationalist" part of Peirce's theory is his view that the mind produces relational structures of ideas. The "empiricist" part is his insistence that the mind alone cannot distinguish the full meaning of any idea and must therefore defer to subsequent experience in determining truth or falsity.

Certain conceptions are formed and found to hold true in a wide variety of circumstances, by virtually all inquirers. Such conceptions are formulations of *laws*. Peirce distinguished between two kinds of laws:

> those which in a different state of things would continue to hold good and those which in a different state of things would not hold good. The former we call *formal* laws, the latter *material* laws. The formal laws do not depend on any particular state of things, and hence we say that we have not derived them from experience; that is to say, any other experience would have furnished the premises for them as well as that which we have experienced. . . . [the formal laws are] therefore not laws of *nature* but of the conditions of knowledge in general.(W 1:422)

The most fundamental laws, which must be true in any world whatever, are reflected in the categories. They apply to the course of thought itself, and it is irrelevant whether what is being thought about has anything to do with the existent world. Mathematics studies such laws, and is the source of our most basic formal conceptions.

Peirce's classification of the sciences embodies the notion that there are *formal* and *material* elements in every science. The application of this principle to logic allows him to escape the paradox of the origin of the categories. The categories have both formal and material aspects. Their general forms can be discovered rationally, but their material instantiation must be experienced. The categories are first disclosed in the mathematics of logic, and not by the logic which is normative for thought. Peirce could thus have his cake and eat it too: our knowledge of the categories as formal laws of the conditions of thought *derives from* mathematical logic; but these categories are *presupposed by* the normative logic peculiar to any particular stage of inquiry.[6] In good scholastic form, Peirce dissolved the paradox by making a distinction. His classification of the sciences was designed to show that this distinction is plausible.

Peirce's Conception of Science

By 1902, Peirce had all he needed to attempt his definitive classification of the sciences. Perhaps most importantly, he was professionally familiar with a number of sciences. He had made contributions in astronomy (photometric researches), geodesy (pendulum researches), metrology (proposing that the standard meter be defined in terms of a wavelength of light), experimental psychology, chemistry, economics, mathematics, and logic. He had worked as a consulting engineer, statistician, and etymologist. He had participated in several international research efforts while with the U.S. Coast and Geodetic Survey. In addition, he had privately studied classificatory biology with Louis Agassiz and maintained a lifelong interest in physics, history, and linguistics.[7] In short, Peirce was no armchair scientist. He was in as good a position as anyone to survey and "take note of all the valuable ideas in each branch of science."

He was also well versed in the philosophy of science. He had delivered invited lectures on the logic of science in 1865 and 1866, and his 1877–1878 "Illustrations of the Logic of Science" series is an important nineteenth-century contribution to this field.[8] His approach to the task of classifying the sciences was fully informed by this background, including the crucial insight that the sciences could be arranged according to their order of dependence.

Peirce's intimate acquaintance with the day-to-day work of active scientists left him with a disdain for the "encyclopedic" conception of science prevalent in the nineteenth century. According to this view, science consists of the corpus of its established facts. The project of researchers is to utilize the scientific method to establish facts, which are then coordinated into a monolithic system of definitive knowledge. Alasdair MacIntyre points to Thomas Spencer Baynes, editor of the Ninth Edition of the *Encyclopaedia Britannica,* published in 1873, as a leading proponent of this view: "In his preface to the first volume of the Ninth Edition, Baynes made it clear that he intended his contributors not merely to provide detailed information on every major topic but to do so within the framework of a distinctive architectonic of the sciences as that had emerged in the late nineteenth century."[9] In this view, science progresses by accumulating facts about all aspects of the human and natural world and presenting them in a work that, as MacIntyre suggests, was intended eventually to replace the Bible as the canonical work of the culture.[10]

Peirce rejected the view that science is an accumulation of facts. He insisted that science must be characterized as "a living historic entity," which "does not consist so much in *knowing,* nor even in 'organized knowledge,' as it does in diligent inquiry into truth for truth's sake" (CP 1.44). The way to draw distinctions among the various sciences is not by looking at the products of the science (the body of facts that constitute the special knowledge of biology or physics or mathematics, for example) but rather by examining the relations and demarcations between "the different groups of men who devote their lives to the advance of different studies" (SS 79–80). A scientist is identifiable as a person "belonging to a social group all of the members of which sacrifice all the ordinary motives of life to their desire to make their beliefs concerning one subject conform to verified judgments of perception together with sound reasoning, and who therefore really believes the universe to be governed by reason." (SS 75). A particular science, in short, is distinguished by the *idea* that motivates those who conduct research in an area, the common interest that leads them to form a community of inquiry.

Natural Classes and Genealogy

Peirce prefaced "A Detailed Classification of the Sciences" with an extensive discussion of the principles of classification. The key concept for any classification is the *natural class.* A natural class is not a "metaphysically real class" as traditionally defined. His concern was with natural classes "in another and purely experiential sense" (CP 1.204).[11] A thing belongs to a natural class by virtue of its realizing the same final cause as all the members of that class. Lamps of whatever variety, for example, belong to the class of lamps because they are all designed to provide illumination. In the more problematic case of a class of natural objects, Peirce recognized that we cannot usually discern the final cause that its members all realize. Nonetheless, he held that the same principle applies. In biology, for example, "evolution is nothing more nor less than the working out of a definite end" (CP 1.204). We might object that where no final cause can be described, we cannot be sure that one is at work. Peirce's concept of the natural class may be hard to apply in biology, but in the case of objects made with a general purpose in mind, "as is, of course, the case with the sciences," such a concept provides a good basis for classification (CP 1.205).[12]

Final causation is "that mode of bringing facts about according to which a general description of result is made to come about, quite irrespective of any compulsion for it to come about in this or that particular way" (CP 1.211). A final cause is not necessarily a conscious purpose, though that is the form most familiar to us. Rather, it is an idea, a projected state of affairs, which confers on the individual members of a class the power of working out results in the world (CP 1.220). The final cause is what makes a living, thinking human qualitatively different from the pile of chemicals that is a corpse. It is the guiding idea that makes a scientific research program qualitatively different from a long series of random observations carried out by a dilettante. "Efficient causation is that kind of causation whereby the parts compose the whole; final causation is that kind of causation whereby the whole calls out its parts" (CP 1.220). A final cause is not some force working *independently* of efficient cause, but rather an idea around which efficient forces are organized toward the realization of an end.

Peirce noted three characteristics of a final cause: It is general, it is vague, and its manner of realization varies from one particular situation to another. That a final cause is *general* means that it calls only for some *kind* of result to be brought about. To say that illumination is needed only says that some device that provides light should be produced, not that it must be an electric table lamp (CP 1.205). That a final cause is *vague* means that the realization of the end will follow one of a large number of possible paths: The means of satisfying the final cause is *variable* (CP 1.206). Finally, the actual means of satisfaction will be determined largely by the circumstances in which the final cause must operate. There may be an ideal object that would fulfill the final cause perfectly (a lamp of infinitely variable brightness that costs nothing to produce or operate, for example), but such an object does not usually exist. Compromise and deviation from the ideal are inevitable, and various characteristics will be emphasized or subordinated depending on the situation in which the final cause operates. The actual objects we encounter "will cluster about some middling qualities, some being removed this way, some that way, and at greater and greater removes fewer and fewer objects will be so determined. Thus, clustering distributions will characterize purposive classes" (CP 1.207).

Classification, then, does not look for *essential* features of objects (i.e., characteristics that are necessary and sufficient for a thing's inclusion in a class) because there is no essence that makes a thing what it is. Rather, it is a combination of a general "desire," vague specifications for satisfying it, and various limitations on the resources available to meet those specifications that make a thing what it is. In classifying objects, we look for the broad similarities that identify the members of a class. As Ludwig Wittgenstein later put it, the members of a class bear a "family resemblance" to one another.

Classification is inherently uncertain. In many cases an object exhibits features characteristic of more than one class. Unless we have more information (of the object's history, for example) it may be impossible for us to be sure what its primary purpose is (CP 1.208). All we can do in setting out to classify objects is to look for their apparent similarities and try to identify as best we can the final cause that similar objects fulfill. Objects that share a common final cause, and hence exhibit similar features, are included in the same natural class. Clearly, in many cases the final cause will be unknown, and mere similarity of objects' features does not allow us to describe natural classes. It is an inconvenient fact of nature that everything exhibits *some* similarities to anything else we may choose. Lacking additional information, we have no way to tell which ones are the "important" characteristics of an object, for purposes of classification. In extreme cases where we have no information about why a thing was created or how it was to be used, we have almost no basis for determining what its natural classification is.

Rather than starting at the top of the taxonomic tree, with a sure identification of the final cause that brings a broad class of objects into existence, we are often forced to start instead at the bottom, with a sampling of particular objects that we *suppose* might belong together, and look for shared qualities. This requires that we first form a hypothesis about the final cause, or some part of it, that is apparently at work. We then examine our sample objects, and others selected at random, for occurrence of the characteristics that would be relevant to fulfilling that final cause. This *genealogical* method (which Peirce saw exemplified in Charles Darwin's biological investigations) allows us to distinguish types within the broader sample. Types are various manifestations of a general kind, produced under the influence of the same unidentified final cause. Genealogical information allows us to "trace the genesis of a class and ascertain how several [classes] have been derived by different lines of descent from one less specialized form" (CP 1.222). Genealogy provides us with an account of what classes there are, and an explanation of why there are those particular classes rather than others. We can also see how the various classes are related to one another. With the classes so distinguished, we have some guidance in venturing a classification on the basis of similar characteristics. We know which characteristics would be functionally important in various classes, if our hypothesis were correct, and we can look for them in the objects before us.

Classification is not primarily a matter of definition. Only *after* the classes have been found, either by the top-down method of identifying the final cause or by the bottom-up method of constructing a genealogy, is it appropriate to venture abstract definitions of the classes (CP 1.222).

> All natural classification is essentially, we may almost say, an attempt to find out the true genesis of the objects classified. But by genesis must be understood, not the efficient action which produces the whole by producing the parts, but the final action which produces the parts because they are needed to make the whole. Genesis is production from ideas. It may be difficult to understand how this is true in the biological world, though there is proof enough that it is so. But in regard to science it is a proposition easily enough intelligible. A science is defined by its problem; and its problem is clearly formulated on the basis of abstracter science. (CP 1.227)

The classification of sciences proceeds via genealogy, which describes the interrelations of the various sciences. The construction of a genealogy of the sciences is not an endeavor for the historian of science, on this view. To the historian it is quite important that the physicists' paradoxical concept of instantaneous velocity led to the development of the calculus, for example. But that it in fact took the findings of a physical science to suggest the need for certain mathematical tools is unimportant to the Peircean genealogist. The important point is that the physical problem itself remained a paradox until the mathematical tools for understanding it were developed. The physicists' concept was not fully intelligible, and could not provide the basis for experiment, until the mathematical concepts of the calculus were in place. Historically, the physicists' paradoxical *questions* preceded the mathematical one; genealogically, the mathematical *ideas* of the infinitesimal calculus produced the intelligible ideas of Newtonian physics.

A classification of the sciences, then, must identify the central problems and the guiding ideas of the various sciences. A science's central problem is its final cause. The ideas that allow us to clearly formulate that problem have their origin in another, more basic science. Peirce's classification sets out to articulate the defining problems and the structure of dependence among the various sciences.

The Classificatory Scheme

Figure 2.1 shows the schema of Peirce's classification of the sciences.[13] Peirce's main distinction is between theoretical or heuretic sciences (also called sciences of discovery), and practical sciences. The fundamental purpose of theoretical science is "simply and solely knowledge of God's

Fig. 2.1 Peirce's Classification of the Sciences

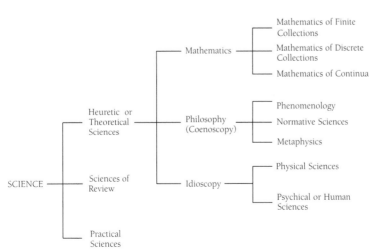

truth," while the purpose of practical science is "for the uses of life" (CP 1.239). Peirce supplied a list of practical sciences to indicate the sort of thing he included: It begins with "pedagogics, gold-beating, etiquette, pigeon-fancying" and continues to great length (CP 1.243). He apparently did not attempt to classify the practical sciences at all.

Figure 2.1 shows the sciences of review as an independent branch of science.[14] Peirce defines a science of review as "the business of those who occupy themselves with arranging the results of discovery, beginning with digests, and going on to endeavor to form a philosophy of science" (CP 1.182). It includes the project of forming a classification of sciences. Its purpose is "to sum up the results of all the theoretical sciences and to study them as forming one system" (CP 1.256).[15]

The first among the three sciences of discovery is mathematics. It is not usual to consider mathematics a science of discovery, but in Peirce's view it does rely on a certain kind of observation: "it makes constructions in the imagination . . . and then observes these imaginary objects, finding in them relations of parts not specified in the precept of construction" (CP 1.240). In dealing only with imagined objects, it "does not undertake to ascertain any matter of fact whatever, but merely posits hypotheses, and traces out their consequences" (CP 1.240). The purpose of mathematics, then, is to study "what is and is not logically possible, without making itself responsible for its actual existence" (CP 1.184). Peirce placed mathematics first among the sciences because it provides concepts (e.g., number, possible kinds of relation) that are essential to every other science (CP 1.245, 362–63). Because it is free to investigate any idea that may happen to arise, in any way that may prove practicable, mathematics is not dependent on any other science for the formulation of its problems.

Philosophy is the second science of discovery.[16] It, too, is observational, but "contents itself with observations which come within the range of every man's normal experience" (CP 1.241). The purpose of philosophy is "to find out all that can be found out from those universal experiences which confront every man in every waking hour of his life" (CP 1.245). There is a peculiar difficulty in this study, however, because a truly common experience is one of the hardest things to *observe*: "These observations escape the untrained eye precisely because they permeate our whole lives, just as a man who never takes off his blue spectacles soon ceases to see the blue tinge" (CP 1.241). Philosophy derives its fundamental concepts from mathematics, and has no particular need to draw on the special sciences "except as a sort of condiment to excite its own proper observation" (CP 1.241).

The third branch, comprising the special or idioscopic sciences, includes the physical and psychical (i.e., human or social) sciences. Both subclasses of idioscopy depend upon special observation "which travel or other exploration, or some assistance to the senses, either instrumental or given by training, together with unusual diligence, has put within the power of its students" (CP 1.242). The purpose of the special sciences is to discover the particular causal order working in the world. The physical sciences investigate efficient causation; the psychical sciences investigate final causation (CP 1.242). These sciences draw their fundamental concepts from both mathematics and philosophy.

Mathematics and Logic

Peirce took up the problem of the role of logic in discovering the categories in "A Guess at the Riddle." He finally resolved the problem nearly fifteen years later, in his 1902 classification of the sciences. Following Kant, he maintained that the categories are in some sense "derived" from logic. By 1902, though, he brought some subtle distinctions to this assertion. First, he distinguished the metaphysical significance of the categories from their function as the elementary forms of thought. The categories of metaphysics are indeed derived from the categories of logic. The categories of logic, however, are themselves derived from a more elementary manifestation of the three categories. This move involves a second distinction: that between *the mathematics of logic* ("the simplest mathematics" and the first science), and *the mathematical part of logic* (the formal or symbolic "logic of relatives"). These are two distinct but closely related areas of inquiry. In fact, because these areas are of interest primarily to the same investigators, the two are nearly indistinguishable under Peirce's definition of a "science." The details of Peirce's solution to the problem of the categories will unfold as we explore the major divisions of mathematics.

Besides the conviction that infinitesimals are real, Benjamin Peirce's definition of mathematics may well be the most important thing he left to his son. Charles' view that mathematics is an observational but purely hypothetical discipline has already been mentioned. It is a refinement of Benjamin's definition, published in 1881, of mathematics as "the science which draws necessary conclusions" (CP 5.8). In 1902, Charles recast this definition in terms of the object of mathematical inquiry: "Mathematics is the study of what is true of hypothetical states of things" (CP 4.233).

Mathematics is the province of "precise necessary reasoning," which according to Peirce always proceeds along the following lines:

> It consists in forming an image of the conditions of the problem, associated with which are certain general permissions to modify the image, as well as certain general assumptions that certain things are impossible. Under the permissions, certain experiments are performed upon the image, and the assumed impossibilities involve their always resulting in the same general way. (CP 5.8)

Mathematical reasoning, then, is entirely unrestricted except by hypothetical permissions and restrictions that the reasoner chooses to introduce. These may differ from the apparent "permissions" and "restrictions" of the actual world; in many fruitful mathematical experiments (such as those concerning non-Euclidean geometries) they often do so differ. The only indispensable rule for mathematical reasoning is that we consistently obey the stipulated conditions. "Such reasonings and all reasonings turn upon the idea that if one exerts certain kinds of volition, one will undergo in return certain compulsory perceptions" (CP 5.9). Mathematics, then, discovers what we are compelled to think, *if* particular conditions are admitted, without restriction upon the conditions to be admitted or excluded. Mathematics is applicable to "every other science without exception" (CP 1.245).

Figure 2.2 indicates Peirce's main division of mathematics into mathematics of finite series, mathematics of infinite discrete series, and mathematics of continua and pseudo-continua, along with subdivisions of each (CP 1.185, 1.283). The mathematician is free to stipulate any hypothetical conditions whatever as the defining conditions for reasoning about a problem. On the other hand, the particular hypothetical conditions that are stipulated will in part determine the problems that offer themselves for investigation. Peirce urges that mathematics, then, should be divided "according to the nature of its general hypotheses," rather than by the various methods (such as algebraic or geometrical) that it may employ (CP 4.247–48). "Mathematics may be divided according to the degree of complexity of its hypotheses" (NEM 1:256), that is, according to the multitude of units admitted in the hypothetical universe of reasoning (CP 4.248).

Fig. 2.2 Divisions of Mathematics

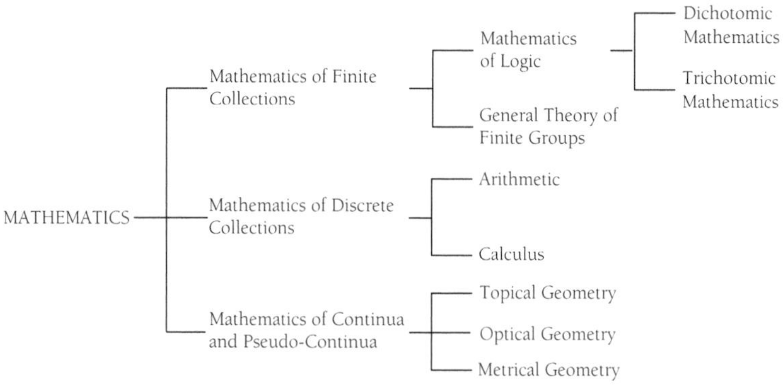

The division according to *multitude* of units is not identical to division according to *number* of units postulated in the mathematical universe. A universe containing three objects obviously has a different number of objects from one containing three thousand. Because the set of objects in the universe is countable in both cases, however, both have the same multitude—both are *enumerable*. Besides enumerable multitudes (of which any finite collection is an example), Peirce identified two other grades of multitude for collections of discrete objects. A *denumerable* multitude is the lowest grade of infinite multitude, corresponding to what is naively called "infinity": It is the smallest grade of uncountable collection. There are grades of infinite discrete collections larger than denumerable, however, which Peirce designated as *abnumerable* multitudes. The first of these is the Cantorean continuum; Peirce refers to this and all other abnumerable multitudes as "pseudo-continua." These are distinguished from the kind of multiplicity he calls true continua, which are not exactly collections as they are not composed of discrete units at all.[17]

The most elementary division of mathematics is also the most fundamental science. According to Kant, it is in the most fundamental science that the table of categories is disclosed. In Peirce's scheme, this science concerns the necessary properties of enumerable finite collections. Within this field, the consideration of those systems grounded on the simplest possible hypotheses constitutes its own study. Peirce identified this branch as *mathematics of logic* and claimed that, although it is indispensable to logic, it is "hardly worth consideration" by the mathematician owing to its simplicity from the mathematical point of view (CP 4.227). It is in the mathematics of logic, and specifically in dichotomic and trichotomic mathematics, that the categories are discovered. Because mathematics per se is concerned only with the activity of reasoning rather than its analysis, though, the analysis of the categories is left to logic.

Peirce's description of the simplest mathematics proceeds step-by-step through the only possible hypotheses, until all the "interesting" possibilities have been identified. Concerning the simplest conceivable universe, Peirce says:

> Were nothing at all supposed, mathematics would have no ground at all to go upon. Were the hypothesis merely that there was nothing but one unit, there would not be a possibility of a question, since only one answer would be possible. Consequently, the simplest possible hypothesis is that there are two objects. (CP 4.250)

The mathematics of a one-object universe consists of a single proposition:

> Nothing whatever can be predicated of [the single object] *A* and it is absolutely indistinguishable from *blank nothingness*.
>   For if anything were true of *A, A* would have some character or quality which character or quality would be something in the universe over and above *A*. (NEM 4:165)

41

The two areas of mathematical inquiry that Peirce called "dichotomic" and "trichotomic" mathematics comprise the mathematics of logic (CP 4.307). Dichotomic mathematics posits a universe of two things, distinct from one another. If we designate the things as B and M (for *bonum* and *malum*), then

> the problem of this mathematics will be to determine in regard to anything unrecognized, say *x*, whether it is identical with B or identical with M. It would be a mere difference of phraseology to say that there are countless things in the universe, *x*, *y*, *z*, etc. each of which has one or the other of the two values B and M. (NEM 4:165)

The most important application of this system is in the theory of traditional two-valued logic where any unknown *x* may be supposed to be either true or false (CP 4.250). In the dichotomic universe, of course, there can only be dyadic relations among the "primary substances." Peirce commented that "the Boolian algebra of logic is a mere application of this kind of pure mathematics. It is a form of mathematics rather poverty-stricken as to ideas" (NEM 4:165).

Trichotomic mathematics introduces a third thing into the universe. With this, there are not only the possibilities for a number of dyadic relations among the primary substances, but also triadic relations among them. In a dualistic universe, there are only four dyadic relations that can obtain among the objects. To get a more interesting situation, Peirce suggested that we consider the possibility of relations among the different dyadic relations. Once this "virtual introduction of an entire new kind of *abstractions*" (NEM 4:166) is allowed, though, we have left the province of traditional logic. This opens to us a qualitatively complex universe, describable by the logic of relations. In it, we encounter triadic and even higher-order relatives which may obtain among the new abstractive entities. The number of such entities expands exponentially as we pass through higher levels of abstraction. The analysis of a trichotomous universe is requisite to comprehending the complex world of the logic of relations.[18] Trichotomic mathematics is central to Peirce's system, based as that system is upon the logic of relatives.

Inclusion of three rather than two objects in the hypothetical universe introduces possibilities for triadic relations in addition to dyadic relations. Introduction of any more than three objects (as virtually occurs when we admit abstractive entities into the dichotomous system) increases the number of possible *instances* of relations, but introduces no new *kinds* of relations. Peirce argues that no matter how complex our N-valued mathematical universe becomes, all polyads higher than triads can in principle be reduced to complexes of monadic, dyadic, and triadic relatives. This point will be considered more closely in chapter 3; here we note only Peirce's contention that any kind of relation that could occur in a more complex universe of discrete elements is present in the simplest supposable universes, which he conceives as the universes of traditional syllogistic and of the modern logic of relations, respectively. We shall see that the novel kind of relation among the parts of a continuum, which denies that such parts are even discrete elements, is itself a case of a triadic relation.

With the discovery of monadic, dyadic, and triadic relatives in the logic of mathematics, we have the formal concepts of the three cenopythagorean categories. The question of their material applicability remains to be addressed in phenomenology; that of their necessity and sufficiency as logical categories must await analysis in the mathematical part of logic proper.

One last point concerning Peirce's discussion of trichotomic mathematics should be noted here. Just as the two values of dichotomic mathematics could be interpreted as "true" and "false," the three values of trichotomic mathematics may likewise be interpreted as truth values. In 1902 Peirce wrote that trichotomic mathematics "is not quite so fundamentally important as the dichotomic branch," and rhetorically asked "how is the mathematician to take a step without recognizing the duality of truth and falsehood? Hegel and others have dreamed of such a thing; but it cannot be" (CP 4.308). Yet this does not exclude the possibility of the three-valued logic. Carolyn Eisele has briefly sketched the evolution of Peirce's thought on multi-valued logic, and her findings suggest that it was only a short time after writing the above passage that he came upon the genuine possibility for a triadic logic and began to explore its implications. In a draft for his 1903 Lowell Lectures, Peirce mentions a "different conception" of truth values, in which we "consider that a proposition is never, or hardly ever, perfectly true."[19] The question to be settled concerns what interpretation to place upon the third truth value. The answer appears in a subsequent draft:

> We cannot reason or think at all without making the distinction between truth and falsity; while we can perform some elementary kinds of reasoning. . . without absolutely excluding the possibility of an intermediate state between the two, say the state of being sometimes true and sometimes false. The principle of contradiction is more elementary than that of excluded middle, so that we may begin by considering the consequences of the former while leaving the latter out of account.[20]

By 1909, Peirce's continued work on the problems of true continua and his insights in trichotomic mathematics led him to develop a viable system of triadic logic, which allows for the suspension of excluded middle. The third value in the system (L) characterizes a "limit-case" between truth and falsity.[21]

The mathematics of the simplest finite collections and of continua are by far the most important branches of mathematics for Peirce's philosophy.

Between these, however, falls the mathematics of infinite discrete collections. Peirce saw the mathematics of infinite collections as an underdeveloped area of study. Arithmetic is the study of "the least multitudinous of infinite collections," the natural numbers; and calculus is "the study of collections of higher multitude." Peirce observed that at the time of his writing, calculus had not been applied to any collections except that whose order of multitude immediately succeeds the natural numbers (CP 1.283). This application has still not been made, primarily because most mathematicians identify this collection as *the* continuum.

This brings us to Peirce's third division of mathematics. According to what has come to be the accepted view, there should not *be* a third division of mathematics, if the divisions are made according to multitude of elements admitted in the mathematical universe. Peirce, however, disagreed with Cantor about the nature of the continuum. He proposed that there is another order of number beyond the infinite series of infinite, discrete collections that commences with the set of natural numbers. In this maximal collection, which he calls the "true continuum" to distinguish it from Cantor's ("pseudo-") continuum, cardinality or "roominess" ceases to be a meaningful concept. According to the techniques applicable to discrete series, the true continuum is apparently larger than any other collection. The defining characteristic of this collection is not its size, but rather the mode of connection among its parts. As mentioned before, the parts of the true continuum are not discrete. The study of the true continuum is the science of topical geometry, or *synectics,* still a young science today (CP 1.283).

Before discussing Peirce's divisions of philosophy, it will be helpful to establish his account of the difference between mathematics and logic in general, and the difference between mathematical logic and normative logic in particular. Peirce noted that "mathematics has such a close intimacy with one of the classes of philosophy, that is, with logic, that no small acumen is required to find the joint between them" (CP 1.245).

Two things allow us to distinguish mathematics from logic. The first is a difference in their central concerns, and the second is a difference in the application of their results. Mathematics is the science that *draws* necessary conclusions, not the science of *how to draw* them. The mathematical branch of the latter science is deductive logic (especially in its modern guise as the formal or symbolic logic of relatives).

> The logician does not care particularly about this or that hypothesis or its consequences, except so far as these things may throw a light upon the nature of reasoning. The mathematician is intensely interested in efficient methods of reasoning, with a view to their possible extension to new problems; but he does not, *quâ* mathematician, trouble himself minutely to dissect those parts of this method whose correctness is a matter of course. (CP 4.239)

Peirce illustrated the difference in terms of what the logician and mathematician value in an algebra of logic. The mathematician wants an elegant system, one that will allow the shortest possible proof of a conclusion from given premises. The logician, interested in the process of reasoning rather than the result, wants a system that exhibits every intermediate step between premises and conclusion (CP 4.239).

A second notable difference is that while mathematics is purely hypothetical, logic aims to make categorical assertions: logic in the broad sense is a normative discipline. "The problem of the logician is to determine the general conditions of the attainment of truth" (NEM 4:196). Logic has something to say about how thought ought to proceed, and must rely on ethics for help in stating the end toward which thought ought to strive (CP 4.240).

Logic does rely on mathematics in proving certain of its claims, as does any other science (CP 4.240). Peirce identified this part of the science as formal or deductive logic; it is grounded in dichotomic and trichotomic mathematics. The broader science of logic, which makes use of deductive logic as well as of inductive and abductive inference, is the normative theory of inquiry.

Mathematics does not depend on logic at all. It embodies and obeys the rules of deductive reasoning, of course, but Peirce's point is that it never needs to refer to any formal statements of those rules: "mathematics performs its reasonings by a *logica utens* which it develops for itself, and has no need of any appeal to a *logica docens*; for no disputes about reasoning arise in mathematics which need to be submitted to the principles of the philosophy of thought for decision" (CP 1.417). Mathematics is not the science of reasoning, but a science that reasons. It is guided by long practice and highly developed good sense about drawing conclusions, but not an explicit theory of right reasoning. "[J]ust as it is not necessary, in order to talk, to understand the theory of the formation of vowel sounds, so it is not necessary, in order to reason, to be in possession of the theory of reasoning" (CP 4.242). Logic affords a conscious awareness of the rules that direct reasoning, and with this awareness comes responsibility to apply the rules correctly. Thus logic in the broad sense is a normative science of reasoning, and is distinct from mathematics, a non-normative science that reasons.

The principles that constrain mathematical reasoning are the inherent rules governing the possibility of any consistent thought whatever. These rules are explored in mathematical or formal logic (CP 4.240). Because the hypothetical universes that the mathematical logician studies actually *do* turn out to correlate in important ways with the universe of actual experience (a finding established in phenomenology, the first division of philosophy), the rules that govern thought in them have fruitful application in the real world. This, however, is not the mathematician's concern.

The wide applicability of its discoveries makes mathematical or formal logic an interesting and important area of study, but Peirce insisted that formal logic "is by no means the whole of logic, or even its principal part" (CP 4.240). If we take formal logic for the whole of logic, we neglect the normative factor that directs us toward the proper use of logical reasoning. Mathematical reasoning is a powerful tool, but used alone, without ethical direction, it may turn out to be "a great hindrance to right reasoning" (CP 4.242). Peirce's view on the proper use of logic is reminiscent of Socrates' view concerning the proper use of rhetoric. Employing logic without the knowledge of why truth is valuable is much the same as employing persuasive techniques without knowledge of what it is good to persuade people to believe. "Logic has to define its aim; and in doing so is even more dependent upon ethics, or the philosophy of aims, by far, than it is . . . upon mathematics" (CP 4.240).

The Divisions of Philosophy

Mathematics, taken as a whole, is an extended hypothetical syllogism: *If* we suppose a particular sort of universe, then certain consequences necessarily follow. If we suppose a different sort of universe, then other consequences necessarily follow. Mathematics seeks discoveries about universes of pure thought, which do not necessarily have anything to do with the actual world. The remaining two branches of the science of discovery, philosophy and idioscopy, inquire into the nature of things in the actual world.

Philosophy involves the most general kind of inquiry about the world. It "deals with positive truth, indeed, yet contents itself with observations such as come within the range of every man's normal experience" (CP 1.241). Its purpose is "to find out all that can be found out from those universal experiences" (CP 1.246).

The first branch in figure 2.3 illustrates Peirce's three divisions of philosophy, each of which correspond to one of the three categories. He briefly described them in the following passage from 1903:

> Philosophy has three grand divisions. The first is Phenomenology, which simply contemplates the Universal Phenomenon and discerns its ubiquitous elements, Firstness, Secondness, and Thirdness, together perhaps with other series of categories. The second grand division is Normative Science, which investigates the universal and necessary laws of the relation of Phenomena to *Ends*, that is, perhaps, to Truth, Right, and Beauty. The third grand division is Metaphysics, which endeavors to comprehend the reality of Phenomena. (CP 5.121)

Just as philosophy is dependent on mathematics for its fundamental ideas, each division of philosophy is likewise dependent on its predecessor.

Fig. 2.3 Divisions of Philosophy

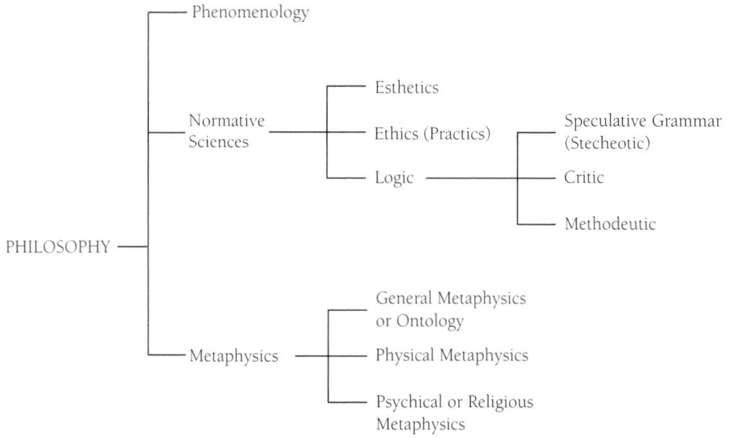

```
                    ┌── Phenomenology
                    │
                    │              ┌── Esthetics
                    │   Normative  │
                    │   Sciences ──┼── Ethics (Practics)      ┌── Speculative Grammar
                    │              │                          │   (Stecheotic)
                    │              └── Logic ─────────────────┼── Critic
PHILOSOPHY ─────────┤                                         │
                    │                                         └── Methodeutic
                    │
                    │              ┌── General Metaphysics
                    │              │   or Ontology
                    └── Metaphysics ┼── Physical Metaphysics
                                   │
                                   └── Psychical or Religious
                                       Metaphysics
```

PHENOMENOLOGY

Phenomenology examines what is given in common experience: It "just contemplates phenomena as they are, simply opens its eyes and describes what it sees. . . [Its concern is] simply describing the object, as a phenomenon, and stating what it finds in all phenomena alike" (CP 5.37). Phenomenology approaches the field of common experience in its Firstness, but as we have seen it does not start its investigation of experience entirely without preconceived ideas or expectations about what it may find. On the contrary, it sets out armed with the hypothetical findings of mathematics— especially the mathematics of logic. Phenomenology must,

> if it is to be properly grounded, be made to depend upon the Conditional or Hypothetical Science of *Pure Mathematics*, whose only aim is to discover not how things actually are, but how they might be supposed to be, if not in our universe, then in some other. A Phenomenology which does not reckon with pure mathematics, a science hardly come to years of discretion when Hegel wrote, will be the same pitiful club-footed affair that Hegel produced. (CP 5.40)

The discoveries of pure mathematics describe what could possibly be discovered in any universe, and suggest what may be fruitfully sought in the broad patterns of actual experience. The hypothetical investigations of mathematics serve to direct the attention of the phenomenologist. The kinds of relations described in dichotomic and trichotomic mathematics may very well obtain in actual experience, and the phenomenologist looks specifically for these relations. Firstness, Secondness, and Thirdness are thus to be anticipated in phenomena. Because the actual world is more complex than the limited two- and three-element universes of the simplest mathematics, though, he leaves the door open for discovering other series of categories, "consisting of phases of evolution" (CP 5.38). In practice Peirce was well enough occupied by the three universal categories, "all of which apply to everything," and was little concerned with discovering any others (CP 5.38).

THE NORMATIVE SCIENCES

While phenomenology considers the Firstness of common experience, that is, how it merely appears to the mind, the normative sciences consider the Secondness of common experience, or what is in any way compelling about it. Normative science "investigates the universal and necessary laws of the relation of Phenomena to *Ends,* that is, perhaps, to Truth, Right, and Beauty" (CP 5.121). These sciences are normative because they study what ought to be, *in the nature of things,* and not just as seen from the anthropological or psychological standpoint: "A subtle and almost ineradicable narrowness in the conception of Normative Science runs through almost all modern philosophy in making it relate exclusively to the human mind" (CP 5.128). Peirce identified esthetics, ethics, and logic as sciences because they strive to state and explain the results of *experimental* inquiry into the nature of what is good, right, and true.

At first sight the claim that experiment can reveal anything to us about these intangibles may be surprising. The first step toward understanding Peirce's normative sciences is to realize that esthetic, ethical, and logical goodness are not exactly intangible. They are important and acknowledged features of everyday lived experience. As such they are subject to inquiry; and for Peirce, genuine inquiry *always* proceeds by experiment. The second step toward understanding the normative sciences is to recognize that each of us is capable of exercising some control over our own desires, conduct, and the course of our thought. The normative sciences simply investigate ideals so that control can be exercised to make our desires, conduct, and thought better conform to them.

A passage written on ethics (or practics, as Peirce sometimes called the second normative science) provides our point of departure. It sketches the process by which we can come to exercise proper control over our own conduct. A similar process applies to controlling our desires and the course of our thought. Peirce begins by distinguishing uncontrolled conduct from deliberate conduct, which is directed toward an ideal:

> Every action has a motive, but an ideal only belongs to a line [of] conduct which is deliberate. To say that conduct is deliber-

ate implies that each action, or each important action, is reviewed by the actor and that his judgment is passed upon it, as to whether his future conduct is to be like that or not. His ideal is the kind of conduct which attracts him upon review. His self-criticism, followed by a more or less conscious resolution that in its turn excites a determination of his habit, will . . . *modify* a future action. (CP 1.574)

An angry child, for example, hits another child. In our example, this is an "uncontrolled" act—it is not done in conformity to an ideal. After the incident, perhaps facing a parent's condemnation, the child feels remorse and makes a decision: In the future, anger will not lead to rash and violent actions. Perhaps the child even resolves to be the kind of person who will never resort to violence. This identification of an ideal is the first step toward determining a habit of nonviolence, which will modify the course of future actions. The child may reflect before acting next time. Whatever action ensues will be more deliberate, carried out with an awareness that it either conforms to the child's own ideal or violates it in some way. In the course of future experience, the ideal may become more refined (if, for example, the child decides not to fight *except* in self-defense). This process of refinement is carried out in light of "experimental findings" that come as the habit arising from the ideal is tested in a variety of situations.

The general pattern of how deliberate control is established is simple enough. In the following formulation, the pattern is made applicable to all three normative sciences. Esthetics examines what is compelling (i.e., desirable) about possible ends; practics, what is compelling about possible actions; and logic, what is compelling about possible courses of thought. Something is unreflectively desired, done, or concluded in response to a situation. Afterward, the desire, act, or conclusion is reconsidered and criticized: Does the person want future desires, acts, or conclusions to be like this one or not? Does the person want to *be* like that? The answer, whether positive or negative, leads the person to formulate a general ideal, a standard or norm, to which future desires, acts, or conclusions should conform. As experiences accumulate, the ideal is refined and modified so as to become more workable. All along, there is a conscious attempt to conform to this self-imposed and accepted ideal. Note that even if the criticism originally comes from another, as in my earlier example, the ideal is self-imposed because the individual finally must accept the ideal as his or her own. The person deliberately forms habits of desiring, acting, or thinking which further the realization of that ideal the experiment indicates is "the best way to be."

Practics is the science that studies "the conformity of action to an ideal" (CP 1.573). Its aim is to describe the ideal conduct, based on experience. Peirce suggested that an individual setting out to determine the ideal of conduct would be wise to consult the prevalent view of the community—

especially if it happens that a novel ethical theory leads to an unconventional conclusion (for example, that incest is a moral duty) (CP 1.661-62). As William James suggested, society itself may be seen as a long-running experiment aimed at identifying the best kind of conduct, and its conventional mores deserve a great deal of respect.[22] Practics by itself tells us only "that we have a power of self-control, that no narrow or selfish aim can ever prove satisfactory, that the only satisfactory aim is the broadest, highest, and most general possible aim" (CP 1.611). It tells us that our conduct should always conform to the highest ideal, but the conception of that ideal is developed in esthetics.

Esthetics examines phenomena as possible ends. It asks what is desirable in all the worlds of fact and fancy that are before us. We should note that for Peirce, esthetics is not primarily the study of "the beautiful." It is certainly not concerned to discover rules for the production of beauty (the concern of the "fine arts," which would be classified as practical sciences in Peirce's schema). Esthetics, rather, examines phenomena and tries to discern what is *good* in the broadest sense. The ultimate aim of Peirce's esthetics, as Vincent Potter puts it, is "to analyze the *summum bonum,* the absolutely ideal state of things which is desirable in and for itself regardless of any other consideration whatsoever."[23]

Before the summum bonum can be identified, however, we must determine what constitutes goodness in the broadest sense. Esthetics deals with the inherent qualities of phenomena, independent of the relations of those phenomena to actions. "[I]n order to state the question of esthetics in its purity, we should eliminate from it, not merely all consideration of effort, but all consideration of action and reaction, including all consideration of our receiving pleasure" (CP 2.199). When we strip away these considerations, it appears that any phenomenon that possesses inner unity and completeness qualifies as esthetically good: "[A]n object, to be esthetically good, must have a multitude of parts so related to one another as to impart a positive simple immediate quality to their totality; and whatever does this is, in so far, esthetically good, no matter what the particular quality of the total may be" (CP 5.132). Potter observes, "Everything is what it is, and as such has some quality pervading its totality."[24] In so far as a phenomenon *is,* as a unified whole, it possesses esthetic goodness, or what has been called "ontological goodness." Esthetics is not a theory of "beauty," but of what is inherently admirable in something's being the way it is. The inherently admirable may include ugly, disturbing, or frightening qualities. Such an object "remains none the less esthetically good, although people in our condition are incapacitated from a calm esthetic contemplation of it" (CP 5.132).

Although all phenomena exhibiting inner unity are ontologically or esthetically good, there are differences among phenomena. In determining the summum bonum, we consider various phenomena as possible ideals toward which we might strive, and seek to comprehend an ideal that stands out as categorically good. This value distinction goes beyond asserting the ontological goodness of all that is, but does not yet reach the level of distinguishing relative goodness and badness. Questions of relative goodness depend on how suitable a thing is for realizing some purpose; the summum bonum is "a state of things that *reasonably recommends itself in itself* aside from any ulterior consideration" (CP 5.130). It is that purpose which *can* be pursued, without contradiction of effort, in every circumstance.

Peirce's description of the summum bonum clearly owes a great deal to Kant's categorical imperative. Recourse to Kant may help set the stage:

> Rational nature is distinguished from the rest of nature by the fact that it sets itself an end. This end would be the matter of every good will. But in the idea of an absolutely good will— good without any qualifying condition (of attaining this or that end)—complete abstraction must be made from every end that has come about as an effect (since such would make every will only relatively good).[25]

At the natural level, all things are ontologically good. Rational agents with the capacity for self-control, however, establish purposes to which their energies may be directed. An act such as cutting open a human abdomen is *relatively* good or bad, depending on the particular project the act furthers. The same act may be performed in an appendectomy or in a murder. The absolute end, the highest good, is that to which *all* our particular projects must answer.

Peirce's ultimate end corresponds to Kant's ultimate end. In one formulation, Kant describes the ultimate end as a "possible kingdom of ends" in which any rational agent is simultaneously sovereign, legislator, and subject. It is characterized by "completeness of its system of ends," a harmony of all the particular projects its subjects pursue.[26] In Peirce's system, phenomenology discovers Thirdness, the operation of laws, in the universe. Given this discovery, we will sooner or later conceive the possibility of a perfectly rational, law-governed, orderly universe. Such a universe would not be pure idea, or pure law, but a universe of law-governed existents exhibiting all the reasonableness of the abstract world of mathematics.[27] Though it is clearly a product of imagination, this conception is an idea, a phenomenon. From the human vantage point, this ultimate end is unrealizable; but it may serve as the goal toward which all our actions—all *action,* in fact—ought to be directed.

The summum bonum, accordingly, is not the perfect state of the world itself but rather that deliberate process, guided by reason, which could bring us closer to such a state. It is "that process of evolution whereby the existent comes more and more to embody those generals [real universals] which were just now said to be *destined,* which is what we strive to express in calling them *reasonable*" (CP 5.433). Human effort contributes to this process. The ideal of bringing about greater reasonableness in the existent universe is a standard against which all our actions can be judged, and to which we may deliberately try to conform our actions. At the very least, we should never deliberately do anything to inhibit it. This is the principle behind Peirce's most famous moral utterance, which he said "deserves to be inscribed upon every wall in the city of philosophy: Do not block the way of inquiry" (CP 1.135).

One does not, however, just intuit the summum bonum and immediately recognize it as the highest good, the norm toward which all thought and action should be directed. "If conduct is to be thoroughly deliberate, the ideal must be a habit of feeling which has grown up under the influence of a course of self-criticisms and of hetero-criticisms; and the theory of the deliberate formation of such habits of feeling is what ought to be meant by *esthetics*" (CP 1.574). It is the role of esthetics, the first of the normative sciences, to identify and explain the summum bonum. One who is familiar with the discoveries of esthetics presumably should not hesitate to become the source of "hetero-criticisms" when appropriate.

Ethics or practics is "the theory of self-controlled, or deliberate, conduct" (CP 1.191). It is the task of ethics to determine which sorts of action ought to be deliberately pursued. These, of course, promote the summum bonum identified in esthetics. Ethics does not concern casuistry, "the determination of what under given circumstances ought to or may be done" (CP 1.577). Nor does it concern what is good, although as late as 1903, in the passage from which the previous quotation was taken, Peirce affirms that it is. The nature of the *good* is properly the concern of esthetics. Peirce came to see that, in Potter's words, ethics "is not concerned directly with pronouncing this course of action right and that wrong, but with determining what makes right right and wrong wrong."[28]

Ethics, then, aims to describe the *kind* of conduct that actually promotes the highest good, and to understand how it does so. Though he wrote little about ethics, Peirce investigated the relation of kinds of conduct to the realization of ends enough to arrive at one key conclusion: a theory of conduct is needed because *individual* conduct must be evaluated in terms of its contribution to a *collective* aim, the aim of the infinite community of inquiry. As esthetics sets up norms for judging ideals that offer themselves as ends of action, ethics or practics sets up norms for judging conduct, whether one's own or another's, in terms of its contribution to the communal project of bringing reason into the existent world.[29]

Deliberate action is the practical expression of an idea. To say the same thing another way, *thought* is a kind of action that does not have existential effects in and of itself. It is preparatory to the kind of action that does have such effects. Thought may be subjected to deliberate self-criticism, just as action may be. Logic is the theory of critical thought: "surely *logic,* or the doctrine of what we ought to think, must be an application of the doctrine of what we deliberately choose to do, which is Ethics" (CP 5.35). Logic, then, is the normative science of right thought. It "sets up norms for deciding what thoughts we should entertain and what arguments we should accept, what procedures we should adopt" in thinking.[30]

Normative logic articulates a broad theory of inquiry, and is a positive science. Its goal is to discover how thought works, and to establish standards by which we may evaluate the validity of our thinking. Because, according to Peirce's view, all thought proceeds in the media of signs, normative logic may also be called normative semeiotic. "If we can find out the right method of thinking and can follow it out—the right method of transforming signs—then truth can be nothing more nor less than the last result to which the following out of this method would ultimately carry us" (CP 5.553). Truth stands as the objective toward which thought ought to progress, and all thought is judged in terms of its conformity to those methods of inference which bring us closer to truth. Logic thus parallels ethics in its normative force. Peirce makes this clear in the following passage:

> just as conduct controlled by ethical reason tends toward fixing certain habits of conduct, the nature of which (as to illustrate the meaning, peaceable habits and not quarrelsome habits) does not depend upon any accidental circumstances, and *in that sense* may be said to be *destined*; so, thought, controlled by a rational experimental logic, tends to the fixation of certain opinions, equally destined, the nature of which will be the same in the end, however the perversity of thought of whole generations may cause the postponement of the ultimate fixation. (CP 5.430)

Esthetics, ethics, and logic each formulate a general conception of the ideal state of the world. Ethics and logic also provide norms which, if followed, would further the realization of that ideal. In ethics, presumably, one must have not only a general conception of the ideal and an account of what sort of action promotes its realization, but also a general theory of action. In logic, likewise, a conception of the ideal and of the kind of thought which leads toward it must be supplemented by a general theory of thought. Peirce's theory of thought is nothing other than his general semeiotic, or general theory of signs and sign functions. This branch of logic is *stecheotic,* or speculative grammar. *Critic* describes the logical ideal of truth, and *methodeutic* or speculative rhetoric explores the kind of thought or sign transformations that lead to truth.

The mathematics of logic outlines the formal aspects of the categories, their function in thought as hypothetical concepts of relation. Phenomenology discovers features in experience that correspond to these formal aspects of the categories. The Firstness, Secondness, and Thirdness discovered in phenomena provide the basis for developing a theory of the material aspects of the categories, which is the concern of the normative sciences. Esthetics discovers the ideal state of the world in its Firstness, as a comprehensible and compelling possibility. Ethics explores this ideal in its Secondness, seeking to discover what kinds of actions promote it. Normative logic or semeiotic explores the Thirdness of the ideal discovered in esthetics, beginning with the analysis of the categories in the formal logic of relatives (deductive logic). Semeiotic develops the guidelines for thought about actions, providing both a general theory of thought and, ultimately, a conceptual model of the ideal. The process of thought is described in terms of a limitless series of sign transformations, which may be characterized as a "semeiotic stream." The ideal is the state of complete information, truth, and reality toward which this stream flows.

The hypotheses of the continuum and the infinitesimal, which are developed in his mathematical thought and identified as centrally important in phenomenology, come to their full fruition in semeiotic. Peirce's conception of the ideal state of the world has its roots in his mathematical conception of the continuum. The ideal is characterized in semeiotic terms as a continuum of thought governing the course of events, a self-sufficient representation of the universe, which would in fact *be* the universe. It is conceived as a perfectly continuous sign. Semeiotic thus provides a theoretical framework within which we can describe both the ideal state of things, the universe of the true continuum, and the manner in which communities of inquiry work toward that ideal. As subsequent chapters will show, the parallels between the semeiotic stream and the mathematical concept of the continuum, and between isolated sign-cognitions and the infinitesimal, are deliberate and systematic.

METAPHYSICS

If Peirce's mathematical hypotheses of continuity and the infinitesimal come to fruition in semeiotic, the harvest takes place in metaphysics. Metaphysics is the last coenoscopic science, and should have been the capstone of Peirce's philosophical edifice. Metaphysics is, however, the most problematic part of Peirce's mature philosophy. Peirce certainly left a wealth of metaphysical writings, but if there is any area that deserves the reputation of inconsistency which has sometimes been attached to his work as a whole, it is his metaphysics. Debate may continue indefinitely, for example, over the question of whether his philosophy is ultimately "idealistic" or "realistic."[31] In another vein, there is little in his logical work to prepare the casual reader for his metaphysical doctrine of "evolutionary love." Although it is not the purpose of this study to undertake a thorough reconstruction of Peirce's mature metaphysical views, no discussion of Peirce's philosophy can omit consideration of his metaphysics and of the outstanding interpretive problems it presents.

Metaphysics appears in the 1902 Carnegie Application as an example of a subject to which Peirce's methodeutic is amenable, but little more is said of it there (NEM 4:17, 32). In the 1903 "Outline Classification of the Sciences," one of the sources on which the present exposition is based, Peirce identified three divisions of metaphysics: "i, General Metaphysics, or Ontology; ii, Psychical, or Religious, Metaphysics, concerned chiefly with the questions of 1, God, 2, Freedom, 3, Immortality; and iii, Physical Metaphysics, which discusses the real nature of time, space, laws of nature, matter, etc." (CP 1.192). This promising systematic division seems to be largely formal. Peirce does not follow it elsewhere, and his extant metaphysical writings would seem to require some modification of these descriptions. As Murphey notes, Peirce devoted little attention to the questions of freedom and immortality, and there is no mention in this classification of one of his abiding interests, cosmology.[32] In the "Outline Classification," Peirce was apparently concerned to complete a sketch of his system. The divisions of metaphysics given there seem to have been developed purely on the basis of what the three categories (and Kant's famous formula concerning God, Freedom, and Immortality) suggested. The divisions of metaphysics given in figure 2.3 follow Kent's arrangement, though not her characterizations of the subject matter.[33] The first division, general metaphysics or ontology, aims to develop a general theory of reality based upon the discoveries of semeiotic. Physical metaphysics concerns the nature of dynamical (dyadic) relations in the universe of phenomena, and psychical metaphysics concerns the nature of interpretive (triadic) relations in that universe.

Peirce wrote that "[t]he third grand division [of philosophy] is Metaphysics, which endeavors to comprehend the reality of Phenomena" (CP 5.121). His other accounts of the subject matter of metaphysics tend to be equally as general—consider such statements as "Metaphysics seeks to give an account of the universe of mind and matter" (CP 1.186), and "Metaphysics has to account for the whole universe of being" (CP 6.214). A more precise conception of the science of metaphysics can be developed, however, by examining its place in the architectonic. Metaphysics depends on logic for its fundamental concepts, and in turn provides the fundamental concepts for the special or idioscopic sciences.

In a fragment dated around 1903, Peirce says that metaphysics studies "the most general features of reality and real objects" (CP 6.6). He often denounced metaphysics as idle speculation, but such criticisms are always directed at those who step beyond the boundaries of the experienceable world, beyond the limits of knowable reality. Peirce acknowledged the possibility of a legitimate science of metaphysics, and even offered a list of questions that fall under its purview.

Whether or no there be any real indefiniteness, or real possibility and impossibility? Whether or not there is any definite indeterminacy? Whether there be any strictly individual existence? Whether there is any distinction, other than one of more or less, between fact and fancy? Or between the external and the internal worlds? What general explanation or account can be given of the different qualities of feeling and their apparent connection with determinations of mass, space, and time? Do all possible qualities of sensation, including, of course, a much vaster variety of which we have no experience than of those which we do know, form one continuous system, as colors seem to do? . . . What is consciousness or mind like; meaning, is it a single continuum like Time and Space, which is for different purposes variously broken up by that which it contains; or is it composed of solid atoms, or is it more like a fluid? (CP 6.6)

The original list is twice this length.

All of Peirce's metaphysical questions concern the operation of *laws* in the universe of common experience. The special sciences, of course, also inquire into the operation of laws. The difference between metaphysics and the special sciences is accordingly not easily discerned. Metaphysics approaches the universe in a manner which "is nearly that of the special sciences (anciently, *physics* was its designation), from which it is mainly distinguished, by its confining itself to such parts of physics and of psychics as can be established without special means of observation" (CP 1.282). One way to put the difference between metaphysics and the special sciences is to say that, while metaphysics studies the most general features of reality, idioscopy studies the special features of classes of real objects, that is, physical realities (like molecules) and psychical realities (like history). Metaphysics, then, does not study the laws governing reality, but rather the laws governing the operation of laws themselves. Metaphysics seeks to comprehend the operation (and absence) of laws in the real world. This endeavor, given Peirce's conception of reality *as* lawfulness, certainly qualifies as the study of "the most general features of reality and real objects."

Such, then, is the relation of metaphysics to idioscopy. On the other side, metaphysics derives its principles for explaining reality directly from logic or semeiotic, which depends on the normative sciences, on phenomenology, and on mathematics for its fundamental concepts. Phenomenology studies the Firstness of the world (qualities and possibilities in experience), normative science the Secondness (the compelling aspects of experience), and metaphysics the Thirdness (the operation of law in experience). "Metaphysics is the science of Reality. Reality consists in regularity. Real regularity is active law. Active law is efficient reasonableness, or in other words is truly reasonable reasonableness. Reasonable reasonableness is Thirdness as Thirdness" (CP 5.121). General semeiotic provides a model for understanding the material aspects of the categories, and normative logic directs thought toward greater reasonableness. Metaphysics seeks to understand the universe as a whole, which means understanding the evolutionary process by which reasonableness comes to be embodied in existence. Peirce regarded process as the continuous semeiotic transformation of thought.

Metaphysics follows out the ontological implications of logical principles: "Metaphysics consists in the results of the absolute acceptance of logical principles not merely as regulatively valid, but as truths of being" (CP 1.487). Because these principles are normative, Peirce's metaphysics inherits a normative aspect: it not only provides an explanation of the world as it is, but also goes further to give an account of how it is evolving toward what ought to be.

> Synechism is founded on the notion that the coalescence, the becoming continuous, the becoming governed by laws, the becoming instinct with general ideas, are but phases of one and the same process of the growth of reasonableness. This is first shown to be true with mathematical exactitude in the field of logic, and is thence inferred to hold good metaphysically. (CP 5.4)

In the architectonic, then, there is a direct chain linking mathematics to metaphysics. The hypothesis of true continuity is the metal from which that chain is forged.

Our discussion of Peirce's architectonic classification of the sciences cannot end without a cautionary note. The classification is a blueprint, showing the interrelations and interdependence among various areas of inquiry. It is an unfortunate feature of all blueprints that they only present simplified images of the structures they represent. Just as a floorplan loses a great deal in portraying a three-dimensional structure on a two-dimensional medium, the classification of sciences loses a great deal in representing the dynamic, social activity that is science in the medium of a static and essentially linear classificatory scheme. The architectonic should not be seen as portraying a structure of pigeon-holes ready to be stuffed full of bits of knowledge. Rather, it is a schematic diagram showing paths of influence, channels by which ideas are exchanged among groups of inquirers working in different areas.

In a heroic attempt to give a more accurate image of the network of relations that make up the Peircean classification, Beverley Kent presents several complex figures onto which we might project the various sciences.[34] She observes in connection with one of these that "[i]t is difficult to convey the three-dimensional array on a two-dimensional surface, and an attempt at actual construction might be like trying to realize an Escher drawing."[35] The observation is quite suggestive. M. C. Escher's well-known image "Ascending and Descending" takes advantage of the distortions of his two-dimensional medium to show monks traveling along a staircase that leads upward to its own foot, or downward to its own head. A better image of the inversion of the order of being and the order of knowing is hard to find. This same inversion must be seen in Peirce's architectonic, except that the order is less a simple inversion than a complex involution at almost every level. If we consider the relation between mathematics and metaphysics, for example, it is clear that the mathematician as a thinking, historically situated person inevitably approaches the science with certain (though perhaps ill-defined) metaphysical conceptions about the nature of number, class, function, and so forth. Peirce would be the last to deny this fact, and his arrangement of the sciences should certainly not be understood as depriving the mathematician of all metaphysical conceptions, or of isolating the theoretical scientist from the practical sciences. As inquirers, we begin with a stock of beliefs or presuppositions. We can no more remove our active inquiries from the medium of these presuppositions than a swimmer can remove her backstroke from the medium of water. Science is a dynamic social activity, in other words. The classification of the sciences no more restricts the inquirer to moving through the classification one time in a straight line, than the blueprint of a house restricts the inhabitant to moving through it in two dimensional space.

Part Two
Mathematical Hypotheses

CHAPTER 3

The Mathematics of Logic: Formal Aspects of the Categories

According to the architectonic presented in chapter 2, the universal categories of thought are first encountered in the hypothetical reasoning of the simplest branch of mathematics, which Peirce identified as the mathematics of logic. In this chapter I will examine his formal conceptions of the three categories, outline his arguments for the irreducibility and completeness of the categories, and show how triadic relations introduce the concept of continuity in his system.[1]

I begin with a short account of the path by which Peirce arrived at his description of the formal aspects of the categories. Peirce came to his philosophical views about the categories, semeiotic, and metaphysics well before he developed his philosophical architectonic. In the 1867 "On a New List of Categories," Peirce had cut Kant's list of twelve categories to five, and shortly after that he eliminated Being and Substance from the list. The remaining three categories, Quality, Relation, and Representation, were subject to some modification over the years, but Peirce never let go of his early conviction that there are three categories, that they are in some sense "derived" from logic (the mathematics of logic, as it turned out), and that they find their most significant application in semeiotic.

The architectonic that makes the categories central to phenomenology, the normative sciences, and metaphysics was not developed before the late 1890s. Common sense would suggest that the architectonic ought to have preceded the development of the main features of a philosophical system such as Peirce's. Peirce's philosophy, in short, was born out of order: categories, semeiotic, and metaphysics first; mathematical foundations, phenomenology, normative sciences, and architectonic last. Peirce began with certain insights or hypotheses, derived mainly from his reading of Kant and of post-Kantian idealists, which were attractive because of their potential explanatory power. He worked with them, explored their connections to various areas of thought and their usefulness in answering traditional philosophical problems, and constantly made adjustments as he attained new insights. It was only after many of the details of his system were settled that he could see its whole structure sufficiently well to describe it in the architectonic.

Peirce did not see himself as setting out to *create* a novel philosophy, but rather as attempting to describe the features of that philosophy Kant called "a *conceptus cosmicus*."[2] Peirce greatly admired the chapter on architectonic in Kant's first *Critique* in which this description of philosophy is offered. He agreed with Kant that a philosopher is like any other scientist who aims to describe the real workings of the experienced world rather than to make up a fiction about it, however charming such a fiction might be. Peirce's adherence to the categories throughout his career, and his reluctance to admit isolated objections to it, can be explained quite simply: He thought he was on the right track, and he felt sure that once his system was more fully developed it would be clear that such objections were mistaken.

The Origin of the Categories in the Logic of Mathematics

The most dramatic adjustments in Peirce's philosophy involve his reconception of the categories after 1885. He retained the view that there are three and only three universal categories, but both the logic from which they are derived and his understanding of their nature were revised. In a manuscript entitled "One, Two, Three: Fundamental Categories of Thought and of Nature," Peirce first introduced his strategy of deriving the categories from the mathematics of logic.[3] In this first attempt at such a derivation, he asserted that "the whole organism of logic may be mentally evolved from the three conceptions of first, second, and third, or more precisely, An, Other, Medium" (MS 901, p. 21). He observed that "if these conceptions enter as we find they do as elements of all conceptions connected with reasoning, they must be virtually in the mind when reasoning first commences. In that sense, at least, they must be innate ideas" (MS 901, p. 22). This is followed by a psychological investigation of the elementary conceptions, and some speculation about their physiological basis. The surviving manuscript fragment breaks off, dramatically, with the following: "I cannot help guessing that [a cell] may contain all the fundamental elements of the uni-" (MS 901, p. 38). In later efforts, Peirce left off the psychological and physiological investigations, and focused instead on the a priori elements of thought as presented in "the simplest mathematics" and elaborated in phenomenology and formal logic.

By his own testimony, Peirce had been vaguely aware of this formal approach since the late 1860s. The mathematician Augustus De Morgan had sent him a copy of his groundbreaking paper on the logic of relations in 1866,[4] and Peirce said in 1905 that it was only "a short time" after reading it that he arrived at the conclusion that there are exactly three classes of indecomposable relations (CP 1.562).

It is not clear precisely when he became confident that these three classes corresponded to his three categories. In a fragment from the "One, Two,

Three" group, Peirce associated Thirdness with continuity (CP 1.337). This association seems to have emerged during his work on the logic of relatives while at The Johns Hopkins University. It is likely he first began to reflect seriously on the nature of triadic relations in that period, when he was surrounded by the outstanding students whose work was published in the 1883 *Studies in Logic*. In a 1905 reflection on De Morgan's influence Peirce noted that his own understanding of genuine triadic relations as always involving an element of thought is *not* implied by De Morgan's work (CP 1.562). The logic of relations apparently suggested this idea, however, and Peirce had clearly become convinced of it by the time he began work on "One, Two, Three."[5]

At the same time, Peirce and his students were working to develop a theory of quantification for the Boolean calculus.[6] This development suggested to Peirce the possibility that his category of Secondness could be associated with existent individuals, whose distinguishing feature is their *haecceity*, or "thisness" (a term borrowed from Duns Scotus).[7] Just as De Morgan's work on relatives had suggested but did not require a connection between triads and continuity, the theory of quantification suggested but did not require a connection between Secondness and individuation.

These correlations appeared promising to Peirce, but nothing in logic itself could validate or refute them. He could *assert* that dyadic relations are associated with individuation, existence, and indexicality, and that triadic relations are associated with continuity, reality, and symbolicity. He could further *assert* that the former associations belong together as aspects of Secondness, and that the latter are aspects of Thirdness. The problem, though, was that he could not show why there should be these associations, nor sufficiently explain what Secondness and Thirdness *are* without an appeal to experience. In the 1890 "Logic of Mathematics" manuscript, for example, Peirce resorted to utterly un-mathematical descriptions of the categories in his effort to explain the fundamental differences between monadic, dyadic, and triadic relations (CP 1.424, 457, 473).

By 1901, he had dealt with the problem by separating what was earlier referred to as "the logic of mathematics" into three distinct areas of inquiry. The *mathematics of logic* explores the structure of formal relations without reference to their application. *Phenomenology* investigates modes of relation encountered in experience. *Deductive* or *formal logic,* part of the normative sciences, develops the symbolic system used to articulate and analyze these experienced relations. Peirce could thus formally examine monadic, dyadic, and triadic relations in their own right, and leave the question of their material aspects (and the descriptive language) to phenomenology and the normative sciences. The result of this approach was that he could separate his hypotheses about the material or experiential significance of dyadic and triadic relations from their importance in the mathematics of relations—where his hypotheses could find neither justification nor refutation. On the formal side, he came to see three-term relations as necessary and sufficient for any comprehensive logical system one might develop.

Peirce also found that irreducible three-term relations embody *connection* or *combination*, a relation that goes beyond genuine and degenerate dyadic relations. The two uncombined terms of a genuine dyad are *merely* other, we might say—they do not even speak to one another. We must be careful here, however. Even to *conceive* them as co-existing "others" supposes they are combined in a thought or universe. That thought or universe is itself a third, and introduces a triadic relation. We thus cannot really conceive of genuine dyadicity—though we do have experiences of otherness, like banging a shin against a table in the dark, that come close. Three-term relations express combination. As it turns out, combination is the basis of the principle of continuity, but it is left for phenomenology to investigate the experiential significance of individuation, continuity, and the intellectual element in triadic relations. Deductive (or "formal" logic), the "mathematical part of logic," then systematizes these findings as part of a theory of reasoning.

Monadic, Dyadic, and Triadic Relatives

Peirce tended to think of language on the model of the chemical atom (CP 1.289, 1.346, 3.421, 3.468, 4.309, MS 908). Just as nineteenth-century chemists learned to classify elements according to valence, the number of open bonding sites on the atom, Peirce classified relatives, the relational elements of a proposition, according to the number of open places for inserting an indexical sign. A relative having no open places is called a "medad," from the Greek for "nothing" (CP 1.465). Any completed proposition or proper name is a kind of medad, of course, but the process of learning or recognizing such a medad involves mentally *filling* some relative with proper indexical signs (CP 3.463). Were an idea to arrive in the mind with *no* open sites for attachment of an indexical sign, it would amount to "an indecomposable idea altogether severed logically from every other. . . . a flash of mental 'heat-lightning' absolutely instantaneous, thunderless, unremembered, and altogether without effect" (CP 1.292). The medad is the logical analogue to a noble element. A medad either emerges at the end of a process of thought (in which case it was not *originally* a medad), or is altogether incapable of initiating a thought process. A true medad clearly can have no role in the process of thought, though it exists as a logical possibility.

A relative with valence of one is a *term* (CP 1.515). It expresses a property of something: '____ is white', or '____ is large', for example (CP 1.370). The monad, the saturated "singulary" relation, represents "something *which is what it is without reference to anything else* within it or without it, regardless of all force and all reason" (CP 2.85).[8] As an example, Peirce asks "Why should the middle part of the spectrum look green rather than violet? There is no conceivable reason for it nor compulsion in it" (CP 2.85). The monadic relative '____ is green' is an absolute term, in just this sense.

A relative with valence of two, if it expresses a genuine binary or dyadic relation, introduces a subject, and the logical form of the *proposition* (CP 1.515). An example is the relation '_____ strikes _____', or '____ is the brother of ____'. Peirce described the genuine dyad, the saturated binary relation, as "two objects which are not merely *thought* as two, but of which something is true such that neither could be removed without destroying the fact supposed true of the other" (CP 2.84). In such a relation, there are really two subjects, "each a sort of mimic monad, but the two are of different kinds, one being active, the other passive" (CP 1.515). If A strikes B, we cannot transpose the places of A and B without changing the meaning of the proposition: the relationship is not commutative.

A relative with valence of two may, however, be degenerate. The designations of "genuine" and "degenerate" relatives are borrowed from plane geometry, where the terms are used to distinguish those figures that are not reducible to simpler figures from those that are. A genuine relative, analogously, is not reducible to a complex of simpler relatives, while a degenerate relative is so reducible.[9] Peirce characterized the distinction between genuine and degenerate dyadic relatives as the difference between *real relations* and *relations of reason*: "A real relation subsists in virtue of a fact which would be totally impossible were either of its related objects destroyed; while a relation of reason subsists in virtue of two facts, one only of which would disappear on the annihilation of either of the relates" (CP 1.365). In the preceding example, if either A or B were destroyed prior to their violent encounter, it would not be true to say that A is a striker of B or that B is struck by A. Genuine or *external* dyads "are constituted by external fact, and are true actions of one thing upon another" (CP 1.365). Degenerate or *internal* dyads consist merely in bringing two monads together in the same thought. This act of mind accounts for the name "relations of reason." The relation 'A is sharper than B' is a degenerate dyad. Were either A or B destroyed, the remaining object would still retain whatever sharpness it originally had.

Triadic relations, too, may take either genuine or degenerate form. There are two ways in which a triadic relation may be degenerate. A triad which is degenerate in the second degree, or is *doubly degenerate*, involves neither any true element of combination nor any true element of action. 'A is taller than B and shorter than C' is an example. A triad degenerate in the first degree, or *singly degenerate*, can be reduced to a pair of dyadic relations. One of Peirce's favorite examples involves the merchant who accidentally kills the genie's son in the *Arabian Nights*. 'The merchant (accidentally) killed the son with a date-stone' can be reduced to the pair of dyadic relations (1) 'the merchant threw away the date-stone' and (2) 'the date-stone struck and killed the genie's son' (CP 1.366). The genie's charge of murder in the tale is unjustified, because there was no intention, no mental element binding the two actions together in a genuine triadic relation. A relative with valence of three, if it represents a genuine ternary or triadic relation, introduces a mental element or *intention* as an essential part of the relation itself (CP 2.86).[10] The mental element is what makes a genuine triadic relation. "Just as a real pairedness consists in a fact being true of A which would be nonsense if B were not there, so we now meet with Rational Threeness which consists in A and B being really paired by virtue of a third object, C" (CP 2.86). 'The attacker murdered the victim with a rock' would be such a case. We can try reducing this statement to the two dyadic relations 'the attacker threw a rock' and 'the rock struck and killed the victim', but in doing so we lose the intentional element that joins the attacker, the rock, and the victim in the relation of "murder." If we eliminate any of the three, we eliminate the murdering relation altogether.[11]

NECESSITY AND SUFFICIENCY OF THREE CLASSES OF RELATIVES
   In chapter 2, I discussed Peirce's account of mathematical reasoning as involving observation. Though all mathematical observation concerns "imaginary objects," the various branches of mathematics employ different aids to observation (CP 1.240). In geometry one normally constructs and modifies a figure that bears letters designating its various parts; in algebra a combination of numbers, letters, and other symbols are used to represent relationships among different elements in an equation (CP 4.233). In any case, there must be clearly stated conventions for constructing and modifying the diagram, and the diagram *itself* (as a particular thing) is not the medium in which mathematical operations are performed. *That* medium is general, an ideal construct; the diagram is a particular representation of it. Peirce refers to such representations as *replicas* or *instances* of the general medium (CP 4.395).[12] A carefully constructed symbolic system, suitable for representing the objects of thought, is essential to successful mathematical reasoning.
   The language most commonly used in symbolic logic today is derived from the system developed by Alfred North Whitehead and Bertrand Russell in *Principia Mathematica,* and it employs an algebraic notation.[13] Peirce developed and published an algebraic notation in 1870 (W 2:359–429). The system was expanded to include quantifiers during his work at The Johns Hopkins, and was published as "Note B: The Logic of Relatives" in the 1883 *Studies in Logic* (W 4:453–66).
   Peirce did not favor his algebraic logical system, however. Because the aim of logic is to investigate the *process* of inference rather than to provide a calculus for *drawing* inferences in the shortest fashion possible, he considered a symbol-system that conveniently exhibits every step in the reasoning process more desirable (CP 3.485, 4.373). He developed his system of existential graphs to this end. In his own evaluation, "Existential Graphs is the

most perfect system hitherto proposed for the analytical representation of ratiocinative thought" (MS 905, page dated 1907 Dec. 7). Peirce the humble fallibilist did not claim it is a *perfect* system, of course, only that it was the *most perfect* so far devised.

Proofs in existential graphs are performed by means of drawing two-dimensional images, which function as replicas of the mental symbols observed in mathematico-logical reasoning, and then modifying the images according to a set of permissions and restrictions. Peirce suggests that if the graphical premises of a proof are scribed on one sheet, and each successive transformation is scribed on subsequent sheets, then a rapid scan through the whole stack would produce "a veritable moving picture of the mind in reasoning" (MS 905, page dated 1907 Dec. 7).[14] The first two parts of the system of existential graphs, Alpha and Beta, have been proven to be complete and consistent formulations of the propositional and predicate calculus, respectively.[15] Peirce's system has enjoyed some attention in recent years both from logicians and from persons working in artificial intelligence.[16]

All this is to prepare the way for Peirce's argument, based on the demands of his formal logic, that an adequate and complete logical system must contain exactly three kinds of relation: monadic, dyadic, and triadic. The argument that at least three elementary relations are necessary is summarized as follows:[17]

> In existential graphs, a spot with one tail —X represents a quality, a spot with two tails —R— a dyadic relation. Joining the ends of two tails is also a dyadic relation. But you can never by such joining make a graph with three tails. (CP 1.346)

Any attempt to construct a spot with three tails must involve some form of branching. The simplest such diagram would be formed by joining one tail from each of two dyads to the same tail of another dyad. But any branching diagram would represent a situation in which one term (C) operates simultaneously on two others (A and B), and this is precisely what Peirce means by a triadic relation: it "consists in A and B being really paired by virtue of a third object, C" (CP 2.86). The *possibility* of branching, at least an incipient triadicity, must be inherent in the system from the outset—it cannot be artificially introduced or constructed.[18]

Peirce, then, held that not all three-termed relations are reducible to pairs of dyadic relations. This position is contrary to the common view of contemporary symbolic logic. Quine, for example, argues that once we have defined dyadic relations in terms of ordered pairs of objects [so that the relation Rzw is defined as the ordered pair (z;w)], it is easy to conceive triadic relations on the same model. The relation Tyzw can be reduced to (y;(z;w)), where the pair (z;w) is conceived as an object in dyadic relation with y.[19] In Quine's algebraic system, this approach apparently suffices. In Peirce's graphic system, however, it is less clear that such a reduction of triadic relations is always legitimate. Although the reduction certainly works for a logical system conceived merely as a set of rules for manipulating marks on paper, Peirce insisted that such a system is inadequate for representing thought. Examples of genuine triadic relations, such as the case of murdering, suggest that their irreducibility is not just an accident of Peirce's graphic method of symbolization.

Peirce offered the following argument that the conception of combination expressed in triadic relations is necessary and irreducible. In what follows, "Phaneron" may be read as "the collective total of all that is in any way or in any sense present to the mind, quite regardless of whether it corresponds to any real thing or not" (CP 1.284).

> [U]nless the Phaneron were to consist entirely of elements altogether uncombined mentally, in which case we should have no idea of a Phaneron (since this, if we have the idea, is an idea combining all the rest,) which is as much as to say that there would be no Phaneron, its *esse* being *percipi* if any is so; or unless the Phaneron were itself our sole idea, and were utterly indecomposable, when there could be no such thing as an interrogation and no such thing as a judgment . . . it follows that if there is a Phaneron . . . or even if we can ask if there be or no, there must be an idea of *combination* (i.e. having *combination* for its object thought of.) Now the general idea of a combination must be an indecomposable idea. For otherwise it would be compounded, and the idea of combination would enter into it as an analytic part of it. It is, however, quite absurd to suppose an idea to be a part of itself, and *not the whole*. Therefore, if there be a phaneron, the idea of combination is an indecomposable element of it. This idea is a triad; for it involves the ideas of a whole and of two parts. (MS 908, pp. 7–8)

There are two arguments offered here: one seeks to establish that the concept of combination is presupposed by the very possibility of there being anything present to the mind, the other asserts that this concept is irreducible.

If there is a phaneron—if there is *anything* present to the mind—or if we can even conceive of the phaneron well enough to ask the question, then the phaneron must fall under one of three general descriptions. In the two extreme cases, it would consist *either* of a radical plurality of ideas, none associated with any other, *or* of a single monolithic idea not compounded of any others. Any other conception of the phaneron must involve some combination or synthesis of ideas. If what is present to the mind is a radical plurality, there would be not even the faintest conception of "the collective total" of things that are or could be present to the mind. The phaneron apparently is not a radical plurality, then, as it is (at least) the subject of this sentence, and that subject names a collection of ideas. On the other hand, if the phaneron were our *sole idea* we could not ask the question whether it exists, or form any judgment about it. Any such judgment or interrogation about an object involves an idea other than the idea of the object: the idea of its properties, for example. By elimination, we must conclude that the phaneron, whatever it contains, involves combination. Moreover, the *idea* of combination (an idea having *combination* as its object) is bound up with the idea of the phaneron, because if we understand what is meant by "the phaneron" at all, we understand it as the synthesis of whatever is present to the mind.

The second argument establishes that the idea of combination is not (completely) reducible to other ideas. If it were, it would itself prove upon inspection to be a compound idea. A compound idea involves two or more ideas that are associated or joined in the mind. To say that the ideas are in any way joined together, however, introduces the very concept of combination which we are analyzing. There must then be an *irreducible* idea of combination if there is *any* idea of combination, and there must be an idea of combination if we have a concept of the phaneron at all.

In chapter 1, we saw that Peirce rejected the possibility of a transcendental justification for his list of categories. The preceding arguments are the strongest arguments Peirce can offer for the necessity and irreducibility of the concept of combination or thirdness. They are not, however, transcendental. In fact, they are circular in the sense that each one is a deductive argument, and deduction itself presupposes the principle of combination. They proceed by explicating the idea of the phaneron, and showing that it involves the concept of combination. But for such an explication to occur at all, the idea of the phaneron as a combination of ideas present to the mind must be understood. Peirce cannot then offer an argument to show that such an idea must necessarily be present to *any* mind whatever. We might for the sake of argument try to *suppose* that there is a mind that contains only a radical plurality of ideas, but there would be no unity to such a mind. It would apparently be no mind at all. A similar problem arises if we try to imagine a mind that contains only one monolithic idea: Here we find unity, certainly, but there would be no activity of thought, no process of synthesis, learning, or growth. Peirce's arguments are directed toward genuine minds, not toward logically extreme absurdities, though he introduces these figments for the sake of thoroughness. His argument establishes that, for real minds, the concept of combination is "necessarily" present. Combination is not transcendentally necessary, but rather is necessarily present *if* certain kinds of mind exist. That they do exist is a practical or metaphysical truth, to be empirically verified by anyone who questions Peirce's arguments. There is thus a recognized pragmatic element to the necessity and irreducibility of the concept of combination.

What has been said so far suggests that three primitive relational symbols are needed to represent the operations of thought. Once three-termed relations are admitted into the system, however, we discover that they are the primitive relatives. From triads one can construct monads and dyads, although the reverse is not the case. Peirce presents the following diagrams to show that, by joining the tails of one or more triadic relations in the appropriate way, the lower-order relatives can be constructed (CP 3.484). Figure 3.1(a) shows the construction of a dyad from two triads; figure 3.1(b) shows the construction of a monad from one triad by joining two of the triad's tails together. Of course, many alternative ways of constructing lower-valence relations can be found. Those in figure 3.1 are the simplest.

Fig. 3.1 Construction of Monads and Dyads from Triads

(a)   (b)

Thus we have seen Peirce's arguments, first, that triadic relations are necessary for a complete logical system, and second, that they are primitive in the sense that lower-order relations can be constructed from them. All that remains is to examine his claim that there is no need for any higher-order relation than the triadic in order to provide a complete formal system.

Peirce's *reduction thesis* claims that all higher-order polyads can be reduced to triads; conversely, all higher-order polyads can be constructed from triads (CP 3.483; 1.347, 363).[20] Figure 3.2 provides a graphic representation of how tetrads and pentads are constructed from triads.

Fig. 3.2 Construction of Tetrads and Pentads from Triads

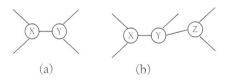

(a)   (b)

The process can easily be extended so as to construct a polyad of any higher value whatever, and as will become clear once Peirce's notion of a *continuous relation* has been explained, each bond among the central clusters of triadic relations (x, y, z) can be conceived as infinitesimally short (NEM 4:307). The bonds, so conceived, effectively vanish; the relatives themselves can then be pictured in the more convenient forms given in figure 3.3. Peirce's logic of relatives need only admit the triadic form of relation, then, in order to construct forms with every possible valence.

Fig. 3.3 Standard Representation of Tetrad and Pentad

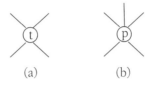

(a)   (b)

TRIADS, COMBINATION, AND CONTINUITY

There is a genuine triadic relation in any expression, if it is an expression of a thought.[21] We never in fact conceive *purely* medadic, monadic, or dyadic relations:

A man cannot conceive of a one-subject fact otherwise than as more or less vaguely analogous to a feeling of his own. He cannot conceive of a two-subject fact otherwise than as analogous to an action of his own. A three-subject fact is comprehensible and is analogous to an utterance, a speech, a thought. (CP 6.323)

Our conceptions of medads, monads, and dyads are always mediated, or triadic. On the other hand, Peirce notes that genuine triadic relations always involve "some relation of an intellectual nature, being either constituted by an action of a mental kind, or implying some general law" (CP 1.562). Peirce's assertion that triads are the primitive relatives in a formal system reflects his view that the mediation of thought is ubiquitous.

Peirce notes that the idea of *combination* is triadic, "for it involves the ideas of a whole and of two parts" (MS 908, p. 8). Though not all triadic relations represent genuine combination, the idea of combination is expressible only in a triad. Such triadic relations as 'A murders B with C' do not refer to combination, but they do presuppose it. On closer analysis, it turns out that all *other* relations also presuppose combination and hence triadicity. This point carries Peirce from the position that triadic relations are formally necessary and sufficient for logic, to the position that *continuity* is bound up, a priori, with the possibility of thought.

Consider the proposition that some roses are red. Logically, this proposition could be stated so as to involve any number of relational subjects:

1. 'some *roses* are red'
2. 'some *roses* possess *redness*'
3. 'some *roses* are in the relation of *possession* to *redness*'
4. 'some *roses* are related to the *relation* of *possession* of *redness*'

Such an expansion is both open-ended and trivial. It is trivial because no matter how many times we stipulate "relatedness" by making it into a substantive, we can never exhaust the basic combinatory relation expressed in the word "are" in line 1. Peirce says,

> to be in relation to X, and to be in relation to a relation to X mean the same thing. If therefore I were to put "relation" into the subject at all, I ought in consistency to put it in infinitely many times, and indeed this would not be sufficient. It is like a continuous line: no matter what one cuts off from it a line remains. So I do not attempt to regard "A is B" as meaning "A is identical with something that is B." I call "is in relation to" and "is identical with" Continuous Relations, and I leave such in the Predicate. (MS 611, pp. 14–15).

The most basic relations (of mere co-being or of identity, for example) imply genuine combination and triadicity. This is the case even though they are commonly expressed in dyadic form: 'A is related to B'; 'C is identical to D'.

In the preceding passage Peirce makes explicit reference to continuity, comparing simple relations to a continuous line. Much more will be said about Peirce's thought concerning infinity and continuity in chapter 4. For now let it suffice to say that the reference to a line is more than a convenient image. There is a significant difference between infinite relations and continuous relations. All that the above argument apparently justifies at this point in our study is the assertion that *infinity* is bound up, a priori, in the possibility of there being anything at all. The attempt to understand Peirce's qualification, that to put the word "relation" into the expression infinitely many times would not be sufficient, leads us to take up the mathematics of transfinite multitudes and continua in the next chapter.

Three-Valued Logic

The concept of combination also affects the postulation of truth-values in logic. Ordinary logic has only the two values *true* and *false*. In chapter 2 we saw that Peirce identified dichotomic mathematics as the theory of operations in such a system, and that trichotomic mathematics suggested to him the possibility for a three-valued system. Peirce suggested that in a triadic logic the principle of excluded middle could be suspended, and the notion of a degree of truth intermediate between the standard two could be introduced. The third truth value is a kind of combination of truth and falsity. Such a system would be needed in analyzing any universe that contained objectively indeterminate entities: potentialities, real possibilities, universals, or any other *generals*.[22] That there are such entities at least in some universes of discourse, Peirce was certain: "A triangle in general is not isosceles nor equilateral; nor is a triangle in general scalene" (CP 5.505). Peirce foreshadows the development of multi-valued logic in a passage published in *The American Journal of Mathematics*[23] in 1885:

> According to ordinary logic, a proposition is either true or false, and no further distinction is recognized. This is the descriptive conception, as the geometers say; the metric conception would be that every proposition is more or less false, and that the question is one of amount. At present we adopt the former view. (CP 3.365)

Peirce took up the question of three-valued logic in earnest around 1901 or 1902. His article "Mathematical Logic," published in *Baldwin's Dictionary* in 1902 says that, of the possible logical systems having a finite number of values, "only that of the system of three values seems likely to repay study" (NEM 3:742). Chapter 3 of the 1902 "Minute Logic" contains a section on trichotomic mathematics (CP 4.307–323), and in the 1903 Lowell Lectures, Peirce referred to a three-valued system, "which has been in some measure developed" (NEM 3:358).

Peirce recorded little more of his thought about the three-valued logic beyond these references, until he made some short entries in his "Logic Notebook" in 1909. Max Fisch and Atwell Turquette have discovered several pages of notes concerning triadic logic, including matrices that define operators for a projected logical system.[24] At the top of the first sheet is written "Let the system of values be V, L, F." V and F correspond to true and false; L is a limit-case between V and F. Peirce was apparently not satisfied with his first approach, however, and wrote on the sheet "All this is pretty close to nonsense." He fared better on the second attempt, and constructed matrices defining six operators. It is not clear whether he was aware of his accomplishment, but in fact the operators he defined are adequate to establish a functionally complete system for three values.[25] Peirce's successful use of matrices to define operators for a three-valued system predates the better-known and more thorough work of Jan Lukasiewicz and Emil Post, both of whom developed the technique in 1920.

Peirce summarized his work in the third entry, which bears the heading "Triadic Logic" and the date Feb. 23, 1909:

> Triadic Logic is that logic which, though not rejecting entirely the Principle of Excluded Middle, nevertheless recognizes that

every proposition, S is P, is either true, or false, or else has a lower mode of being such that it can neither be determinately P nor determinately not P, but is at the limit between P and not P.[26]

Peirce estimated the importance of his new triadic logic in a comment at the bottom of the page: "Triadic Logic is universally true. But Dyadic Logic is not absolutely false, it is only L."

It is likely that Peirce considered his triadic logic "universally true" because it would allow us to deal not only with all the states of affairs that can be handled by two-valued logic (the value L is simply not assigned), but also with any objectively indeterminate states of affairs. Peirce believed that there are such indeterminate cases: His epistemological doctrine of fallibilism and his metaphysical doctrine of tychism are based on this belief.[27]

The Generative Potency of the Number Three

The importance of the third category of relation for Peirce's architectonic cannot be overemphasized. This category, as we have noted, is not required by the logic of relations as De Morgan originally presented it. Peirce argued that it is required, if we are to have a logic capable of representing all orders of polyads. The formal categories of the mathematics of relations are clearly developed with an eye to their potential for adequately characterizing experience. Experience, as phenomenology will show, is not easily reducible to categorical dualisms like true-false or agent-patient. The notion that the world we confront in experience is *not* fully determinate is one of Peirce's basic contentions. He maintains that the gradual emergence of law, and of greater determinacy in the order of things, can and ought to be promoted. This requires that we have some means for comprehending and coping with real indeterminacy, with what William James characterized as the vague and inarticulate fringes that hang about the edges of our supposedly clear-cut experience. Peirce's inclusion of the third category, and with it the fundamental conception of combination, provides the basis for a logical system (in the form of multi-valued logic) and ultimately a metaphysics that accommodates the shadings, ambiguities, and continuities encountered in experience.

Firstness and Secondness are indecomposable ideas, distinct from Thirdness. They are not, now or at the end of the evolution of thought, absorbed into a Hegelian Absolute. My focus on the third category in this study should *not* be taken to suggest that Thirdness and continuity comprise the whole of Peirce's philosophical system, or that they supersede Firstness or Secondness. Such is clearly not the case. However, the third category introduces Peirce's notion of continuity, and it is his insistence upon the principle of continuity that differentiates Peirce's philosophy from many others—such as the pragmatism of Dewey or James, or the mechanistic

Cartesianism that Peirce rejected.[28] It is the principle of continuity that grounds Peirce's metaphysical doctrine of synechism and his religious philosophy.[29] Peirce's categories of Firstness and Secondness, of possibility and existence, are in their general features familiar to most metaphysics. It is Thirdness that demands special attention, and this requires an understanding of infinity and continuity as Peirce conceived them.

CHAPTER 4

Infinity and Continuity

In chapter 1 we saw that the interrelated concepts of infinite inquiry, infinite community, and infinite information are all involved in Peirce's notion of reality. Peirce's theories of cognition and representation, as well as his account of the perceptual judgment, involve the conception of a continuous process rather than one having a discrete beginning, intermediate states, and end. Peirce looked to the developing mathematics of transfinite set theory for the theoretical framework that would make such concepts intelligible.[1] What he found there was adequate to make sense of the paradoxes of the infinite (i.e., set theory shows that one *can* talk meaningfully about degrees of infinity), but he found the prevalent theory of the continuum inadequate to ground his philosophical conception of Thirdness. Characteristically, Peirce departed from the prevailing theory and developed a conception of continuity that better accommodated his philosophical insights. To understand what he did, however, requires some familiarity with the theory he rejected.

Cantor's Theory of the Infinite

Peirce recognized Georg Cantor (1845–1918) as the single most important figure in the history of thought about mathematical infinity.[2] Cantor's work introduced Peirce to rigorous thought about infinity and continuity.[3] Moreover, much of what is distinctive in Peirce's thought arises out of his specific disagreement with Cantor about the nature of the continuum. My brief exposition of Cantor's work will consider his two methods of describing series of infinite multitudes and his well-known "continuum hypothesis." For a more rigorous and thorough presentation of Cantorean set theory, the reader is referred to the works by Abraham Fraenkel, Robert B. Stoll, and A. W. Moore, which provided the material for this section.[4]

SETS, POWER-SETS, AND TRANSFINITE CARDINALS

Although one of the basic disputes in set theory concerns the proper definition of a *set,* a somewhat informal definition from Cantor will serve our purposes here. It reads as follows: "A set is a collection into a whole of definite, distinct objects of our intuition or of our thought. The objects are called the elements (members) of the set."[5] Sets may contain anything whatever as elements, and a set is constituted entirely by its elements. Because the mathematician does not care whether it is a set of apples or of nations that is being considered (since the nature of individual elements does not affect the mathematical properties of their collections), Cantor developed the concept of *cardinality* as a way of abstracting from what a set contains. "The cardinal of a set S is the set (class) of all sets that are equivalent to S."[6] In general, the cardinality of a set is a representation of its size. A set of ten apples is the same size, that is, contains the same number of elements, as a set of ten nations. Both have the same cardinality, specified by the number '10'. Any two sets that admit of one-to-one mapping from the elements of one to the elements of the other, where no elements in either set are left unmapped, are said to be *equivalent,* and equivalent sets have equal cardinals.[7]

A *finite* set is one for which there is an integer *n,* such that the set contains *n* members. The null-set, containing no members, is also defined as a finite set.[8] In a finite set of *n* members, *n* is the cardinal number of the set. The concept of cardinality is of relatively little interest when applied to finite sets, but becomes rather more important when considering infinite sets. An infinite set N may be defined as a set that has a proper subset M that is its equivalent.[9] For M to be a *proper subset* of N means that every element of M is also a member of N, and there is at least one element of N that is not an element of M.[10] That there are such sets is easily demonstrable, for example, by arranging the set of positive integers, I, on a line, the positive even integers, E, on another line, and mapping the two series onto one another in the relation that maps every number *n* of the first line to the number *2n* on the second line:

$$I: \quad 1 \quad 2 \quad 3 \quad \ldots \quad n \quad n+1 \quad n+2 \quad \ldots$$
$$E: \quad 2 \quad 4 \quad 6 \quad \ldots \quad 2n \quad 2(n+1) \quad 2(n+2) \quad \ldots$$

This simple array shows that the set of even integers, a proper subset of the positive integers, is equivalent to the set of positive integers.

The cardinal of an infinite set is called a *transfinite cardinal.* Cantor introduced the convention of using the Hebrew letter aleph, with subscript, to denote a transfinite cardinal. The first transfinite cardinal, Aleph-null ($\aleph_0$), denotes the cardinality of the smallest transfinite set—the set of natural numbers. Because E is equivalent to I in the preceding diagram, its cardinal is likewise $\aleph_0$. *Any* set that can be put in one-to-one correspondence with I has $\aleph_0$ as its cardinal. Such sets are called *denumerable* sets.[11]

The most significant application of Cantor's work is in the description of various degrees of infinity. $\aleph_0$ is the cardinal number of a denumerable infinite set, but Cantor proved that there are infinite sets containing more members than are contained in a denumerable set. The standard "diagonal method" proof of this is well known, and Peirce developed his own proof as well.[12] One way to construct a set of higher cardinality than $\aleph_0$ is to distribute the members of the denumerable set I into all the possible subsets of I, including the null set and I itself. The collection of all the resulting subsets (called the power-set of I) has the cardinality of $2^{\aleph_0}$.[13] *Cantor's Theorem* states that the power-set of any set S is strictly larger than S itself.[14]

A special application of the "diagonal method" is also used to prove that the set of real numbers on an interval (say, between 0 and 1) is greater than the set of natural numbers.[15] It can be shown, furthermore, that the cardinality of the set of reals is $2^{\aleph_0}$.[16] Cantor identifies the set of real numbers as *the continuum*. That is, the set of reals can be used to describe *all* the points on a continuous line or any other continuous geometrical construction. However, $2^{\aleph_0}$ is by no means the greatest transfinite cardinal.[17]

Recall that the cardinality of a power-set is always greater than that of the set whose power-set it is. It can be proven that, for any set T with the cardinal t, the power-set of T has the cardinal 2^t. Further, it can be proven that $2^t > t$ for *any* cardinal t, including transfinite cardinals.[18] Given this theorem, we can construct a series of transfinite cardinals beginning with $\aleph_0$.

$$\aleph_0,\ 2^{\aleph_0},\ 2^{2^{\aleph_0}},\ \ldots$$

This, then, is the first method for generating transfinite cardinals. It will here be referred to as the *power-set method*.

NUMBER-CLASSES AND TRANSFINITE ORDINALS

Cantor's other method for describing a series of transfinite cardinals is based on his theory of ordinal numbers. The cardinal of a set is obtained by abstracting from the nature of the elements of the set, and from their arrangement in the set. The resulting property of the set, its cardinality, can be intuitively understood as its *size*. The *ordinal* of a set is likewise obtained by abstracting from the nature of its elements, but not from their arrangement.

An *ordered set* is one for which there is a rule that will tell, for any two distinct members of the set, which one precedes the other.[19] Two ordered sets are said to be *similar* if a one-to-one mapping can be performed between the two sets, preserving their order.[20] All similar sets are equivalent, then, but not all equivalent sets are similar. Consider the following sets:

$$I = (1, 2, 3, \ldots)$$
$$P = (\ldots 6, 4, 2)$$

I and P both have the same cardinal, $\aleph_0$, but the first member of I cannot be mapped to the first member of P. Hence I and P are equivalent but not similar.

The concept of similarity is used to define *order-type*, in the same way that equivalence is used to define cardinality. Two ordered sets S and T are said to have equal order-types if S is similar to T.[21] Intuitively speaking, the order-type of a set is what it has in common with any set that is the same both in the number of its elements and in their arrangement.

One last definition is needed before the concept of an ordinal number can be explained. An ordered set W is *well ordered* if every non-empty subset of W has a first member.[22] Thus the infinite sets I and E, above, are well ordered, but the equivalent set P is not well ordered. I is similar to E, but not to P. The order-type of a well-ordered set is an *ordinal number*; if the set is infinite, the order-type is a *transfinite ordinal*.[23] The ordinal number tells the *size* and the *shape* of a well-ordered set, while the cardinal number tells the size of a set, without regard to ordering.[24]

In the case of finite sets, ordinals are straightforward. The ordinal of a finite set is a positive integer, and is always the same as its cardinal: for F = (0, 1, 2, 3) the ordinal and the cardinal are both 4. The simplest ordinals, then, are natural numbers. Now the set of natural numbers, N = (0, 1, 2, 3, . . .), is itself well ordered and has an ordinal number. This number is the first number succeeding all the natural numbers. By convention it is known as ω. Consider now the well-ordered set N_1 = (1, 2, 3, . . . , 0). N_1 differs from the set of natural numbers, because it has a last element. Though the same size, it has a different shape and must therefore have a different ordinal. The ordinal of N_1 is $\omega + 1$. In similar fashion, the ordinal of the set N_2 = (2, 3, 4, . . . , 0, 1) is $\omega + 2$. Ever larger ordinals may be generated in this way until we arrive at $\omega + \omega$, or 2ω, which would be the ordinal of (2, 4, 6, . . . , 1, 3, 5, . . .). After this comes $2\omega + 1$, $2\omega + 2$, . . . until we arrive at 3ω, $3\omega + 1$, . . . and, eventually, ω^2. The pattern continues through such numbers as $\omega^2 + \omega$, ω^3, ω^ω, ω^{ω^ω}, . . . until we reach the first ordinal after all *these* numbers, ϵ_0.[25] There is, in short, an inexhaustible supply of ordinals.

We note two things about the series of transfinite ordinals. The first is that its manner of construction shows that there is a rigorous way to describe every number greater than what is naively called "infinity," the limit of the series of natural numbers. The second is that, because all these ordinals are strictly countable, they all describe denumerable sets. Paradoxical as it seems, sets describable by ω, ω^2, or even ϵ_0 are all equivalent to the set of natural numbers.

The concept of *number-classes* allows us to impose some order on this profusion of ordinals. The set of all ordinals that have a common cardinal, ordered by multitude, is normally called the number-class for that cardinal. For the sake of convenience, however, the finite ordinals 0, 1, 2, . . . (each natural number being a distinct ordinal) are grouped together as the *first number-class*. All the sets described by the series of ordinals (ω, $\omega + 1$, $\omega + 2$, . . . , ϵ_0, $\epsilon_0 + 1$, $\epsilon_0 + 2$, . . .) are denumerable, and they all have the cardinal $\aleph_0$. This ordered set of transfinite ordinals is known as the number-class of $\aleph_0$, or the *second number-class*. The initial number of the second number-class is ω, which can be specified as ω_0.

It is possible to construct a well-ordered set of all the ordinals of the first two number-classes. This will be the set of all denumerable ordinals, and *it* must be describable in terms of size and shape, that is, it must have its own ordinal. ω_1 is the first *non*-denumerable ordinal. Abstracting from the order of the set it describes, we get a cardinal, $\aleph_1$.[26]

An Aleph, with subscript, can be understood as the size specified by the initial ordinal in a given number-class.[27] We can generate a series of Alephs using this *number-class method*. The series begins with $\aleph_0$, which corresponds to ω_0. The series runs as follows:

$$\aleph_0, \aleph_1, \aleph_2, \ldots$$

The series continues indefinitely, using finite and then transfinite ordinals as subscripts for the Alephs.[28]

CANTOR'S CONTINUUM HYPOTHESIS

Cantor's theory of transfinite sets thus provides two independent methods for generating transfinite cardinals, the power-set method and the number-class method. The first produces the series $(\aleph_0, 2^{\aleph_0}, 2^{2^{\aleph_0}}, \ldots)$ and the second produces the series $(\aleph_0, \aleph_1, \aleph_2, \ldots)$. Cantor and subsequent theorists labored to determine how these two series compare, *if* they compare, without success. Unable to prove the nature of the relation between these series of cardinals, Cantor stated his famous "continuum hypothesis." This is a conjecture that $2^{\aleph_0} = \aleph_1$.[29] Because Cantor identifies the set of real numbers as the continuum, his hypothesis implies that the size of the continuum is $2^{\aleph_0}$, or that the *next* transfinite multitude larger than the natural numbers is the continuum.

Peirce on Infinity and Continuity

The preceding sketch of Cantor's theory of transfinites will serve as a point of reference for understanding Peirce's own theory. For the most part, Peirce embraced Cantor's discoveries. He welcomed Cantor's work as opening the way to a mathematically rigorous investigation of an ancient and intractable set of philosophical problems concerning the infinite.[30] For all his admiration of Cantor, Peirce did differ from him on several points. In a 1911 article entitled "On Multitude (in Mathematics)" written with H. B. Fine for the second edition of J. M. Baldwin's *Dictionary of Philosophy and Psychology*, Peirce distinguished among multitude, cardinal number, and ordinal number in the following way. *Multitude* is "that relative character of a collection which makes it greater than some collections and less than others" (CP 3.626). Peirce then says that Cantor "confounds" multitude with cardinal number. The difference, according to Peirce, is that while multitude is a property of a collection, *cardinal numbers* are "a series of vocables the prime purpose of which, quite unlike any other words, is to serve as an instrument in the performance of the experiment of counting; these numbers being pronounced in their order from the beginning, one as each member of the collection is disposed of in the operation of counting" (CP 3.628). The cardinal number is used to represent the multitude of a collection, "by virtue of the theorem that a collection the counting of which comes to an end, always comes to an end with the pronunciation of the same cardinal number" (CP 3.628). Finally, the *ordinal numbers* are the cardinal numbers treated "simply in themselves, as objects of mathematical reasoning, stripped of all accidents not pertinent to such study" (CP 3.629).

Whereas Cantor's ordinal names a collection by specifying its size and shape, Peirce's ordinal merely names a place in a sequence.[31] A single infinite collection can be ordered differently, so as to terminate with ω, $\omega + 1$, or any other Cantorean transfinite ordinal. Thus, as we have seen, Cantor was able to show that in respect to size, $\omega = \omega^2$. In the case of an infinite collection with the ordinal ω^2, this is the last ordinal in the count of that particular arrangement of the collection. What Peirce distinguished as the "multitude" of a collection, however, is not the last ordinal in a given count but rather the *least* ordinal that *could* be used to count it. Ordinals name places in a sequence, cardinals are the ordinals as used in counting, and multitude is the size of a collection, as named by the least ordinal needed to count it (the ordinal so used being a cardinal). Peirce's theory of ordinals thus has no way to name the shape of a collection.

Peirce differed from Cantor on one other important point. We have seen that Cantor's "continuum hypothesis" postulates a relation between the different series of transfinite cardinals generated by the power-set method and by the number-class method. The hypothesis identifies the cardinality of the set of real numbers, the continuum, with the cardinality of the first nondenumerable number-class. Peirce denied that the continuum could be identified with the set of real numbers, and ultimately denied that the continuum appears in either of these series at all. As we shall see, he conceived the continuum as something analogous to a set, but to which the concept of size or cardinality does not strictly apply. He referred to the Cantorean transfinites as "pseudo-continua," and argued that the "true continuum" is ultimately different from a set of points, however large.[32]

Peirce's theory of the transfinite depends entirely on the power-set method of generating cardinals. He neglected the theory of ordinals, for the most part, and the concept of number-classes was apparently never quite clear to him.[33] His work on the power-set method is correct, however, and was sufficient to clarify his thought on transfinite multitudes and continua. In the remainder of this chapter, I look at Peirce's application of the power-set argument and Cantor's Theorem, and then turn to his major point of disagreement with Cantor: Peirce claimed that *no* collection of discrete points can constitute a continuum.

PEIRCE'S ACCOUNT OF TRANSFINITE MULTITUDES

The most important conclusion Peirce drew from Cantor's Theorem is that there can be no greatest multitude.[34] The series of cardinals generated by the power-set method is unending, and Peirce introduced his own nomenclature for discussing transfinite multitudes. Following Cantor's original terminology, he called finite multitudes (having a finite cardinal) *enumerable*, and the lowest grade of infinite multitude (having $\aleph_0$ as its cardinal) *denumerable*. Although Cantor called the multitudes larger than denumerable multitudes "non-denumerable," Peirce coined the more precise term *abnumerable* for this grade of infinite multitude. These terms name *kinds* of infinite collections. Peirce introduced variants on them to refer to *particular* multitudes of various kinds. He named the smallest infinite multitude, the denumerable multitude equivalent to the set of natural numbers, the *denumeral* multitude. Cantor's theorem, though, guarantees the existence of larger abnumerable multitudes. The smallest abnumerable multitude has the cardinal $2^{\aleph_0}$. Peirce called it the *first abnumerable* multitude, or the *primipostnumeral* multitude. $2^{2^{\aleph_0}}$ is the *second abnumerable,* or *secundopostnumeral* multitude, followed by the *tertiopostnumeral* (third abnumerable) and *quartopostnumeral* (fourth abnumerable) multitudes, and so on (CP 3.631, 4.200–17).

It can be said that Peirce naively accepted Cantor's continuum hypothesis. Recall that this hypothesis posits a relation between the series of transfinite cardinals generated by applying Cantor's theorem and the series of Alephs applicable to the number-classes discovered in his theory of ordinals. We have seen already that Peirce's ordinals are essentially the same as cardinals, abstracted from their use in counting. Peirce did not develop the notion of number-classes, and so may not have seen the specific point of Cantor's continuum hypothesis as a very significant or problematic claim. In his 1911 article "On Multitude," in fact, Peirce devoted only one line to this issue. He wrote that the series of infinite multitudes (denumeral, primipostnumeral, secundopostnumeral, and so on, which properly name the "power-set" series of transfinite cardinals) "seem to be the same multitudes that are denoted by Cantor as *Alephs*" (CP 3.631). But of course the Alephs, for Cantor, are number-classes, and the whole point of the continuum hypothesis is explicitly to *posit* the correspondence between the two transfinite series that Peirce simply *assumes*.

ANALYTIC VERSUS TRUE CONTINUITY

This naive acceptance of what is a controversial hypothesis suggests that Peirce was indeed unclear about Cantor's whole theory of ordinals.[35] Peirce's misunderstanding of the theory of ordinals and the claim of the continuum hypothesis itself are less important for reading his philosophy, however, than the fact that he let such a misunderstanding arise in the first place. For someone as enamored of Cantor's work as Peirce was to make such an error might indicate that his real concern was with some other feature of Cantor's theory. I suggest that it was: Peirce was worried about Cantor's identification of the set of real numbers ($2^{\aleph_0}$, the primipostnumeral multitude) as the continuum. This issue is more fundamental, for Peirce, than the question whether $2^{\aleph_0} = \aleph_1$. Both $2^{\aleph_0}$ and $\aleph_1$, or for that matter any other Cantorean transfinite multitudes, are conceived as collections of discrete elements or numerical points. *This* is the bone Peirce wants to pick with Cantor.

Peirce was concerned with the proper mathematical treatment of the continuum from early in his career. He frequently discussed Zeno's paradoxes of motion as a prelude to setting forth his own views on the nature of continua. These references are always unsympathetic.[36] Zeno's characterization of space and time as static series of points and instants rankled Peirce, and he saw this view as important, being perhaps the least satisfactory approach to the problem. Karl Weirstrass' widely accepted "analytic" approach to problems of motion, based on the theory of limits, is a considerable improvement over Zeno. Cantor's identification of the set of reals as the continuum conforms with this method of analysis. Peirce, however, found this approach lacking as well, and developed an alternative conception of continuity.

In "Grounds of Validity of the Laws of Logic," published in 1869, Peirce summarized his principal objection to Zeno's view. His objection to Cantor's view is essentially the same, so it will be helpful to see what Peirce had to say about Zeno.

> All the arguments of Zeno depend upon supposing that a *continuum* has ultimate parts. But a *continuum* is precisely that, every part of which has parts, in the same sense. Hence, he makes out his contradictions only by making a self-contradictory supposition. In ordinary and mathematical language, we allow ourselves to speak of such parts—*points*—and whenever we are led into contradiction thereby, we have simply to express ourselves more accurately to resolve the difficulty.
>
> Suppose a piece of glass to be laid on a sheet of paper so as to cover half of it. Then, every part of the paper is *covered,* or *not covered*; for "not" means merely outside of, or other than. But is the line under the edge of the glass covered or not? It is no more on one side of the edge than on the other. Therefore, it is either on both sides, or neither side. It is not on neither side; for if it were it would be *not* on either side, therefore not on the covered side, therefore not covered, therefore on the uncovered side. It is not partly on one side and partly on the other, because it has no width. Hence, it is wholly on both sides, or both covered and not covered.
>
> The solution of this is, that we have supposed a part too narrow to be partly uncovered and partly covered; that is to say, a part which has no parts in a continuous surface, which by definition has no such parts. The reasoning, therefore, simply serves to reduce this supposition to an absurdity. (W 2:256–57)

The passage suggests rejecting continuity as a relation among discrete parts: while it is often *convenient* to speak of ultimate parts in a continuum, it is not *accurate* to do so. A point or a line having no width (and likewise an instant having no duration) is an abstraction, a mere convenience of speech. It is not an ultimate indivisible part of a continuum, since a genuine continuum of the kind Peirce posits *has* no such indivisible parts.

The question whether *the line* at the edge of the glass is covered or not is therefore nonsensical, since it rests on a contradictory assumption. Properly speaking, there is no way to identify the line, the individual geometrical entity that has no width, in the continuous surface. What there is, instead, is a topological feature (constituting what Peirce called a relative discontinuity) marked by the edge of the glass. This feature is indeed thinner than any specifiable width, but it is not without width: it has infinitesimal width. The abstract "line" may be spoken of *as if* it were there, but it does not exist in the continuous surface.

Zeno's arguments, according to Peirce, always rest on the same error of substituting a mathematical abstraction—a point, line, plane, or instant—for a real topological feature of a continuum. These mathematical abstractions land us in contradiction. On Peirce's view, statements about actual topological features of infinitesimal width do not lead to contradiction, because they are not necessarily subject to all the usual principles of logic.[37] The topological feature marked by the edge of the glass is too narrow to be quantified, but is "wide enough" that it may be thought of as being both covered and not covered, or neither fully covered nor fully uncovered.

Another of Peirce's examples, from the 1902 article "Mathematical Logic" in Baldwin's *Dictionary,* is given in conjunction with a discussion of the method of limits. The method of limits offers an improvement over Zeno's methods of analysis because it posits events as occurring not in a denumerable system of points or instants, but in an "analytic continuum" of $2^{\aleph_0}$ values.[38] The following passage considers an event occurring in a continuous system, and highlights Peirce's dissatisfaction with the method of limits.

> Suppose, for example, a ball rolling on a billiard table to come to rest. The system of dates in time (not of *assignable* dates, since these can only form, at most, a first-abnumerable system, but of instants such as our conception of flowing time supposes) is a system of values [which does not admit of individuals]. That ball is moving down to a certain instant, and [at] all subsequent instants is at rest. It cannot, however, absolutely move through *all* the time previous to that instant and be at absolute rest during all subsequent time, without at that instant being in a state which is neither one of absolute motion nor one of absolute rest. The method of limits would explain this, were it applicable; but it is only applicable to a collection of assignable

instants, which is a very limited kind of multitude. If time flows, no instant has an absolutely independent identity. It is so far independent that an instantaneous state of things may be supposed to exist absolutely at that instant alone. But a duration which begins or ends at that instant cannot properly be said absolutely to contain or absolutely to exclude that instant. (NEM 3:747)

Just as the line at the edge of the glass is neither entirely in the covered region of the paper nor in the uncovered region, the moment at which the ball ceases rolling is neither a moment of absolute motion nor of absolute rest.

Peirce notes that the method of limits could be used to identify this instant "were it applicable," but he clearly believed that the method is not entirely appropriate for analyzing such events. To get clear on the disagreement, let us first consider how the method of limits would apply in this case. Suppose the ball to be moving in a Cantorean analytic continuum consisting of $2^{\aleph_0}$ discrete temporal instants. The instant at which the ball stops rolling would have an assignable date, though perhaps not one that appears in a denumerable set of values. The method of limits affords a way to *use* a denumerable series of values in order to specify the instant in question. If v is the velocity of the ball and t is time, then time can be expressed as a function of velocity: $f(v) = t$. If we designate the instant at which the ball's velocity reaches zero as t_1, then it is possible to associate a denumerable series of values that corresponds to the decreasing velocity of the ball with a denumerable series of instants leading up to t_1.

Say the initial velocity (at time t_0) is one inch per second, and zero at t_1. Then the function $f(v)$ has the limit t_1 as v approaches zero. Now, the instant t_1 in our example may not appear in a denumerable series and so cannot always be represented by a rational value. But it can be specified with as much precision as desired, simply by choosing a suitably small value for v. We can specify a denumerable set of decreasing numbers $(1, \frac{1}{2}, \frac{1}{4}, \ldots)$ that may be substituted for v in the equation. As these values approach zero, the values for t approach a limit, the value of t_1. If the value for t in a substitution is not sufficiently small for our purposes, we may always choose a smaller value for v and obtain a closer approximation of t_1.

To speak of t_1 as being precisely identified implies that the denumerable series $(1, \frac{1}{2}, \frac{1}{4}, \ldots)$ has been completed, and the limit of the series actually reached.[39] But this involves a contradiction, since the series is infinite. This is made clear where t_1 is irrational: The limit of the series cannot be stated exactly, but only approximated. We then suppose we have completed *all* possible approximations, including not only the hundredth, thousandth, and so forth, but also the "infinity-eth." In Latin, this would be the *infinitesima* approximation, and to suppose it actually to exist "is to accept infinitesimals in the Leibnizian sense" (NEM 3:745).

That the method of limits is counterintuitive has been noted by generations of calculus students. Why not simply let v equal zero, and say that t_1
equals the resulting value?[40] One reason has been suggested already: in case
t_1 is irrational, its value cannot be stated with absolute exactitude, and
something like the method of limits must be used to get ever more accurate
approximations. The more compelling philosophical reason, though, is that
if we suppose the limit to be reached we face the problem of deciding
whether the ball is in motion or at rest at t_1. The best answers (that it is
both, or not quite either) violate the principles of contradiction and excluded middle, respectively. Rather than throw out these "laws of logic," mathematicians have usually opted to throw out infinitesimals. The method of
limits allows as precise an approximation of values at a limit as may be
needed, but escapes the paradoxes associated with positing a state of affairs
at the limit point. This consistency comes with a price however: Strictly
speaking, we lose the right to say (for example) that the ball ceases motion
exactly one-half second after its velocity measures one inch per second.

Peirce allowed that the method of limits and Cantor's analytic continuum meet the needs of those who merely want a method for analyzing
motion. He did not, however, accept that the analytic continuum accurately
portrays the real world. His fundamental objection to analytic continuity
was philosophical. If mathematics is to serve as the basis for philosophy,
including metaphysics, then we ought not to limit ourselves arbitrarily to a
narrow mathematical world, ruling out alternative mathematical conceptions of continuity simply because they appear unneeded at present.
Because hypotheses direct our observation, and because mathematics has to
do with the production and investigation of hypotheses, narrow mathematical conceptions are likely to lead to narrow observations and, ultimately, a
narrow conception of reality. The method of limits can be applied to any
system of discrete values,[41] but to accept it as an entirely accurate mathematical representation of reality excludes the possibility that reality consists,
in whole or in part, of values that are *not,* in principle, distinct. As Peirce
says, "Cantor's theory . . . is a perfectly reasonable supposition. But why
limit ourselves to two *classes* of *infinity?* This limitation springs from no
more being needed in mathematics, nothing else" (NEM 4:xxiv).[42]

In his discussion of the billiard ball, Peirce merely *asserted* that the
method of limits is not applicable because in the flow of time no instant
has absolutely independent identity. The true nature of time, of course, is a
problem for metaphysics. In the context of his article for Baldwin's
Dictionary, Peirce simply introduced time as an example of a true continuum that is not fully amenable to the method of limits. More will be said
about the continuity of time in the presentation of Peirce's definition of true
continuity, and in the next chapter. Even without raising the question
whether there *are* non-analytic continua such as Peirce here supposes time
to be, however, the mathematician must ask whether analytic continuity is

satisfactory as a hypothesis, and whether other coherent conceptions of continuity are possible.

Peirce argued that the analytic continuum would not meet the needs of topical geometry, and offered the following paradox that arises for the geometer working with an analytic continuum:[43]

> Suppose a filament to occupy the whole of a limited line and to be restricted to that line. Let the terminal particle which occupies an absolute point, be thrown off. Then, according to our ordinary idea of space, will that filament remain without any terminal particle? No. But if it now had *another* particle as its termination, it would consist of particles next to one another, and so not be continuous. (NEM 3:747)

Peirce's solution holds that the conception of continuity here is at fault, much as it was at fault in Zeno's paradoxes. The problem, again, lies in conceiving a continuum as *consisting* of ultimate parts. In response to the preceding paradox, Peirce wrote that "we are forced to say that it is *the same* particle which remains after being thrown off, —in short, we must admit that, according to our ordinary idea of space, points and particles occupying points have no absolute identity" (NEM 3:747–48).

Peirce thus offered two reasons to look for continua that do not consist of collections of discrete elements, however multitudinous such collections might be. First, there is the philosophical desire to keep all the doors open, to develop a number of hypotheses before turning to phenomena to investigate whether they are true. On Peirce's view, Cantor's continuum hypothesis blocks inquiry into the properties of continua of nondiscrete elements. As Potter and Shields note, Peirce must have been uneasy with the idea that the continuum contains *only* $2^{\aleph_0}$ elements, when larger collections are clearly conceivable.[44] Second, Peirce maintained that to take the analytic continuum as an accurate model of reality lands us in paradoxes analogous to and as pernicious as Zeno's, though at a higher level of mathematical sophistication.

Of course, it was up to Peirce to show that his own method involves no equally undesirable paradoxes. It has been noted already that, in Peirce's view, the principle of excluded middle does not apply to assertions about the state of affairs at a limit-point. Such a violation of a fundamental principle of logic is usually considered undesirable, and one of the things that makes the doctrine of limits attractive is that it avoids this consequence. We have seen that Peirce's triadic logic includes a third truth-value, *L*, in addition to the usual values for True and False. Peirce clearly thought that logic could get along just fine without universal adherence to the principle of excluded middle. The limit-case of an event in a true continuum is thus the geometrical instantiation of a certain feature of his logical system and, in

Peirce's architectonic, such hypothetical states may well foreshadow meta-physical realities. This is clearly the case here. The possibility of suspending the traditional "laws of logic" in such special cases is to be seen as an asset, a needed feature for any logic or mathematics that will prove adequate to ground a theory of reality.

THE DEFINITION OF TRUE CONTINUITY

In the 1902 article "Mathematical Logic," immediately after concluding that "points and particles occupying points [in a continuum] have no absolute identity," Peirce wrote, "Kant defines a continuum as that of which every part consists of parts, and though he confuses this definition with infinite divisibility, it is really a different hypothesis, and may (in the present writer's opinion) be accepted as an approximate definition of a continuum" (NEM 3:748).[45] To say that a continuum is infinitely divisible is to say that it has no ultimate parts. This is one of the two defining characteristics of a continuum. The other concerns the way parts are related: They are connected, so that they combine or "stick together."

If all the approximations represented by the limit-series of a function were completed, we would obtain an exact value for the function in question at that point. In an analytic continuum, however, we cannot do so. For a limit function (e.g., $f(v)=t$ as v approaches 0), the series of values that can be substituted for the independent variable v (the abscissa sequence) are denumerably infinite. There is an infinite supply of values that can be run through without reaching the limit point. To suppose the abscissa sequence actually completed, then, is generally considered contradictory.

If we wish to develop a conception of the continuum that will allow for an *exact* value for t at the limit-point ($v=0$), we must suppose that the abscissa sequence is *not* an infinite series. Clearly it will not do to suppose, as a solution, that the abscissa series is finite. Peirce therefore suggests that we not think of the values to be substituted for the independent variable as a series of *distinct* values in the first place. This is what Peirce means when he says that the continuum is not composed of ultimate parts. In Peirce's approach, then, the abscissa sequence is not taken as an accurate representation of reality. There is no set of independent values that will accurately represent a true continuum, as it does not consist of independent points.

The first of the two defining characteristics of a true continuum, then, is that it is not an aggregate or collection of distinct parts. It is, rather, an entity upon which individuals may be marked: Any true continuum is a continuum of possible determinations.[46] Several observations may be made about the first defining characteristic. First, although it is not composed of parts, a continuum may be divided into parts. Such a division occurs when something external to the continuum marks a topical singularity on it. The billiard ball ceases its motion, and that cessation effectively divides the temporal continuum into two parts: The time before the motion stopped, and the time after it stops. Second, a true continuum is *infinitely* divisible. A line, for example, may be divided. Then each part is a continuous line, which may likewise be divided, and so on. We never reach a part so small that it is not itself divisible. Third, *every part* of a continuum is divisible in this way. This means not only that every part, no matter how small, is divisible (which merely repeats the second point), but also that a continuum is infinitely divisible at every place along its extension. As Peirce states it, "all the parts of a perfect continuum have the same dimensionality as the whole" (CP 4.642).

In a note dated May 26, 1908, Peirce wrote, "my notion of the essential character of a perfect continuum is the absolute generality with which two rules hold good, first, that every part has parts; and second, that every sufficiently small part has the same mode of immediate connection with others as every other has" (CP 4.642). The second defining characteristic of a continuum, then, concerns the way parts of a continuum are related. Peirce explicates the notion of *immediate connection* with reference to the continuity of time, but such an appeal to phenomenological evidence is out of place at this point in our exposition. Indeed, temporal continuity may turn out to be the closest thing to true continuity there is in our experience, and hence be the most suitable standard of reference for discussing other kinds of continuity. Nonetheless, it may also be that time itself is not a perfect example of continuity.[47] At this point we need to clarify the notion of "immediate connection" among parts.

Peirce offers the following definition of *parts* of an entity:

> The *material parts* of a thing or other object, W, that is composed of such parts, are whatever things are, firstly, each and every one of them, other than W; secondly, are all of some one internal nature (for example, are all places, or all times, or all spatial realities, or are all spiritual realities, or are all ideas, or are all characters, or are all relations, or are all external representations, etc.); thirdly, form together a collection of objects in which no one occurs twice over and, fourthly, are such that the Being of each of them together with the modes of connection between all subcollections of them, constitute the being of W. . . . It will be seen that the definition of Material Parts involves the concept of *Connexion,* even if there be no other connexion between them than co-being; and in case no other connexion be essential to the concept of W, this latter is called a *Collection.* (CP 6.174)

Clearly, then, not everything that has material parts is a continuum.[48] Let us consider what must be true of two material parts, A and B, which are continuous. If A and B are "sufficiently small parts" and are continuous, they must be "immediately connected." Immediate connection is a kind of relation, but a rather peculiar kind. That the connection is *immediate* suggests that there is no need of a third, C, which mediates the relation of A to B. Not only does this exclude the possibility that there is anything located *between* A and B, it also excludes the possibility that A and B are related only in virtue of belonging to some general class of objects. In the case where A and B are connected *only* in co-being, for example, the third is that which brings the two independent things together in a collection: My dog and my hat are "connected" in the sense that both are elements of the set of things in the house as I write this sentence.

Suppose that two things, A and B, have some part in common. If that part is the *region of intersection* of A and B, then the region acts as a third and the relation is mediated by that third. Now suppose that A and B have *everything* in common. This means that A and B are *the same*. In fact, the relation of immediate connection appears to be tied up with the relation of identity. Roughly speaking, the "mode of immediate connection" between sufficiently small neighboring parts of a continuum is that such parts are in some sense identical.

If I read Peirce correctly, he is here flirting with what would appear to be a disastrous contradiction: *neighboring parts of a continuum may be the same in every respect, including location.* But if all neighboring parts of a continuum are thus identical, there seems to be no way to explain how they make up a continuum rather than collapsing into a single point. How is it that we get from the identity of neighboring points to a line with a left hand and a right hand region? Peirce escapes the paradox by denying that the relations of identity and otherness strictly hold in respect to sufficiently small neighboring parts of a continuum (NEM 3:747). This assertion demands some elaboration.

Peirce's escape may be through a loophole in Leibniz's Law. According to this law, "A is the same as B" means that A can be substituted for B in any proposition whatever, and the truth of the proposition will be preserved.[49] A closely related principle is the Identity of Indiscernibles: if there is no respect in which A is *discernibly* different from B, then A and B are the same. Peirce says of two things having identical properties that "They are like two ideal rain drops, distinct but not different. Leibniz's 'principle of indiscernibles' is all nonsense" (CP 4.311). If Peirce does escape contradiction in his discussion of immediate connection, he is able to do so because in Leibnizian terms difference is equated with discernible difference, that is, a difference that *in principle* could become apparent to a mind.[50]

Now let us suppose that A and B are neighboring parts of a continuous line, and that they are sufficiently small to be immediately connected. Both parts have the same internal nature—both are continuous, one-dimensional geometric entities. Suppose them to be shorter than any specifiable positive length. There then can be no discernible difference in their length. The only difference between A and B must be in their location on the continuous line of which they are parts. Because they are neighboring parts and are connected, they have parts in common; because they are immediately connected, they have *all* their parts in common.

Let us consider briefly the analogous situation in the macroscopic world. For two parts of *specifiable* positive length (call them X and Y), there are three ways they may be related so as to have parts in common. First, X may be wholly enclosed within the extremities of Y, so that any part of X is part of Y, but some parts of Y are not parts of X. Second, X and Y may exactly coincide, so that *every* part of X is part of Y, and vice versa. Third, X and Y may overlap, so that some parts are common to both, some parts of X are not parts of Y, and some parts of Y are not parts of X.

For the indefinitely small parts A and B, however, the distinctions among these possible relations disappear. Because A and B have no specifiable length, it is meaningless to say that A is smaller than B, or that A could be wholly enclosed within B. This would require that B is *longer* than A, but B itself has no quantifiable length and so cannot meaningfully be said to be "longer than" anything. For A and B to be exactly coincidental means that any part of A is a part of B, and vice versa. This is meaningful: It says that A and B are the same, according to the Identity of Indiscernibles. In such a case, A can clearly be substituted for B in any proposition (or equation) and the truth of the proposition will be preserved.

This explains what it means for A and B to coincide, to share all their parts. Now, A and B are supposed to be *neighboring* parts of a continuous line. In what sense might they differ in location (which must be what is meant by being neighboring parts) and still be immediately connected? Consider the following case, based on an example offered in the third of Peirce's 1898 Cambridge Conferences Lectures.[51] Suppose a point is marked on a continuous straight line. The line is then cut at that point, so as to produce a left-hand region (L), and a right-hand region (R). The original marked point thereby becomes *two* points: the point at the right end of L, and the point at the left end of R. If the ends are then rejoined, they become again *one* single point. It is clear that if the original "point" thus admits of being divided, it must be divisible into parts of the kind we have been discussing. This example illustrates that the immediately connected neighboring parts A and B (which are at the same "point" before the cut) must be ordered. This requires a closer look.

Say that A and B are ordered by the relation "A is r to B for C"; that, for example, proceeding along the line from C (a point which is not immediately connected to A or to B) to the right, one reaches A before reaching B.[52] Then A and B are ordered with respect to C. It is this ordering that ensures that, if the line is cut at this point, A ends up in the region L and B ends up in the region R. Is this ordering, which serves to differentiate A and B when the cut is made, compatible with A and B being the same? Peirce would say that it is, as A and B are by hypothesis immediately connected and hence indiscernible before the cut. A is a specifiable distance to the right of C, and B is adjacent to A. The difference in their distance from C is infinitesimal, and so it is correct to say they are the same before the cut. When the cut occurs, however, their order becomes apparent: as the result of an outside imposition of discontinuity, the difference *becomes* discernible. A and B as distinct points on a continuum are only potentially distinct, then, prior to the cut. The cut is a determinative act that serves to distinguish the two points.

We might again raise the question: If all neighboring parts of a continuum are identical, how is it that we ever get a continuum with differentiable parts, rather than one dimensionless point? The response is that in this discussion we *started* with a continuum, and were inquiring into the relation that obtains between very small neighboring parts. We do not *need* to work our way back up, from the small parts to the whole continuum, by adding them together. To do so, in fact, would violate the first defining characteristic of a continuum. To try to build up a continuum in this way is to suppose that we are working with its ultimate constituent parts, but there *are* no such ultimate parts. The point that is cut is not, after all, a point. It is a place, an infinitesimally small part of a continuum, and so is itself a continuum capable of infinite division.[53]

The parts A and B can be considered different in their location on the line (because of a specifiable ordering relation), but the difference is infinitesimally small. They may be thought of as "overlapping," so that they occupy different places. The difference is infinitesimal, however, so it is in principle indiscernible. If the difference is indiscernible, then we may as easily say that A and B are the same.[54] The lengths of A and B are indeterminately small: A and B are objectively indeterminate quantities, and the place of their occurrence in the continuum is a general.[55] Peirce says that the principle of excluded middle does not apply to general terms (CP 5.448, 505). Here, in the mathematics of continuity, we encounter an instance of this exception to the principle. It is neither entirely true nor entirely false to say of two immediately connected parts of a continuum that they are the same in every respect including location. This is indeed a difficult conclusion to accept, accustomed as we are to thinking in terms of determinately sized objects. As Peirce puts it, though, "The definitions of otherness and of identity proper (identity ἀρθμῷ) presuppose a universe of individuals; in a universe not consisting of individuals, where every part consists of parts of the same kind, they are only applicable so far as that universe admits of individuals" (NEM 3:747).

INFINITESIMALS

The continuous system Peirce envisions does admit of "individuals," of course. Though a line extending through Dallas and Wichita is continuous, the two cities are certainly located at different places, and these places can be distinguished. Likewise, even though time may be continuous, tomorrow really is another day. Such spatial or temporal "individuals" are distinct, however, because we impose the distinction for most purposes. They are in fact not metaphysically individual; they are *singular parts* of the spatial or temporal continuum (CP 3.93). It is not that these singulars exist in ultimate component parts of the continuum which are themselves absolutely distinct from one another. Relations of otherness and identity apply perfectly well to singulars so conceived, which is what we mean when we speak loosely of "individuals." With respect to a continuous system ("a system of an infinite multitude of dimensions") Peirce says, "[g]eneral logic applies . . . provided we take care not to assume that objects have independent identity, after it has already been assumed that they have not" (NEM 3:748).

It is when we look for such things as the absolutely determinate point at which two lines intersect, or the instant when a billiard ball stops rolling, that the general logical relations of otherness and identity break down. The *absolute* point or instant eludes thought structured in these terms.[56] The reason is that we do not encounter absolute points or instants at all when we pass below the threshold of determinate quantity. Here we enter the world of infinitesimals.

An infinitesimal is simply a positive quantity which is less than any specifiable quantity. The discussion of the "small parts" A and B in the previous section is a description of the nature of infinitesimals. A few words are now in order about how *not* to conceive infinitesimals.

Cantor rejected the notion that infinitesimals, as just defined, have any place in mathematics.[57] Until recently, most mathematicians followed Cantor in this view. The prevalent reasons for rejecting infinitesimals are legitimate, within the proper bounds, and it is important to see why they would not affect Peirce's conception. Fraenkel sets forth the Cantorean view in these terms:

> After the introduction of transfinite numbers by Cantor such attitudes [belief in the legitimacy of infinitesimals] pretended to be justified by set theory because there ought to exist reciprocals (inverse ratios) to the transfinite numbers, namely the ostensible infinitesimals of various degrees representing the ratios of finite to transfinite numbers.[58]

We can try to define this reciprocal using transfinite cardinals, so that it is "one divided by $\aleph_0$," (or some other transfinite cardinal). The problem with such an expression is that it does not make sense to divide by a transfinite cardinal number. If we conceive an infinitesimal as the quotient of "one over infinity," then there are indeed no infinitesimals.

Cardinal numbers, for Cantor, describe the size of sets by abstracting from the nature of the sets' elements and their arrangement. Not all the usual mathematical operations *work* for cardinal numbers so defined, and when they do work, they often yield unexpected results. This is especially true for transfinite cardinals. The size of the set obtained by adding all the odd integers to all the even integers, for example, is $\aleph_o + \aleph_o = \aleph_o$.[59] Addition is thus possible, but unusual. *Division* by cardinals, on the other hand, is generally disallowed. Cardinals describe the size of sets, and sets are either empty or they contain whole elements. We can certainly divide the number 1 by the number 3, but not by the *cardinal* number 3. To divide 1 by a cardinal suggests that the resulting ratio is also a cardinal. Now a set of three oranges has the cardinal 3. We can normally divide 1 by 3, but it makes no sense to speak of a set whose cardinal is $\frac{1}{3}$. A set containing one-third of an orange would contain *one* element (a chunk of an orange), not one-third of an element. If we object that it contains *no* (whole) oranges, the result is still unsatisfactory: the cardinal would be 0, which still is not $\frac{1}{3}$. Cantor's rejection of infinitesimals is thus justified, *if* infinitesimals are conceived as the quotient of 1 divided by a transfinite cardinal. It is a rule of set theory that one cannot find the inverse ratio of a transfinite cardinal.[60]

This objection cannot be raised against Peirce's conception of infinitesimals, however. First of all, we must note that Peirce's notion of the cardinal numbers is not the same as Cantor's. For him, the cardinals are merely the counting numbers, and might be amenable to division. Likewise, his different conception of ordinals (the ordinals are merely the cardinals as actually *used* in counting) would allow division.[61] Peirce would probably not find this approach acceptable, though, and he apparently never sought to define the infinitesimal as the reciprocal of a transfinite number. To do so would have run counter to his whole notion of continuity: The infinitesimal is an indeterminately small part of a true continuum, not of any discrete multitude identifiable by a cardinal number.[62] Peirce's true continuum is not identifiable by its multitude, so there is no particular cardinal associated with it. Hence Peirce could not, and did not, define the infinitesimal as the reciprocal of the cardinal for the continuum.

The Hypothesis of True Continuity

Peirce's concept of true continuity is a fascinating hypothesis about the properties of certain ideal mathematical objects. Though it is used to furnish virtually every room of Peirce's philosophical house, we will first consider its virtues as a mathematical speculation. Mathematics, again, "merely posits hypotheses, and traces out their consequences" (CP 1.240). The key hypothesis behind true continuity is that *the continuum is not composed of discrete parts*. As a mathematician, and by his own account of mathematics,

Peirce is free to posit anything whatever as a hypothesis and to devote his energy to investigating its consequences. Clearly, though, there are specific concerns that led Peirce to fix on this particular idea. One of these concerns has served as our point of focus: Peirce found Cantor's identification of the set of real numbers as the continuum to be inadequate.

We have already noted that Peirce was willing to concede that the analytic continuum is adequate for the usual needs of mathematics. He did predict that it would prove inadequate for the development of topology, but history has shown Peirce to be wrong on that point. We now ask what there is within the scope of mathematics (as Peirce conceived it), which would motivate anyone to follow him in adopting this hypothesis. Aside from the concern about topology, there are two things which must have made the continuity hypothesis attractive to Peirce. First, it allows a precise understanding of the concept of *combination,* which he found indispensable for logic. Second, Peirce's concept of true continuity is a broader theory than Cantor's analytic continuity. It opens more possibilities for inquiry, and—provided it proves *plausible*—should be preferred on that account. To restrict our notion of continuity to a system of discrete elements, while there is the possibility that such a system is merely one aspect of a more general system, is to block the way of inquiry into the properties of that broader system.

In Peirce's logic, the triad is the primitive relative. The peculiar virtue of the triad is that it can represent genuine combination. In chapter 3 a passage from MS 908, pp. 7–8, was presented in which Peirce argues, in effect, that if there is thought of anything whatever, then that thought is synthetic and presupposes combination. Thus for Peirce, combination or triadicity is necessarily a component of our thinking, if we are aware of anything at all. The account of continuity develops the meaning of combination: Parts that are immediately connected in a continuum are *combined.*[63]

The ubiquity of continuity is illustrated by its appearance in the most fundamental of logical relations:

> [T]o be in relation to X, and to be in relation to a relation to X mean the same thing. If therefore I were to put "relation" into the subject at all, I ought in consistency to put it in infinitely many times, and indeed this would not be sufficient. It is like a continuous line: no matter what one cuts off from it a line remains. So I do not attempt to regard "A is B" as meaning "A is identical with something that is B." I call "is in relation to" and "is identical with" Continuous Relations, and I leave such in the Predicate. MS 611, pp. 14–15)

When Peirce says that even to put the word "relation" into the subject an infinite number of times would not be sufficient, he has in mind the difference between discrete multitudes (however large) and a true continuum.

Just as no collection of points by its size alone can constitute a continuous line, no number of repetitions of the word "relation" can weld the idea of redness to the idea of the rose when we say "the rose is red." They are connected from the beginning. True connection, combination, or continuity is qualitatively different from mere crowdedness in a transfinite set. Individuation, or Secondness, can never attain to real combination, or Thirdness.

If the earlier account of the relation between neighboring infinitesimals is correct, we can consider it an elaboration of what Peirce means by "continuous relation" in the above passage. The parts A and B, taken in one light, are identical; taken in another light, they occur in an ordered relation. This is possible if they are immediately connected in the way we have suggested. Likewise, the concepts joined in the statement, "The rose is red" are immediately connected, or welded together. They arrive as one idea, but may be distinguished if necessary.

The elementary logical concept of "being related to," which is necessary to any thought whatever, reappears in the geometrical concept of immediate connection within a continuum. Peirce's existential graphs are meant to exploit this affinity between the fundamentals of geometry and the fundamentals of logic. He considered the graphs far superior to algebraic logical notation, as they provide a better iconic representation of the object of logic. Peirce believed that object to be propositions and, in turn, the world. J. Jay Zeman scratches an otherwise untouched surface in Peirce's thought with his observation that "The Peirce of the existential graphs. . . is as well the Peirce of synechism, the metaphysical doctrine asserting the reality of continua and the continuity of reality."[64] Logic is to be the basis for metaphysics, and Peirce's preferred logical system is thoroughly imbued with the principle of true continuity. Unfortunately, we cannot here go into a thorough exposition of the system of existential graphs, much less the metaphysical interpretation that Peirce designed into them.

I will only note that in the existential graphs system there are several symbols which are of particular interest with respect to the notion of combination. The first such symbol is the "sheet of assertion" itself, upon which graphs are scribed. In the Alpha and Beta graphs, the blank sheet of assertion "represents simply a universe of existent individuals, and the different parts of the sheet represent facts or true assertions made concerning that universe" (CP 4.512). In the Gamma graphs (Peirce's unfinished modal system) the empty sheet of assertion is conceived as a map of the multidimensional continuum of true assertions which are or could be developed (CP 4.512–13). In general, the sheet is understood as a representation of "an external continuity" among true assertions, "and especially, a continuity of experiential appearance" (CP 4.561n.1). Because it represents in two dimensions "a field of Thought, or of Mental Experience, which is itself directed to the Universe of Discourse," the sheet of assertion is "the most appropriate

Icon possible of the continuity of the Universe of Discourse" (CP 4.561n1).

Given an icon of the universe of discourse itself, one may make a particular assertion with only the simplest possible modification of the surface of the sheet: though short phrases or capital letters are typically used for this purpose, a simple spot or mark on the map can designate any chosen proposition (for example, a premise of an argument). Another, different mark, can be placed anywhere else on the sheet to make another assertion. Suppose we have asserted, out of the whole universe of possible assertions, that something is a Rose and that something is Red:

——————— is a Rose   ——————— is Red

If we wish to assert the identity of these two things, to say that the Rose is Red, we can do so by drawing a ligature connecting the open positions on each monadic relative:

——————— is a Rose   ——————— is Red

The ligature or "line of identity" asserts that the two concepts are continuous, that Rose and Redness, in this particular case, are connected in the concept of the single individual about which the assertion "There is a Red Rose" is made. The line of identity represents the continuous connection of the concepts, but this is not the same continuity as is iconically represented in the two-dimensional sheet of assertion. The line of identity is one-dimensional, and "represents Identity to belong to the genus Continuity and to the species Linear Continuity" (CP 4.561n1). It derives its continuity from that of the sheet, or universe, in which it occurs. Thus even though triadic relatives might appear only rarely in using existential graphs (monadic and dyadic relatives appear more frequently), the principle of combination that they represent is nonetheless *always* present. The continuity involved in the sheet of assertion and in the line of identity is a triadic phenomenon. The intended parallel is clear: Just as the graphs take advantage of an antecedent continuity in the sheet of assertion for their operation, the mind takes advantage of the antecedent continuity of the universe of thought for its operation.

Peirce's conception of the continuum and its infinitesimal parts also provides an instance where the third value in his triadic logic must be assigned. Eisele points out that "were a proposition to be false up to a certain instant and thereafter to be true, at that instant it would be both true and false" (NEM 3:xvii). The instant of change is a limit-case parallel to the case of the rolling billiard ball. If we ask what the state of affairs is at the instant of change, trying to determine the truth or falsity of the proposition that the ball is at rest, then we need to introduce a third truth value. The principle of excluded middle demands that we answer either true or false. In Peirce's system, though, the answer is *L*—a truth value that is objectively neither True nor False.[65]

Peirce's second reason for favoring his "true" continuity over Cantor's analytic continuity is that *if* it is a logically consistent concept, then it offers a broader hypothesis with which to initiate mathematical inquiry. If we follow Cantor, mathematical and scientific investigation is restricted to systems of discrete individuals. Peirce's hypothesis offers an additional avenue: We may investigate systems of discrete individuals, or we may investigate truly continuous systems. One may always *choose* to restrict inquiry to the properties of the analytic continuum, or any other pseudo-continuum, simply by positing that the true continuum has been marked with the appropriate multitude of points.[66] To mark points on a continuum merely means that continuity has been *broken* at those points.[67] What is originally continuous, in other words, may be ruptured. But what is originally *discontinuous* cannot by brute force be made continuous. This wider possibility for inquiry would make Peirce's hypothesis about the nature of the geometric manifold preferable over Cantor's.

There is a lurking concern, however. For Peirce's hypothesis to be acceptable, we need a rigorous demonstration that the concept of a continuum composed of nondiscrete parts is not self-contradictory. In the 1898 Cambridge Conferences Lectures, Peirce stated that his logic of relations is the perfect tool for proving the concept logically consistent, and said "that apparatus not only absolutely refuses to pronounce this self-contradictory but it demonstrates, on the contrary, that it is not so" (NEM 4:343). In his lectures and publications he declined to present the proof, however, claiming that it would be too tedious and involved for his audience.[68] In 1900 he again expressed confidence in the consistency of infinitesimal theory: "Not only is this view admissible without any violation of logic, but I find— though I cannot ask the space to explain this here—that it forms a basis for the differential calculus preferable, perhaps, at any rate, quite as clear, as the doctrine of limits" (CP 3.569). To my knowledge, however, no proof of the logical consistency of infinitesimals has been identified in Peirce's published or unpublished writings.

Mathematicians may be excused for skepticism about true continuity and infinitesimals as long as no rigorous proof of consistency was forthcoming. Fraenkel expresses the dominant mid-century view of the value of infinitesimals in these terms:

> [The admission of infinitesimals has] been thoroughly rejected by Cantor and by the mathematical world in general. The reason for this uniformity was not dogmatism, which is a rare feature in mathematics and then almost invariably fought off; nobody has pleaded more ardently than Cantor himself that

liberty of thought was the essence of mathematics and that prejudices had but a short life. The argument was not even that the admission of infinitesimals was self-contradictory, but just that it was *sterile and useless*.[69]

This comment brings out the other side of the issue: Though we have no proof from Peirce's hand that the concept is consistent, neither did anyone meet his challenge to prove its inconsistency.[70]

Whether he actually proved it or not, it turns out that Peirce was right to insist that a consistent theory of infinitesimals could be developed. In the 1960s, Abraham Robinson used the apparatus of modern symbolic logic to develop a theory called "nonstandard analysis."[71] The system posits a mathematical universe that includes, besides the standard real numbers, nonstandard "pseudo-real" numbers—including infinitesimal and infinite quantities. The system disposes of the central paradox which plagued earlier uses of infinitesimal quantities in the calculus:

> Leibniz, like de l'Hospital after him, stated that two quantities may be accounted equal if they differ only by an amount which is infinitely small relative to them. And on the other hand, although he did not state this explicitly within his axiomatic framework, de l'Hospital, like Leibniz, assumed that the arithmetical laws which hold for finite quantities are equally valid for infinitesimals. It is evident, and was evident at the time, that these two assumptions cannot be accommodated simultaneously within a consistent framework. They were widely accepted nevertheless, and maintained themselves for a considerable length of time since it was found that their judicious and selective use was so very fruitful. However, Non-standard Analysis shows how a relatively slight modification of these ideas leads to a consistent theory.[72]

The inclusion of nonstandard numbers in the system allows many proofs about standard mathematical objects to be constructed in a shorter and more intuitively appealing way. Moreover, as Peirce suspected might happen, the nonstandard numbers present a new field for study in and of themselves. Their inclusion opens the doors to entirely new areas of inquiry, such as nonstandard probability, dynamics, economics, and algebra, which simply are not possible in the standard universe.[73]

Whether Robinson's work constitutes a "vindication" of Peirce is a question I will not here pretend to answer, for several reasons. Most importantly, Peirce's claimed proof of the consistency of infinitesimal theory is not available for comparison to Robinson's work. If a valid proof from Peirce's hand is ever discovered, a chapter in the history of logic and mathematics will have to be supplemented, if not rewritten.[74] It is clear that Peirce would have used the logic of relatives, perhaps in the form of the Alpha and Beta parts of his Existential Graphs, to present the proof. This system was substantially developed by 1897, the year before he claims to have a proof (CP 4.422), and is equivalent to the apparatus of predicate calculus which Robinson used to develop nonstandard analysis. It is highly unlikely that Peirce's proof would closely resemble Robinson's work, however, because Robinson relies heavily on the theorems of *completeness* and *compactness*, which were not discovered until after Peirce's death.[75] It is virtually impossible, then, that Peirce anticipated nonstandard analysis in any *specific* sense.

Nonetheless, Robinson's theory can be seen as a rigorous formulation of the kind of system Peirce envisioned, showing that such a system is logically consistent. Peirce might see in Robinson's theory the evolved and developed form of his own conception. Though there is apparently no line of direct influence from Peirce to Robinson, he uses symbolic logic to resolve the mathematical question of infinitesimals.[76] Peirce would no doubt be gratified by its results.

Mathematical Hypotheses and Philosophical Conceptions

> If I were to attempt to describe to you in full all the scientific beauty and truth that I find in the principle of continuity, I might say in the simple language of Matilda the Engaged, "the tomb would close over me e'er the entrancing topic were exhausted"—but not before my audience was exhausted. So I will drop it there. (CP 1.171)

It is time to put Peirce's conception of continuity in perspective. Mathematics, after all, is only the entrance hall to Peirce's philosophical house. In chapter 3, we saw how the simplest branch of mathematics, the mathematics of logic, suggested three things of philosophical importance to Peirce. First, there are three irreducible forms of relation, which find material application in deductive logic. Monadic relatives are absolute terms, or simple predicates. They express the relation of a property to a subject: "the leaf is green." Genuine dyads express an existential relation between two subjects, a relation that would not obtain if either subject were removed: "The acorn strikes Jones." Finally, a genuine triad expresses a relation among three objects that would not obtain if any of the three were removed: "the attacker murdered the victim with a rock."

Peirce also found that any relation of higher valence than three could be reduced to some combination of these three irreducible kinds of relation, just as degenerate triads and dyads may be reduced to combinations of lower-valence relations. All this suggested to Peirce that he ought to look for three and only three categories of phenomena.

Peirce's second discovery in the mathematics of logic is that, though the *kinds* of relations represented in monads, dyads, and triads are distinct, it is in fact possible to construct monads, dyads, and all polyads using one or more triads. Thus the triad can be considered the primitive relative. This mirrors Peirce's view of our understanding of monadic and dyadic relations in the sphere of deductive logic: though they are logically necessary and prior to triads, they cannot in fact be conceived by us in their pure form (CP 1.362, 6.323). Any conception of the lower-order relations is mediated by the mind, and involves a triadic element. The quality of sound a tree makes when it falls in an empty forest is expressible in a monadic relative; its impact on the ground is expressible in a dyadic relative. But in so far as these relations are *conceived as* a quality of sound or a brute crushing impact, they are represented in a mind. Semeiotic will show that this representation itself is triadic, and the fact that the triad is formally primitive will reappear in the theory of mind, in the principle that mind itself consists of triadic sign-relations.

The third mathematical hypothesis Peirce developed and which finds application in formal logic is that a three-valued logic is indeed possible and should be developed. Once mediation is introduced as a formal category, the possibility of a third truth value that mediates between truth and falsity emerges. If there is any objective indeterminacy in the world our logical system describes, the third truth-value will be needed (though logic itself cannot determine whether it will in fact be needed). The hypothesis that there may be a third logical state of affairs led Peirce to describe genuine indeterminacy in the mathematics of the continuum. Objective indeterminacy will appear elsewhere, as well, especially in the theory of knowledge and in metaphysics.

The distinguishing feature of triadic relations is that they involve combination or connection among elements: the combined terms are continuous. It has been shown in this chapter that Peirce's principle of continuity rests upon the concept of infinitesimally small parts that may be immediately connected in such a way that they are both identical (according to Leibniz's principle) and occur in an ordered arrangement. It is this concept of continuity that Peirce referred to as "the master-key of philosophy" (MS 949, p. 1).

Peirce's discovery of the three categories of logical relation, and the conception of continuity developed in the mathematics of supermultitudinous collections, are both hypothetical speculations. Peirce saw that they would provide conceptual resources for his philosophy that are lacking in the nominalist and mechanistic philosophies he rejected. He maintained that the principle of continuity is logically consistent, and that the triad is an irreducible and necessary relative. On the one hand, however, certainty about such matters is hard to come by—Peirce was keenly aware that even the best logical reasoning can go disastrously astray. On the other hand, he was aware that no matter how interesting these concepts might be in mathematics, there is no assurance that they have any application in the world outside mathematics. *Relevance,* in Peirce's view, is not the mathematician's problem. For that, one must step outside mathematics. Let Peirce himself set the stage for us to take up phenomenology, the first of the philosophical sciences:

> The essence of continuity, by G. Cantor's and by Mr. Peirce's own studies, having been determined, it remains to ask what reason we have, or, for that matter, even can have, for believing that things really are continuous. . . . For a long time doubt as to evidence of the existence of continuity interfered with the development of my speculations. But that doubt has at length been overcome. (MS 949, p. 2)

Part Three

The Categories
in Experience

CHAPTER 5

Phenomenology

Peirce's work in the mathematics of logic suggested that exactly three kinds of relation are necessary to construct a formal system of relations. Further, he found that of the three simplest logical relatives, the triad is elementary. In his system of deductive logic, the triad represents combination or synthesis in its simplest aspect. The reduction thesis maintains that relatives combining more than three terms introduce no more sophisticated form of combination than this, but only compound the triadic form. The relations of "identity" and "relatedness" suggest the idea of *continuous relations,* for which no list of the particular relationships among terms can be exhaustive. To say that A is identical to B is to make a general statement: Even an infinite list of the attributes shared by A and B would not establish that the two are truly identical, because there may be elements that are not included in a given infinite list. The general proposition of identity asserts that the concepts of A and B are continuous, fully synthesized to one another.

Cantor's work on the theory of transfinite sets opened the way for Peirce to explicate the difference between infinite multitudes and continuous multiplicities. The notion of continuity he developed is central to his logical notion of continuous relations. Peirce proposed that we conceive a true continuum as qualitatively different from an analytic continuum, as not composed of discrete parts. Continuity, he argued, does not depend on the size of a collection but rather on the mode of connection among its parts. The mode of connection among parts of a continuum is *immediate connection,* and our analysis of immediate connection shows the basis for Peirce's affirmation of the legitimacy of infinitesimals.

Infinitesimals, conceived as parts of a linear continuum, are the formal mathematical paradigm for very small parts of any continuum. Neighboring infinitesimals are indiscernible and hence identical; yet because they are potentially ordered, they are potentially different. As William James puts it, the mathematical notion of the infinitesimal embodies "the whole paradox of the same and yet nascent other, of an identity that won't *keep* except insofar as it keeps failing."[1] In chapter 4 I described how Peirce might have reasoned through this paradox. The merits of that argument could be discussed at length, but the important thing here is to recognize that for Peirce the paradox was only apparent. There is, in his view, a perfectly consistent conception of mathematical entities that embody both identity and difference, whose mode of relation is genuinely triadic, and which are truly continuous.

So far in Peirce's architectonic, the subject matter has been formal and the discussion has been hypothetical in nature. At this point in the system, discussion moves beyond mathematical speculation to the study of common experience—to the *coenoscopic sciences,* or philosophy. The first philosophical science in Peirce's schema is phenomenology, or phaneroscopy. The thrust of the present chapter is captured in one of Peirce's own statements, when he reached the present stage in an exposition of his thought: "it is proper to consider the evidences for the reality of continuity. That we have a perfectly consistent conception of it has been shown. But what evidence is there that it is real? The author maintains that it is a datum of direct presentation" (MS 397, pp. 10–11).

Phaneroscopy

Peirce introduced phenomenology into his system in 1902, at the same time that he separated the formal and normative aspects of logic.[2] Normative logic derives its principles of right and wrong thought from ethics, and ethics in turn derives its principles of good and bad from esthetics. Phenomenology is the bridge, then, between the speculative "could be" of the mathematical sciences and the "ought to be" of esthetics and the other normative sciences. Phenomenology examines "what is" (where the *is* carries no special ontological significance), but passes no evaluative judgment. Phenomenology "just contemplates phenomena as they are, simply opens its eyes and describes what it sees; not what it sees in the real as distinguished from figment—not regarding any such dichotomy—but simply describing the object, as phenomenon, and stating what it finds in all phenomena alike" (CP 5.37).

Peirce distinguished his science of phenomenology from what Hegel undertook in the *Phänomenologie des Geistes:* "I will not restrict it to the observation and analysis of *experience* but extend it to describing all the features that are common to whatever is *experienced* or might conceivably be experienced or become an object of study in any way direct or indirect" (CP 5.37). Perhaps as a way to emphasize his difference from Hegel, Peirce coined the word "phaneroscopy" as the name for this science. "The word θανερόν is next to the simplest expression in Greek for manifest. . . . There can be no question that θανερόν means primarily *brought to light, open to public inspection throughout.* The *manifest* is that which a person who does not willfully shut his eyes to has no choice but to believe in" (MS 337, pp. 4-5).[3] The object of study in phenomenology is whatever emerges in the field of awareness: "Phaneroscopy is the description of the *phaneron;* and by the *phaneron* I mean the collective total of all that is in any way or in any sense present to the mind, quite regardless of whether it corresponds to any real thing or not" (CP 1.284). The aim of phaneroscopy is to describe what features are present in all phenomena, based on careful examination of particular phenomena.

The student of phaneroscopy must possess three faculties above all others: first, "the faculty of seeing what stares one in the face," which Peirce likened to the artist's observational ability; second, "a resolute discrimination," which can detect a general feature of diverse phenomena "beneath all its disguises"; and finally, "the generalizing power of the mathematician who produces the abstract formula that comprehends the very essence of the feature under examination purified from all admixture of extraneous and irrelevant accompaniments" (CP 5.42). At the same time, the student must endeavor to negate the influence of "any tradition, any authority, any reasons for supposing that such and such ought to be the facts, or any fancies of any kind, and to confine himself to honest, single-minded observation of the appearances" (CP 1.287).

This is not to say that phaneroscopy proceeds without *any* antecedent preparation: "in order that a work of observation should bring in any considerable harvest, there must always be a preparation of thought, a consideration as definite as may be, of what it is possible that observation should disclose. That is a principle familiar to every observer" (MS 908, p. 4). The preparation for phaneroscopy is mathematical analysis of hypothetical states of affairs.[4] What Peirce's work in the mathematics of logic indicates, above all, is that the phenomenologist will do well to look for *modes of relation* in experience, rather than metaphysical modalities such as Aristotle's substance and accident. Mathematics suggests that we will find evidence of three kinds of relatedness. Moreover, we may expect to find that the "substantial" things in phenomena are in fact relational continua.

Peirce often referred to the three kinds of relation in mathematics and in formal logic as categories, but it may be more accurate and less confusing, in light of his mature writings, to apply the term *category* to these conceptions only when they are considered as applicable to phenomena.[5] Peirce here saw himself following in the footsteps of Aristotle, Kant, and Hegel, in attempting to provide a list of categories conceived as the most general features discernible in phenomena (CP 5.42). Phaneroscopy shows that the formal relations studied in mathematical logic have material correlates in experience.

Peirce identified two orders of categories. The *universal categories* of Firstness, Secondness, and Thirdness "belong to every phenomenon, one being perhaps more prominent in one aspect of that phenomenon than another but all of them belonging to every phenomenon" (CP 5.43). The universal categories correspond to the three stages of thinking Hegel identified, but Peirce denied that Hegel directly influenced his conception of the categories (CP 5.38; MS 305, p. 10). The universal categories are distinguished from the *particular categories,* "the series of categories consisting of phases of evolution" (CP 5.38). Only one of the particular categories appears in any given phenomenon (CP 5.43). Peirce says little more about the particular categories than this, except to indicate that the divisions in Hegel's *Encyclopædia* constitute a mistaken list of them, and to say that he himself has been unable to compose a satisfactory list (CP 5.38, 5.43). The universal categories, however, are by far the most important aspect of Peirce's philosophical architectonic.[6]

Before turning to phenomenology proper, a point that has been made before should be reinforced: The list of categories is necessarily fallible. Phaneroscopy is a kind of scientific inquiry and as such is never capable of absolute certainty in its conclusions. Phaneroscopy is not Cartesian introspection, meant to lead the investigator to indubitable ideas. Peirce emphasized that his audience should confirm his findings by carrying out their own investigations into phenomena.[7] Rosenthal notes that "Peirce nowhere indicates that his categories are absolute or eternal and in fact states quite clearly that though his selection seems the most adequate, alternative series of categories are possible."[8] Beyond this consideration, the categories themselves are subject to modification over time, as the nature of mind evolves. The formal aspects of the categories are discovered in the "a priori observation" of mathematics, and then confirmed in experience. The list thus has an excellent pedigree: A priori concepts are the most secure concepts we have. But because mind is a product of the contingencies of nature, it might have developed differently, and might yet develop into something with different a priori structures. A different kind of mind (whatever that would be) might well yield a different list of categories, both as discovered a priori and in phaneroscopy. Every age thus should undertake to develop philosophy anew, from the ground up. The findings of previous thinkers, however authoritative they may have once been, should be accepted only if they accord with the findings of honest and careful philosophy in the present age.

What Is in Any Way Present to the Mind

Let us carry out a brief phenomenological investigation, then, in order to establish a concrete reference for Peirce's stated conclusions. Because the universal categories are all present in any phenomenon whatever, it should not matter which particular phenomenon we choose to examine. Because nothing is so vividly present to the mind as a surprise, however, I will focus on the perception of a common and mildly surprising event:

> While writing with a pencil, the tip of the lead snaps and the remaining stub gouges the paper.

The reader may wish to sharpen a pencil to a fine point and become freshly acquainted with the phenomenon before proceeding.

There seem to be two parts in the perception of this phenomenon. The first is awareness of *interruption,* signaled by the sound of the lead breaking, the tactile sensation of the hand and the pencil moving in an unintended and unexpected direction, and the visual awareness of a stray mark on the paper. The second is evaluative. In my experiment, only the sharp point of the lead snapped, leaving a rather blunt but serviceable end on the pencil. This second part of my perception of the event involved (1) evaluation of damage to the pencil, (2) evaluation of damage to the paper, to see whether the stray mark was likely to interfere with the legibility of the word and would need to be erased, and (3) evaluation of where the pencil line had been interrupted, simultaneous with a return of the pencil tip to that point and a continuation of the writing.

The whole complex process, of course, takes place in a very short time.[9] I will not venture to estimate the lapse of time the event occupied, though it could certainly be measured. The point of phenomenological investigation is not to analyze an event in terms of abstract categories such as "objective time" or "subjective time" for, as William James pointed out, at the level of immediate experience we do not encounter the dichotomy of subject and object. This distinction is introduced subsequent to the event itself.[10] The categories of "objective time" and "subjective time" are, in fact, applied only in a few cases, for special purposes. What is encountered in immediate experience is simply an event in an ongoing flow—in this case an event characterized primarily by a sense of shock or interruption.

Let us then concentrate on the first element of perception of the event, the mere awareness of interruption. This stage is surely less complex than the evaluative stage, though it is far from simple.[11] The perception of the pencil tip's snap consists of certain peculiar qualities of sensation. The sound of the lead as it breaks is a combination of pitch, volume, and timbre that is perhaps unique to this kind of event. The jarring movement as the pencil gives way, likewise, is difficult to simulate except by snapping another pencil lead in the same way, and the mark or gouge made by the pencil tip is not quite identical to any other sort of visual phenomenon. Furthermore, these three sensations (together with others that are less prominent) arrive in experience as a unified package: It seems especially difficult to separate completely the sound and the feel that accompany the snap.

In general, any phenomenon will exhibit "qualities of feeling or sensation each of which is something positive and *sui generis,* being such as it is quite regardless of how or what anything else is" (CP 7.625). The sound, for example, though closely associated with the sensation of jarring movement, might have been quite different. There is no a priori *reason* for it to be a dull pop rather than, say, a bell-like chime or even mere silence. The qualities peculiar to these sensations are "self-sufficient"; they simply *are* the way they are. "On account of this self-sufficiency, it is convenient to call these the elements of 'Firstness'" (CP 7.625). They are the experiential correlates of *priman,* expressed logically in the monadic relative.

In the phenomenon, though, these elements are not merely felt; they are felt *together,* and as *contrasting with* other qualities. The sound of the break contrasts with the soft scraping sound of lead on paper just prior to the break. The jarring motion of the hand contrasts with the small controlled movements of normal writing. The smudge on the paper contrasts with the line of normally formed letters. The perception of these differences signals that what Peirce calls *connectives* are part of the phenomenon. Different qualities are "connected" in that they are perceived to be *with* one another in the experience. "These connectives are directly perceived, and the perception of each of them is a perception at once of two opposed objects,—a double awareness. In respect to each of these connections, one part of the percept appears as it does *relatively to a second part.* Hence, it is convenient to call them elements of 'Secondness'" (CP 7.625). This double awareness corresponds to *secundan,* expressed in the genuine dyad of formal logic.

The sensed qualities, together with their connections and contrasts, comprise the "brute fact" of the event in question. We suppose that events occur that are *only* brute facts, which consist only of qualities and connectives. Such events must remain entirely unperceived, however—there would be, in Peirce's terminology, a *percept* but no *perception* (CP 7.626). The perceived phenomenon is not merely an assemblage of qualities, but one with an attached meaning or significance.

Perception requires that the percept be experienced as meaningful. That is, a *perceptual judgment* must be formed about the percept. Peirce noted, with respect to visual phenomena, that "One can . . . escape the percept by shutting one's eyes. If one *sees,* one cannot avoid the percept; if one *looks,* one cannot avoid the perceptual judgment" (CP 7.627). There is, in short, awareness that the lead has snapped.[12] The combined sensory qualities of the percept have meaning; they signify a state of affairs that is perceived as some *kind* of event. While the percept simply happens, the perceptual judgment *represents* that something has happened: "In a perceptual judgment the mind professes to tell the mind's future self what the character of the present percept is" (CP 7.630). This involves Thirdness or mediation, wherein one thing (the event) is represented to another (the future self) by a third (the present self's perceptual judgment). This structure corresponds to *tertian,* represented in logic by the genuine triad.

The process of representation occupies some span of "objective time," of course, and the representation follows the percept. In the actual experience, however, there is seldom explicit awareness of the passage of time. The percept and the perceptual judgment occur as one event, which Peirce called the *percipuum* (CP 7.629). In the percipuum, three elements are always present: qualities, connectives, and representation of the event as meaningful, as a specific instance of a general kind of event. These are the universal phenomenological categories of Firstness, Secondness, and Thirdness.[13]

Any perception, any phenomenon, is perceived as meaningful. The meaningfulness of a phenomenon consists in its being potentially related to other phenomena in some way. This is true even for "nonsensical" or bizarre phenomena. To perceive an event as irrational or mysterious involves the prediction that it will not fit with other phenomena. The observation that phenomena are partially apprehended in terms of their present and potential relations to other phenomena brings us to consider the question of experienced time.[14]

That time is a general phenomenon rather than a distinctly experienced event does not make it inappropriate for analysis—it indicates only that the phenomenon of time is not primarily characterized by particularity, or Secondness. Rather, time is dominated by Thirdness. Concerning inquiry into the phenomenon of time, Peirce observed:

> If we wish to know what the percipuum of the course of time is, all we have to do is to abstain from sophisticating it, and it will be plain enough. No more than the present moment directly confronts us. The future, however little future it may be, is known only by generalization. The past, however little past it may be, lacks the explicitness of the present. Nevertheless, in the present moment we are directly aware of the flow of time, or in other words that things can change. (CP 7.649)

The percipuum arrives as a "bud" or "drop" of perception, to borrow an image from James. When we examine the passing moment of any event, we find that *as perceived* in itself, it involves a sense of development. There is a beginning, middle, and end to any phenomenon. This quality of development signifies the passage of time. The sensation is that one thing *determines* another, meaning that "the former not only follows the latter, but follows it according to a general rule" (CP 7.349). We have seen this to be the case in simple perception. A perceptual judgment is determined by a percept according to a general rule: *This* combination of qualities signifies *this* kind of occurrence, and this kind of occurrence signifies *these* potentialities. For Peirce, what occurs in perception is a kind of inference that differs from reasoning only in the respect that it cannot be consciously controlled. Ideas occur in ordered succession, and there is a real connection among them in time.

A phenomenon is never completely isolated, though we may focus attention on "the single event" and thereby abstract it from other events. When the pencil lead snapped, the event occurred in the context of the writing that preceded it and the range of potential events that could follow it. "On the whole, then, the percipuum is not an absolute event. There is no span of present time so short as not to contain something remembered, that is, taken as a reasonable conjecture, not without containing something expected for the confirmation which we are waiting" (CP 7.675). There is never an experience of an absolute instant. The passing moment is *thick,* always involving a process of presentation and representation that occupies time and refers beyond itself even to the remote past and future.[15]

Peirce says that "if there is no such thing as an absolute instant, there is nothing *absolutely present* either temporally or in the sense of confrontation. In fact, we are thus brought close to the doctrine of Synechism, which is that elements of Thirdness cannot entirely be escaped" (CP 7.653). Experience is experience of the passing moment, which might be said to "contain" the temporal and confrontational (ontological) present, and much else besides. In the next section we will consider the first of these senses of *presence*. This will allow us to elaborate the phenomenon of continuity as it appears in relation to time and as it functions in the categories.[16]

The Continuity of Time

Time, as experienced, is almost perfectly continuous according to the definition of "true continuity" given in chapter 4. A true continuum is not composed of *ultimate* parts, and sufficiently small neighboring parts are immediately connected in such a way that the relations of identity and difference do not strictly apply.

The passing moment is not an instant or a point in time, but rather a "field of the immediate present." The moment at which the pencil lead snapped, for example, was originally considered as a single event consisting of two phases or elements—the snap, and the evaluation of the snap. Yet even in these very brief elements there is a "beginning" and an "end." Though there is probably no original awareness of any parts in the "snap," we clearly could investigate, for example, the "first part" of the event in a repetition of the experiment. We might focus on that part of the event during which the pressure on the pencil lead increased to a critical level. The "second part," in which the break occurred, could be disregarded. The focus could be narrowed further, limited only by our capability to mentally discriminate an interval of time, or by our ability to build instruments to measure small intervals of time. And although there no doubt are limits to our measuring instruments and to our capacity to focus attention in experience, there apparently is no intrinsic limit to the potential subdivision of a temporal duration. Time is infinitely divisible because every part of a lapse of time in the percipuum is itself a lapse of time (CP 7.651–52). There are no *ultimate* parts, or instants, which do not themselves exhibit beginning, middle, and end.

The various parts of the field of the immediate present are immediately connected. In the original experience of a brief event, the relations of identity and difference do not strictly obtain. We do not *register* the beginning, middle, and end of a brief experience as strictly separate. They are immediately connected phases or parts of the event. The original experience is simply that *the lead snapped while writing*, for example. The event is perceived as one occurrence, appearing in experience in full dress, as it were. The difference between phases becomes clear upon reflection, of course, but what happens "upon reflection" is a process of establishing distinct relations among the "first" and "second" parts of the event. This indicates that the parts were originally at least potentially ordered, and subject to the determination of sequential relations. It does *not* imply that the parts are originally distinct and separate, that the incipient ordering relations are in any sense absolute and merely unnoticed at first. That they are *not* absolute becomes clear if we attempt to pinpoint the boundary between the two phases: there *is* no absolute, objective boundary, even after the distinction between the two phases has been made. There is a change between phases, but they melt into one another.

We see in the structure of an event the experienced manifestation of infinitesimals. Instants or "points in time" may be distinguished because the parts of the temporal flow are ordered, or potentially ordered. On closer examination, however, the "point in time" is found to be a fiction. To speak of the point at which the lead snapped, for example, is merely a shorthand way to separate the parts of experience coming "before" and "after" the snap. The "point" at which the lead snapped is itself a span of time capable of infinite division, of further determination of relations among *its* parts. There is no such individual point. The case exactly parallels Peirce's discussion of absolute points on the geometrical continuum (CP 7.656–57).

Experienced time is homogeneous. All of its parts are of the same nature, and have the same dimensionality (CP 4.642). It is regular, in that all its parts are related in the same manner. The experienced temporal continuum, in short, is a *general*: "it everywhere follows a law; that is, the same thing is true of every portion of it" (CP 7.535). Peirce does not include *process* as a separate category in his system, but it should be clear that what is true of all intervals of time is that they involve process, change, or development of some kind.[17] Time is continuous or general in that it allows for any number of particular determinations to be made. Such determinations may, as we have seen, be the determination of dates, of "points" of relative discontinuity. We speak of "the point" that divides time into the intervals before and after the lead snaps, the drought ends, or two persons are married, for example. These determinations are imposed so as to structure a history, but they are not metaphysically absolute.

The notion of time as general, however, is more radical than such examples suggest. The law of time is the law of change or development. Change or development takes place with and through the determination of relations. The radical dimension of our statement that time is the general form of change becomes apparent when we note that the relations that distinguish subject and object are not absolute facts given in the immediate field of the present. Part of the general continuity of temporal experience is the continuity of subject and object. The distinction that separates the two comes "upon reflection," and itself involves the determination of a relation.[18] Clearly, then, it makes little sense to conceive the process of "determining relations" as something carried out by an active subject on the material of a passive world. We ought not to give in too quickly to the familiar image of the human mind shaping history the way a potter shapes clay. There is truth in this image, but it cannot account for the process in which potter and clay, or mind and history, are rendered distinct.

The temporal continuum of change contains within it the potentiality for particular determinations of relations, of discrete cuts. As time is continuous, no multitude of such determinations can exhaust all possibilities. In the phenomenon of time, we encounter process and see that phenomena must be generated by general principles and possibilities which are constitutive of temporally structured phenomena. These general principles and possibilities are the phenomenological categories of Firstness (positive possibility), Secondness (individuating existence), and Thirdness (law-governedness).

The Phenomenological Categories

Peirce's statement that there is nothing *absolutely present* in experience served as our point of departure for the consideration of the phenomenon of time. The present moment was found to be better described as a thick "field of the immediate present" than as an instantaneous "point in time." The field of the immediate present is constituted through the determination of relations in a temporal flow, a flow characterized by change or development. Relations are not determined by an agent acting on a passive world-stuff. Phenomena then, on Peirce's view, do not emerge in the encounter between a Kantian transcendental ego and a noumenal world, structured according to categories of the ego's reason. Experience is indeed structured according to universal categories, and Peirce does suggest that space and time are analogous to the Kantian forms of intuition. They are the continua in which the relations that constitute the world emerge.[19]

Peirce differs from Kant, however, in insisting that time, space, and the categories are inherent in nature, and that the constituting agent must itself be a phenomenon constituted in the ongoing process of the world. Time and space are not forms of intuition that introduce continuity into nature; they are in *no* sense subjective (NEM 4:343). Rather, "[t]ime and space are continuous because they embody conditions of possibility, and the possible is general" (CP 4.172). Thus even the continua of time and space turn out to be understandable as instances of *possibility* and *generality*, which we recognize as the categories of Firstness and Thirdness involved in the percipuum.

I now return to a closer consideration of the three universal phenomenological categories. In phenomena, there are always qualities, dyadic relations of "withness" among qualities, and some significance that accompanies combinations of qualities. Here are the three categories in rough outline. Peirce has suggested, moreover, that all phenomena occur "in" the continua of time and space, which embody not only the *present* (as actual) but also indefinite possibilities for determination of other presents, other actualities. The following description of the phenomenological categories is presented in terms of the manifestation of possibility and actuality in experience.

> Let us begin with considering actuality, and try to make out just what it consists in. If I ask you what the actuality of an event consists in, you will tell me that it consists in its happening *then* and *there*. The specifications *then* and *there* involve all its relations to other existents. The actuality of the event seems to lie in its relations to the universe of existents. . . . Actuality is something *brute*. There is no reason in it. I instance putting your shoulder against a door and trying to force it open against an unseen, silent, and unknown resistance. We have a two-sided consciousness of effort and resistance, which seems to me to come tolerably near to a pure sense of actuality. On the whole, I think we have here a mode of being of one thing which consists in how a second object is. I call that Secondness. (CP 1.24)

Actuality, as such, is characterized by resistance or reaction (CP 5.66). The present, the brute fact that stands out in an experience, is defined by its occurrence in the context of an existential network of other brute facts. Something is identifiable *as* a thing when a cluster of qualities persist in association with one another in experience. It is distinguishable from other things or clusters of connected qualities, against which it may react by virtue of being "with" them in phenomena. The actual is the most obtrusive part of experience, and existent things can be identified by their stubborn resistance to one another and to our will.

If Secondness is the category of the actual, the other two categories must concern the possible:

> Firstness is the mode of being which consists in its subject's being positively such as it is regardless of aught else. That can only be a possibility. For as long as things do not act upon one another there is no sense or meaning in saying that they have any being, unless it be that they are such in themselves that they may perhaps come into relation with others. The mode of being a *redness,* before anything in the universe was yet red, was nevertheless a positive qualitative possibility. And redness in itself, even if it be embodied, is something positive and *sui generis*. That I call Firstness. We naturally attribute Firstness to outward objects, that is we suppose they have capacities in themselves which may or may not be already actualized, which may or may not ever be actualized, although we can know

113

nothing of such possibilities [except] so far as they are actualized. (CP 1.25)

Suppose we have an unfamiliar metal coin, and prepare to drop it on a hard tabletop. The coin is an actual existent thing, having a determinate size, shape, weight, color, texture, and so forth. We suppose that it also possesses the capacity to produce a sound when dropped, though we do not know what *particular* sound it will produce. There is a range of possible qualities of sound we expect, of course, but our knowledge of the coin's sound is vague (in Peirce's technical sense). Strictly speaking, we confront a whole universe of possibilities when we speculate about the sound it will produce. This universe includes silence, a ring, a click, and even the sound of a locomotive whistle. If the first or the fourth of this list were to be actualized, we would certainly consider it problematic. We would probably search for unnoticed facts about the coin which act as efficient causes of the unusual effect. As mere possibilities, however, even these absurd sounds are among the things that "may be."

We admit the absurd sounds as possibilities, but not as *real* possibilities. These possibilities seem to hang at the fringe of our awareness, but scarcely belong to the phenomenon. They are mere Firstness. What distinguishes absurd possibilities such as these from more acceptable or realistic possibilities is that we know, looking at the coin before it drops, that things like *this* do not tend to make sounds like *that*.

> Now for Thirdness. Five minutes of our waking life will hardly pass without our making some kind of prediction; and in the majority of cases these predictions are fulfilled in the event. Yet a prediction is essentially of a general nature, and cannot ever be completely fulfilled. To say that a prediction has a decided tendency to be fulfilled, is to say that the future events are in a measure really governed by a law. If a pair of dice turns up sixes five times running, that is a mere uniformity. The dice might happen fortuitously to turn up sixes a thousand times running. But that would not afford the slightest security for a prediction that they would turn up sixes the next time. If the prediction has a tendency to be fulfilled, it must be that future events have a tendency to conform to a general rule. . . . A rule to which future events have a tendency to conform is *ipso facto* an important thing, an important element in the happening of those events. This mode of being which *consists,* mind my word if you please, the mode of being which *consists* in the fact that future facts of Secondness will take on a determinate general character, I call a Thirdness. (CP 1.26)

General laws distinguish the possibilities that tend to become actualities from those that do not. That we are *aware* of the operation of such laws, that they affect *us* as well as the events they guide, should be clear. This awareness is what makes the proposal that a small coin will produce a deafening whistle-blast when dropped appear prima facie absurd. It is a possibility, but not a real potentiality. There is no general tendency, no rule governing the course of events, that would bring about such an actuality.

The category of Secondness applies to those features of phenomena that traditional metaphysics, following Aristotle, explains in terms of efficient causation. This principle, the heart of Newtonian physics, tells us that physical actions are set in motion by other physical actions. The category of Thirdness applies to those features of phenomena that defy explanation in terms of efficient causation, features that were accounted for by final causation in traditional metaphysics. Peirce noted that we do believe "firmly and without doubt that to some extent phenomena are regular, that is, they are governed by general ideas; and so far as they are so, they are capable of prediction by reasoning" (CP 2.149). The problem with purely mechanistic philosophies is that there is more in experience than physical action and reaction. Physical actions and reactions are *regular,* and this regularity itself is something to be explained.

Peirce argued that there are ultimately only two ways to account for the widespread regularity of events we observe, both in the physical world and in our own actions. The regularity may be due to pure chance, akin to the case of the dice that turn up sixes a thousand times running, or it may be the result of "some *active general principle*" that influences the course of events (CP 5.100). We must suppose either that there is *no* reason for things to happen the way they do, or that there is *some* reason in events that accounts for their unfolding. According to Peirce, "every sane man will adopt the latter hypothesis," because it would be impossible to live in the world if one genuinely thought the world a thoroughly irrational place (CP 5.101). This may seem too easy an escape, but I think Peirce's point will sustain criticism. If we thought the world's uniformities were *entirely* fortuitous, we could not walk across the room without experiencing a real and genuine fear that the floor might swallow us up, or the roof fall in, or the air turn to deadly poison. Sane persons do live without these fears, and so betray a faith that physical events are governed by regularities. Even the skeptic who outwardly denies the real power of general tendencies betrays what George Santayana called an "animal faith" in their reality, by trusting to them in virtually every action.

Thirdness, then, is the category of regularity in experience. We are always aware, if only vaguely, of general principles or laws that will approximately determine the outcome of future events. The experience of Thirdness is thus awareness of a *teleological* element in our own actions and in the natural world. Actuality, the course of natural events, tends to conform to an idea that in some way regulates them. It is an important and controversial matter to ask how far this teleology extends, and how powerful it is. These questions, like so many others that arise in phenomenology, will receive no answer from phenomenology. They are metaphysical questions, and we need to examine the notion of teleology further before they can be addressed. I note here that the very possibility of an awareness of teleology presupposes a felt continuity of present and future. There must be a connection between the general tendencies of the present and the actualities of the future. With this, I turn to consider the manifestation of continuity in the phenomenological categories.

CONTINUITY IN THE CATEGORIES

A mere complication of Category the Third, involving no idea essentially different, will give the idea of something which is such as it is by virtue of its relations to any multitude, enumerable, denumerable, or abnumerable or even to any super-multitude of correlates; so that this Category suffices of itself to give the conception of True Continuity, than which no conception yet discovered is higher. (CP 5.67)

Thirdness consists in the general tendencies or laws that guide the actualization of possibilities. A general law influences not only all past occurrences of some type, but all such occurrences that might conceivably take place. The multitude of such occurrences transcends any multitude that might be specified. Thirdness governs a continuous multiplicity of events, whose similarities and differences shade into one another. "[T]he general is seen to be precisely the continuous" (MS 397, p. 11). The operation of law in phenomena, the Thirdness operative in even the simplest prediction about events, involves true continuity.

The continuum of time is a species of generality, and is present in any event whatever. Moreover, time is the most perfect continuum in experience. Accordingly, when Peirce defined a continuum as that which, first, has no ultimate parts, and second, exhibits immediate connection among sufficiently small neighboring parts, he appealed to the experience of time to illustrate the notion of immediate connection. Time serves as the experienced standard of continuity, through which we envisage all other continua (CP 6.86)

There is an apparent circularity in using time to define continuity. The definition of continuity involves the idea of immediate connection, immediate connection is clarified by an appeal to the concept of time, and time is conceived as continuous (CP 4.642). In chapter 4, I sought to clarify the notion of immediate connection *without* an appeal to time, so as to break this circle. With the mathematical account of immediate connection in hand, though, we can see that Peirce's appeal to time identifies it as the experiential standard of continuity, as the most perfect manifestation of the formal concept of continuity. Peirce asserts that to say time is continuous is "just like saying the atomic weight of oxygen is 16, meaning that that shall be the standard for all other atomic weights. The one asserts no more of Time that the other asserts concerning the atomic weight of oxygen; that is, just nothing at all" (CP 4.642).[20]

Time, the standard of continuity, is the "most perfect" continuum in experience, but should not be taken as an absolutely perfect continuum. The perfect *true continuum* is only described hypothetically in mathematics. Peirce observed that time is in all likelihood not "quite perfectly continuous and uniform in its flow" (CP 1.412). Phenomenological time does exhibit the properties of infinite divisibility and immediate connection, but is probably *not* best conceived as an unbroken and absolutely regular thread. The only constant we have noted in time is the regularity of development or change, but change is not smooth. Changes differ from one another. The "regular" phenomenon of change consists, on closer examination, of numerous (perhaps infinite) parallel courses of development with different patterns and histories that interweave and diverge.

Bertrand Helm suggests that Peirce conceived time on the model of a continuous fifty-foot rope, which on examination is found to contain no fifty-foot fibers.[21] Another suitable image is Heraclitus' river, in which "different and different waters flow. . . . They scatter and . . . gather . . . come together and flow away . . . approach and depart."[22] The experienced continuum of time itself consists in the lawlike association of "different and different" courses of events, all under the unifying form of time (CP 6.87). Peirce might say, with Heraclitus, that "[t]hings taken together are wholes and not wholes, something which is being brought together and brought apart, which is in tune and out of tune; out of all things there comes a unity, and out of a unity all things."[23]

Time thus represents continuity *almost* to perfection. Likewise, "[c]ontinuity represents Thirdness almost to perfection" (CP 1.337). The phenomenological category of Thirdness, of triadic combination, may be approached by retracing our steps in the architectonic, in a process of successive generalization from certain ubiquitous features of experience. We move from experienced time, to mathematical continuity, to the fundamental concept or category of perfect Thirdness.[24] All phenomena occur in time; time embodies continuity; and continuity in turn embodies the ideas of generality and potentiality that are constitutive of Thirdness. Now this process of generalization is itself a phenomenon, and the "abstract" ideas it produces would be present to any mind that undertook this particular line of investigation. The whole process of generalization involves the very principle of Thirdness it is meant to clarify, but it should not be construed as question-begging. There is at least nothing viciously circular in discovering a principle whose presence is tacitly assumed at the outset, via a process that presupposes that principle.

Peirce's answer to the charge of circularity would have to be the same as that given by any hermeneutic thinker. What is ultimately discovered was indeed given, imprecisely, in the object of study at the outset, but it was not illicitly introduced by the investigator. Moreover, Peirce's logical work describes a precedent for this situation. In 1865 he noted that the validity of each of the leading principles of the three different kinds of inference could be proven only by using the form of argument that each principle makes possible (W 1:280). The categories, like the leading principles, are irreducible; none can be understood in terms of the others. The recurrence of this "hermeneutic circle" in the discovery of the category of Thirdness is yet another illustration of the pragmatic view that we must begin inquiry not with feigned doubt and a tabula rasa, but with genuine questions and the given material of experience for thought.

The upshot of all this is that continuity, regularity, law, the tendency of events to conform to general patterns Peirce calls "habit," are all present in experience as facets of a universal and irreducible principle. Thirdness can be described succinctly as the principle that softens the edges of individuation and impels things toward greater unity.

Thirdness is not the only category in which continuity is to be found, however. It is merely the category that embodies it most perfectly. Once the principle is apprehended under the head of Thirdness, its place in the other two categories becomes apparent.

The category of Firstness was first apprehended in the notion of a quality which is what it is sui generis, independent of any other factor. The color of red velvet in sunlight, the feel of soap on one's hands, the sound of a brass chime—all these simply are what they are. These are actually experienced qualities, of course, but if we reflect on the way in which we conceive the notion of possible qualities, "[w]e can hardly but suppose that those sense-qualities that we now experience, colors, sounds, feelings of every description, loves, grief, surprise, are but the relics of an ancient ruined continuum of qualities. . ." (CP 6.197). Our conception of qualities is determined by those qualities we have in fact experienced, and those we suppose we could experience. But this conception of Firstness is apparently imperfect. We know there are sounds beyond human hearing, wavelengths of light beyond the visible spectrum, tactile stimuli below the threshold of perception.

> Of the continuity of intrinsic qualities of feeling we can now form but a feeble conception. The development of the human mind has practically extinguished all feelings, except a few sporadic kinds, sounds, colors, smells, warmth, etc., which now appear to be disconnected and disparate. (CP 6.132)

Between those qualities actually experienced, we suppose there is a continuum of possible qualities. In a famous passage in the *Enquiry Concerning Human Understanding,* David Hume found himself at a loss to explain how we could conceive a shade of blue we had never experienced. Peirce is able to answer the question, holding that we experience such gaps as interruptions of continuity. "It follows . . . from the definition of continuity, that when any particular kind of feeling is present, an infinitesimal continuum of all feelings differing infinitesimally from that is present" (CP 6.132). The actual is experienced in the context of a continuum of the possible, which includes qualities falling "between" those actually experienced and qualities extending "beyond" the threshold of the actually perceivable. We conceive Firstness as a continuum of possible qualities, a universe partially beyond our ken.

Secondness is also conceived under the form of continuity. Secondness is the category of brute reaction, wherein one thing exists in virtue of its relations to another. Existence and individuality "are essentially the same thing" (CP 3.613). The existent thing is a distinct combination of qualities, a determinate individual. The principles of contradiction and excluded middle apply to descriptions of existent things. For example, the door I encounter is either locked or not. Here the existent state of affairs is defined in relation to my efforts to open it. There is a dyadic relation between my will or my physical effort, and the resistance of the door. It is in virtue of this relation that the door and its lock are recognized as individual things distinct from myself.

Secondness may be understood, on this side, as the category of discontinuity. There is a rupture between myself and this particular piece of the world, the door. Yet the discontinuity is always relative, not absolute. The door exists as an individual thing only so far as it is constituted in a continuum of relations. "[E]verything whose identity consists in a continuity of reactions will be a single logical individual" (CP 3.613). The door as an individual thing is not merely a brute substance; it is a system of qualitative relations that endures through time and space.[25] There is continuity "internal" to it as a thing, but relative discontinuity in some of its "external" relations to myself. It is an independent thing, experienced as "one in number from a particular point of view" (CP 3.93), that is, from my "external" point of view. Nonetheless, it is not an *absolute* individual: it exists in the same time and space as myself, or I could never become aware of it.

Nor is its individuality absolute even when considered from the "internal" perspective. The locked door exists as a determinate set of relations in space and time. As such, it is not in itself absolutely indivisible (CP 3.93). We have already, in passing, distinguished the door and the latch that holds it. "The locked door" may be considered as one thing, or it may be considered as "a closed door" *and* "a locked latch." Moreover, the system of qualities constituting the individual may change in the course of time, yet it is the same individual door that was once closed and locked, but is now unlocked and open.

Secondness, the category of existent individuality, is thus the category of *relative* discontinuity. Even here we find no absolute individuality. The absolute individual is a thing appearing nowhere in the field of experience. Like an isolated quality or perfect continuity, it is a generalized conception, a limit-point of abstraction whose meaning and significance must be elaborated in metaphysics.

THE INTERRELATIONS OF THE CATEGORIES

None of the categories, then, is absolutely distinct in experience. They may be distinguished in reflective thought and considered apart, but they may never be finally divorced from one another. All three are given simultaneously in phenomena. Mere possibility, actuality, and potentiality (the principle of Thirdness, which leads some possibilities to tend toward actualization) all figure into the constitution of any phenomenon, even when that phenomenon appears on its face to be a brute, individual existent fact. "[I]ndividual existence depends upon the circumstance that not all that is possible is possible in conjunction. But existence is continuous as far as the nature of the case admits. At every point of it, it reunites all qualities each in some degree" (MS 942, pp. 13–14).

A few words are in order concerning abstraction, the mental separation of concepts, which is employed in the phenomenological account of the categories. In the 1867 "On a New List of Categories," Peirce identified three ways in which concepts may be distinguished (W 2:50–51). The most complete separation is *dissociation,* "that separation which, in the absence of a constant association, is permitted by the law of association of images. It is the consciousness of one thing, without the necessary simultaneous consciousness of the other." The concept of red, for example, can be dissociated from the concept of blue or any other color. Peirce calls the formal separation of concepts *discrimination,* which "has to do merely with the essences of terms, and only draws a distinction in meaning." Color can be formally discriminated from space (and vice versa), for example, but the concepts cannot be completely dissociated (since color cannot be conceived apart from space). Finally, *abstraction* or *precision* of concepts is that kind of mental separation, "which arises from *attention to* one element and *neglect* of the other." Precision "supposes a greater separation than discrimination, but a less separation than dissociation." While color and space can be formally discriminated, color cannot be prescinded from space; one always conceives color in terms of a colored space. The reverse is not true, however. Space *can* be prescinded from color, "as is manifest from the fact that I actually believe there is an uncolored space between my face and the wall."

In phenomenology the three categories are prescinded. "Prescision is not a reciprocal process. It is frequently the case, that, while A cannot be prescinded from B, B can be prescinded from A" (W 2:51). Such is the case with the three categories. Firstness may be prescinded from the other two categories: We can conceive a continuum of possible qualities without supposing them to be actualized. Secondness, however, presupposes Firstness: In order for anything to be actual, the qualities it possesses must be possible. On the other hand, we *can* prescind Secondness from Thirdness. Actuality does not *logically* presuppose any tendency toward enduring existence (though such a world would give us only "flashes" of disconnected existence). Finally, Thirdness cannot be prescinded from Firstness or Secondness. For there to be potentialities, real tendencies or regularities in the actual, there must be both actualities and possibilities.

These distinctions, which describe the interdependence among the categories, are merely the product of analysis, however. In the field of the immediate present there is no separation of the categories. The categories may be *prescinded,* in other words, but not *dissociated.* "Not only does Thirdness suppose and involve the ideas of Secondness and Firstness, but never will it be possible to find any Secondness or Firstness in the phenomenon that is not accompanied by Thirdness" (CP 5.90). Phenomena are shot through with Thirdness. Aspects of continuity are everywhere. Any quality, any individual, appears in the midst of an ongoing process occurring in the continuous forms of time and space. Peirce suggests that the process itself is best understood on the mathematical model of a continuum that allows for the generation of determinate cuts in itself.[26] The "cuts" are places of relative discontinuity; they are "marked" not by dimensionless interruptions but by continua of lower dimensionality.[27] The generative source of such interruptions is the category of Secondness, or the principle of *haecceity*: "Secondness, or bare brute action and reaction, is a distinct analytic element within the ongoing process of a concretely rich processive continuum."[28] The operation of Secondness, of course, logically presupposes Firstness or possibility.

Peirce's favorite illustration of the interweaving of various dimensionalities of continua involves a clean chalkboard that is divided by a chalk line, itself continuous. "There is a certain element of continuity in this line. Where did this continuity come from? It is nothing but the original continuity of the blackboard which makes everything upon it continuous" (CP 6.203). Thirdness, perfect continuity, is the principal category, though not in the sense that it (or any of the categories) is *temporally* prior to the others. It is principal in the sense that Secondness and Firstness may be comprehended only approximately, through the lens of continuity. "[T]he third is of its own nature relative, and this is what we are always thinking, even when we aim at the first or second" (CP 1.362). Thus phenomenology parallels a finding in the logic of relations. Monads and dyads may be constructed by the artificial restriction and combination of triads, but triads cannot be constructed out of monads or dyads. Likewise, if continuity were not immediately given in phenomena, we could not construct the category of Thirdness out of pure Firstness and pure Secondness.

We have discovered near-perfect continuity in the phenomenon of time, and it characterizes space as well. These were each found to be continuous because they are general, embodying conditions of potentiality (CP 4.172). Is there a phenomenon of generality more primordial than time? Peirce suggested that there is. Contrary to what his definitions might suggest, his argument for the reality of Thirdness does not finally rely on the perfection of temporal continuity.

The Continuity of Inference

We apparently have no direct experience of any perfect continuum. It is remarkable, then, that the third universal phenomenological category would be best conceived under the form of continuity, a complex mathematical concept, and that Thirdness seeps into our conception of the other categories as well. Some degree of continuity is given in experience, but we seem to inject a more perfect continuity into our conceptions than is given in experience.

Peirce suggested that continuity is a characteristic of *ourselves,* as thinking and acting beings in the world:

> For how should the mind of every rustic and of every brute find it simpler to imagine time as continuous, in the very teeth of the appearances,—to connect it with by far the most difficult of all the conceptions which philosophers have ever thought out,—unless there were something in their real being which endowed such an idea with a simplicity which is certainly in the utmost contrast to its character in itself. (NEM 4:344–45)

The self, in short, is a continuum. Peirce originally took this to mean that there is *continuity of individual consciousness* that would account for the unity of the self. He later turned to the notion that the self is a *sign* in a continuous semiotic flow. The last step in our examination of Peirce's phenomenology will lead us to inquire into the nature of inference, or sign cognition, as the vehicle of change not just in our own minds, but in the living temporal flow of the world itself.

"The extraordinary disposition of the human mind to think of everything under the difficult and almost incomprehensible form of a continuum can only be explained by supposing that each one of us is in his own real nature a continuum" (NEM 4:345). On first approach, it seems promising to characterize the continuity of the self in terms of a continuous ego or consciousness. For Peirce, as we shall see, the fundamental insight here is correct, but to conceive the continuous self as an individual consciousness is a common but dangerously misleading philosophical convenience.

The notion of self as consciousness may appear so natural as to be accepted as a direct datum of experience, although I have already observed that in the immediate field of the present there is no clear self-other distinction. As Sandra Rosenthal observes, there is a unity of awareness and its field, a unity of knowing and ontological presence, in the immediate present.[29] The distinction between consciousness and its object is secondary, but extremely useful.

It perhaps seems almost inevitable that something like "individual consciousness" will be discovered when we introspect, but even early in his work Peirce saw consciousness as an explanatory hypothesis developed by a mistaken psychology:[30]

> Now so long as we suppose that what is present to the mind at one time is absolutely distinct from what is present to the mind at another time, our ideas are absolutely individual, and without any similarity. It is necessary, therefore, that we should conceive a process as present to the mind. And this process consists of parts existing at different times and absolutely distinct. And during the time that one part is in the mind, the other is not in the mind. To unite them, we have to suppose there is a consciousness running through time. (CP 7.350)

This observation was made in 1873. The mistake identified here is that of considering ideas as distinct individuals. If this assumption is made, consciousness must be introduced to provide continuity of ideas and of the self. Peirce moved away from the problematic concept of consciousness in his last period, at about the same time James published his pivotal essay "Does 'Consciousness' Exist?"[31] Before that time, Peirce endeavored to restructure the concept so as to exclude the erroneous assumptions. His observations on consciousness are nonetheless important for our study. They present an approach to understanding the continuity of the self that paves the way for his mature semeiotic account of the self.

Peirce's best attempt to salvage the notion of consciousness appears in "The Law of Mind," published in 1892. In this article, Peirce described consciousness as a continuum of ideas of infinitesimal duration. Immediate consciousness covers only an infinitesimal interval of time. A past idea may be present as memory, though not *immediately* present.

> In an infinitesimal interval we directly perceive the temporal sequence of its beginning, middle, and end—not, of course, in the way of recognition, for recognition is only of the past, but in the way of immediate feeling. Now upon this interval follows another, whose beginning is the middle of the former, and whose middle is the end of the former. Here, we have an immediate perception of the temporal sequence of its beginning,

123

middle, and end, or say of the second, third, and fourth instants. From these two immediate perceptions, we gain a mediate, or inferential, perception of the relation of all four instants. This mediate perception is objectively, or as to the object represented, spread over the four instants; but subjectively, or as itself the subject of duration, it is completely embraced in the second moment. (The reader will observe that I use the word *instant* to mean a point of time, and *moment* to mean an infinitesimal duration.) (CP 6.111; emphasis in original)

Figure 5.1 illustrates the sequence of inference described in the preceding passage.

Fig. 5.1 The Sequence of Infinitesimal Cognitions

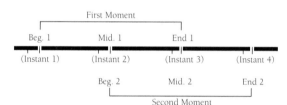

The account goes on to explain how it is that memory of the past is possible:

Now, let there be an indefinite succession of these inferential acts of comparative perception, and it is plain that the last moment will contain objectively the whole series. Let there be, not merely an indefinite succession, but a continuous flow of inference through a finite time, and the result will be a mediate objective consciousness of the whole time in the last moment. In this last moment, the whole series will be recognized, or known as known before, except only the last moment, which will be absolutely incognizable to itself. (CP 6.111)

In terms of the notion of continuity, phanera that neighbor one another in the temporal flow are infinitesimally brief, immediately connected, both the same and different. Being conscious of a moment, a day, or a lifetime simply indicates that an arbitrarily long chain of continuous phanera has been highlighted.[32]

With this account of consciousness, Peirce eliminated several of the major flaws that attend prevalent accounts of the continuity of the self. First, the notion that ideas and perceptions are individual, atomic data is destroyed by Peirce's insistence that the act of cognition or perception is an infinitesimal part of a continuous thought process. Second, an implicit ambiguity in the term "consciousness" has been cleared up: "consciousness" is commonly taken to refer both to *immediate awareness in the present,* and to *the faculty that unifies the whole history of a life.* The infinitesimal account shows that in fact these are two sides of the same coin. It shows how the whole history of a life may be mediately present in the latest infinitesimal cognition.

The "Law of Mind" account, then, represents a step away from what Peirce saw as the mistakes of associationist and empiricist psychologies. Nonetheless, Peirce considered even this revised account of consciousness problematic. In spite of the improvements, consciousness still appears to be something utterly private, mysterious in its unifying power, and not, after all, given in the immediate field of the present. If we are to approach the problem of the continuity of the self as psychologists at all, we ought to be careful not to include any more faculties or principles than are necessary and justified for the theory in question. Phenomenology provides three categories in terms of which things might be explained, and Peirce came to see how the category of Thirdness would allow him to move beyond talk of "individual consciousness."

The insight for psychology was stated by James in his 1890 *Principles of Psychology:* "The only thing which psychology has a right to postulate at the outset is the fact of thinking itself, and that must first be taken up and analyzed."[33] We may view phenomenology as Peirce's own analysis of "the fact of thinking itself," without the usual presuppositions of psychology. He discovered that the self or stream of thought can be analyzed without recourse to the hypothesis of individual consciousness. Recall our earlier discussion of the act of perception. In the field of the immediate present there is a unity of percept and perceptual judgment, and the latter is triadic in structure: "In a perceptual judgment the mind professes to tell the mind's future self what the character of the present percept is" (CP 7.630). Perception involves a process of representation, occupying (at least) an infinitesimal duration of time. Logical inference, deliberate reasoning, likewise involves a process of representation, though it proceeds according to rules that can undergo deliberate modification when necessary.

The relation of representation turns out to be fundamental. All thought has the same triadic structure exhibited in a perceptual judgment: a phaneron (or idea) that is present to the mind represents some other phaneron to the mind's future self. The self can be characterized as a continuous chain of presentation and representation of phenomena. The ubiquitous feature of this continuum of inference is change, in which what is present to the mind grows out of what was immediately and mediately past, and grows toward what will be in the immediate and mediate future.

This last point needs emphasis. A present representation points beyond itself to past and future. The immediate field of the present offers unlimited possibilities for the determination of relations, for how the past will be linked to present and future. Not just *anything* will emerge from the present phaneron: not just any sound will be produced when I drop an unfamiliar coin on the table. In the "Law of Mind," Peirce used the word *personality* to identify the general idea, the element of Thirdness, which directs the self's action in the immediate field of the present and determines which among infinite possible associations will be actualized (CP 6.155). Personality is the connection among ideas; it is a developmental teleology, the general principle of which determines that some possibilities will be actualized and others avoided or neglected. "A general idea, living and conscious now, it is already determinative of acts in the future to an extent to which it is not now conscious" (CP 6.156). Personality is the continuum of potentiality that lives in the present and is most readily identified as the self.

Peirce retained the concept of personality even after he ceased to talk of individual consciousness, and in his last period he began to speak even more broadly of the personality of the cosmos (CP 6.502). Personality is simply another name for the unifying element in the stream of thought, the general principle that guides development in the temporal continuum of inference. The meaning a situation has, we may say, depends largely on the personality of the interpreter; the same kind of event may be an obstacle to one person and an opportunity to another. The difference among personalities lies in the general rules that shape the significance of the present phenomenon. In the broadest sense, personality may be characterized as the patterns by which ideas are associated, the set of good or bad rules of inference that govern one's thought.

Now we come to the bedrock beneath pragmaticism. All phenomena, so far as they are meaningful, may be treated as representations, or triadic signs of other phenomena. The result of any process of representation is determined both by what is represented and by the rules of transformation that are applied to that kind of representation. The process, whatever its particular structure, is conceived as continuous.[34] The problem of the continuity of consciousness and personality are psychological aspects of a fundamental philosophical problem: How does inference operate? We need to describe the continuity of inference and develop a model of representation as a prolegomenon to addressing this problem.

Peirce's phenomenology provides an account of the manifestation of the three categories in experience. It reveals the need for a general theory of representation, and this theory will contain a normative aspect. It is not enough to describe how inference in fact proceeds, because there is a teleological element to representation. We must ask toward what it is, or ought to be, directed. As the architectonic indicated, we now leave the descriptive work of phenomenology behind, and venture into the normative sciences of esthetics, ethics, and logic conceived as semeiotic.

CHAPTER 6

The Normative
Sciences and Semeiotic

All phenomena exhibit the three universal categories. First, any event, actual or potential, is characterized by qualitative aspects that might have been other than they are; thus every phenomenon presupposes and retains a penumbra of mere possibility. Second, all phenomena exhibit some element of actuality. Even if the phenomenon is a thought of merely possible qualities, we conceive them as inhering in actual objects and not in a vacuum. A continuum of possible colors, for example, is imagined as embodied in a kind of color strip or other spatial entity. If we think of metaphysical universals or general laws, we conceive them as (at least potentially) having concrete instantiation in particular events. Finally, all phenomena exhibit a degree of Thirdness, or regularity. This follows from the definition of *phenomenon* as anything in any way present to the mind. As Kant showed, every phenomenon must occur in the forms of time and space, which are for Peirce the paradigms of regular continua. Phenomenology identifies these three universal elements of the phaneron as the categories, which serve as fundamental conceptions in any specialized analysis of the features of experience.

The Normative Sciences

There is no treatment of the valuational aspect of experience in Peirce's phenomenology, though we do note that events are always evaluated. Any phenomenon emerges within a context of relations—to other phenomena, to other possibilities, actualities and potentialities, to past and future developments. Any event that reaches the level of conscious awareness is experienced as meaningful in some degree, and its meaning consists in its particular contextual relations.

The meaning of any event consists in three general components. There is the overall *feel* of an event or situation. It is more than a mere figure of speech to say, for example, that the fog itself (rather than the person experiencing it) is romantic, or that a celebration is joyous. There is also the factual *impact* the event has at the existential level. A dense fog, however it feels, will keep one's plane from landing safely. Finally, there is apprehension of the likely *consequences* (always conceived in more or less general terms) the event has for the realization of potentialities. A plane that lands late will likely mean missed connections and a delay in one's travel plans. In broad terms, any phenomenon may be judged as relatively positive or negative in each of these three respects, which correspond to Firstness, Secondness, and Thirdness. The study of our judgment, our appraisal of the positive or negative significance of various phenomena, is the province of the normative sciences: esthetics, ethics, and logic.

There is evaluation of phenomena in any case, but the evaluation may be either "instinctual" and unconscious (and hence haphazard and arbitrary, if one's instincts are not reliable) or it may be *scientific* in Peirce's sense: deliberate, reflective, and directed by the principles of reason. In the normal course of events, there will be relatively few cases where the latter approach is required, or even appropriate. Most judgments can be carried out at the level of "instinct," though philosophers may hesitate to dignify such cases by the name *judgment.* I normally do not need to make a conscious decision about what to do, for example, when I encounter a long line at the cashier's station in a store. My judgment that it is better to wait in line than to leave without paying is certainly an acquired response to the situation, but such an internalized judgment as this is considered *instinctual* in Peirce's sense (CP 2.170). Situations in which momentous consequences will follow from an evaluation *do* involve judgment in the usual sense. A medical team routinely makes decisions that affect the long-term quality (or continuation) of a patient's life. Judges, especially in a newly established legal system or in the high courts of an older system, make decisions that will have long-term effects on the understanding of the code of law.

Peirce's account of experimental inquiry in the normative sciences was outlined in chapter 2. A judgment is made, and its consequences play themselves out. In light of these consequences, it is possible to reconsider and criticize the ideal, the end toward which the judgment in fact points. Upon deliberate reflection, the judgment and its implicit ideal may be either rejected, adjusted, or accepted for future implementation. In the course of this ongoing process (carried out by individuals as members of a community) ideals evolve, become more clearly understood, and then affect future judgments of a similar type.

There is a hierarchical relation among the three normative sciences. Esthetics concerns the criticism of possible ends, the inquiry into the nature of what is good in and of itself. The summum bonum is "the absolutely ideal state of things which is desirable in and for itself regardless of any other consideration whatsoever."[1] We have already seen that the summum bonum is not a finished state of the universe, an arrangement of elements that will persist forever in perfect harmony. To put it in these terms is to conceive the world entirely under the category of Secondness. This "Platonic" version of the good represents the perfection of Secondness; unfortunately it implies the extinction of Thirdness, of process, altogether. There would be no time, and hence no reality, in such a universe (NEM 4:300). The summum bonum, then, is a process rather than a finished state of affairs. It is the process of deliberately controlled action and thought, which has as its sole purpose the increase of its own influence (CP 5.433).

Ethics or practics is the inquiry into the principles of action that promote the summum bonum. Practics informs us that our actions are indeed within our own control and that they can be directed toward realizing the Beautiful and the Admirable. Echoing Kant, Peirce suggested that the true freedom of the will is the freedom to control our actions in just this way: "[T]here is but one thing that raises one individual animal above another,—Self-Mastery" (SS 112).

Ethics promotes the kinds of actions that simultaneously realize two ideals: the satisfaction of one's own desires and the furtherance of good for the larger community. The first of these ideals is often overlooked in discussions of Peirce's philosophy. He tended to emphasize the goals of the community rather than individual desires, and he rejected any philosophy encouraging merely selfish actions. He referred to the nineteenth-century idea that progress takes place through the efforts of individuals to satisfy their own desires as "the Gospel of Greed," in contrast with the gospel of Christ (CP 6.294).[2] Nonetheless, Peirce recognized that the springs of action lie within the individual:

> The art of conduct can only be the art of attaining nothing else than that which will best satisfy himself. There is no selfishness or Epicureanism in a man's devoting all his energies exclusively to that end, since he neither can, nor, as a being endowed with Freedom and Reason, ought if he could, to be moved by any other impulses than such as he has made his own. (MS 649, p. 19)

The caveat is that although action must be grounded in the individual's desires, only those desires that are in accord with the summum bonum are sanctioned by reason and the broader community. Ethics teaches that there is ultimately no conflict between rational desires and the good of the greater community. This notion has appeared throughout the history of Western ethical thought. Peirce added nothing new, except perhaps a tendency to extend the notion of the greater community beyond the specifically human realm. The best life is that which exhibits the selflessness appropriate to the "scientific" thinker, whose work is meant to advance a project of inquiry extending far beyond his or her own interests. Such a mind is "obedient to that great world-vitality which is bringing out a cosmos of ideas, which is the end toward which all the forces and all the feelings in the world are tending" (MS 439, p. 9). Peirce's few utterances concerning ethics are summarized in the following passage:

> The function of a person is . . . threefold; to work out his own nature and impulses, to aid others, and to contribute to the fulfillment of the destiny of his generation. The ultimate utility to him of his experience is to enable him to do this. (MS 299, p. 20)

Actions, then, ought to aim at the increase of self-controlled reason in the constantly evolving cosmos. Self-control comes through reflection on past experience and the adoption of principles that will direct action in the future. Such principles are ideals, incorporated into acquired habits or general rules, which ensure that the ideals are expressed in action. Thought or reason, Thirdness, in this way closes the gap between the Firstness of the merely possible summum bonum and the Secondness of particular actions.[3] Logic is the normative science of thought, and Peirce extended the usual conception of logic so as to include the study of *judgment,* the science of the development of principles. Peirce conceived of logic as "the Ethics of the Intellect,—that is, in the sense in which Ethics is the science of the method of bringing Self-Control to bear to gain our Satisfactions" (SS 112).

A more precise account of the findings of the normative sciences can now be given in terms of the principle of continuity and the three phenomenological categories. This account explains Peirce's identification of logic as semeiotic, and brings out semeiotic's importance as the highest normative science, the keystone in the construction of his philosophical system. The discussion of semeiotic will allow us to sketch Peirce's semeiotic characterization of the summum bonum and his account of the means for realizing it in the ongoing inquiry of the infinite community.

In the 1892 essay "The Law of Mind," Peirce stated "there is but one law of mind, namely, that ideas tend to spread continuously and to affect certain others which stand to them in a peculiar relation of affectibility. In this spreading they lose intensity, and especially the power of affecting others, but gain generality and become welded with other ideas" (CP 6.104). Later in the essay he elaborated: "[W]herever ideas come together they tend to weld into general ideas; and wherever they are generally connected, general ideas govern the connection; and these general ideas are living feelings spread out" (CP 6.143). Finally, toward the end of the essay, he referred to the continuous system of "welded" ideas that the law of mind strives to realize as "the celestial and living harmony" (CP 6.153).

Here we have not only Peirce's conception of thought as a continuum of ideas, but also the precursor of his mature account of the summum bonum. The theory of continuous semeiosis refines the image of a continuum of welded ideas, but the basic view that the ultimate end of all activity is to increase connectivity in thought remains central. Here we may note again Peirce's insistence that the system of "thoughts" toward which events ought to be directed is *not* a static system but a "living harmony." Individual ideas and experience are not anonymously absorbed into an unchanging Absolute, but are brought into communication with one another within a larger system. The law of mind "does not so much as demand that the special ideas shall surrender their peculiar arbitrariness and caprice entirely; for that would be self-destructive. It only requires that they shall influence and be influenced by one another" (CP 6.153).

In 1898, Peirce devoted the greater part of his third Cambridge Conferences lecture to developing the mathematical notion of continuity, setting the stage for several statements concerning the nature and purpose of life. These statements are unusual in their expression, though what they express is not unfamiliar in the history of philosophy. The first echoes the assertion in "The Law of Mind" that a general idea is a continuum of feeling. Peirce cited his "extreme form of realism," which holds that "every true universal, every continuum, is a living and conscious being" (NEM 4:345). As noted at the conclusion of chapter 5, humans are continua. We now see the other side of the coin: If there are continua *other* than human minds, these, too, are (in some sense) living entities.[4] Peirce did not elaborate this view, but continued with a second point: "I will content myself with saying that the only things valuable, even here in this life, are the continuities" (NEM 4:345).

Systems of thought, of material production, of politics, indeed any systems characterized by Thirdness that bind together disparate parts so as to allow for their communication and interaction ought to be encouraged; systems that thwart such an increase in continuity ought to be discouraged (NEM 4:346). The arbitrary, irrational, destructive aspects of the individual components are "ground off" in the evolution of reasonableness, while healthy growth, evolution toward greater harmony and rationality, are promoted. The summum bonum is the concretion of Reasonableness in existent events. Peirce says that the work of society "cannot but be helped by regarding [continuity] as the really possible eternal order of things to which we are trying to make our arbitrariness conform" (NEM 4:346).[5] The lesson of esthetics is that "Generalization, the spilling out of continuous systems, in thought, in sentiment, in deed, is the true end of life" (NEM 4:346). In a passage that elaborates this notion, Peirce wrote

> your quite highest business and duty [is] . . . to recognize a higher business than your business, *not* merely an avocation after the daily task of your vocation is performed, but a generalized conception of duty which completes your personality by melting it into the neighboring parts of the universal cosmos. . . . [T]he supreme commandment of the Buddhisto-christian religion is, to generalize, to complete the whole sys-

tem even until continuity results and the distinct individuals weld together. (CP 1.673)

The lesson of ethics is that our actions ought always to be guided by the principle of continuity, that all our actions ought to contribute to the establishment of greater rationality and greater continuity in the world of experience.

In terms of the three categories, this means that the merely possible Firsts that are admirable in and of themselves ought to be brought into actual existence, and that the resultant Seconds will be embodiments of continua, of rationally evolved ideals. The element of Thirdness, reason, is crucial. It is only in reason or thought, actively mediating between the actual and possible universes, that living continua can arise and grow. Peirce offers a definition of Thirdness as comprising "everything whose being consists in active power to establish connections between different objects, especially between objects in different Universes" (CP 6.455) To act in accordance with the summum bonum is to promote the evolution of continuous systems; and what promotes continuous systems is whatever has its being in establishing connections or communication among disparate parts. We may therefore characterize the summum bonum as the growth of Thirdness, in whatever form it may take.

There are countless examples of entities that have their being in so far as they effectuate continuity through triadic action, that is, whose mode of action exhibits purpose and cannot be adequately characterized in terms of efficient causation. Logic broadly conceived is the science of the principles of such action, of the action of Thirdness.[6] Peirce offered several examples: "Such is everything which is essentially a Sign. . . . Such, too, is a living consciousness, and such the life, the power of growth, of a plant. Such is a living constitution—a daily newspaper, a great fortune, a social 'movement'" (CP 6.455). Because there are a staggering variety of kinds of triadic action, we ought to expect a variety of "logics" investigating principles of self-regulation in the various kinds of activity. Special sciences seek to describe such "internal logics": economics, for example, may study the principles of a market exchange system; politics, the principles of representative democracy; anthropology and sociology, the principles of the practice of a religion. Evolutionary biology and ecology are among those disciplines that (on Peirce's view) study the action of Thirdness in the "natural world." The branch of modern theoretical physics known as cosmology, which seeks to describe the origin and development of the universe itself (both the stuff of which it is made and the principles governing its activity), is thoroughly Peircean in its aims. There are numerous other such disciplines, and there are vast numbers of systems whose internal principles are the special subject of no particular discipline, but which are known tacitly by those who live and work within them.

Logic Conceived as Semeiotic

Just as we may seek a general ethical theory that would apply to various areas of action, or a general esthetic theory that would apply to various cases of qualitative feeling, we may look for a general logic, a normative logic of *events* that would abstract from the particular subject matter of the more specialized areas of inquiry.[7] This discipline will be far broader in scope than logic is usually considered to be—textbooks in logic concern the logic of written or spoken arguments, and many are confined exclusively to the formal logic of deductive arguments. Peirce's philosophy, on the other hand, conceives logic in more Hegelian terms, as the science of triadic action. In practice, Peirce found that his proposed discipline of logic is virtually identical with general semeiotic.

> Now it may be that *logic* ought to be the science of Thirdness in general. But as I have studied it, it is simply the science of what must be and ought to be true representation, so far as representation can be known without any gathering of special facts beyond our ordinary daily life. It is, in short, the philosophy of representation. (CP 1.539)

Peirce's reasons for asserting that his broad conception of logic may be virtually identified with semeiotic deserve some special attention. Examination of his thought on this matter leads to one of the most fundamental and difficult questions in Peirce scholarship: how broad is the scope of semeiotic? Clearly, semeiosis is a paradigm of triadic action for Peirce, providing an excellent instance of causation other than physical causation. "According to the physical doctrine, nothing ever happens but the continued rectilinear velocities with the accelerations that accompany different relative positions of the particles. All other relations, of which we know so many, are inefficient. Knowledge in some way renders them efficient" (SS 31). Peirce argues that the "inefficient" relations among things must be constituted by an active principle of Thirdness, and that *all* such action can be described in terms of the triadic sign-relation. "It appears to me that the essential function of a sign is to render inefficient relations efficient,—not to set them into action, but to establish a habit or general rule whereby they will act on occasion" (SS 31).

This claims more than that the operation of a sign is a sufficient *analogue* to any other triadic action (e.g., inference). This correspondence would be merely fortuitous. The similarity between the principles of semiosis and other triadic actions would then be no more worthy of consideration than a noted similarity between the Dow Jones stock average and rainfall patterns in Scandinavia. Semiosis is not merely a model of triadic action; it is *the* model in the sense that it is the generalized "pure case" of such action. Peirce wrote that if we abstract from "the psychological or accidental human element" in cognition "we see the operation of a sign" (CP 1.537). The principle applies not only to the triadic action of the human mind—the same can be said if we abstract from the accidental features of *any* triadic action: "*signification,* meaning the action of a sign, covers *all* connexions" not reducible to dyadic relations (NEM 4:297, second emphasis added).

The fundamental question concerning the scope of semiosis amounts to this: Did Peirce mean to assert that all triadic action, all Thirdness whatsoever, whether associated with a human mind or not, is *essentially* semiotic? Or did he mean to make the weaker claim that all operations of Thirdness could be *treated as* semiosis, that this is the most perfect conception we can form of such action, and that it is natural for us to conceive a general theory of triadic action in semiotic terms? There is no doubt that Peirce's theory, "semeiotic," has metaphysical implications; the question is what they are. The stronger claim implies that semeiotic is itself a general metaphysical theory. The weaker claim implies that any metaphysical theory we develop will do well to draw on the ideas of semeiotic, but not necessarily that actual events in the world are ultimately events of signification. Peirce tended to favor the stronger claim, but sometimes expressed uncertainty. A 1906 passage nicely shows Peirce walking this conceptual tightrope. He stated it as a fact

> that the entire universe—not merely the universe of existents, but all that wider universe, embracing the universe of existents as a part, the universe which we are all accustomed to refer to as "the truth"—that all this universe is perfused with signs, if it is not composed exclusively of signs. (CP 5.448n.1)

I mention the problem mainly to emphasize the central role of semeiotic in Peirce's philosophy and not because I have the solution to this metaphysical dilemma. It is only recently that this problem has been recognized, reflecting a belated recognition that semeiotic is the key to Peirce's metaphysics. Felicia Kruse has focused attention on this matter in two essays.[8] In the second of these essays she asks, "is there nothing in Peirce's universe but signs?" She concurs with David Savan in reasoning that there must be extra-semiotic factors in the cosmos, even if the cosmos is conceived as essentially semiotic.[9] These factors are prerequisites for semiosis and therefore resist intelligibility, which must involve representation. Kruse and Savan argue that Peirce's insistence that Firstness and Secondness are never *completely* subsumed into Thirdness makes them just such extra-semiotic factors. On the other hand, one who wished to defend the more radical metaphysical claim (which Savan calls "strong semiotic idealism") could respond that non-semiotic elements only enter into reality, and hence become knowable, through participation in semiosis. This reflects the phenomenological principle that the categories of Firstness and Secondness can only be *imperfectly* conceived—in terms of continuity, which is central to the category of Thirdness. The corresponding situation appears in semeiotic: the ostensively non-semiotic entities may be understood as imperfect instances of perfect semeiotic phenomena.[10] A better conception of the place of the theory of signs in Peirce's system, and of how the details of his theory are related to the phenomenological categories, is needed before the metaphysical question can be settled.

For the purposes of developing an account of Peirce's theory of signs it is not necessary to determine the ontological status of signs. We recognize that there *are* signs, and that they are the paradigm of those things "whose being consists in active power to establish connections between different objects" (CP 6.455). *Sign* and *semiosis* are defined as follows:

> by "semiosis" I mean . . . an action, or influence, which is, or involves, a coöperation of *three* subjects, such as a sign, its object, and its interpretant, this tri-relative influence not being in any way resolvable into actions between pairs. Σημείωσις in Greek of the Roman period, as early as Cicero's time, if I remember rightly, meant the action of almost any kind of sign; and my definition confers on anything that so acts the title of a "sign." (CP 5.484)

We may accept this as a stipulative definition, and bear in mind that "we ought not to think that what are signs to us are the only signs; but we have to judge signs in general by these" (NEM 4:297). With these notes in mind, let us explore Peirce's science of semeiotic.

Divisions of Semeiotic

Logic or semeiotic is the third of the normative sciences, and Peirce consistently identified three divisions within semeiotic. His first account of the three divisions appears in the Harvard "Lectures on the Logic of Science" of 1865, where they are identified as Universal Grammar, Logic, and Universal Rhetoric (W 1:175). The terms preferred in the present study appear, along with others, in Peirce's post-1902 writings. The first division of semeiotic (Speculative Grammar) is *Stecheotic*; the second is Logical Critic or simply *Critic*; the third (Speculative Rhetoric) is *Methodeutic*.[11]

Though Peirce's division of semeiotic into three parts is consistent throughout his career, his conceptions of semeiotic and of its relation to what is usually understood as "logic" are not. There are various discussions of the divisions of semeiotic in Peirce's writings, most of them clear in presentation and all of them expressed in his usual authoritative tone. We must recognize, however, that Peirce's conception of semeiotic changed over the nearly five decades he spent working on the philosophy of representation.

In particular, fundamental shifts in his thought about semeiotic occurred in the mid-1880s and around 1902. Peirce's consistent division of semeiotic into three parts threatens to mask these fundamental changes in his thought.[12]

Peirce defined a sign as something that has the capacity to establish a triadic relation among (1) an *object* of representation, (2) a particular existent sign-vehicle, or *representamen,* and (3) an *interpretant,* a thought in which the representamen and its object acquire meaning. For example, a fresh footprint in mud is a representamen, its object is the person (or at least the foot) that created it, and its interpretant is the idea that someone has recently walked in that spot. The *sign* (in Peirce's special sense) is not to be identified with any of the three relates; it is the relation itself in which the now-absent foot, the existent footprint, and my thought about them are brought together. The sign is irreducibly triadic: If any one of the three correlates is absent, then representation or semiosis does not occur. This rough characterization of the definition of *sign* provides sufficient background to trace the development of Peirce's conception of the science of semeiotic.

Peirce's first conception of semeiotic as an area of inquiry appears in his writings from 1865 until the mid-1880s. It is based on the insight that there are three general ways in which a sign may be related to its object. In two works from 1865, Peirce identified semeiotic as the science of representations, and identified the three kinds of representation as *signs,* "[r]epresentations by virtue of a convention"; *symbols,* "[r]epresentations by virtue of original or acquired nature"; and *copies,* "[r]epresentations by virtue of a sameness of predicates" (W 1:304, see also W 1:170). In this early approach to the classification of signs we already see distinctions made in terms of the relation of a sign to its object. Peirce says that a proper name is an example of a *sign* in this sense. The distinguishing thing about a *sign* is that it refers to an individual. Peirce apparently did see the flaw in this definition: representation "by virtue of a convention" soon becomes the definition of a symbol. *Sign* is redefined as something existentially connected to its object, making individual things the only possible objects of a sign. A *copy* represents its object via shared qualities—a portrait resembles a person in this manner. Finally, a *symbol* operates via laws of association of ideas, which are general and not confined by resemblance or by existential connection to an individual. A word, for example, has a nature "such that when it is brought before the mind certain principles of its use—whether reflected upon or not—by association immediately regulate the action of the mind; and these may be regarded as laws of the symbol itself which it cannot *as a symbol* transgress" (W 1:173).[13]

Within semeiotic, then, there would be three separate sciences: the science of copies, the science of signs, and symbolistic (W 1:174, 1:304). The account of the three types of signs is revised in "On a New List of Categories" in 1867. Peirce there introduced the term *likeness* in place of *copy*, and *index* as an alternative to *sign* (W 2:56). In later writings, *icon*, *index*, and *symbol* become standard. Peirce in this period freely ignored the sciences treating the first two kinds of signs, and argued that logic is exclusively concerned with symbols. He made no mention of what disciplines might be concerned with the other two sciences during the first two periods of his thought on semeiotic.

Peirce identified further divisions within "symbolistic" (W 1:175, 1:304). First, we may study the formal conditions of a sign's being suitable to function as a sign, considered in itself. A random scattering of letters rattled out on a typewriter violates the basic rules of written language. Ordered arrangements do not, and may be taken as symbols even if we do not happen to understand their meaning. Some inscriptions, for example, are orderly enough in arrangement to indicate that they embody meaning even if no one living is able to read the language. It is presumed in such cases that the language *can* be decoded, because the inscriptions are recognized as suitable vehicles for conveying some meaning and, we suppose, must therefore have been used to do so. The science that studies the conditions of something's being serviceable as a symbol is Universal Grammar.

Something that is clearly fit to be a symbol, such as the written statement 'It's raining', may or may not accurately represent its object, however. The second division of symbolistic, Logic, examines "the conditions which enable symbols in general to refer to objects" (W 1:175). Logic, in short, concerns the conditions of reference that allow for a symbol's being true.

Finally, the science of Universal Rhetoric explores "the formal conditions of intelligibility of symbols" (W 1:175). These are the requirements that must be met in order for a symbol to convey any meaning to an interpreting mind. These conditions concern the relation of a symbol to the whole system to which it belongs. Such a system may be called a *language* (W 1:304). It is unlikely that Peirce would restrict application of this term to the "natural languages" used by humans. There may be, for example, musical or artistic symbol-systems, perhaps with nonlinguistic vocabularies, that satisfy the Peircean notion of language.[14]

In this early stage of thought about semeiotic, Peirce does not identify logic with semeiotic. Logic is a specialized discipline alongside the grammar and rhetoric of symbols, and is largely independent of these other divisions of symbolistic. Symbolistic, in turn, is an independent area of inquiry within semeiotic, alongside the science of copies and the science of signs. The division of semeiotic during the first period is illustrated in figure 6.1.

The first major revision in Peirce's conception of semeiotic as a science coincides with the period of his work on logical notation carried out at The Johns Hopkins University in the early 1880s. Peirce and O. H. Mitchell introduced a refinement to the algebraic notation of Boolean logic that allowed for the quantification of logical propositions. In an essay "On the Algebra of Logic," published in 1885 (CP 3.359–403), Peirce gave the reasons he deemed such innovations necessary for logic. The essay begins with a brief account of the icon, index, and symbol (in this essay called the *token*). In the sixth paragraph we find the statement that overturns his earlier account of semeiotic: "in a perfect system of logical notation signs of these several kinds must all be employed" (CP 3.363). There follows a short account of the indispensable role of each type of sign in logical thought. "Without tokens [i.e., symbols] there would be no generality in the statements, for they are the only general signs; and generality is essential to reasoning" (CP 3.363).

Fig. 6.1 Divisions of Semeiotic, 1865–1885

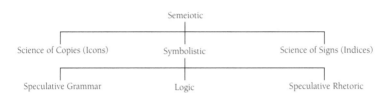

Reasoning, however, is never *completely* general in character. It is always directly or indirectly about some particular thing, so signs other than symbols are necessary to reasoning: "[T]okens alone do not state what is the subject of discourse; and this can, in fact, not be described in general terms; it can only be indicated. The actual world cannot be distinguished from a world of imagination by any description" (CP 3.363). Thus in formal logical notation, we need universal and existential quantifiers; in ordinary language we need indexical signs such as pronouns (as well as paralinguistic indicators such as pointing fingers and the movement of a speaker's eyes) to indicate the subject of discourse. "With these two kinds of signs alone any proposition can be expressed; but it cannot be reasoned upon, for reasoning consists in the observation that where certain relations subsist certain others are found, and it accordingly requires the exhibition of the relations reasoned with in an icon" (CP 3.363). Reasoning requires an icon of some form upon which experiment, observation, and comparison may be based (it makes no difference whether the icon is represented mentally or physically). Thus even pure mathematics is observational, making use of icons such as numbers, equations, and geometric diagrams in its reasoning.

With this account of the necessity of icons and indices for any reasoning whatever, Peirce abandoned his 1865 account of logic as a division of symbolistic that is independent of the science of copies and signs. Logic must in some way include the study of icons, indices, and symbols alike. After the mid-1880s, Peirce viewed logic as including all three divisions of semeiotic; hence logic must be identified with semeiotic. By the late 1890s, Peirce made this shift in his thinking explicit: "Logic, in its general sense, is, as I believe I have shown, only another name for *semiotic* (σεμειωτική), the quasi-necessary, or formal, doctrine of signs" (CP 2.227). The separate studies of icons and indices are not mentioned.

Recall that the earlier account of logic, as a division of symbolistic, defined it as the science of the conditions that allow symbols to refer to objects. After restructuring the science of semeiotic, Peirce retained a place for logic understood in this earlier sense. *Logic proper* (as opposed to logic "in its general sense") "is the science of what is quasi-necessarily true of the representamina of any scientific intelligence in order that they may hold good of any *object,* that is, may be true. Or say, logic proper is the formal science of the conditions of the truth of representations" (CP 2.228). Peirce's application of the term *logic* during the middle phase of his thought about semeiotic can be confusing. Peirce's conception of logic during the period 1885 to 1902 is set forth in the following passage, written about 1896:

> The term "logic" is unscientifically by me employed in two distinct senses. In its narrower sense, it is the science of the necessary conditions of the attainment of truth. In its broader sense, it is the science of the necessary laws of thought, or, still better (thought always taking place by means of signs), it is general semeiotic, treating not merely of truth, but also of the general conditions of signs being signs (which Duns Scotus called *grammatica speculativa*), also of the laws of the evolution of thought, which since it coincides with the study of the necessary conditions of the transmission of meaning by signs from mind to mind, and from one state of mind to another, ought, for the sake of taking advantage of an old association of terms, be called *rhetorica speculativa*, but which I content myself with inaccurately calling *objective logic,* because that conveys the correct idea that it is like Hegel's logic. (CP 1.444)

Speculative grammar here includes the study of all kinds of signs (icons, indices, and symbols), and inquires into the conditions of their embodying any meaning. Logic "in the narrow sense" concerns the conditions of reference necessary for a sign to be true. Speculative rhetoric still concerns the conditions under which a sign may convey its meaning in an interpretant, but this is now explicitly characterized as the study of the laws governing the evolution of thought in a personality or in a larger society. The division of semeiotic during the second period is illustrated in figure 6.2.

The second major revision in Peirce's conception of semeiotic occurred around 1902, and the new structure is retained through his last writings on

Fig. 6.2 Divisions of Semeiotic, 1885–1902

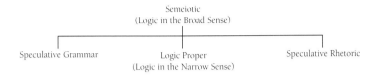

semeiotic. In chapter 2 we saw that Peirce at this time distinguished the *mathematics of logic* from *logic as a normative science,* which includes a "mathematical part"—the formal logic of relations. Logic conceived as semeiotic now becomes normative logic conceived in semeiotic terms. With the introduction of a normative aspect to logic, the divisions of semeiotic fall at last into place. The outline of Peirce's 1902 application for aid to the Carnegie Institution virtually mirrors the architectonic of the 1903 Syllabus (except that the position there occupied by *phenomenology* bears the name *categorics*). In his description of the proposed memoirs, Peirce stated that "Logic will here be defined as *formal semiotic,*" and that "By an application of Categorics, I show that the primary division of logic should be into Stechiology, Critic, and Methodeutic" (NEM 4:20–21). The terminology is new, and it signals a change in the conception of semeiotic—especially with regard to Speculative Grammar.

Stechiology is Speculative Grammar broadened to include not only the study of the conditions requisite to something's being a sign, but also "the general theory of the nature and meanings of signs, whether they be icons, indices, or symbols" (CP 1.191). Stecheotic is meant to be to semeiotic what Euclid's *Elements* was meant to be to geometry: it lays out the general theory of sign-action, establishes definitions, and sets forth the basic principles governing *any* possible form of representation.[15] In a 1911 letter, Peirce characterized this branch of semeiotic (in this instance called *Analytic*) as that which "examines the nature of thought, not psychologically but simply to define what it is to doubt, to believe, to learn, etc." (NEM 3:207). Because Peirce maintained that all thought occurs in the form of sign action, the general account of the nature of thought *is* a general theory of signs.

With the introduction of the term Critic (or Logical Critic) as the name of the second division of semeiotic, Peirce escaped his earlier ambiguous use of the term *logic.* Critic is "logic in the narrow sense" (CP 2.93); it "classifies arguments and determines the validity and the degree of force of each kind" (CP 1.191). While stecheotic presents "the general conditions of symbols and other signs having the significant character," critic raises the issue of the truth conveyed in some representations (CP 2.93). Critic is "the theory of the general conditions of the reference of Symbols and other

Signs to their professed Objects, that is, it is the theory of the conditions of truth" (CP 2.93).

The determinations of validity and strength made in Critic lay the basis for semeiotic to become a normative science, as it is here that good and bad kinds of thought are sorted out. Methodeutic or Speculative Rhetoric is normative semeiotic proper. It concerns "the reference of Symbols and other Signs to the Interpretants which they aim to determine" (CP 2.93). This branch of semeiotic "studies the methods that ought to be pursued in the investigation, in the exposition, and in the application of truth" (CP 1.191). Methodeutic, in short, "shows how to conduct an inquiry" (NEM 3:207).

Thus we see how Peirce's conceptions of logic and semeiotic shifted over the years, and how the structure of three divisions of semeiotic gradually evolved. Throughout his career, though, Peirce was steady in considering semeiotic as the theory of signs and representation, and hence as the theory of thought, where the word "thought" is stripped of its psychological connotations. General semeiotic is primarily the study of the operation of Thirdness in phenomena. Peirce's conception of logic changed, from being the study of the reference of symbols, a part of symbolistic, to being identified with general (coenoscopic) semeiotic. The analysis of the validity and strength of arguments falls under Critic. As Fisch puts it, Peirce moves from a view of *logic within semeiotic* to a view of *logic as general semeiotic.*[16]

There is one loose end to be tied down in this history of Peirce's conception of semeiotic. Semeiotic rightfully encompasses all manner of signs: icons, indices, and symbols. Logic is strictly concerned only with signification as it functions in reasoning, however. This means that logic ought properly to concern itself only with symbols, or with icons and indices that function as constituent parts of symbolic thought. We may well ask what has become of the study of icons and indices in their own right.

The science of copies (icons) and the science of signs (indices) were lost in the first restructuring of semeiotic. They make a rather unexpected return in the last period, however. In the manuscript "Phaneroscopy, **φαν** 1906," Peirce wrote:

> it seems to me that in the present state of our knowledge of signs, the whole doctrine of the classification of signs and of what is essential to a given kind of sign, must be studied by one group of investigators. Therefore, I extend logic to embrace all the necessary principles of semeiotic, and I recognize a logic of icons, and a logic of indices, as well as a logic of symbols; and in this last I recognize three divisions. (CP 4.9)

The three divisions are none other than Stecheotic, Critic, and Methodeutic. In a letter to Lady Welby dated 14 March 1909, Peirce repeated the point:

studies of the limits of the sciences in general convinced me that the Logician ought to broaden his studies, and take in every *allied* subject that it was no business of anybody else to study and in short, and above all, he must *not* confine himself to *symbols* since no reasoning that amounts to much can be conducted with[out] *Icons* and *Indices*. (SS 118)

The 1906 passage clearly indicates that stecheotic, strictly speaking, is the general theory of *symbols* but not necessarily the general theory of *signs*. The logician *qua* logician, in other words, is still interested primarily in symbols. These two passages stress that the study of icons and indices ought properly to be given status as independent inquiries. Logic, as the study of symbols, would draw on the findings of these inquiries. Lacking this independent status, though, the studies fall to the logician by default. No other investigator is better suited to adopt these orphaned studies. Because icons and indices *are* necessary allies to symbolization, they are to be included in the logician's study of stecheotic: "My studies must extend over the whole of general Semeiotic" (SS 118). For practical purposes, then, Stecheotic or Speculative Grammar is the general theory of sign action, as it was in the 1903 classification of sciences. The final account of the divisions of semeiotic is illustrated in figure 6.3.

Fig. 6.3 Divisions of Semeiotic, 1902–1914

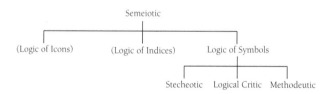

Speculative Grammar: The New Elements of Semeiotic

Just as phenomenology depends upon mathematics for its guiding hypotheses, the general theory of signs depends upon phenomenology for its guiding hypotheses about the kinds of signs that might be discovered in the world. Semeiotic is the science of triadic action, and its first division, stecheotic, provides a model of forms of triadic action. Its aim is to articulate a formal theory of sign action, which is in effect a formal model of phenomena. It proceeds in two stages, as does all inquiry. First, it adopts the findings of its predecessor in the classification of sciences as hypotheses to guide inquiry, deduces the consequences of these hypotheses for the special subject matter at hand, and formulates these in a general theory.[17] This part of the inquiry may be described as a priori speculation, grounded in the best available hypotheses. The next stage requires that the speculative theory be tested against experience and observation.

> The principles and analogies of Phenomenology enable us to describe, in a distant way, what the divisions of triadic relations must be. But until we have met with the different kinds *a posteriori*, and have in that way been led to recognize their importance, the *a priori* descriptions mean little; not nothing at all, but little. Even after we seem to identify the varieties called for *a priori* with varieties which the experience of reflexion leads us to think important, no slight labour is required to make sure that the divisions we have found *a posteriori* are precisely those that have been predicted *a priori*. (CP 2.233)

The process of inquiry, the refinement of hypotheses through observation, is open-ended. Peirce makes it clear that his own efforts in semeiotic are only the first steps toward a developed theory of signs. He describes his work in semeiotics as that of "a pioneer, or rather a backwoodsman, in the work of clearing and opening up what I call *semiotic*" (CP 5.488). He never presented his findings in any single, systematic work. In his writings we find formulations, revisions, insights later abandoned or neglected, and dead ends. We also find, I argue, a core of consistent method and theory that develops in sophistication over the years, just as his conception of semeiotic itself developed. Since Peirce's death, a number of persons have devoted much effort toward revising the theory of signs he sketched. Peirce's "science of representation" has emerged as a discipline in its own right.[18] There is a great deal of literature available on the theory of signs, and many advances have been made beyond Peirce's theories. Happily, much recent scholarship is also devoted to the explication of Peirce's own pioneering work. This literature is a valuable resource for the present study, where our concern is to reconstruct the systematic core of Peirce's mature semeiotic and to show how it arises from and contributes to his architectonic philosophy.

The Definition of "Sign"

A rough definition of *sign* was given earlier; here I examine several of Peirce's definitions, to draw out as accurate a conception of the sign as possible. The following passages provide the basis for our definition.

[Definition 1]:
A sign, or *representamen,* is something which stands to somebody for something in some respect or capacity. It addresses somebody, that is, creates in the mind of that person an equivalent sign, or perhaps a more developed sign. That sign which it creates I call the *interpretant* of the first sign. The sign stands for something, its *object.* It stands for that object, not in all respects, but in reference to a sort of idea, which I have sometimes called the *ground* of the representamen. (CP 2.228, ca. 1897)

[Definition 2]:
A *Sign,* or Representamen, is a First that stands in such a genuine triadic relation to a Second, called its *Object,* as to be capable of determining a Third, called its *Interpretant,* to assume the same triadic relation to its object in which it stands itself to the same Object. . . . A *Sign* is a Representamen with a mental Interpretant. Possibly there may be Representamens that are not Signs. (CP 2.274; 1902)

[Definition 3]:
A sign is . . . an object which is in relation to its object on the one hand and to an interpretant on the other in such a way as to bring the interpretant into a relation to the object corresponding to its own relation to the object. I might say 'similar to its own' for a correspondence consists in a similarity; but perhaps correspondence is narrower. (SS 32; 1904)

[Definition 4]:
I define a Sign as anything which is so determined by something else, called its Object, and so determines an effect upon a person, which effect I call its Interpretant, that the latter is thereby mediately determined by the former. My insertion of "upon a person" is a sop to Cerberus, because I despair of making my own broader conception understood. (SS 80–81; 1908).

My examination of these definitions will take up, in turn, the notion of the object of a sign, the notion of interpretant, and finally, the nature of the sign itself.

THE OBJECT

The sign represents an object, Peirce says in Definition 1, "not in all respects" but in reference to an *idea* of the object which may be called the ground of the sign or representamen. The simple case of a footprint in mud illustrates this point. The whole person who created the footprint is not represented in any detail. To the expert tracker, the footprint will represent a person of some approximate weight and frame, who made the footprint at some approximate time in the past. The *ground* of the representamen is this vague conception of an individual, not the actual person in all his or her particular features. Not even Sherlock Holmes could discover, from a footprint alone, the number of teeth that its maker possesses.

The ground of a sign is thus an abstraction from the complex, dynamic, particular thing the sign represents. Peirce calls the ground the *immediate object* of the representation. It is distinguished from the *dynamical object,* "the Object as it is regardless of any particular aspect of it, the Object in such relations as unlimited and final study would show it to be" (CP 8.183).[19] The dynamical object is the actual thing, conceived as that larger determinate reality from which certain properties are abstracted and represented in a given sign.

Any actual sign falls short of representing its object in its complete dynamical reality, of course. If we ask what the ideal would be, we find that a sign that represented its object without abstraction from it, that is, a sign whose immediate object coincides with its dynamical object, would be a perfect representation of all that *is* (CP 2.407). The "individual" who makes the footprint is defined by his or her relations to all the rest of the existent universe. The same is true for any dynamical object. A *perfect* representation of an object would then embody all the relations that constitute the universe. Any object of representation, "even if we are talking of Hamlet's madness," is part of "one and the same Universe of being, the 'Truth'" (NEM 4:239).[20] Thus, though it is tempting to speak of the dynamical object of a sign as that particular thing which the sign represents, it is ultimately not possible to dissociate "that particular thing" from all of reality.

The crucial distinction with respect to objects is between the world, or some part of it, "*as* the sign represents it to be" and the world as it exists independent of its representation in any finite number of signs. The dynamical object, moreover, is not a noumenal reality which lies somehow "behind" its representation in phenomena. The dynamical object is the reality, all that is the case, as it would be represented in a perfect representation. The perfect representation may be conceived as a sign that is the summation of all the information embodied in an infinite number of representations. To anticipate, it is what would be embodied in the ultimate *interpretant* of infinite, continuous semiosis.

THE INTERPRETANT

"The whole purpose of a sign is that it shall be interpreted in another sign; and its whole purport lies in the special character which it imparts to that interpretation" (CP 8.191). A sign is something related to its object in such a way that the ground of representation is communicated to an "interpreter" of the sign. This process of communication is completed when the ground and its vehicle, the sign or representamen, are represented in an *interpretant*. Definition 2 and Definition 3 indicate that the resulting interpretant (itself a sign) stands in the same relation to the original object as did the first sign. This provides the basic conception of sign action, but it is not quite adequate to Peirce's conception of semiosis, which requires that subsequent representations *may* provide more or less information about the object than did the original.

This basic model does point out one crucial aspect of semiosis, however. It is necessarily an infinite process: A sign is "Anything which determines something else (its *interpretant*) to refer to an object to which [it] itself refers (its *object*) in the same way, the interpretant becoming in turn a sign, and so on *ad infinitum*" (CP 2.303). Each subsequent interpretant is required as the completion of the previous sign-function; and each in turn, as a sign, requires the production of a further interpretant sign. In the simplified account of semiosis of Definition 2 and Definition 3, each sign is determined by its predecessor to stand in the same relation to the object that its predecessor did. This simplified account of semiosis is diagramed in figure 6.4. On this conception, the last interpretant would stand in the very same relation to the object as the first sign did. This is indeed conceivable if we postulate that each sign-function is an infinitesimal process. There might be no discernible difference between successive interpretations that are immediately connected.

Fig. 6.4 Simplified Model of Semeiosis

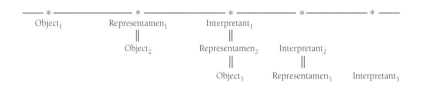

Over the long run, however, it is likely that development will occur, so that the first sign's relation to the object will differ from that of the hundredth, for example. If semeiotic is meant to model the process of thought, it must allow for development in interpretation over time. The language of Definition 1 requires this possibility. If semiosis is conceived as a *continuous* process, on the model of the mathematical continuum, then there is room for gradual change over the course of the whole process even though neighboring interpretations are not discernibly different in their relation to the object. The interpretant sign is not always a perfect duplicate of the original sign. In many cases, the interpretant adds to or reduces the information conveyed in the original sign. Its relation to the object is thus *similar* to the original sign, but the similarity may or may not amount to equivalence. Development in information occurs so naturally that it may very well be inevitable. The model of an interpretant sign that is equivalent to the original sign may be an ideal case.

Development of information in successive interpretants is possible, and may be inevitable, because of one feature that the simplified conception of semiosis omits. The dynamical object of each successive representation in the process is necessarily different from that of its predecessor. The dynamical object of the first representation is the real universe at that time, and the immediate object is an abstraction consisting of some aspects of this reality. The next representation, however, *cannot* have exactly the same dynamical object. The real universe is at that point populated by at least one additional entity—the first representamen itself. Every successive representation in the semeiotic process thus has as its dynamical object not just the universe which the first representamen represented, but that universe *plus* the first representamen itself. The ground of each successive sign is an abstraction from a more complex universe than that from which the predecessor sign abstracted. The object *necessarily* grows and develops over time, if semiosis takes place at all. Figure 6.5 shows how, in a process of semiosis, each stage represents not just the original object, but all those representations that intervene. (Terms joined by a double vertical line name the same thing, considered as belonging to different representation relations.) The original object is thus mediately present in successive interpretants, but information may also enter or drop out due to the repeated abstractions which occur at each step.

Fig. 6.5 Model of Semiosis

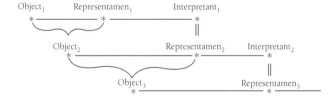

Semiosis, then, is necessarily a developmental process rather than a static affair. The existence of one sign whose purpose "is that it shall be interpreted in another sign" implies, as Hanna Buczyńska-Garewicz notes, that "the plurality of signs is logically prior to a single sign."[21] The basic concept of Peirce's semeiotic is not the sign, but the process of *semiosis* in a continuous, infinite, self-generative system of signs.

In semiosis we find a process (graphically presented in figure 6.5) that should be familiar by now. Semiosis is an infinite, continuous process that can in principle have no absolute beginning or end. The "first representation" of the dynamical object involves an infinite process of representation. It is clear that no actual representation can be adequate to the dynamical object—such a representation would be the embodiment of Absolute Knowledge. We certainly cannot *begin* the process of representation with Absolute Knowledge. Only some aspects of the dynamical object, the abstracted ground, can ever be represented.

What is the "process of abstraction" that provides the ground for a representation? It necessarily consists in the selection of certain features of reality and the neglect of others. Because it is clear that we never have access to a representation of the whole of reality, though, the "reality" whose features are abstracted is itself already an abstraction. The selection of features for representation of the dynamical object has *always already occurred,* no matter how far "back" in the series of representation we may go. In the semiotic activity which is human thought, we sooner or later come to a level where the abstraction apparently occurs before consciousness appears on the scene. We may then say that physical conditions such as spatiotemporal location or the operation of the autonomic nervous system and the sense organs do the abstracting. Yet this explanation of the origin of semiosis is no explanation at all, as the abstraction has merely been relegated to the preconscious arena of the perceptual judgment.[22] Our attempt to conceive an absolute beginning to semiosis is always frustrated.[23] Semiosis is in principle without absolute beginning, as well as without end.

Peirce's model of semiosis is precisely analogous to his model of the continuous line, whose parts are infinitesimals, and to the model of cognition presented in "The Law of Mind."[24] I contend that the similarity is anything but coincidental. All are expressions of the principle of continuity, the fundamental concept that finds application in every part of Peirce's architectonic. Semeiotic is the science of Thirdness; Thirdness is the category of perfect continuity, which is an irreducible element of phenomena; and the mathematical definition of a perfect continuum is precisely that whose parts (including its apparent termini) are all continuous in the same manner as the whole. The process of abstraction that leads to the "first representation" is itself a continuous semiotic process, and is in fact no different from the process of abstraction that occurs in any subsequent representation. Semiosis, as an objective process, is a continuum of representation and interpretation. It reflects the continuous processive nature of phenomena, and provides a set of terms and principles that are applicable to virtually every other process. This, in rough outline, is what makes semeiotic the very heart of Peirce's philosophy.

What is still missing from this account, however, is that semiosis is a self-directing process. In Definition 4, Peirce says only that the interpretant is mediately determined by the object. This is a very loose formulation, and it would apparently allow us to say that even utterly incongruous signs may be related as representamen and interpretant, as long as there is *some* association between them.

Signs, however, are teleological. A sign's purpose is not only to determine an interpretant; "its whole purport lies in the special character which it imparts to that interpretation" (CP 8.191). Peirce stipulates that a sign, B, in order to be considered an interpretant of another sign, A, must come into being "without violation of its, A's, purpose, that is, in accordance with the 'Truth'" (NEM 4:239). The *telos* of any given sign is to generate an interpretant sign that represents not only the first sign's *immediate* object, but also its *dynamical* object as accurately as possible.[25] The proper *telos* of a sign is discovered in ethics and esthetics. Attempts at representation that promote the summum bonum are ethically good; the summum bonum is that which is admirable in and of itself. This, as we have indicated before, is the process of expressing truth. Thus a sign whose *telos* is to represent the summation of an inquiry into truth is esthetically and ethically good; one that has some other aim is not. Likewise, an interpretant that violates the *telos* of a representamen is not in fact a legitimate interpretant, and it undermines the semiotic process of which it is supposed to be a part.

In order to understand more clearly the teleological aspect of semiosis, we require a more refined notion of the interpretant. In the broadest sense, an interpretant is the effect produced by a sign. We have confined our discussion so far to the *logical* effect of the sign, but there are clearly many possible effects a sign might produce. Any of these *may* function as interpretants. Peirce's analysis of the interpretant is complex, as it must be if it is to account for the wide variety of possible effects of signification.

The *immediate interpretant* is "the interpretant as it is revealed in the right understanding of the sign itself" (CP 4.536). The term "immediate interpretant" refers to "the Quality of the Impression that a sign is fit to produce, not to any actual reaction" (CP 8.315). The immediate interpretant is the effect that the sign in itself is suited to bring about. It is a possibility—nothing guarantees that the immediate interpretant will ever be realized. Everyone just might "miss the point" of a given sign. The *dynamical interpretant* is "the actual effect which the Sign . . . really determines" (CP 4.536). It is "whatever interpretation any mind actually makes of the sign" (CP 8.315). The dynamical interpretant is the totality of whatever effects the sign produces in the interpreter—it may fulfill the purpose of the sign and realize the immediate interpretant, or it may not. The dynamical interpretant almost certainly involves effects beyond the scope of the immediate interpretant. Finally, the *normal* or *final interpretant* is "the effect that would be produced on the mind by the sign after sufficient development of thought"

(CP 8.343). "The Final Interpretant does not consist in the way in which any mind does act but in the way in which every mind would act" if interpretation, synthesis of information about the Truth, were carried on indefinitely (CP 8.315). The dynamical interpretant, conceived as the effect of a sign on a *passive* mind, "indefinitely approaches the character of" the immediate interpretant; conceived as the *active* work of the mind on material provided for it in the sign, it indefinitely approaches the character of the final interpretant (CP 8.315).[26]

Peirce offered another division of interpretants that has been the source of considerable confusion. "The first proper significate effect of a sign is the feeling produced by it. There is almost always a feeling which we come to interpret as evidence that we comprehend the proper effect of the sign, although the foundation of truth in this is frequently very slight" (CP 5.475). Peirce calls the quality of feeling produced by a sign the *emotional interpretant*. Some signs, he notes, are intended to produce emotional interpretants almost exclusively. Such is the case with a musical performance. "If a sign produces any further proper significate effect, it will do so through the mediation of the emotional interpretant, and such further effect will always involve an effort" (CP 4.475). An interpretant characterized by an effort of the will, whether it is a physical or a mental effort, is an *energetic interpretant*. A shouted command to "Drop your weapon!" is meant to produce an energetic interpretant, as is the cautionary "Don't think that way."

Finally, if a sign has an effect beyond mere reaction in the interpreter, this effect must amount to the modification of "a person's tendencies toward action," that is, it must establish a rule that can affect action in the future (CP 5.476). This is the *logical* or *ultimate interpretant* of a sign.[27] The logical interpretant of a sign is a sign that can be expressed as a rule of action, a habit. The intended logical interpretants of the Golden Rule or the utilitarian principle, for example, are ways of thinking that will influence one's behavior in the future. "As Thirdness, habit has the same nature as a sign and owing to that it can be an interpretant. But due to its actualization as Secondness, it can be a link between the universe of signs and the world of experience," or action.[28] A given sign may be intended to produce any one or perhaps all of these three kinds of interpretant.

Most early commentators assumed that the division into emotional, energetic, and logical interpretants was meant to be identical to the division into immediate, dynamical, and final interpretants.[29] In contrast, John J. Fitzgerald suggests that energetic, emotional, and logical interpretants be understood as varieties of dynamical interpretants.[30] The dynamical interpretant, as an actual experienced effect, must always be characterized by a quality and a reaction of the interpreter. It may be that every actual interpretant also involves an implicit rule that could, if it were adopted, effect a change in habit, though this is less clear. Certainly there are some dynamical interpretants that do involve habit change. Fitzgerald is correct to point out that the two sets of divisions are not *identical,* since the dynamical interpretant *at least* involves an emotional and an energetic interpretant, and possibly a logical interpretant as well.

Thomas L. Short goes further, to suggest that the emotional-energetic-logical distinction is a subdivision applicable not only to the dynamical interpretant, but to the immediate and final interpretants as well.[31] This is more satisfactory than Fitzgerald's reading, which makes energetic, emotional, and logical interpretants aspects of only the dynamical interpretant. It appears that the immediate interpretant of a sign, as a possibility, may be describable in terms of its *intended* emotional, energetic, and logical effects. Depending on the nature of the sign, some of these categories may be irrelevant—we may be unable to specify the intended logical interpretant for most paintings, for example. Likewise, the emotional and energetic aspects of a sign's final interpretant may be impossible to imagine—how *would* it feel to know the full truth that Milton's *Paradise Lost* was intended to express? Nonetheless, the immediate interpretant of a painting is largely a quality of feeling, and the final interpretant of *Paradise Lost,* according to its author, is the ultimate truth of Christianity, which would be a logical interpretant.[32] Peirce himself developed his theory of signs with barely a mention of the emotional-energetic-logical distinction, however, and the nature of a sign's intended interpretant is normally clear enough for our purposes that careful analysis is not needed.

When all goes well, the immediate interpretant determines the dynamical interpretant, at least in part. The dynamical interpretant, in turn, contributes to the realization of the final interpretant. It is the essential nature and purpose of a sign to further the process of semiosis by generating such interpretants. The process of semiosis has its own *telos* as a total system, which is reflected in the *telos* of each part of the system. Like the continuous line, each part of the semiotic continuum has the same nature as the whole; its purpose is to realize the summum bonum, conceived in semiotic terms.

> The purpose of every sign is to express "fact," and by being joined with other signs, to approach as nearly as possible to determining an interpretant which would be the *perfect Truth,* the absolute Truth, and as such (at least, we may use this language) would be the very Universe. Aristotle gropes for a conception of perfection, or *entelechy,* which he never succeeds in making clear. We may adopt the word to mean the very fact, that is, the ideal sign which should be quite perfect, and so identical,—in such identity as a sign may have,—with the very matter denoted united with the very form signified by it. The entelechy of the Universe of being, then, the Universe *quâ* fact, will be that Universe in its aspect as a sign, the 'Truth' of being.

The 'Truth,' the fact that is not abstracted but complete, is the ultimate interpretant of every sign. (NEM 4:239–40)

The summum bonum, in semeiotic terms, is the realization of Truth in and by the infinite process of representation and interpretation. "[T]hought passing always from object to interpretation at its extremest point reaches the absolute reality of objectivity. The real and true thing is the thing as it might be known to be" (NEM 4:300).

SIGN AND SIGN VEHICLE

We have examined the notions of *object* and *interpretant* in Peirce's definitions of the sign, and turn now to the notion of the sign itself. This will lead us directly to Peirce's classification of signs, the heart of his stecheotic. Our use of the term "sign" has been ambiguous up to this point. We defined a sign as something the purpose of which is to generate an interpretant sign. We have also spoken of the sign as something that has its being in so far as it does generate an interpretant sign. In one sense, a sign is anything that *can* represent an object to an interpretant. In another sense, a sign is an essentially triadic entity—something that *must* represent its object to an interpretant. Semeiotic, as the study of signs in the second sense, can be described as the theory of triadic action, of Thirdness. A sign that strictly fits this definition is called, in the detailed classification of signs, a *legisign*. To avoid getting too far ahead, however, I will in this section refer to the genuinely triadic legisign as a *Sign*. The Sign is ideal; it belongs to the category of Thirdness. The actual existent *signs* (with lower-case 's') we encounter belong primarily to the category of Secondness.

Peirce dealt with the distinction between the Sign and its existent vehicle in a variety of contexts and via several distinctions in terminology. Two of these sets of terminology are synonymous, and these will be presented here. A more complex account of the distinctions among various kinds of signs emerges in the classification of signs, in chapter 7.

One of Peirce's well-known distinctions is between *type* and *token*. Precisely synonymous to this is the distinction between a *Sign* and its *replicas*.[33] "[A] *sign* is not a real [i.e., existent] thing. It is of such a nature as to exist in *replicas*. Look down a printed page, and every *the* you see is the same word, every *e* the same letter" (NEM 4:238–39). A replica is the vehicle of a Sign. It is composed of ink, sound waves, or some other physical stuff. The replica or token is an individual physical thing which "embodies" the Sign or type. The Sign "has a real being, *consisting in* the fact that existents *will* conform to it" (CP 2.292). A replica is not essentially triadic, while the Sign is. A metal stop sign does not generate an interpretant without the law that caused it to be manufactured to certain specifications and placed at the intersection. A replica's status as a representamen or signifier is entirely derivative from the Sign that governs it; its status as an existent thing, however, may be conceived independently from its relation to the Sign. The stop sign certainly exists in its own right as a sheet of painted metal, even though its characteristics may have been originally specified in a law. Likewise, the Sign's status as a representamen is independent of its embodiment in any replica, even though it requires replicas to become an existent thing.[34]

What has been said so far applies to semiosis in its most perfect form. We have examined the theory of sign action as it applies to Signs, which are *essentially* triadic signs. With the introduction of the Sign-replica distinction, however, we enter upon a more complex area of semeiotic. Not all things capable of representing other things are essentially triadic. In the experienced world, semiosis involves a number of different kinds of signs, all interacting and operating in the three "universes" of Firstness, Secondness, and Thirdness. A systematic account of the possible kinds of signs will help us to keep our bearings.

CHAPTER 7

Logic Conceived as Semeiotic

The Classification of Signs

Peirce attempted the classification of signs several times, and a great deal of secondary literature has been devoted to explicating these classifications. Two of Peirce's classifications are of special interest. The first is from around 1903, and is by far the more clear of the two. The second is from 1908. It is more complex than the earlier classification, and its presentation (in private letters to Victoria Lady Welby) is incomplete.[1] The methodology in both cases is the same. Peirce distinguished the possible kinds of being that a sign's *object*, a sign's *interpretant*, and the *sign itself* (the *representamen*) may possess, according to whether each of these phanera is characterized primarily by Firstness, Secondness, or Thirdness.

The first approach obtains three trichotomies of classification according to the mode of being of the representamen, its relation to the object, and the nature of the object as represented in the interpretant. The second classification includes the division of objects into immediate and dynamical objects, and of interpretants into immediate, dynamical, and final interpretants. Peirce apparently intended to take into account the mode of being of each of these six components, as well as four relations of the sign: to its dynamical object, to its dynamical interpretant, to its final or normal interpretant, and to its dynamical object and normal interpretant taken together. The partial classification he outlined gives ten trichotomies of signs.[2]

Given the problems in interpretation that attend the second classification and the fact that it is essentially an incomplete elaboration of the earlier classification, we will focus attention on the 1903 classification.

> Signs are divisible by three trichotomies; first, according as the sign itself is a mere quality, is an actual existent, or is a general law; secondly, according as the relation of the sign to its object consists in the sign's having some character in itself, or in some existential relation to that object, or in its relation to an interpretant; thirdly, according as its Interpretant represents it as a sign of possibility or as a sign of fact or a sign of reason. (CP 2.243)

A quality or feeling (e.g., a characteristic color, sound, or taste) may serve to represent something other than itself. Such a representamen is a *qualisign.* A qualisign cannot act unless it is embodied, but the embodiment of a color—in glass or metal, for example—has nothing to do with the character of the color that suits it, potentially, to act as a sign (CP 2.244). A concrete existent thing or state of affairs (e.g., a footprint) that represents something other than itself is a *sinsign* (singular sign). A sinsign necessarily possesses certain characteristic qualities, and hence must involve qualisigns, but its being as an existent thing is something over and above these qualities (CP 2.245). A general type (e.g., a typical pattern of behavior such as a dog's cowering at loud noises, or a word considered apart from its replicas) that represents something other than itself is a *legisign.*

> The difference between a legisign and a qualisign, neither of which is an individual thing, is that a legisign has a definite identity, though usually admitting a great variety of appearances. Thus, &, *and,* and the sound are all one word. The qualisign, on the other hand, has no identity. It is the mere quality of an appearance and is not exactly the same throughout a second. Instead of identity, it has *great similarity,* and cannot differ much without being called quite another qualisign. (CP 8.334)

A legisign requires embodiment in a replica in order to signify, but the replica would be meaningless without the influence of the legisign. Each replica is a sinsign, which in turn involves qualisigns (CP 2.246). The physical world is populated with sinsigns, since these are the only *existent* kind of sign.

The relation of the representamen to its object may also be characterized predominantly by Firstness, Secondness, or Thirdness. An *icon* represents its object in virtue of possessing qualities or characteristics that resemble or duplicate those of the object (e.g., the arrangement and tones of color in a photo-realistic painting make it an icon of the original scene). "Anything whatever, be it quality, existent individual, or law, is an Icon of anything, in so far as it is like that thing and used as a sign of it" (CP 2.247).

An *index* represents its object in virtue of an existential connection between itself and the object (e.g., a fingerprint signifies the existence of a particular finger). An index is itself an existent thing, a sinsign, and is in some respect caused to be as it is by its object. "In so far as the Index is affected by the Object, it necessarily has some Quality in common with the Object, and it is in respect to these that it refers to the Object. It does, therefore, involve a sort of Icon" (CP 2.248). The fingerprint is like the finger in that it presents a reverse image of the ridges on the fingertip. Due to the existential determination of the index by its object, however, it is more than a mere icon of its object—a "swirled" fingerprint may be an icon of a hurricane, but not its index.

Finally, a *symbol* represents its object in virtue of a convention that governs how the symbol will be used. The only connection between the symbol and its object is that it *will* be associated with the object in an interpretant; it is "a law, or regularity of the indefinite future" (CP 2.293, 299). The only connection between the word "cat" and the animal to which it refers is that conventional English usage ensures that the word will tend to be used this way. Any sign that is related to its object in the manner of a symbol is itself a general type or law, and the only vehicle capable of bearing this kind of relation to an object is a legisign. Symbols, being legisigns, must act through existent replicas or sinsigns (CP 2.249).

The object of a sign may be represented to its interpretant as something that is characterized predominantly by Firstness, Secondness, or Thirdness (CP 2.250–53). A sign that represents its object as a feeling or quality (e.g., a laugh or bright smile expressing joy) is a *rheme*. A sign that represents its object as an existent state of affairs, as a particular fact (e.g., a proposition such as "the air temperature is 47°F") is a *dicent*. An *argument* represents its object as a general tendency, a law, or a disposition of things to operate in a certain way. An example is the statement "seatbelts save lives." What the argument expresses is a general rule, known by inductive inference.

Any sign involves some combination of object, representamen, and interpretant in one relation. If all combinations were possible, we would obtain twenty-seven classes of signs from the three trichotomies just outlined. However, not all combinations of object, representamen, and interpretant are possible. The nature of the object limits the kind of representamen that may possibly represent it, and the nature of the representamen limits the kind of object it may represent to an interpretant (CP 8.177). In short, there are rules limiting the combination of object, representamen, and interpretant: A *possible* can determine nothing but a *possible*, and a *general* can be determined by nothing but a *general*.[3]

The possible combinations of signs and their relations to their objects are presented in table 7.1, where impossible combinations are indicated with an 'X'.

Table 7.1 Relation of Sign to Object

		Representamen:		
		Qualisign	*Sinsign*	*Legisign*
Associated with Object by:	*Resemblance*	Icon	Icon	Icon
	Connection	X	Index	Index
	Convention	X	X	Argument

Table 7.2 summarizes the possible combinations of representamen and interpretant, with impossible combinations again indicated by an 'X'.

157

Table 7.2 Representation of the Object

		Representamen:		
		Qualisign	Sinsign	Legisign
	Quality	Rheme	Rheme	Rheme
Represents Object to Interpretant as:	Fact	X	Dicent	Dicent
	General	X	X	Argument

The limiting rules, that a possible can determine only a possible and a general can be determined only by a general, operate in the composition of the two classifications presented in tables 7.1 and 7.2. They function also in the composition of the a priori list of ten classes of signs that Peirce gives at CP 2.254–64. That list results from the combination of the two tables. An Icon can give rise only to a Rheme, and only a Symbol can give rise to an Argument. The ten classes of signs are presented in Table 7.3. Essential parts of the name of each class are italicized.

Table 7.3 Ten Classes of Signs

	I	II	III	IV
Representamen:	Qualisign	Sinsign	Sinsign	Sinsign
Assoc. with Object by:	Resemblance	Resemblance	Connection	Connection
Represents Object to interpretant as:	Quality	Quality	Quality	Fact
Class of sign:	Rhematic Iconic Qualisign	Rhematic Iconic Sinsign	Rhematic Indexical Sinsign	Dicent Indexical Sinsign

	V	VI	VII	VIII
Representamen:	Legisign	Legisign	Legisign	Legisign
Assoc. with Object by:	Resemblance	Connection	Connection	Convention
Represents Object to interpretant as:	Quality	Quality	Fact	Quality
Class of sign:	Rhematic Iconic Legisign	Rhematic Indexical Legisign	Dicent Indexical Legisign	Rhematic Symbol Legisign

	IX	X
Representamen:	Legisign	Legisign
Assoc. with Object by:	Convention	Convention
Represents Object to interpretant as:	Fact	General
Class of sign:	Dicent Symbol Legisign	Argument Symbolic Legisign

This much we can do by drawing upon "the principles and analogies of phenomenology," but the newcomer to the thicket of signs in Table 7.3 is likely to agree wholeheartedly with Peirce's statement that the a priori descriptions mean little (CP 2.233). Peirce offers examples of each of the ten classes, and it is in the a posteriori consideration of examples that the theory takes on life. The editors of the *Collected Papers* introduced examples, drawn from elsewhere in Peirce's writings, into the discussion of the ten classes of signs that appears at CP 2.254–63. A brief survey of these examples will provide a concrete illustration of the above classes. Undoubtedly it would be rewarding to consider the various ways one might classify one and the same sign, and to search for instances of signs that do not fit into the theoretical schema well at all. This would flesh out the a posteriori side of the inquiry, and it would likely suggest some revisions of the classification before us. Such an undertaking would be a massive effort, however, and would not directly contribute to our present task of explicating Peirce's thought. I have therefore contented myself with a list of the suggested examples:

I.	Qualisign	A feeling of 'redness,' conceived apart from the circumstances of its appearance
II.	Iconic Sinsign	An individual diagram, as a particular thing made of ink on paper
III.	Rhematic Indexical Sinsign	A spontaneous cry of pain, as a response to some stimulus
IV.	Dicent Sinsign	A weathervane
V.	Iconic Legisign	A diagram or design, conceived apart from its individual replicas
VI.	Rhematic Indexical Legisign	A demonstrative pronoun, such as 'this' or 'that'
VII.	Dicent Indexical Legisign	A street cry (abstracting from its replicas), such as 'Getcher paper here!'
VIII.	Rhematic Symbol	A common noun
IX.	Dicent Symbol	A proposition
X.	Argument	A syllogism

Note that while *any sign that actually signifies* is triadic, not all the classes of signs are such that they will actually signify on every occasion. Only the symbol is *necessarily* triadic. An index may be existentially connected to its object even if there is no interpretant that cognizes the connection. In such a case the index is only a potential sign, since it fails to signify in actuality. Likewise, an icon may resemble its object in some respects without functioning as a sign of that object.[4] The relation between a symbol and its object, however, is different. The connection here consists in the fact that an interpretant will arise that establishes the connection. Thus the symbol is the only genuinely (i.e., irreducibly) triadic sign. Potential icons and indices may exist without generating an interpretant. If a symbol comes into being, however, so does an interpretant of it. The symbol is thus the paradigmatic semeiotic entity.

There are two standpoints from which we may regard nonsymbols. Robert Marty has observed that a symbol "in itself" is a triadic relation, an irreducible relation among three phanera.[5] Likewise, we may conceive the index as a relation among two phanera, and the icon as a monadic phaneron. The index considered "in itself" is an existential relation among things; the icon is a portrayal of some quality or qualities. If we consider the various kinds of signs from this standpoint, they may become the objects of special study that would *not* be semeiotic as Peirce conceived it, the science of Thirdness. The first standpoint from which we may regard nonsymbols would consider them in themselves, as independently subsisting relations among phenomena. The logic of icons and the logic of indices, which Peirce included in his 1906 division of semeiotic, take just this view of signs. The second standpoint from which we may regard nonsymbols is the standpoint within semeiotic proper. Nonsymbols are then conceived as degenerate cases of symbols, as *incomplete* symbols, which may potentially enter into semeiosis but do not necessarily do so. Our main interest is in this latter standpoint, but a few words are in order concerning the logic of icons and the logic of indices.

Peirce said almost nothing about these areas of inquiry, but I think that we can identify what they would involve and even provide an example of each. Taking the easier case first, the logic of indices would study those things characterized by existential relations that make them suitable as representations of other things (their objects). The aim of the logic of indices would be to describe the principles by which one thing's existential connections to another may be discovered and legitimately interpreted. The logic of indices may be characterized as the science of particular connections. The sciences that treat of physical evidence explore things in this way, as potential signs of other particular things or states of affairs. The forensic branches of chemistry, medicine, and ballistics, for example, have strict procedures for investigating physical evidence. When followed, these procedures allow investigators to draw conclusions about the events that are connected with the physical evidence. The body of theory behind forensic science is a species of the general logic of indices.

The logic of icons, analogously, would treat of the relations among things that are associated not by physical connection but by shared qualities. Its aim would be to describe the principles by which one thing's qualitative associations with another may be discovered and legitimately interpreted. Artists are conspicuously concerned with the principles of legitimate association of qualities. Any painter must learn the tricks of the trade—dark colors are more "massive" than light colors, for example. The study of perspective in drawing and painting is another example of the logic of icons. The theory of perspective resulted from careful inquiry into the way that relative size and placement of an image could convey the sense of three-dimensional space in a two-dimensional medium. Nonperspectival painting has its own conventions, of course, and these, too, are iconic. A large image does not necessarily represent an object as "nearer," but perhaps as "more important." In medieval and Renaissance Europe, musical modes or "moods" (Doric, Ionian, etc.) were identified according to their emotional qualities. The musical system was integral to a logic of icons which directed, for example, that some musical modes were appropriate for joyous Psalms, and others were appropriate for more somber passages.

The logics of icons and indices explore nonsymbolic signs in themselves, and describe the principles by which they may be legitimately associated with their objects. The logic of indices might be used to show, for example, that a certain fingerprint is admissible in a court of law as evidence that a person touched a certain surface. This means that the fingerprint is a sign that is suited to be included in an argument for someone's guilt or innocence. This argument is a symbol. It is the purpose of a trial to generate such a symbol, and it is the purpose of the symbol to generate an interpretant: a verdict of guilty or not guilty. Likewise, the logic of icons might indicate to us that a sign has a quality that makes it suitable as a sign of a certain other quality—that "triumphant" music is suitable as a sign of Christ's triumph over death, for example. This means that it may be included in an Easter mass, a symbol of the Resurrection meant to generate an interpretant in the minds of worshippers. What becomes apparent here is that the logics of icons and indices study signs that do not attain their full significance when taken in isolation. For them to enter into the thought of the community and have any effect in the world, they must be incorporated with other signs into a complete symbol. The study of icons and indices is carried out for the sake of something else, for the sake of the growth of symbols. This brings us to the other standpoint from which nonsymbols may be regarded.

From the standpoint of semeiosis (the science of symbols or Thirdness), icons and indices are degenerate cases of genuine semeiotic entities (NEM 4:241–43). These classes of signs may remain merely potential, failing to generate an interpretant. In such cases, they never enter into thought and remain literally insignificant. If we aim to develop a theory of genuine semeiosis, our first concern must be with symbols. As we have seen, icons and indices *may* be incorporated into symbols. Semeiotic discovers that they *must* be so included, if a symbol ultimately is to refer to things in the world (CP 3.363). Accordingly, Peirce includes the logics of icons and indices as divisions of semeiotic in his mature philosophy.

Symbols are the proper subject matter of the science of Thirdness. As the classification of signs shows, though, a symbol can have only a legisign as its representamen. A system that consisted entirely of symbols and legisigns could represent any kind of object to an interpretant—symbolic legisigns may be rhemes, dicents, or arguments. But if the system is confined to conventional representations *of* qualities, things, and ideas *to* ideas, it is locked into a rather sterile form of idealism. Things and qualities would have status *only as represented*; their effects could only be effects on ideas. Peirce's semeiotic provides a more robust account of signs than this, however. Any legisign that actually functions in semeiosis must have an instantiation, which can only be a sinsign. Likewise, no sinsign can exist without embodying some qualities or other. A legisign hence requires sinsigns and qualisigns if it is to function in semeiosis at all. The paradigm of semeiosis is a system of ideas, of symbols, but the paradigm is not the whole picture. The ideal system of legisigns functions as a system that governs the production of its own replicas, in the field of existence. The continuum of legisigns and symbols, in other words, acts through final causation to bring into being a world of determinate qualities and existents which is its embodiment. The basic account of the phenomenological categories virtually requires just this result. Just as all three categories are always present in varying degrees of prominence in any phenomenon, all three forms of representamens (legisign, sinsign, qualisign) are always present in varying degrees of prominence in any sign. There is more to the semeiotic universe than ideas.

The same principle yields similar results when applied to the other components in the triadic analysis of sign. A pure symbol would be a vacuous thing without the icon and index. The purely symbolic statement "Cain killed Abel" cannot be understood unless the interpreter has some acquaintance with the subjects of the proposition—Cain, Abel, and Killing. To provide this acquaintance to someone who lacked it, we would need to provide an icon that shows the relation of Cain to Abel, "in so far as this relation was *imaginable* or imageable" (SS 70). Further, we would need an index to provide "the necessary acquaintance with any single thing," which full comprehension of the statement requires. Finally, "[t]o convey the idea of causing death in general," that is, to provide acquaintance with the subject *killing* (which is a general idea), we would need to use a symbol (SS 70). Without the introduction of icon, index, and symbol to acquaint one with the subjects in the statement, it must appear as an utterly meaningless series of sounds or marks. "Strictly pure Symbols can signify only things familiar, and those only in so far as they are familiar" (CP 4.544n.1). The point is that without icons and indices, we could not acquire knowledge of any things not presently before us and intuitively understood—and, given Peirce's objections to the notion of immediate intuition, perhaps not even of these. Icons and indices are then indispensable elements of any symbol.

The rheme and dicent have a similar constitutive role in the argument. An argument presents its object as a tendency of things to occur according to a general law. If we remove the generality (say, from the statement of the law of gravity) we have a dicent, a proposition about a particular object. If we remove the denotative parts of a proposition, we are left with a term or rheme, which makes no existential claim and is hence an expression of mere possibility (NEM 4:243–44). The interdependence is clear: Without a fund of rhemes or terms as possible subjects, there could be no proposition expressed in a dicent; without factual propositions, there could be no generalizations about existence.

Fig. 7.1 Internal Structure of a Complete Symbol

Relationship to Object	Representamen	Representation of Object
Symbol ———————	Legisign ———————	((Argument))
Index	Sinsign	(Dicent)
Icon	Qualisign	Rheme

Such are the constituent parts of a sign as an irreducibly triadic entity, as a symbolic legisign. The diagram of the internal structure of a complete symbol (figure 7.1) shows a complex interaction of components belonging to each of the three categories, in each of the three components of the representation relation. In figure 7.1, argument and dicent are in brackets to indicate that they may or may not be present in a given symbol. If the symbol is a dicent, it requires at least one rheme; if it is an argument, it requires at least one dicent as well. A very complex sign (such as a book or a trial) might well involve millions of signs, from each of the ten classes, as its constituent parts. An argument, Peirce writes, may involve almost *any* kind of sign as "enacting a rôle in it" (MS 640, p. 7). Clearly, a complete logic conceived as semeiotic must concern itself with a comprehensive theory of signs.

Signs and Mind

The classification of signs provides us with the "new elements" for a semeiotic model of phenomena. The ten classes of signs may be treated as a taxonomy of the relations that can occur in phenomena.[6] The qualisign is characterized by almost perfect Firstness, the dicent sinsign by almost perfect Secondness, and the argument by almost perfect Thirdness. The various other classes of signs indicate the other possible admixtures of the categories that might appear in a phaneron.

Peirce remarks that his conception of phaneron is similar to what the British empiricists mean by *idea*, except that "they have restricted the meaning of it too much to cover my conception . . . besides giving a psychological connotation to their word which I am careful to exclude" (CP 1.285).

Because Peirce defines *phaneron* as that which "is in any way or in any sense present to a mind, quite regardless of whether it corresponds to any real thing or not," we are naturally led to ask what Peirce's nonpsychological conception of mind is. Semeiotic provides the basis for Peirce's account of mind, and his frequent statements to the effect that an interpretant is the effect of a sign on a mind introduce only an apparent circularity in the definitions of sign and of mind. His comment that the reference to a mind in the definition of *sign* is "a sop to Cerberus, because I despair of making my own broader conception understood" suggests that the formulation might be better turned around (SS 81). The broader conception of *mind,* which Peirce sometimes calls "Quasi-mind" (CP 4.536), then includes anything capable of producing an interpretant of a sign.

Peirce does recognize and often discusses individual consciousness, of course, and it is crucial for us to understand the place of individual consciousness in his system. Briefly put, individual consciousness is primarily characterized by Firstness. The broader conception of mind, as anything capable of interpreting a sign, is primarily characterized by Thirdness. Individual consciousness may be prescinded from the broader conception of mind, but cannot be entirely dissociated from that broader conception. In other words, mind in the broader sense is logically prior to mind as individual consciousness, just as the whole system of signs is logically prior to any individual sign.

John Locke says that "Consciousness is the perception of what passes in a Man's own mind," and Thomas Reid defines it as "that immediate knowledge which we have of our present thoughts and purposes and, in general, of all the present operations of our minds".[7] The mind that is conscious in this sense may be described in Peirce's terms as the simple, immediate awareness of a phaneron. Abstaining from the psychological language of perception and sensation, consciousness can then be described as the awareness of a *quale*:

> There is a peculiar *quale* to *purple,* though it be only a mixture of red and blue. There is a distinctive *quale* to every combination of sensations so far as it is really synthesized—a distinctive *quale* to every work of art—a distinctive *quale* to this moment as it is to me—a distinctive *quale* to every day and every week—a peculiar *quale* to my whole personal consciousness. . . .
>
> Each *quale* is in itself what it is for itself, without reference to any other. (CP 6.223–24)

A quale, then, is characterized by Firstness, and "consciousness, so far as it can be contained in an instant of time, is an example of quale-consciousness" (CP 6.231). Clearly, though, consciousness cannot be *abso-*

lutely severed from past and future and conceived as occurring in a succession of discrete instants. Even in the discussion of perception it is necessary to introduce a temporal or processive dimension: "In a perceptual judgement the mind professes to tell the mind's future self what the character of the present percept is" (CP 7.630). Purely individual and isolated quale-consciousness is a psychological myth. The "individual consciousness" is a singularity discerned within a broader continuum of mind, just as an "individual point" is a topological singularity located in a geometrical continuum. We will return to the notion of individual consciousness once we explore the broader, semeiotic conception of mind.

On the broader conception, mind is conceived primarily as Thirdness: mind is anything capable of producing an interpretant. Recall that a sign may give rise to an emotional interpretant (a feeling), an energetic interpretant (a physical or mental reaction), or a logical interpretant (a rule expressed in habit). The only one of these that seems to *require* a conscious mind as the interpreter is the emotional interpretant (CP 5.492). There may be energetic or logical interpretants that are not associated with the thoughts of any individual human mind. Peirce indicated that our investigation of signs ought to take conscious mind as the paradigm of the interpreter, however, as we are most familiar with this kind of interpreter. The methodological hypothesis for semeiotic is that any interpreter is "a sufficiently close analogue of a modification of consciousness" that a theory developed on this model will adequately convey how other kinds of interpreters operate (CP 5.485).

How might a representamen be interpreted by something other than a human mind, then? The first possibility is that it will generate an energetic interpretant in another living thing. Peirce proposes the following situation in which a plant is a representamen, and its interpretant is another plant:

> [I]f a sunflower, in turning towards the sun, becomes by that very act fully capable, without further condition, of reproducing a sunflower which turns in precisely corresponding ways toward the sun, and of doing so with the same reproductive power, the sunflower would become a Representamen of the sun. (CP 2.274)

Clearly there is no conscious apprehension of the "meaning" of the first flower by the second flower; nonetheless, the processes that generate the second flower are describable in semeiotic terms. The first flower brings the second flower to stand in a relation to its object, the sun, which is similar to the first flower's own relation to the sun. Semiosis thus may occur in a biological system, without conscious thought. Consider also a second case, in which Peirce argues that patterns of deductive reasoning can be found functioning in the quasi-mind of a physical system:

> We all think of nature as syllogizing. Even the mechanical philosopher, who is as nominalistic as a scientific man can be, does that. The immutable mechanical law together with the laws of attraction and repulsion form the major premise, the instantaneous relative positions and velocities of all the particles whether it be "at the end of the sixth day of creation," . . . or whether it be at any other instant of time is the minor premise, the resulting accelerations form the conclusion. (NEM 4:344)

As a matter of fact, there is little thought involved in the production of *any* merely energetic interpretant. A conditioned response in a human subject is highly efficient because it does bypass the need for a conscious decision to act.

Nor is the logical interpretant an exclusively mental thing, in spite of its name. The ultimate logical interpretant of a sign is a habit, a general rule that governs future actions. The psychological account of an acquired habit is instructive in this respect. Suppose I have quit my job as an oilfield worker and am now working in a day care center. I wish to alter some of my habitual forms of expression. There are certain reasons that compel me to do this, and I may have to remind myself of them when I slip and address one of the children or a co-worker inappropriately. Others may help to remind me of the reasons: "Say that again and you're fired!" serves as a premise for an inference in *modus tollens*. I supply the other premise: I don't want to be fired. The conclusion is a rule, which is an *argument* (identified in table 7.3 as a class X sign) in Peirce's classification: I won't say that again. The simple pattern of reasoning, taken as a whole, is a sign that is summarized in the conclusion. Its logical interpretant is the rule as it operates in regulating my future speech. This habit, the ultimate or logical interpretant of the argument, is "by no means exclusively a mental fact" even though my first awareness of the rule that it embodies is conscious (CP 5.492). The habit is the means by which Thirdness reaches into the sphere of Secondness, the means by which an idea can affect the order of existence.

We need not refer to conscious mind in the general account of habit, then, but only in the account of the *formation* of some habits in the human sphere.[8] What is characteristic in the establishment of a habit is not that an element of consciousness be present, but that an element of Peircean "reasoning" be operative in arriving at a rule that affects subsequent events. The physical world indeed exhibits Peircean habits: "[W]e find that some plants take habits. The stream of water that wears a bed for itself is taking a habit. Every ditcher so thinks of it" (CP 5.492). The natural world can be frustratingly persistent in its habits, as any gardener or builder knows. The tendencies of physical nature can be modified to our purposes, but only with great effort and not permanently. The deeply established habits known as "physical laws," gravity and the rest, eventually win out.

Thus, although some kind of sentient mind may be necessary for producing an emotional interpretant of a sign, energetic and logical interpretants may arise in nonmental systems. This suggests that semeiosis is a very wide-ranging process indeed. Peirce makes the implications explicit in the following passage from 1906:

> Thought is not necessarily connected with a brain. It appears in the work of bees, of crystals, and throughout the purely physical world; and one can no more deny that it is really there, than that the colors, the shapes, etc., of objects are really there. . . . Not only is thought in the organic world, but it develops there. But as there cannot be a General without Instances embodying it, so there cannot be thought without Signs. We must here give "Sign" a very wide sense, no doubt, but not too wide a sense to come within our definition. Admitting that connected Signs must have a Quasi-mind, it may further be declared that there can be no isolated sign. Moreover, signs require at least two Quasi-minds; a *Quasi-utterer* and a *Quasi-interpreter*; and although these two are at one (*i.e., are* one mind) in the sign itself, they must nevertheless be distinct. In the Sign they are, so to say, *welded.* (CP 4.551)

The Quasi-mind required for semiosis is part of a law-governed physical, chemical, or biological system. Semiosis is a model of the process of growth or development in general, and is conceived on the model of true continuity, as the above passage makes clear. The Quasi-utterer and the Quasi-interpreter are one mind in the sign, yet are distinct. They are, Peirce says, "welded" in the sign. This is exactly the same image he often uses to describe the relation of immediately connected parts of a continuum. What we identify as individual consciousness, or quale-consciousness, is but an artificially isolated fragment of a broader system: "just as we say that a body is in motion, and not that motion is in a body we ought to say that we are in thought and not that thoughts are in us" (CP 5.289n.1). Individual immediate consciousness is a hypothetical construct, a mind composed entirely of qualisigns. As our discussion of the relations among the various classes of signs shows, however, qualisigns are ultimately part of the much more complex semiotic system that is the developing universe in its aspect as a sign.

The elements of semeiotic allow us to describe the world as a living continuum of symbols.[9] It generates its own interpretants, thereby extending the process into the infinite future. As a system of symbols, it requires icons and indices in its constitution: Firstness, Secondness, and Thirdness are all essential to the system. The element of Firstness appears as a world of pure possibility, embodied in qualisigns. The element of Secondness appears as *haecceity,* or the principle of existence, and is embodied in sinsigns. The governing principle of a semiotic flow is Thirdness, continuity, the incorporation of signs generated by other semeiotic processes into ever more comprehensive symbols, or legisigns. Secondness functions both to actualize and to limit the world of possibility: "individual existence depends upon the principle that not all that is possible is possible in conjunction. But existence is continuous as far as the nature of the case admits. At every point of it, it reunites all qualities each in some degree" (MS 942, pp. 13–14).

The natural *telos* of a semiotic system is the realization of a perfect symbol, a symbol of the Truth, a complete representation of the dynamical object of all signs. Such a perfect symbol would embody in itself all the icons and indices that are required for its explanation. Each component of the complete symbol would have some other part of the symbol as its object, making the sign, effectively, a sign of itself (CP 2.230). Stecheotic provides the "new elements" for an account of the universe as an argument, "a vast representamen, a great symbol of God's purpose, working out its conclusions in living realities" (CP 5.119). The final interpretant of any sign is some aspect of the vast truth that would be the conclusion of this cosmic argument. That vast truth would be the completely rational, habit-governed universe, conceived in its aspect as a sign.

"[T]here is in the being of things something which corresponds to the process of reasoning . . . the world *lives*, and *moves*, and *has its being*, in a logic of events" (NEM 4:344). Since the universe can be conceived as a vast argument, and since we are a part of that universe and can affect its course of development, we are bound by the self-interest that is at the root of all action to reason well. When we act, we contribute to the argument, and good reasoning can enable our actions to better conform to the ideal of the summum bonum. With this, our discussion of stecheotic comes to an end. The elements for a semiotic conception of phenomena are before us, and we now turn to the normative branches of semeiotic: critic and methodeutic.

Logical Critic

The most comprehensive sign is the argument, and as figure 7.1 shows, the complete argument involves signs of every other form. Only the argument is capable of representing an object as a general law. It is thus the most powerful kind of sign, the only one capable of communicating the content of a complete process of thought. All forms of representation, all phenomena, may ultimately be assimilated to arguments. Additionally, since the argument represents a rule capable of determining habits, the argument is the form of symbol through which all other phenomena may realize their ultimate meaning. Note that an argument in this sense need not be expressed in syllogistic or symbolic form: "An 'Argument' is any process of thought reasonably tending to produce a definite belief. An 'Argumentation' is an Argument proceeding upon definitely formulated premisses" (CP 6.456).

The second branch of semeiotic, logical critic, "classifies arguments and determines the validity and the degree of strength of each kind" (CP 1.191). Critic investigates the relation of arguments to their proper object, the Truth. It describes the processes by which the truth may come to be represented.

Peirce spent much of his adult life exploring the nuts and bolts of valid inference, and it is no exaggeration to say that volumes of his writings are pertinent to critic. This section presents only an overview, based primarily on two documents that were intended to summarize his understanding of critic. Both are somewhat less technical than other presentations, having been written for persons who were neither experts in logic nor familiar with Peirce's philosophy. The first is the draft of the 1902 application for aid to the Carnegie Institution (NEM 4:13–73). The second is the draft of a long letter to J. H. Kehler dated 22 June 1911 (NEM 3:159–210).[10]

In the Carnegie Application Peirce proposed seven memoirs concerning logical critic. The first of this group, Number 20 in the whole series, is described only as a discussion of "the nature, division, and method of critical logic" (NEM 4:24). Though he gives no further details, we can infer what Peirce's conception of critic is, based on its location in the architectonic and his comments elsewhere. Esthetics and ethics inform us that the constructive process of inquiry into truth is the highest aim of thought and action; stecheotic provides the elements for a detailed semeiotic account of thought and action. The aim of logical critic is to identify the forms of inference that can represent the truth, so they can be deliberately adopted in thought. Critic investigates the principles that lead to valid interpretations of anything that may be taken as a sign contributing to an argument.

Critic classifies arguments according to their leading principles. In his mature philosophy, Peirce retained the classification of arguments he first published in "On the Natural Classification of Arguments" and "On a New List of Categories," in 1867 (NEM 4:22). Peirce identified three basic forms of inference: *deduction, induction* (or *adduction*), and *retroduction* (or *abduction*).[11] Throughout his career he maintained the view that any argument belongs to one of these three forms, or is a mixed argument incorporating more than one form.

Memoir 21 was to be titled "Of First Premisses," and its main point would have been to outline the theory of perceptual judgments (NEM 4:24, 4:57). We have discussed Peirce's account of perceptual judgments in chapter 1, and will here note only its most obvious implications. The theory rejects absolute foundations, whether of the Cartesian rationalist sort or of the British empiricist sort. We have no clear, distinct, and apodictic ideas with which to commence inquiry; nor do we have any indubitable, ultimate "sense impressions." The perceptual judgment is the acritical limit-case of retroduction. It is a representation of some aspects of the world, which may serve not as an *indubitable* foundation for thought, but as an *undoubted* starting point for thought in particular circumstances. If we entertain doubts about the veracity of something perceived, we may carry out more careful observations until we reach a percept that we do *not* doubt. There will always be some point at which we cannot help but accept what appears: We will sooner or later reach a compelling perceptual judgment. It is characterized by the very fact that our acceptance of it cannot be controlled, which puts it beyond the sphere of critic. It is nonetheless a representation, not an elemental sense impression. It is an interpretation of the world delivered by the senses.

The fact that what appears evident must be acritically accepted also limits what critic has to say concerning the basis of deductive inference. The sketch of Memoir 22, "The Logic of Chance," indicates that where there can be no judgment about the truth of a conclusion there is no role for critic. Peirce's work on formal algebraic and graphical systems for deduction may have shown him what is well known today: A symbolic system for deductive logic eliminates the need for judgment in deciding whether a conclusion validly follows stated premises.

The only judgment necessary in a formal deductive system is the simple judgment whether the system's well-defined rules have been followed, and this decision procedure can be reduced to a mechanical process of elimination: It can, in fact, be carried out by a machine. "Deduction, as such, is not amenable to critic; for it is necessary reasoning, and as such renders its conclusion evident. Now it is idle to seek any justification of what is evident. It cannot be rendered more than evident" (NEM 4:59, cf. 4:69). As concerns necessary deduction, then, the task of critic is largely the descriptive task of identifying valid deductive forms. In the 1902 "Minute Logic," Peirce wrote that in his discussion of critic he would "endeavor to include every form of necessary reasoning known to me. . . . I need hardly say that ordinary syllogistic will be but a small fraction of my doctrine. The main substance of that need hardly fill a page" (CP 2.100). In the Carnegie Application, Peirce noted that critic does also "treat of meaningless and absurd terms, of irrelevant definitions, of fallacious definitions, and of probable deductions."[12] In addition to identifying valid deductive forms, then, critic is also concerned to identify common sources of error in necessary deduction. Probable deduction, the last item just mentioned, is discussed more fully later.

The main concern of critic is with the principles of probable inference, which can yield only an approximate representation of the truth. The great importance of sound principles of inference is that they allow such approximations to be refined indefinitely. An individual probable inference will often be quite wrong, but Peirce maintained that by adhering to the proper *principles* of inference such errors must eventually be overcome. Inaccurate induction can be improved by doing further inductions. Deduction has a place in the pattern of self-correcting inquiry that is outlined in critic, of course, but the acceptance of deductive conclusions per se is not subject to our control.

The bulk of Memoir 22 was to present Peirce's theory of probability, which is crucial to his account of induction and the self-correcting method of inquiry. He describes the theory at some length in his letter to Kehler, and defines the central notions as follows:

> The *probability* that if an antecedent condition is satisfied, a consequent kind of event will take place is the quotient of the number of occasions, "in the long run," in which both the antecedent will be satisfied and the consequent kind of event will take place, divided by the total number of occasions on which the antecedent conditions will be satisfied. (NEM 3:174)

The crucial qualification in this definition is that it is only applicable *in the long run,* by which Peirce means an endless succession of occasions—no one of which has any effect on the outcome of any other—taken in the order in which they occur (NEM 3:173). For any finite number of samples, of course, a *frequency ratio* can be calculated, but there is no assurance that it closely approximates the *objective probability,* the ratio that would emerge in taking an infinite number of samples. This is no problem for the *definition* of probability, but it does restrict our ability to *discover* a probability value through the limited tools of induction. The principle of objective probability only says that where there is a probability, it consists in the tendency of the calculated ratio to converge on a determinate value over the infinite long run. "But, of course, it is only in fictitious cases that we ever know the *exact* value of a probability, and we rarely know one nearer than to the nearest *per cent*" (NEM 3:186).

Memoir 23, "On the Validity of Induction," was to address the problem just noted. Peirce defines induction as "that kind of reasoning which from what is true of a part, concludes what is true of a whole" (NEM 3:182). Objective probability has to do with *what would be true* of an infinite number of samples. The probability of my drawing a blue marble out of a particular bag, for example, is defined as the value to which an infinite series of frequency ratios would be found to converge. Induction concerns *what may be inferred to be true* of a whole from a limited number of samples of its parts, and its most sophisticated form is *quantitative induction,* expressed in the statistical syllogism. Suppose I wish to determine the number of blue marbles in a box of 500. I draw out 50 marbles at random, and find that 12 of these are blue. The leading principle of induction tells us that "presumably and provisionally, until further evidence is obtained," we ought to suppose that approximately 12/50, or 120 marbles in the box, are blue (NEM 3:197).

Logical critic asks *why* we ought to suppose this. It is certainly not because we suppose that one sample gives us good reason to think that there are between, say, 117 and 123 blue marbles in the box. Nor is it because we suppose that this inference has revealed a "natural law" that governs the distribution of blue marbles in the world.[13] We accept the conclusion because of the method that makes the inference possible. It embodies all aspects of the definition of objective probability, except that the series of ratios in an induction can never actually be infinite. The sample is chosen at random and examined for a feature (the incidence of blue marbles) specified ahead of time. The ratio of *occurrences* of the feature to the total number of *possibilities* for it to occur is calculated in the same way. The manner of choosing a sample parallels the randomness involved in the infinite approach to the objective probability value. The procedure can in principle be repeated as many times as needed. With successive samples, we begin to construct a series of frequency ratios for our feature of interest. The higher the number of samples that give something near to a 12/50 ratio, the better we feel about the conclusion.

Even this, however, is not enough to validate the inductive procedure, for it is just possible that we could draw a radically unrepresentative sample five hundred or even five thousand times running. What is decisive is that the procedure could *in principle* be extended into the indefinite future, resulting in an infinite series of frequency ratios that would actually define the objective probability for occurrence of that feature. The method, if persisted in indefinitely, *would* give the true answer, and this is the only method of inference about which this can be said. "Quantitative Induction always makes a gradual approach to the truth, though not a uniform approach" (CP 2.770).

If we conceive the sampling procedure as being carried out by an infinite community of inquirers, the method appears destined to arrive at the truth. Note that the definition of probability postulates an infinite series of frequency ratios, which can be conceived as the result of a continuous, infinite sampling process (NEM 3:174). As a process of sampling is extended into the indefinite future, the quantitative induction becomes more and more accurate. But the possibility of radical error is always there, as long as the number of samples is finite. Quantitative induction is an assured approach to truth only if it is conceived as a part of a process of continuous inquiry. Individual samples are logically insignificant, except when viewed as infinitesimal parts of such a process—they have meaning only as constituent parts of the ideally projected infinite series. The whole series of potential inferences is logically presupposed in ensuring the validity of any single inference. The individual sample and inference would be next to meaningless by themselves.

With this account of quantitative induction before us, we may deal with a potentially confusing point concerning deduction. Peirce identifies two forms of deduction, *necessary deduction* and *probable deduction*. All deductions, of course, are necessary reasonings. A probable deduction is simply a necessary reasoning about probabilities; a necessary deduction is one that can be expressed using categorical propositions. Probable deduction is similar in many respects to quantitative induction. The difference is that deduction establishes nothing new in its conclusion, while induction does.[14] Whereas the inductive procedure allows us to infer an approximate probability based on samples, probable deduction allows us to infer the character of a sample based on prior knowledge of objective probability. Thus if we *put* 120 blue marbles in a box with 380 others, probable deduction tells us that approximately 12 out of a randomly drawn sample of 50 will be blue. Statistical functions allow us to calculate the margin of error for any such sample (NEM 3:194–95). If a probable deduction is stated as a syllogism, with probability expressed as a percentage, the corresponding form of quantitative induction results from interchanging the major premiss and the conclusion:

PROBABLE DEDUCTION	QUANTITATIVE INDUCTION
I. n% of A are B	III. n% of x, y, z (etc.) are B
II. x, y, z (etc.) are A	II. x, y, z (etc.) are A
III. n% of x, y, z (etc.) are B	I. n% of A are B

Peirce says that quantitative induction, expressed in the statistical syllogism, is by far the most powerful form of induction (NEM 3:183). There are, however, two other forms of induction. The first is rudimentary or *crude induction,* which merely infers that a general rule holds good universally on the basis of common experience. If all the swans we have encountered are white, it is a sensible crude induction to infer that there are no black swans. This inference relies merely on the absence of contrary instances in our experience. It is based on the "pooh-pooh argument," which gets its name from the response that greets an unsupported objection to the argument's conclusion (CP 7.111). If we could, for example, say to an eighteenth-century European ornithologist, "There *are* black swans somewhere," the reply might be something like "Pooh-pooh, nobody's ever seen one." The crude induction is a variation of a standard necessary deduction, which involves a universal proposition rather than a statistical proposition (NEM 3:193). In this case, we again interchange the major premiss and the conclusion:

NECESSARY DEDUCTION	CRUDE INDUCTION
I. All A are B	III. x, y, z (etc.) are B
II. x, y, z (etc.) are A	II. x, y, z (etc.) are A
III. x, y, z (etc.) are B	I. All A are B

The difference between Crude Induction and Quantitative induction is clearly not formal, as they have exactly the same structure and leading principle. Each infers to a general rule from a number of "samples." The difference is in *method.* In crude induction, the samples are not selected by truly random sampling. They are chosen because we happen to notice them in everyday experience. Moreover, the character that is predicated of the class in the general rule is not specified for investigation ahead of time, but only *after* and *because* a number of sample cases exhibiting that character have been noted. In a quantitative induction, the character in which we are interested is one that we have some antecedent reason for investigating. The inductive procedure is initiated so as to test our hypothesis about that character. In crude induction, the character of interest is selected by the very fact that it has appeared in some unscientifically chosen samples. Crude induction is a natural part of everyday life, providing us with "rules of thumb" that are immensely important for getting on in the world. It is the basis for most categorical assertions. It is not, however, a reliable guide to knowledge about the real nature of the world.

The third category of induction is *qualitative induction*. Like the others, it may be presented as a variation of the deductive syllogism:

NECESSARY DEDUCTION	QUALITATIVE INDUCTION
I. All A are B	I. All A are B
II. x, y, z (etc.) are A	III. x, y, z (etc.) are B
III. x, y, z (etc.) are B	II. x, y, z (etc.) are A

Reversing the position of the second and third propositions leaves us with a syllogism that is fallacious as a deductive argument, but which may be a legitimate probable inference. The qualitative induction is formally different from the crude and quantitative varieties, and in fact has the same form as retroduction or hypothesis formation (see chapter 1 and NEM 3:203–6). Both qualitative induction and retroduction proceed by noting that a thing has certain qualities, which a known general rule indicates are characteristic of some class. The conclusion asserts that the thing in question is a member of that class. The difference between qualitative induction and retroduction will be addressed in what follows.

Retroduction was to be the subject of Memoir 24, following the memoir on induction (NEM 4:25). Peirce's example of retroduction in the letter to Kehler is the thought of a child who, walking alone at night, sees a menacing object. The unknown thing has a dreadfulness that he knows would be characteristic of a bear, and he concludes that the thing *is* a bear. There is no justification for this hypothesis other than the shared quality (dreadfulness) of the thing and members of the class of bears (NEM 3:204–5). This is a mere iconic relation, and it moreover exhibits the common formal fallacy of affirming the consequent. But it is only by such speculative associations, Peirce says, that we ever find the starting point for a new line of inquiry. "I consider Retroduction . . . to be the most important kind of reasoning, notwithstanding its very unreliable nature, because it is the only kind of reasoning that opens up new ground" (NEM 3:206). The thing might, after all, really *be* a bear! If so, there is no sense in objecting to the formal fallacy involved in the inference that led the child to suppose it *might* be a bear. The logic of hypothesis-formation can give no assurance of the validity of its conclusions, though it is in fact surprisingly effective. Peirce suggests that this effectiveness is due to retroduction's being "the side of human intellect that is exposed to influence from on high" (NEM 3:206).

It is easy to overlook Peirce's claim that there is indeed a difference between qualitative induction and retroduction. Nicholas Rescher, for example, asserts that *abduction* is the process by which hypotheses are generated (which is correct), but then distinguishes this from *retroduction,* which he claims is the process of testing the hypotheses one has generated. He then asserts that *qualitative induction* is the name for the process of hypothesis generation and testing, involving both abduction and retroduction as Rescher conceives them.[15] According to the account in Peirce's letter to Kehler, though, this cannot be right. Abduction and retroduction are two names for the same thing: the speculative process of generating hypotheses. The hypotheses thus generated are extended by qualitative induction, and tested by quantitative induction. Retroduction is a one-time affair in a specific line of inquiry: it provides the starting point for thought.

Qualitative induction, though formally the same as retroduction, can in principle be repeated in order to discover more about a given object. The difference between retroduction and qualitative induction concerns the nature of the assurance we have in the conclusion. Peirce brings out the difference in his discussion of the child's "bear hypothesis":

> Now Adduction is the very coolest of all classes of Reasonings; for its conclusion is accepted provisionally *because* if it deceives us we have only to persist in the same kind of reasoning to be undeceived. Retroduction on the other hand is the most impulsive of reasonings. There is really *no* reason to accept the conclusion except that *we cannot help it* or in its least impulsive form feel that it is the natural, the reasonable, the Human way of thinking. If the child after his first fright begins to look closer and compare the looks of the object before him with the way a bear would look, he is no longer merely *conjecturing*; he is adducing new qualities. (NEM 3:205)

Retroduction compels us to suppose that thing A might be a B; qualitative induction is a process by which other pertinent qualities are identified in A that are similar to the qualities of B's. The former inference is characteristic of a flash of insight that convinces the inquirer that it *must* be so; the latter process is characteristic of the part of inquiry in which evidence is adduced to strengthen a hypothesis.

Peirce summarizes his whole theory of Critic by sketching the relations among the forms of inference:

With [retroduction] investigation starts. Having once formed a conjecture, the first thing to be done is to draw Deductions from it and compare them with observation. So we correct the errors of our Retroductions by processes of Adduction.

So Retroduction comes first and is the least certain and least complex kind of Reasoning.

Deduction follows. It is as certain as are its premisses and no more so.

Finally Adduction ranges in complexity from a simple Crude Adduction up to elaborate Quantitative Adductions which offer new material for Retroductions. (NEM 3:206–7; also 203)

Quantitative induction can provide very specific information about the laws governing events in the universe (which are thus often referred to as "statistical laws"). When this information is surprising, an explanation is needed, and retroduction commences its work again (NEM 4:25). Inquiry proceeds in this pattern indefinitely, constantly producing new hypotheses about the world and opening new areas for inquiry.

Methodeutic

In a draft of his proposal for Memoir 27, "Of Methodeutic," Peirce writes:

In methodeutic, it is assumed that the signs considered will conform to the conditions of critic, and be true. But just as critical logic inquires whether and how a sign conforms to its intended *ultimate* object, the reality; so methodeutic looks to the purposed *ultimate* interpretant and inquires what conditions a sign must conform to, in order to be pertinent to the purpose. (NEM 4:62)

It is not enough for inquiry that an argument represent the truth. There is always in principle an overabundance of true symbols at our disposal, and some are more relevant to an inquiry than others. We must somehow decide which of these to attend to in carrying out a particular course of inquiry. The proper goal of any inquiry is to contribute to the summum bonum, the development of a deliberate and self-controlled system of thought and action. The purpose of any inquiry ought then to be the settling of doubt by developing arguments whose ultimate interpretants (habits) lead to greater reasonableness in the world. Methodeutic outlines the principles for conducting such an inquiry.

In the Carnegie Application, Peirce described seven memoirs, Numbers 27 through 33, which would provide an account of methodeutic. Memoir 27, from which the earlier passage is taken, is simply an overview of methodeutic. Number 28 is "On the Economics of Research." Numbers 29 through 31 were to present Peirce's philosophy of science, his principles for the organization of inquiry. The last two memoirs on methodeutic concern the significance of inquiry in life. Number 32, "On Definition and the Clearness of Ideas" was to present perhaps the best-known aspect of Peirce's whole philosophical system, the pragmatic maxim for ascertaining the meaning of an idea. Number 33, "On Objective Logic," was to deal with the place of ideas and inquiry in the world at large, and would have opened the way to metaphysical inquiry.[16]

There is no space here to give a detailed account of these aspects of Peirce's system. There is a wealth of secondary material dealing with Peirce's philosophy of science and with the principle of pragmatism. There is somewhat less material available concerning his view of the objective status of logical inquiry in the constitution of the world, though any work on Peirce's metaphysics must at least touch upon this matter. There is very little on his theory of the economy of research, though Peirce is recognized as the first person to have explicitly applied economic principles to the problem of organizing research programs.[17] What follows is a brief presentation of aspects of Peirce's methodeutic that pertain to his conception of inquiry as a semeiotic process aimed at realizing the summum bonum.

THE ECONOMY OF RESEARCH

The economy of research is an important component of any theory of inquiry, because inquiry is a social affair. The material support for research must usually be provided by someone other than the individual researchers themselves, and the results of research eventually become the cultural possession of the society as a whole. In allocating resources for research, priorities must be set. The economy of research investigates how to set these priorities rationally.

Peirce was much impressed by the application of mathematical tools to the analysis of political economy, and especially by the pioneering work of David Ricardo.[18] The basic problems of economics have analogues in scientific research:

> The doctrine of economy, in general, treats of the relations between utility and cost. The branch of it which relates to research considers the relations between the utility and the cost of diminishing the probable error of our knowledge. Its main problem is how with a given expenditure of money, time, and energy, to obtain the most valuable addition to our knowledge. (W 4:72)

In the economy of research, knowledge takes the place of honor occupied by material commodities in political economy. Peirce notes that there is very little hope of accurately defining incremental units for measuring an "amount of knowledge," but insists that it is possible "to attach a definite conception to one increment of knowledge being greater than another" (NEM 4:26). All that is needed for the economy of research is this relative scale, by which proposed additions to knowledge can be weighed against one another.

The costs and utilities considered in the economy of research are then the relative costs and utilities of acquiring knowledge. While *costs* are certainly to be measured in terms of money and time expended in investigation, by *utility* Peirce means utility to the scientific community, rather than to society as a whole (NEM 4:27). An increase in knowledge is valuable if it advances knowledge; the value of its practical applications are normally secondary and are usually to be excluded from consideration in the economy of research. The cost and utility of a given piece of information about the world must be considered both on the side of *attaining* the knowledge, and of *diffusing* or disseminating the knowledge. The laws governing these costs and utilities are markedly different from those attending the exchange of material goods, which makes the economy of research a distinct area of inquiry. It is a commonplace, for example, that a material commodity in extreme oversupply reaches a point at which it cannot be *given* away. It is difficult to conceive of an analogous situation with knowledge of astronomy or geology, for example, for even a minuscule increase in knowledge may be of great utility to the community of inquiry.

The economy of research has the greatest application in helping the community of inquirers to choose which among alternative hypotheses they ought to investigate. When a hypothesis arises as the result of retroduction, there is very little to support its truth. Logic itself provides little guidance. "Any hypothesis which explains the facts is justified critically" (NEM 4:62). We can in principle provide an infinite number of hypotheses that would explain any given set of facts, though most would seem fantastic. The point of inquiry is to test *likely* hypotheses, by deducing their consequences and then designing an experiment that will allow us to determine, through induction, whether those consequences in fact obtain in experience. Thus a hypothesis must first of all appear "likely." This is largely a matter of the "feel" of the explanation, of its appeal to what Galileo called *il lume natural* (CP 6.477).

Peirce described this appeal less as a matter of the logical simplicity of the proposed explanation than of what is sometimes called its "elegance." The second character of a good hypothesis is what Karl Popper has called its *falsifiability*.[19] Peirce says that "among justifiable hypotheses we have to select that one which is suitable for being tested by experiment" (NEM 4:62). A hypothesis whose consequences are easily tested ought to be investigated before one whose consequences are difficult to state or to observe, even if the simpler hypothesis seems less likely to be true. "[P]refer the hypothesis which if false can easily be proved to be so; if it can be very easily dispatched, adopt it at once, and have done with it" (NEM 4:63–64). New areas of inquiry ought to be opened up whenever possible, as new areas tend to make rapid progress at little cost (NEM 4:29). The point of the economy of research is to make the most effective use of available resources to enlarge our knowledge about the world.

THE PHILOSOPHY OF SCIENCE

The memoirs on the philosophy of science—"On the Course of Research," "On Systems of Doctrine," and "On Classification"—were to outline the principles for organizing research. Peirce provides scant descriptions of these memoirs, and does not elsewhere seem to have devoted much attention to the subject matter of the first two.[20] The third memoir was to present his theory of classification, which was discussed in chapter 2. The classification of the sciences would no doubt have been the centerpiece of this memoir, though as we have seen, the principles of classification to be presented in the memoir would have been applicable to all objects of study.

In the memoir "On the Course of Research," Peirce proposed to survey virtually all the sciences so as to describe "a general rational course of inquiry" (NEM 4:29). This would apparently have gone beyond an account of the logical relations among abduction, deduction, and induction described in Stecheotic and Critic, to provide practical guidelines for determining the kinds of hypotheses to be investigated and the manner of designing experiments in various disciplines. The memoir "On Systems of Doctrine" would apparently have dealt with the manner in which the results of inquiry ought to be presented so as to constitute a rational system.

The conception of science that underlies this approach is worth noting. Science is conceived as an ongoing process of research that gradually fills in the details of coherent systems of knowledge. Though Peirce was explicitly committed to the view that no discipline can ever be *completed,* he had faith that systems of knowledge may *approach* completion over the very long run. Once a discipline has been established, it progresses by what Thomas Kuhn, in *The Structure of Scientific Revolutions,* calls "normal science":[21]

> [S]cience does not advance by revolutions, warfare, and cataclysms, but by coöperation, by each researcher's taking advantage of his predecessors' achievements, and by joining his own work in one continuous piece to that already done. (CP 2.157)

This view of science (which Rescher calls the "cumulative-convergence view") was typical at the end of the nineteenth century.[22] Most people supposed that physicists, for example, would occupy themselves indefinitely with working out the fine points of Newtonian mechanics. The other sciences sought to emulate the perceived success of physics in this regard. (Many still do, in spite of the revolutions that have since made physics appear rather incomplete in its knowledge of the world.)

It is peculiar, however, to find Peirce promoting this conception of science. He was himself witness to what today are seen as significant revolutions in scientific thought. He saw Kuhnian "paradigm shifts" firsthand in a number of disciplines. As a young man, he absorbed the full intellectual impact of the new theories of evolution proposed by Darwin, Lamarck, and others—at a time when he had been studying with the foremost nonevolutionary biologist in America, Louis Agassiz. He followed the development of non-Euclidean geometries and was aware of their implications for the conception of physical space. He was closely involved in the development of set theory, and especially its application to transfinite sets, which showed for the first time that it is possible to reason with mathematical rigor about infinity. And he was at the forefront of the development of the logic of relatives, the new symbolic logic that displaced the Aristotelian paradigm which had stood in the West for well over two thousand years.

All of these developments were far from what philosophers today would consider "normal science," yet Peirce apparently did not consider them exceptional or "revolutionary." The key to Peirce's attitude is his view of the scientific attitude and its central doctrine, *fallibilism*.[23] Because no finite inquiry can adequately approach truth, but with luck only approximate it, and because there is no way except through the indefinite continuation of inquiry to determine whether current theories do approximately describe reality, the scientist must accept the ever-present possibility that our current knowledge is mistaken. It is assuredly incomplete and mistaken in minor respects; moreover, it may very well be entirely wrongheaded no matter how well it seems to accord with experience. "Our perversity and that of others may indefinitely postpone the settlement of opinion [on the truth]; it might even conceivably cause an arbitrary proposition to be universally accepted as long as the human race should last" (W 3:274). There is no way to eliminate the possibility of radical error. Peirce therefore asserted that "[t]he scientific man is not in the least wedded to his conclusions. He risks nothing upon them. He stands ready to abandon one or all as soon as experience opposes them" (CP 1.634).

Peirce's definition of probability as the frequency ratio that *would* emerge at the end of infinite sampling for a character, and his view that the confirmation of hypotheses can come only through finite induction procedures, combine to make the principle of fallibilism a necessary part of any scientific inquiry. "Revolutions" in scientific thought are not shocking when seen from Peirce's infinitely long-range scientific perspective. They are the natural and expected adjustments that must arise in the cumulative-convergence theory of science. "Revolutions," in short, are a normal and expected part of science, and arise whenever a particularly novel hypothesis abducts ongoing inquiry and takes it on a new course.

INQUIRY IN THE WORLD

The memoir "On the Definition and Clearness of Ideas" was to present the principles by which ideas, the fruit of inquiry, are known. Peirce wrote that the proposed memoir would be a "more accurate" statement of the pragmatic maxim he had published in the 1878 article "How to Make Our Ideas Clear." With a sardonic nod to Descartes, Peirce identified three "grades of clearness" of ideas in that article. "A clear idea is defined as one which is so apprehended that it will be recognized wherever it is met with, and so that no other will be mistaken for it" (W 3:258). This first grade of clearness consists in familiarity with the common uses of a term or nature of an idea (W 3:271). "Iron," for example, names that heavy, malleable metal that is easily distinguished from aluminum or bronze. "A distinct idea is defined as one which contains nothing which is not clear. This is technical language; by the *contents* of an idea logicians understand whatever is contained in its definition. So that an idea is *distinctly* apprehended, according to them, when we can give a precise definition of it, in abstract terms" (W 3:258). This second grade of clearness consists in the technical, abstract definition of an idea. Any chemistry textbook provides such a definition for iron, in terms of its physical and chemical properties and its atomic structure.

Peirce noted that most logicians recognize no higher grade of clearness of an idea than familiarity and definition, but insisted that "a more perfect clearness of thought" exists than these. Indeed, one whose knowledge of iron went no further than familiarity with some of its forms and its abstract chemical definition would be poorly equipped to do anything interesting with it. There must be intimate practical knowledge of what iron does and does not do under a wide variety of circumstances, and moreover, of what these tendencies do *to us*—what habits they elicit. "Thus, we come down to what is tangible and practical, as the root of every real distinction of thought, no matter how subtle [*sic*] it may be; and there is no distinction of meaning so fine as to consist in anything but a possible difference of practice" (W 3:265). The full meaning of what iron is includes not just the chemist's knowledge, but the master blacksmith's as well.

The first statement of the pragmatic maxim, "the rule for attaining the third grade of clearness of apprehension," is one of Peirce's most famous utterances:

> Consider what effects, which might conceivably have practical bearings, we conceive the object of our conception to have. Then, our conception of these effects is the whole of our conception of the object. (W 3:266)

In the proposal for Memoir 32, Peirce expressed his discomfort with this formulation of the pragmatic maxim. He wrote that the paper "was imperfect in tacitly leaving it to appear that the maxim of pragmatism led to the last stage of clearness" (NEM 4:30). Indeed, the phrasing of the maxim is potentially misleading. One might read this statement as providing guidelines for an alternative means of *defining* concepts. If we think of standard dictionaries as giving the "second-grade" linguistic definitions of concepts, we might take the pragmatic maxim as a guide to producing a super-dictionary of "third grade" definitions. Such a book (a "practionary"?) might endeavor to list all the conceivable practical effects a thing could have in experience, and thus furnish the reader with a better conception of the object.

Clearly this is not what Peirce had in mind, though it is a helpful image in its own way. One who has a practical familiarity with an object of thought might well be able to draw up a lengthy list of its practical effects, since he or she has in effect internalized a "dictionary entry" of this sort for the object. The pragmatic maxim, though, refers to the experiential process by which such an internalized entry is formed. The concept is a symbol, and its ultimate logical interpretant is the habit (or habits) of action it produces in an interpreter. The habit that is the ultimate interpretant may be either a habit of action or a habit of thought (CP 5.486–87). In our example, the concept *iron* produces certain expectations, which give rise to particular ways of thinking about or treating the material in various circumstances. These habits could not be absorbed from a linguistic description in a super-dictionary, even if one were available. At most, the inquirer would be forewarned to look for characteristic patterns, and to try various procedures, which earlier inquirers could have discovered only after some experimentation. The third grade of clearness, knowledge of the practical effects, can come only through personal "hands-on" experience with the thing or concept in question.

John J. Fitzgerald writes that the central notion of Peirce's pragmaticism "is that the meaning of a sign or concept consists in the habit to which it gives rise in the interpreter."[24] The ultimate purpose of ideas is thus to effect habit-change. This is different, Peirce insists, from the assertion sometimes attributed to pragmatism that the meaning of an idea consists in action: "I deny that pragmaticism as originally defined by me made the intellectual purport of symbols to consist in our conduct. On the contrary, I was most careful to say that it consists in our *concept* of what our conduct *would be* upon *conceivable* occasions" (CP 8.208). The meaning of a concept now encountered is the habit, the tendency that would guide future actions, which we now conceive that the concept would establish, and this meaning is clearly subject to revision in light of subsequent experience.

Peirce was fully committed to the notion that ideas have a real, indispensable, and decisive effect in the world, through their determination of habits (CP 5.105). Habit is the interface between Thirdness and Secondness: An idea can serve as the basis for establishing a habit in a person or system, and the habit so established will affect events in the future. In the proposed memoir "On Objective Logic," Peirce wanted to emphasize the place of ideas and well-directed inquiry in the world. His sketch of this memoir encapsulates the whole upshot of his philosophy, the practical significance of his elaborate theory of experience and the logic of signs. The account opens by emphasizing the respects in which Peirce's philosophy differs from Hegel's:

> The term "objective logic" is Hegel's; but since I reject Absolute Idealism as false, "objective logic" necessarily means *more* for me than it did for him. Let me explain. In saying that *to be* and *to be represented* were the same, Hegel ignored the category of Reaction (that is, he imagined he reduced it to a mode of being represented) thus failing to do justice to *being,* and at the same time he was obliged to strain the nature of *thought,* and fail in justice to that side also. Having thus distorted both sides of the truth, it was a small thing for him to say that *Begriffe* were concrete and had their part in the activity of the world; since that activity, for him, was merely represented activity. But when I, with my scientific appreciation of objectivity and the brute nature of reaction, maintain, nevertheless, that ideas really influence the physical world, and in doing so carry their logic with them, I give to objective logic a waking life which was absent from Hegel's dream-land. I undertake in this memoir to show that so far from its being a metaphorical expression to say that Truth and Right are the greatest powers in this world, its meaning is just as literal as it is to say that when I open the window to my study, I am really exercising an agency. For the mode of causation in the one case and in the other is precisely the same. In fact, there are two modes of causation, corresponding to Aristotle's efficient and final causation, which I analyze and make clear, showing that both must concur to produce any effect whatever. The mind is nothing but an organism of ideas; and to say that I can open my window is to say that an idea can be an agent in the production of a physical effect. (NEM 4:30–31)

There are a number of noteworthy points in this passage. We will first consider what it suggests concerning the relation between the pragmatic maxim and the semeiotic conception of mind. Other points will be discussed in the concluding section of this chapter.

If it is legitimate to say that a mental intention to open a window leads to the window's being opened, then we have a case of an idea causing a particular event in the world. The idea acts not through efficient causation, but through final causation. The idea that "the window ought to be opened" does not specify the means of making it so: whether I do it myself or ask someone else to do it, use a tool or do it with my bare hands, is unimportant for realizing the intention. Final and efficient causation must act in concert so as to bring about any intended effect. A world that operated entirely by efficient causation would be very unlike the world we know, if such a world were indeed possible. There would be no basis for patterns of events, no tendencies for some events rather than others to come about in given circumstances. Such tendencies, in Peirce's terminology, are all instances of habit. Peirce's philosophy aims to explain the nature and operation of habit, of Thirdness, and this is where the general theory of semeiotic enters in.

The pragmatic maxim says that the meaning of a concept or sign (its ultimate interpretant) consists in the habits it would establish in a mind that rightly interpreted it. The semeiotic conception of mind is much broader than the psychological conception. Anything suited to produce an interpretant of a sign may be considered as an instance of mind. Thus any system capable of taking habits may serve to affect the course of future events through final causation, and be capable of contributing to the rational development of the universe. Indeed, we have already seen Peirce's assertion that the processes of purely mechanical systems exhibit patterns analogous to deductive inference. Immediately following the passage where he makes that assertion, he continues:

> I have not succeeded in persuading my contemporaries to believe that Nature also makes inductions and retroductions. They seem to think that her mind is in the infantile stage of the Aristotelians and Stoic philosophers. I point out that Evolution wherever it takes place is one vast succession of generalizations, by which matter is becoming subjected to ever higher and higher laws; and I point to the infinite variety of nature as testifying to her Originality or power of Retroduction. But so far, the old ideas are too ingrained. Very few accept my message. (NEM 4:344)

Whether or not we accept Peirce's claims about inference in nature, it is the highly volatile and powerful *human* mind that concerns us most. It is this mind that has the greatest potential to affect the course of events in its vicinity, directing them toward good or bad ends, and it is this mind that we can do the most to control. The normative sciences, especially critic and methodeutic, are our best resources for coming to exercise some measure of self-control.

Normative Logic and the Conduct of Life

The whole point of normative semeiotic is to ensure that the ideas that do arise and affect the world are the result, so far as possible, of rational thought, of self-controlled inquiry. Inquiry is a semeiotic process properly aimed at realizing the summum bonum in every area of life. Peirce's discussion of the causal efficacy of ideas indicates that it is not just rational intellectual constructs that inquiry seeks to develop, but, above all, concrete instantiations of rationality in the world of being. The ideas that develop through inquiry take up residence in the actual world, in the form of habits exhibited by persons and institutions. Normative science insists that they ought to promote the evolution of a rational order of things.

In an aside to Lady Welby, Peirce remarked that *life itself* should be recognized as Expression (SS 112). What life seeks to express, and what life forms capable of self-control are best suited to express, are the ideals that are admirable in themselves—Goodness, Beauty, Truth, Rightness, Reality. In the passage from NEM 4:30–31 quoted earlier, Truth and Right are identified as "the greatest powers in this world." They are so because they are the ultimate ideals at which all inquiry aims—not to *know* Truth in an abstract sense (which would be, after all, only the second grade of clearness), but to make Truth an active part of the world of experience. What is sought is practical, "personal" knowledge of the ideals, and the application of this knowledge alongside others in the communal pursuit of the summum bonum. Through self-controlled inquiry, we can come to know these ideals as intimately as an expert mechanic knows the tool-bench.

Reality is defined as what *would* be represented in a perfect argument, at the end of infinite inquiry into the nature of the world—just as objective probability is defined as the ratio that *would* emerge at the end of infinite inductive sampling. Because the process of inquiry into the nature of the cosmos is finite, just as any inductive procedure to determine probability must be finite, a true representation of the Real is an ideal to which we can only indefinitely approximate. This is the basis for the principle of fallibilism: our current state of information is always incomplete, and possibly altogether wrong. The current state of information is but a stage in a great continuum of inquiry, carried on by an infinite community that is far broader than the human community.

> The principle of continuity is the idea of fallibilism objectified. For fallibilism is the doctrine that our knowledge is never absolute but always swims, as it were, in a continuum of uncertainty and of indeterminacy. Now the doctrine of continuity is that *all things* so swim in continua. (CP 1.171)

On the other hand, just as objective probability serves as the idea that validates induction, reality serves as the idea that validates rational inquiry. The ongoing sampling of quantitative induction approaches the objective probability that is *there*, independent of what results the finite inductive procedure discloses. Unless it be supposed that there is such a value, induction has no warrant as a method. Indeed, if we sample a fluctuating system where there is no objective probability of finding a specified character, induction gives no meaningful results. Likewise, unless there is an objective Reality, which would be disclosed at the end of infinite inquiry, our inquiry can give no ultimately meaningful results.[25] Without faith in the ideals of Truth and Reality, an honest commitment to rational thought would not be possible. They are postulates, requisite for any coherent attempt at inquiry.

> I do not say that it is infallibly true that there is any belief to which a person would come if he were to carry his inquiries far enough. I only say that that alone is what I call Truth. I cannot infallibly know that there is any Truth. (SS 73)

If there is to be rational inquiry, however, there must be *faith* that there is such a thing as Truth, the adequate representation of Reality, toward which inquiry strives.

The postulate that continuous inquiry leads to true representations of reality is expressed in Peirce's principle of *synechism*. Stated generally, synechism is "that tendency of philosophical thought which insists upon the idea of continuity as of prime importance in philosophy and, in particular, upon the necessity of hypotheses involving true continuity" (CP 6.169). It "is not an ultimate and absolute metaphysical doctrine; it is a regulative principle of logic, prescribing what sort of hypothesis is fit to be entertained and examined" (CP 6.173). It is the very heart of Peirce's methodeutic.

This faith in the Truth, which appears in logic as a necessary postulate, is closely related to religious faith:

> Every true man of science, i.e. every man belonging to a social group all the members of which sacrifice all the ordinary motives of life to their desire to make their beliefs concerning one subject conform to verified judgments of perception together with sound reasoning, and who therefore really believes the universe to be governed by reason, or in other words by God,—but who does not explicitly recognize that he believes in God,—has Faith in God, according to my use of the term Faith. (SS 75)

Faith in God, faith in reason, faith in our ability to acquire true knowledge of the world, faith in our ability to do good in the world, all come to the same thing for Peirce. Each of these rests on the conviction that continuity, Thirdness, is a fundamental fact of experience and can increase its influence through exertion of its own nature. This effort is especially effective in the form of deliberately controlled inquiry directed at the realization of the esthetic ideals.

Peirce obviously placed great value on the study of logic. We should not get the impression that he saw ratiocination and explicit reliance on a highly sophisticated logic as the solution to our day-to-day problems, however. Logic is the one science of greatest importance in the long run, "for the reason that if we fall into the error of believing that vitally important questions are to be decided by reasoning, the only hope of salvation lies in formal logic, which demonstrates in the clearest manner that reasoning itself testifies to its own ultimate subordination to sentiment" (CP 1.672). There is, in short, more to life in the world than symbols and inference—even if we conceive that life and the world in semeiotic terms.[26] On the other hand, Peirce said that the strongest lesson of sentiment is that the best thing we can do in life is to subordinate our own interests to those of the greater community.

> Thus it is, that while reasoning and the science of reasoning strenuously proclaim the subordination of reasoning to sentiment, the very supreme commandment of sentiment is that men should generalize, or what the logic of relatives shows to be the same thing, should become welded into the universal continuum, which is what true reasoning consists in. But this does not reinstate reasoning, for this generalization should come about, not merely in man's cognitions, which are but the superficial film of his being, but objectively in the deepest emotional springs of his life. In fulfilling this command, man prepares himself for transmutation into a new form of life, the joyful Nirvana in which the discontinuities of his will shall have all but disappeared. (CP 1.673)

Peirce's great hope was that philosophy might come to understand the value of sound reasoning, to put it to work in the service of the highest ideals of Truth and Goodness, and to use its resources to understand these as active, living ideals and not dead abstractions. It is to this end that he developed the synechistic philosophy.

Part Four
The Categories
of Being

CHAPTER 8

Scientific Metaphysics

While Peirce's mathematical hypothesis of continuity comes to philosophical fruition in his semeiotic, its harvest is his metaphysics. Metaphysics is the last of the philosophical sciences. It derives its fundamental concepts primarily from logic or semeiotic, and in turn provides fundamental concepts to the special sciences. The special sciences are concerned to describe how physical and psychical laws operate in the world; metaphysics prepares the way for this sort of inquiry with an account of the nature of law and of the universe(s) in which law operates.

One of the main objectives of the present study is to provide the basis for a sound understanding of Peirce's metaphysics of evolutionary realism. Though much has been written on Peirce's metaphysics, the tremendous importance of semeiotic for Peirce's metaphysical thought has been highlighted only recently.[1] A thorough study of Peirce's metaphysics cannot be provided here. What follows is a sketch of the main features of Peirce's metaphysics, with special attention to one particular problem that emerges under the present exposition of Peirce's philosophy: the question of the ontological status of extra-semeiotic entities in the philosophy of cosmic evolution.

The Science of Metaphysics

Metaphysics aims to provide a thorough and critical account of "the most general features of reality and of real objects" (CP 6.6). This is indispensable for scientific inquiry:

> [T]he special sciences are obliged to take for granted a number of most important propositions, because their ways of working afford no means of bringing these propositions to the test. In short, they always rest upon metaphysics. . . . The philosopher alone is equipped with the facilities for examining such "axioms" and for determining the degree to which confidence may safely be reposed in them. Find a scientific man who proposes to get along without any metaphysics . . . and you have found one whose doctrines are thoroughly vitiated by the crude and uncriticized metaphysics with which they are packed. . . . In short, there is no escape from the need of a critical examination of "first principles." (CP 1.129)

Peirce beheld both tremendous potential and regrettable narrowness in modern science. On the one hand, he saw the self-correcting method of scientific inquiry (which is elaborated in critic and methodeutic) as the best hope for attaining truth in any sphere of inquiry. On the other hand, he saw in the metaphysical assumptions of science a good deal of dogma. The professed materialism of contemporary science, which Peirce saw as a remnant of an older adherence to logical nominalism, must prove a stumbling block in the scientific quest for truth.[2] Peirce's philosophy may be seen as a systematic attempt to rid modern thought of nominalism and materialism, while avoiding the dogmatism of much traditional metaphysics:

[M]y philosophy may be described as the attempt of a physicist to make such conjecture as to the constitution of the universe as the methods of science may permit, with the aid of all that has been done by previous philosophers. I shall support my propositions by such arguments as I can. Demonstrative proof is not to be thought of. The demonstrations of the metaphysicians are all moonshine. The best that can be done is to supply a hypothesis, not devoid of all likelihood, in the general line of growth of scientific ideas, and capable of being verified or refuted by future observers. (CP 1.7)

Peirce insisted on two things, then. First, metaphysics must be admitted as a legitimate subject of inquiry. Second, metaphysics must be treated as a science among other sciences, subject to the same requirements of fallibilism and falsifiability, and proceeding by the same methods of inquiry as the other sciences.

THE LOGICAL DISPUTE: NOMINALISM VERSUS REALISM

Metaphysics is the first science in Peirce's classification that aims to inquire into the nature of the world, rather than into the structures of thought. To put it this way, of course, implies a meaningful distinction between thought and the world, or better, between the subjective and objective features of experience. The root of the distinction is to be found in logic, and is brought out in the scholastic question of nominalism versus realism:

You know what the question was. It was whether *laws* and general *types* are figments of the mind or are real. If this be understood to mean whether there really are any laws and types, it is strictly speaking a question of metaphysics and not of logic. But as a first step toward its solution, it is proper to ask whether, granting that our common-sense beliefs are true, the analysis of the meaning of those beliefs shows that, according to those beliefs, laws and types are objective or subjective. This is a question of logic rather than of metaphysics—and as soon as this is answered the reply to the other question immediately follows after. (CP 1.16)

The question at issue between nominalism and realism concerns whether the truth of laws, and of the deliverances of logical inference, is subjective or objective. The nominalist maintains that the laws science describes are mere names attached to observed regularities or uniformities in experience. Likewise, forms of logical inference are held to be valid, and their results "true," only insofar as there is a consensus to that effect among the community of involved inquirers. Another community, the nominalist maintains, might develop alternate forms of inference and hence legitimately accept other results as "true." The disputes that arise in a confrontation between such alternative systems of reasoning can be resolved only through some process whose outcome is entirely contingent on prevailing circumstances. If one system better serves the ends that a society happens to embrace than an alternative system, then that system will prevail. Given other ends, the other system might well win out.

One radical version of nominalism (suggested by contemporary philosophers of science such as Paul Feyerabend) maintains that the systems that prevail do so only because of sociologically describable power factors. One group controls the publishing and educational institutions, and is able to "freeze out" the other, for example. Whatever its particular form, nominalism maintains that the laws we employ to describe the world, together with the forms of inference by which they are "discovered," are merely human constructs. They can reflect nothing in the way the *world* is, because on this view it makes no sense to talk univocally about "the way the world is."

The realist, on the other hand, maintains that descriptions of laws and logical forms can be true descriptions of universal principles. Although many descriptions of laws or logical forms no doubt *are* mere human constructs, these can sooner or later be distinguished from those that are objectively true. A true statement of the law of gravity, for example, would not only fit the appearances of the attractions among massive bodies, but would accurately and completely represent the features of the natural principle that governs such interactions in the universe. Such a law would be true not because it happens to fit the data before us, but because it is an adequate representation of a real force in nature.

The core of the realist's position, then, is a definition of truth that makes truth independent of what any finite group of inquirers may happen to think. Peirce's definition of truth and his defense of the validity of the laws of logic both admit the nominalists' insight that *knowledge* is a social construct. At the same time, Peirce sought to avoid the great nominalistic error:

the assertion that *truth* is a social construct. The definition of truth as *that opinion which would be affirmed at the end of an infinite process of inquiry* is rooted in Peirce's theory of probability.[3] The relation between the convergence of a frequency ratio (discovered in an ongoing process of quantitative induction) and an objective probability (revealed in a statistical syllogism, or probable deduction) is the paradigm of the relation between the social construction of knowledge and the notion of objective truth. An infinite process of induction would ultimately produce knowledge of any objective probability. The "infinite hope" of logic is that our inferences are valid, and our conclusions about the real state of things are approximately true, even in the short run of finite inquiry (W 2:272).

Peirce the realist agreed with nominalism, then, in saying that our knowledge is a social construct subject to constant revision. He went further, however, to assert that there is an objective reality that would be fully revealed to us only at the end of infinite inquiry, and that is independent of what any number of people may think. This is Peirce's "extreme logical realism" in outline. It provides a definition of truth that makes it independent of any finite opinions. Peirce saw such a regulative ideal as a necessary assumption for logical thought, though logic cannot assure us that there is in fact any such truth to be attained (SS 73).

Peirce believed that when the logical question of the status of laws is answered, the metaphysical question whether there really are any laws or types is also immediately answered (CP 1.16). The definition of truth involved in Peirce's logical realism requires us to suppose that the laws and types described in scientific inquiry are not created by that inquiry. The related metaphysical problem is commonly characterized as regarding the reality of *universals*, of which laws and types are important varieties. Peirce suggested that we understand the concern over the reality of universals in another way, however, since nobody denies that universals or general terms are a real part of thought: "[T]he reality, or as I would say in order to avoid any begging of the question, the value or worth, not merely of the universals, but also that of the individuals was a part of the broad question" for the scholastics (CP 4.1). The part of the dispute that Peirce considered most relevant for modern science concerns the status of general laws.

> Roughly speaking, the nominalists conceived the *general* element of cognition to be merely a convenience for understanding this and that fact and to amount to nothing except for cognition, while the realists, still more roughly speaking, looked upon the general, not only as the end and aim of knowledge, but also as the most important element of being. Such was and is the question. It is as pressing today as it ever was. . . . (CP 4.1)

The modern nominalist, in short, values "facts" that are often spoken of in isolation from the system of thought in which they occur. The realist, on the other hand, considers the whole system of ideas, including the facts, as the primary object of knowledge. This epistemological priority of generals translates into a metaphysical priority, as well. The nominalist values knowledge of particulars, and accords no metaphysical legitimacy to the notion of generals. This accounts for the modern nominalist's fondness for materialism, with its identification of "the real" as particular bits of matter in motion. The realist, however, sees the general as primary, and the general must be conceived in terms of *idea* rather than in terms of *matter*. Peirce's affirmation of metaphysical idealism is thus rooted in his logical realism.

The definition of truth then implies for Peirce that there is an objective reality: "The opinion which is fated to be ultimately agreed to by all who investigate, is what we mean by the truth, and the object represented in this opinion is the real" (W 3:273). The question at issue in logic concerns the definition of truth, which Peirce settled in favor of realism. Metaphysics then aims to give an account of the reality that the definition of truth implies.

Peirce conceived his metaphysics as a scientific inquiry with great human significance, even beyond its importance for the special sciences. Its human significance derives from the fact that humans are, after all, a part of reality. The question whether we are merely bits of matter moving and acting according to mechanically determinant laws, or are integral and active parts of a living universe that is moving toward some good end, for example, is central to one way of asking about the ultimate meaning of life. As Joseph Esposito remarks, knowing the nature of truth and reality, and our relation to them, may be a great aid to helping *realize* truth and reality, and the full meaning of our lives.[4] It is this that led Peirce to characterize his combination of scholastic realism and objective idealism as "a highly practical and common-sense position" (W 2:471).

THE METHODOLOGY OF METAPHYSICS

In Peirce's view, the great failing of most metaphysics is not that it offers nothing significant for human life. Rather, it is that it consists either of reassuring platitudes or terrifying dogma about the nature of ultimate reality. Dogma is all that metaphysics can be, unless it is based on sound principles of scientific inquiry.

The general form of inquiry, again, is to frame explanatory hypotheses, deduce the consequences that would follow if the hypotheses were indeed true, and then look to experience for evidence whether those consequences actually obtain or not. In metaphysics, as elsewhere, the choice of an initial hypothesis is subject to the principles of the economy of research. Peirce praised the nominalistic principle known as Ockham's razor as "a very judicious maxim of logic" in this respect (CP 4.35).[5] The nominalistic hypothesis that facts and particularities are more significantly real than laws and generals is of course simpler than the contrary hypothesis of realism, since nominalism simply disregards universals.

Peirce praised the contribution of stalwart nominalists to the science of metaphysics, "since the only satisfactory way of ascertaining the insufficiency of the theory was to push the application of it, just as they have done" (CP 4.35). Once a hypothesis has been embraced, however, the inquirer must maintain the attitude of fallibilism and be willing to introduce "complications" into the hypothesis if experience shows it to be inadequate as an explanation. One consequence of the nominalistic hypothesis, if it were true, would be that the general tendencies manifest in events (which the nominalist characterizes as mere uniformities constructed and imposed by the mind) are of no real importance except as conveniences for thought. On this view, what matters objectively should be individual events and not resemblances among events of similar type.

Although Peirce's arguments against nominalism are many, one of his most common and accessible characterizations of the inadequacy of nominalism is given in the following observation:

> Five minutes of our waking life will hardly pass without our making some kind of prediction; and in the majority of cases these predictions are fulfilled in the event. Yet a prediction is essentially of a general nature, and cannot ever be completely fulfilled. To say that a prediction has a decided tendency to be fulfilled, is to say that the future events are in a measure really governed by a law. . . . If the prediction has a tendency to be fulfilled, it must be that future events have a tendency to conform to a general rule. "Oh," but say the nominalists, "this general rule is nothing but a mere word or couple of words!" I reply, "Nobody ever dreamed of denying that what is general is of the nature of a general sign; but the question is whether future events will conform to it or not. If they will, your adjective 'mere' seems to be ill-placed." A rule to which future events have a tendency to conform is *ipso facto* an important thing, an important element in the happening of those events. (CP 1.26)

One might ask why the metaphysical significance of so important a class of things as generals has been neglected while nominalism has been allowed to flourish. Peirce offers two responses. His first explanation of the tenacity of nominalism is that it is a well-entrenched view that could not be abandoned without considerable modification to its current proponents' political position (CP 4.35). It is unclear which of his contemporaries Peirce had in mind with this remark, but it does characterize the political position of the original Ockhamists somewhat accurately. This leads us to Peirce's second explanation for the persistence of nominalism.[6] The dispute over nominalism and realism was accidentally associated with the struggle for control of the universities at the beginning of the English Renaissance.

The Scotists, who maintained realism, were then generally in control of the universities. When humanism emerged as a school of thought, its proponents saw the Scotists as the group to challenge.

> So since the great adversaries of the Scotists were the Ockhamists, or terminists, who belonged to the class of *nominales* whom the humanists called nominalists, the humanists allied themselves with the nominalists to cast the Scotists out of the Universities, & not caring a tuppence for the dispute between the two kinds of logicians they conformed to the nominalistic confession in return for the favor of that party; and so, because from that day to this scarcely anybody has examined into the real meaning or merits of the controversy & it was very easy and obvious to say that "Generals are mere words," . . . it follows that everybody has admitted that Nominalism was the correct doctrine. (SS 115–16)

Thus, according to Peirce's account, although realism may have won the logical battle over nominalism, it lost the political war. The followers of Duns Scotus came to be ridiculed as logic-chopping "Dunces," while their opponents' doctrine survived and flourished through an accidental association with the rising philosophy of the Renaissance.

There is yet another reason Peirce might have offered as to why nominalism retained its appeal. According to pragmatism, the importance of any phenomenon is determined by the context of the particular undertaking in which it is encountered. Peirce's observation that a law that governs events is "ipso facto an important thing" is delivered from a post-Kantian perspective on metaphysics. Whatever importance the reality of laws had for the scholastics, its importance in the aftermath of Kant's "Copernican turn" is unquestionable. That it is only from this perspective that laws take on the importance Peirce ascribed to them could have allowed previous thinkers to underestimate their importance.[7]

The crucial insight of Kant's philosophy, Peirce said, is "to regard the reality as the normal product of mental action and not as the incognizable cause of it" (W 2:471). With this turn, the conception of reality as a static order external to the operation of mind is doomed. Reality is henceforth to be conceived as a system closely associated with the activity of mind. In such a system, it is not particular individual things and events that are of primary metaphysical importance, but rather the laws governing *relations* among things and events—and laws are decidedly nonmaterial. The realists' insistence that laws and types, not individuals and isolated facts, are basic to any conception of reality led Peirce to characterize Kant's turn as "the passage from the nominalistic to the realistic view of reality" (W 2:470). Because Peirce conceived the general as a symbol, and because a symbol (a type) is distinguished from its individual tokens, "we may admit, if there be reason to do so, that generals are mere words [i.e., types] without at all saying, as Ockham supposed, that they are really individuals" (CP 2.301).

In metaphysics, as in any science, the pragmatic maxim is essential for clarifying our ideas. The meaning of any idea consists in "our *concept* of what our conduct *would be* upon *conceivable* occasions" (CP 8.208) into which it enters. Meaning is ultimately elaborated in terms of the habits we believe the idea would tend to establish. The meaning of metaphysical ideas, as with any others, must be determined with reference to the purpose that the habits will likely promote. Because metaphysical concepts are of importance primarily for the advance of knowledge through inquiry, their meaning must be considered in the context of what they contribute to the realization of the summum bonum, the growth of reason in the course of inquiry (CP 2.116). This is especially true when we discuss such rarefied notions as the meaning of being, modes of being, and the metaphysical significance of Firstness, Secondness, and Thirdness. Once the pragmatic method is adopted, metaphysical speculation begins to take shape:

> We now begin to see the sense of talking of modes of being. They are elements of coöperation toward the summum bonum. The categories now come in to aid us materially, and we clearly make out three modes or factors of being, which we proceed to make clear to ourselves. (CP 2.118)

The success of realism in the sphere of logic brings certain metaphysical questions to the fore. By the hypothesis of realism (adopted as a result of semeiotic), laws and types are to be considered of primary importance. But the question of the status of particulars (individuals and tokens) in relation to these universals must be addressed, along with the question of how law operates in the unfolding of events in the realm of existence. Additionally, metaphysics must ask whether there is an overall direction in the flow of law-governed events, and if so, what the end of the universe is. The highest level of metaphysics is cosmology, which seeks to give an account of the modes of being of the universe that explains why things are the way they are: why there is law, space, time, and so on.[8] Of course, because metaphysics is an attempt to provide a scientific explanation of the way things are, its suggested answers to such questions must be subject to confirmation or falsification in experience.[9]

Before we leave the subject of methodology, a few words are in order concerning the organization of the science of metaphysics itself. In the classification of the sciences, metaphysics is organized into three branches, according to subject matter. First is general metaphysics or ontology, which describes the modes of being in terms of the categories. This is followed by physical metaphysics, which sets out the fundamental laws governing dyadic or dynamical action, and psychical metaphysics, which sets out the laws of triadic action or semiosis. As noted in chapter 2, however, this division of metaphysics in the classification of sciences appears to be largely formal. Most notably, it makes no place for cosmology, and the arrangement of the branches seems to go against Peirce's view that physical laws are special cases of the more general law of mind.

Unlike his work in semeiotic, Peirce's writings on metaphysics do not fall into the neat divisions of the classification. The structure of the present exposition, accordingly, follows the lead of his methodology rather than of his list. In Peirce's system, each science relies upon its predecessors for its basic concepts. Metaphysics begins with the suggestion that the nature of thought, as described in semeiotic, is sufficiently analogous to the nature of being that the elements of semeiotic may be considered prototypes of the elements of being. Semeiotic then provides four main hypotheses for metaphysics: first, that there is a reality; second, that reality is to be conceived as a *process* similar to the process of semiosis; third, that modes of action or relation are fundamental to understanding modes of being; and fourth, that the elementary metaphysical categories describing these modes of being are variations of the three indecomposable kinds of relation that are manifest in phenomenology and semeiotic. Cosmology is the heart of Peirce's metaphysics, as it is here that the categories' interrelated functioning in the real universe is described.

The Logical Basis of Metaphysics

Peirce's metaphysics must recognize both universal and particular modes of being. Stecheotic provides Peirce with a model of the interrelation of general and particular, in the theory of the complete symbol. Metaphysics accordingly adopts the insights of semeiotic as its starting point. Everything that semeiotic has to say about signs is relevant for metaphysics. Peirce cited strong precedent for basing metaphysics on semeiotic: "[I]t is nothing new to say that metaphysical conceptions are primarily and at bottom thoughts about words, or thoughts about thoughts; it is the doctrine both of Aristotle (whose categories are parts of speech) and of Kant (whose categories are the characters of different kinds of propositions)" (W 2:231). Peirce's metaphysical categories arise when the philosophy of representation is applied to the philosophy of being.

The first principle to be advanced in metaphysics is that there is a similarity between forms of thought and modes of being. Because generals are of the nature of symbols, which are the very medium of mind itself, the conviction that generals are the most important aspects of reality leads Peirce to embrace metaphysical idealism, as we shall see. Idealism serves as a metaphysical hypothesis that explains the similarity between thought and being: the similarity results from the de facto continuity of the two.

THE OBJECTIVE LOGIC OF EVENTS

In an 1896 manuscript entitled "The Logic of Mathematics: An Attempt to Develop My Categories from Within," Peirce stated the basic hypothesis for metaphysics: "Metaphysics consists in the results of the absolute acceptance of logical principles not merely as regulatively valid, but as truths of being" (CP 1.487). Logic in the broad sense, of course, is conceived as normative semeiotic. The adoption of semeiotic as the basis for metaphysics suggests several further hypotheses.

The first is that there is a reality. Peirce's semeiotic involves the regulative ideal of *truth* as the end of semiosis. Signs are teleological, and the unifying factor among the plurality of semiotic processes is that they all share a common purpose. "The purpose of every sign is to express 'fact,' and by being joined with other signs, to approach as nearly as possible to determining an interpretant which would be the *perfect truth,* the absolute truth." (NEM 4:239). Metaphysics looks for a unifying factor analogous to the semeiotic notion of truth: "[I]t is to be assumed that the universe has an explanation, the function of which, like that of every explanation, is to unify its observed variety" (CP 1.487). The unifying concept for metaphysics is *reality,* suggested in semeiotic as the hypothetical *object* that would be represented in a true opinion (W 3:273). In response to the fundamental question "What is reality?" Peirce answered "Perhaps there isn't any such thing at all. As I have repeatedly insisted, it is but a retroduction, a working hypothesis which we try, our one desperate forlorn hope of knowing anything" (NEM 4:343).

The second hypothesis derived from semeiotic is that, because semiosis is conceived as an ongoing *process* of representation and interpretation, reality will likewise be conceived in terms of process, as objective semeiotic. "[I]f there is any reality, then, so far as there is any reality, what that reality consists in is this: that there is in the being of things something which corresponds to the process of reasoning, that the world *lives,* and *moves,* and *has its being,* in a logic of events" (NEM 4:343–44). Metaphysics accepts the proposition that thought, the operation of mind as described in semeiotic, "is the mirror of being" (CP 1.487). Semeiotic, the science of the development of symbols, provides Peirce's general model for any process of development.

The third metaphysical hypothesis derived from semeiotic is that kinds of action (or modes of relation brought about by action) must be considered fundamental to any understanding of the universe, and that the universe exhibits *both* dyadic action and triadic action.[10] Both sorts of action are comprehended under his theory of semiosis: "Every physical force reacts between a pair of particles, either of which may serve as an index of the other. On the other hand, we shall find that every intellectual operation involves a triad of symbols" (CP 2.300). The hypothesis that metaphysics is to be conceived as the objective logic of events shows promise, then. The classification of signs provides categories applicable both to physical and psychical phenomena.

Certainly we observe dyadic or mechanical action in the world. The logic required to describe mechanistic action and reaction is in fact but a small part of semeiotic. Mechanical reactions are necessary actions, and can be adequately characterized in terms of the deductive forms, the forms of necessary reasoning:

We all think of nature as syllogizing. Even the mechanical philosopher, who is as nominalistic as a scientific man can be, does that. The immutable mechanical law together with the laws of attraction and repulsion form the major premise, the instantaneous relative positions and velocities of all the particles whether it be "at the end of the sixth day of creation,"— put back to an infinitely remote past if you like, though that does not lessen the miracle,—or whether it be at any other instant of time is the minor premise, the resulting accelerations form the conclusion. That is the very way the mechanical philosopher conceives the universe to operate. (NEM 4:344)

The interesting metaphysical question, of course, is whether this conception of the logic of events is adequate, or whether events in the world might be more complex than can be described in the lockstep inferences of deductive logic. Peirce suggested that the logic of the world is more complex than the mechanistic philosopher allows:

I have not succeeded in persuading my contemporaries to believe that Nature also makes inductions and retroductions. They seem to think that her mind is in the infantile stage of the Aristotelians and Stoic philosophers. I point out that Evolution wherever it takes place is one vast succession of generalizations, by which matter is becoming subjected to ever higher and higher laws; and I point to the infinite variety of nature as testifying to her Originality or power of Retroduction. (NEM 4:343–44)

In short, that events unfold according to the limited laws of deduction is an unlikely supposition. It would be better to try the hypothesis that "the logic of the universe is one to which our own aspires, rather than attains" (CP 6.189).

Now we turn to the categories, which serve as the basis for the metaphysical conception of modes of being. The mode of being of matter that is entirely governed by mechanical action and reaction is Secondness. To escape the tyranny of determinism, an element of Firstness—spontaneity or absolute chance—must be introduced into our conceptions. Thus Peirce insisted on Tychism, "the doctrine that absolute chance is a factor of the universe" (CP 6.201). He put the problem in terms of the presocratic debate over whether atoms, the ultimate constituent parts of matter, move in a determined direction or whether they spontaneously "swerve." Peirce sided with Epicurus on this issue. What opponents to this notion resist is "the attribution of . . . firstness to things perfectly dead and material. Now I am quite with them there. I think too that whatever is First is *ipso facto* sentient. If I make atoms swerve—as I do—I make them swerve but very very little, because I conceive they are not absolutely dead" (CP 6.201). The inclusion of a degree of Firstness, or spontaneity, in all phenomena corresponds to the view that nature makes retroductions,[11] and entails the rejection of determinism (including all deterministic versions of materialism).

Habit, another nondeterministic element, is also involved:

> [by saying that atoms are not absolutely dead] I do not mean exactly that I hold them to be physically such as the materialists hold them to be, only with a small dose of sentiency superadded. For that, I grant, would be feeble enough. But what I mean is, that all there is, is First, Feelings; Second, Efforts; Third, Habits—all of which are more familiar to us on their psychical side than on their physical side; and that dead matter would be merely the final result of the complete induration of habit reducing the free play of feeling and the brute irrationality of effort to complete death. (CP 6.201)

The element of habit comes in as the teleological factor in metaphysics. A universe of brute reaction, broken up by an occasional chance variation, would exhibit no lawfulness, no discernible order. The teleological influence of habit is essential to Peirce's conception of realism, which emphasizes laws and generals. For this reason Peirce rejected the label Tychism as an incomplete characterization of his system. He preferred instead to call it Synechism, thus emphasizing the importance of continuity or Thirdness (CP 6.202).

These considerations led Peirce to propose a form of idealism as an alternative to materialism (or what is the same thing for him, physicalism).

As we shall see, though, Peirce's idealism is not altogether stripped of materialistic features (CP 6.277).[12] According to materialism, "nothing really exists but matter. . . . [T]he Whole is governed by mechanical forces that are determined by the state of things at the instant they act, without any reference to a purpose of bringing about any determinate state of things in the future" (CP 6.274). The interactions of all phenomena are held to be governed by physical laws (CP 6.24). As attractive as this theory is, with its denial of any fundamental dualism of mind and matter, and even though it cannot be "absolutely refuted," Peirce rejected it as lacking explanatory power (CP 6.274).

Materialist explanations cannot account, he claimed, for the experienced mental realities of intention, purpose, and feeling. Nor can they satisfactorily account for the irreversibility of phenomena that involve the "degradation of energy" described in the second law of thermodynamics. These phenomena involve a *qualitative* change in the net energy of a system, which is most often explained as a *quantitative* change in the "net *usable* energy" of the system. The change from a state of low to high entropy can only be remarked with reference to possible applications of the energy to do work aimed at some end: high entropy energy is unavailable for such applications. In purely physicalistic terms, work is just the transfer of energy from one physical system to another, and is most commonly conceived as the application of energy to move a mass. Work in this sense goes on *whatever* the level of entropy of the system, and of course both sides in the dispute agree that the total amount of matter and energy in the universe remains constant. It is only the amount of low entropy energy available for work directed toward some end that changes. The entropy law thus describes the increasing disorganization of energy, but the concept of *disorganization* is only meaningful with reference to an organizing principle. For Peirce, any organizing principle implies the influence of mind in some form. The fact that phenomena affected by the entropy law are irreversible thus indicated to him that a mental element is presupposed in our very conception of these reactions. There is much disagreement about the philosophical implications of the entropy law, of course, and we should not make too much depend on any interpretation of it. Suffice it to say that to adopt a metaphysical theory that in any way eliminates mental phenomena, or reduces them to physical descriptions, involves a mutilation of experience that Peirce would not tolerate.

The obvious alternative theory, idealism, likewise avoids dualism by asserting that nothing really exists but what is in some manner dependent on cognition and the law of mind:

> [W]e ought to suppose a continuity between the characters of mind and matter, so that matter would be nothing but mind that had such indurated habits as to cause it to act with a

peculiarly high degree of mechanical regularity, or routine. . . . This hypothesis might be called materialistic, since it attributes to mind one of the recognized properties of matter, extension, and attributes to all matter a certain excessively low degree of feeling, together with a certain power of taking habits. But it differs essentially from materialism, in that, instead of supposing mind to be governed by blind mechanical law, it supposes the one original law to be the recognized law of mind, the law of association, of which the laws of matter are regarded as mere special results. (CP 6.277)

The interactions of phenomena are governed by the law of mind, and physical laws are "derived and special" cases of the law of mind (CP 6.24). Peirce held that "[t]he one intelligible theory of the universe is that of objective idealism, that matter is effete mind, inveterate habits becoming physical laws" (CP 6.24). The ossification of the universe into a state governed entirely by physical laws is not absolute, even in the areas where physical law is most powerful: "I would suppose that that result of evolution is not quite complete even in our beakers and crucibles" (CP 6.202).

SEMEIOTIC AND ONTOLOGY

There are then three categories in Peirce's metaphysics, based on the three cenopythagorean categories of Firstness, Secondness, and Thirdness as they are elaborated in the theory of signs. These represent the three metaphysical principles of chance, reaction, and the tendency toward regularity, or habit-taking (CP 1.409). Phenomena are conceived as living events, exhibiting spontaneity, persistence, and order in various degrees.

These three categories correspond to the basic triadic classification of signs. The qualisign is a passing feeling, a quality that simply is what it is. The metaphysical principle of tychism describes the dominant mode of being of the qualisign: nothing external determines the qualisign to function the way it does. Sinsigns are particular existent things, which are what they are only in the context of a system of physical actions and reactions with other existents. The predominant metaphysical feature of a sinsign is that it endures—it resists the forces that would tend to dissipate its being, and its being at any time is determined by the interactions it has entered into with the rest of the actual world. Legisigns are real only to the extent that they tend to bring about the production of replicas. They are thus characterized by the category of habit. These ideas from the theory of signs form the basis of a sophisticated ontology, central to the metaphysical description of a universe in process. The whole of what there is *can* be seen, in short, as the unfolding of an evolutionary process describable as cosmic semiosis: "[A]ll this universe is perfused with signs, if it is not composed exclusively of signs" (CP 5.448n.1).

In this framework, the universe appears under a new aspect. There are positive possibilities, undetermined and unrestricted, yet lacking actuality except as they are brought into being through a decisive action. They are actualized only when they are embodied in sinsigns, and can only then enter into the semiotic flow. There is the material universe of existent things, which, because they can function as sinsigns (and therefore as embodiments of legisigns) may potentially be *more* than mere material things. Finally, there is the general, the medium of the action of *mind*, which "*lives*, and *moves*, and *has its being*" in the continuum of symbols (NEM 4:344). The world so conceived is a complex of possibility, matter, and idea that is in an ongoing process of creative evolution directed toward the summum bonum. The summum bonum, again, is not a final state of Absolute Knowledge, but rather a living *process* that strives toward what that grand idea inadequately expresses.

Peirce suggests in **καινά στοιχεῖα** that the ultimate (but unrealizable) aim of semiosis is to establish a sign whose object comprises all of reality and whose interpretant is absolutely true:

> The purpose of every sign is to express "fact," and by being joined with other signs, to approach as nearly as possible to determining an interpretant which would be the *perfect Truth*, the absolute Truth, and as such (at least, we may use this language) would be the very Universe. Aristotle gropes for a conception of perfection, or *entelechy*, which he never succeeds in making clear. We may adopt the word to mean the very fact, that is, the ideal sign which should be quite perfect, and so identical,—in such identity as a sign may have,—with the very matter denoted united with the very form signified by it. The entelechy of the Universe of being, then, the universe *quâ* fact, will be that Universe in its aspect as a sign, the 'Truth' of being. The 'Truth,' the fact that is not abstracted but complete, is the ultimate interpretant of every sign. (NEM 4:239–40)

Reality, conceived in terms of semeiotic, is both the immediate and dynamical object of the sign that is the *entelechy*, the end of semiosis. Truth, conceived in the same terms, is the immediate, dynamical, and final interpretant of that same sign. Here we have an essential identity of object, sign, and interpretant. In his Lowell Lectures of 1866, Peirce had described this identity as a "divine trinity" of the symbol (W 1:503). Whether or not this *entelechy* is divine, it certainly answers to Peirce's conception of the real and the true, which are conceived as destined to be unified and fully represented at the ideal end of semiosis.

The process of movement toward this ideal is the unfolding of the universe itself, guided by the self-correcting process of semiosis. As Peirce put it in his 1903 "Lectures on Pragmatism,"

> the universe is a vast representamen, a great symbol of God's purpose, working out its conclusions in living realities. Now every symbol must have, organically attached to it, its Indices of Reactions and its Icons of Qualities; and such part as these reactions and these qualities play in an argument that, they of course, play in the universe—that Universe being precisely an argument. (CP 5.119)

Thus all that there is can be described as a component in a universal, continuous, and infinite semiotic flow. The universe is an argument of vast scope, whose end is not a determinate conclusion statable in a proposition (since propositions serve the higher end of *expressing* truth), but is rather the living idea that is reality. The universe is an ever-growing continuum in which thought, matter, and feeling are coming to be welded together into a harmonic state of concrete reasonableness. The ultimate end of this process, the expression of truth, is good not only in logical terms, but also esthetically and ethically. "The Universe as an argument is necessarily a great work of art, a great poem—for every fine argument is a poem and a symphony—just as every true poem is a sound argument" (CP 5.119). For Peirce, then, truth is not something to be grasped or possessed, but is rather something to be *expressed*. In Peirce's evolutionary metaphysics, based as it is on the philosophy of representation, individuals can be considered as infinitesimal parts of the grand continuum in which truth lives. Though the "total effect is beyond our ken . . . we can appreciate in some measure the resultant Quality of parts of the whole" (CP 5.119).

The Metaphysics of Synechism

> Almost everybody will now agree that the ultimate good lies in the evolutionary process in some way. If so, it is not in individual reactions in their segregation, but in something general or continuous. Synechism is founded on the notion that the coalescence, the becoming continuous, the becoming governed by laws, the becoming instinct with general ideas, are but phases of one and the same process of the growth of reasonableness. (CP 5.4)

Peirce called his metaphysical system "synechism," to emphasize the supreme importance in it of the element of Thirdness or continuity (CP 6.202). This should not be taken to imply that all phenomena *are* continuous, something quite contrary to Peirce's thought.[13] Synechism in metaphysics means only that the form of continuous process is indispensable for any attempt to understand reality. Metaphysics, again, is the attempt to develop hypotheses about the nature of the world that afford an explanation, and hence a measure of comprehension, of the way things are. "[T]he only possible justification for so much as entertaining a hypothesis is that it affords an explanation of the phenomena" (CP 6.171).

Synechism is not the simplest available hypothesis about the nature of reality—Peirce knew that extreme nominalism would be far simpler—but he maintained that synechism is the one most appealing to us as scientific inquirers. Several features recommend synechism to *il lume natural,* and render it the most satisfactory hypothesis to adopt. Foremost among these is that it admits no inexplicables, no ultimate principles before which we must simply throw up our hands. This is its great advantage over nominalism, which, Peirce says, "is continually supposing things to be inexplicable" (CP 1.170). Even though there certainly *is* an element of "the inexplicable and ultimate" in the world and in our theories, synechism insists that this element not be allowed to defeat the quest for truth (CP 6.172). The evolutionary theory of mind leaves the door to the future open. We must suppose, on methodological grounds, that what is now inexplicable is in principle capable of explanation, that irrational facts that defy all comprehension can eventually be incorporated into our knowledge. The other side of this coin is that, at any given point, we must suppose our body of knowledge to be incomplete or even mistaken. The hypothesis of synechism thus has "a natural affinity to the doctrine of fallibilism. The principle of continuity is the doctrine of fallibilism objectified. For fallibilism is the doctrine that our knowledge is never absolute but always swims, as it were, in a continuum of uncertainty and indeterminacy" (CP 1.171).

Metaphysics, then, is a high-stakes gamble in the search for truth. By all the indications of the best available metaphysical hypothesis, that very hypothesis itself stands an extremely good chance of being mistaken in some respects, if not altogether. Yet as unlikely as its truth may be, the principle must be adopted if we would have any hope of explaining things. To reject synechism, for Peirce, is to embrace the principle of the inexplicable and ultimately to reject the spirit of the quest for knowledge. The hypothesis that there *is* a reality, a continuum of possibility, existence, and representation toward which all activity must be supposed to be growing, is "our one desperate forlorn hope of knowing anything" (NEM 4:343).

In the project of constructing a metaphysical theory, we must not hesitate to gather up our hypotheses and embark upon speculation. Such an endeavor, however, must be undertaken in a purely scientific attitude. The standards of precise reasoning must be observed, the humble attitude of fallibilism must be adopted in all aspects of the speculation, and the results must be subjected to whatever conditions of verification and falsification can be applied. Peirce's speculative cosmology is just such an endeavor.

SPECULATIVE COSMOLOGY

The hypothesis of synechism offers great explanatory power for metaphysics. It also involves, at its very heart, an assertion that is highly questionable: that the influence of law, of final causation, governs the unfolding of events in the universe. To try to amass direct evidence for or against the reality of law is a pointless endeavor. Every event could well *be* a spontaneous, irrational occurrence, and the world may well be ordered by nothing at all. Existentialism suggests that this hypothesis fits the evidence as well as any other. We simply do not have access to the whole picture of the cosmos, and even if we did, we have no other universe against which we might compare our own. We cannot conduct an empirical comparison of the operation of laws in universes. Although there are apparently elements of order and reasonableness in the world we know, they are certainly balanced by elements of sheer absurdity. This is not an argument against Peirce's ontology, however. He insists that all three metaphysical elements are necessarily present in any event. Spontaneous arising and brute irrational reaction are to be expected alongside orderliness. His hypothesis is only that the universe does not consist *entirely* of the inexplicable and irrational. As we shall see, this hypothesis led Peirce to the *further* hypothesis that the inexplicable and irrational elements are destined to become more intelligible.

Peirce's cosmological speculation aims to show how the three metaphysical principles function together. It asserts an explanatory advantage to admitting the influence of law in the mix of order and absurdity that constitutes the experienced universe. Peirce's designation of cosmology as "mathematical metaphysics" emphasizes its speculative character (CP 6.213). It is an a priori rather than empirical inquiry, in the same sense that geometry and arithmetic are a priori inquiries. Cosmology is subject to confirmation or falsification in a way that mathematics may not be, however, because its conclusions (unlike those of mathematics) are meant to describe the world.[14] The descriptions it offers will eventually prove more or less satisfactory as explanations, and can be modified accordingly.

If we want to admit the element of lawfulness into our explanations, we confront the problem that "conformity with law is a fact requiring to be explained . . . [and] law in general cannot be explained by any law in particular" (CP 1.407). Peirce's cosmological speculation, therefore, aims to show "how law is developed out of pure chance, irregularity, and indeterminacy" (CP 1.407). The mathematics of logic indicates that three categories are necessary and sufficient for constructing a system that can model all possible modes of relation. Phenomenology finds that there are elements in experience that correspond to the three formal categories. Semeiotic details the way in which these constituent elements function in the continuous process of representation and interpretation, governed by the ideal of expressing complete truth. Drawing upon the insights of semeiotic, Peirce proposed that the three fundamental elements in the ultimate constitution of the universe are chance, reaction, and habit-taking. The leap into metaphysics comes with the "guess" that these elements are all part of the unfolding of reality, the object of a true representation.

> Such is our guess of the secret of the sphynx [sic]. To raise it from the rank of philosophical speculation to that of a scientific hypothesis, we must show that consequences can be deduced from it with more or less probability which can be compared with observation. We must show that there is some method of deducing the characters of the laws which could result in this way by the action of habit-taking on purely fortuitous occurrences, and a method of ascertaining whether such characters belong to the actual laws of nature. (CP 1.410)

In developing his cosmological account of law or regularity, Peirce insisted that we not "exaggerate the part that law plays in the universe" (CP 1.406). We are predisposed to do so, because it is only "by means of regularities that we understand what little we do understand of the world" (CP 1.406). In the vast plurality of events, however, "uniformity is seen to be a highly exceptional phenomenon" (CP 1.406). If we were to take a scattering of events at random, it would almost always prove difficult to discover any significant connection among them. Not everything, after all, has anything to do with the price of tea in China. The first thing to bear in mind, then, is that "conformity to law exists only within a limited range of events" (CP 1.407).

Moreover, we should assume that law's influence on events is imperfect. Tychism, the principle of absolute chance, suggests this assumption. In response to the question whether there is any evidence for it, Peirce noted that classical physics postulates that molecules of gas move "irregularly, substantially as if by real chance," and pointed out that "by the principles of probabilities there must occasionally happen to be concentrations of heat in the gases contrary to the second law of thermodynamics, and these concentrations, occurring in explosive mixtures, must sometimes have tremendous effects" (CP 6.47). Very rarely, something probably blows up for no reason at all. Science recognizes that laws are valid only as statistical generalizations. They are not expected to hold with absolute precision in every particular case.[15] In sum, Peirce says, "I do not believe that anybody . . . can maintain that the precise and universal conformity of facts to law is clearly proved, or even rendered particularly probable, by any observations hitherto made" (CP 6.48).[16] Thus the conformity of events to law is on the one hand exhibited only in a limited number of events, and on the other hand, is most likely imperfect even then (CP 1.407). Our cosmology must provide an account of the origin of law that conforms to these observations about its scope.

The overall picture of the evolutionary development of the universe is that such laws as do govern events have arisen through the tendency of spontaneous events to take habits. "A Guess at the Riddle" asserts:

> At present, the course of events is approximately determined by law. In the past that approximation was less perfect; in the future it will be more perfect. The tendency to obey laws has always been and always will be growing. We look back toward a point in the infinitely distant past when there was no law but mere indeterminacy; we look forward to a point in the infinitely distant future when there will be no indeterminacy or chance but a complete reign of law. But at any assignable date in the past, however early, there was already some tendency toward uniformity; and at any assignable date in the future there will be some slight aberrancy from law. (CP 1.409)

Peirce's cosmological ideas will be presented here largely in his own words. Most of the material is drawn from "A Guess at the Riddle" and the drafts for eight lectures he proposed to deliver in Cambridge in 1898.[17] An entry on "Modality" in the manuscript "Prescott Book" from 1907 and a key passage from the 1908 "Neglected Argument for the Reality of God" are also used. With a minimum of explanatory and transitional comments, and some rearrangement to eliminate redundancy and digression, these texts adequately convey the main features of Peirce's mathematical metaphysics.

A word of caution before we begin: Cosmology is literally "prescientific" in that what it seeks to explain are the very elements of our scientific conceptual vocabulary. Plato expressed his cosmology in the form of quasi-mythical accounts; Peirce likewise observed that "[o]ur conceptions of the first stages of the development, before time yet existed, must be as vague and figurative as the expressions of the first chapter of Genesis" (CP 1.412).

Peirce began by postulating a state of *complete* indeterminacy, a "zero-state" antecedent to the appearance of the three categories:

> If we are to proceed in a logical and scientific manner, we must, in order to account for the whole universe, suppose an initial condition in which the whole universe was non-existent, and therefore a state of absolute nothing.
>
> . . . .
>
> But this is not the nothing of negation. . . . The nothing of negation is the nothing of death, which comes *second* to, or after, everything. But this pure zero is the nothing of not having been born. There is no individual thing, no compulsion,

outward nor inward, no law. It is the germinal nothing, in which the whole universe is involved or foreshadowed. As such, it is absolutely undefined and unlimited possibility—boundless possibility. There is no compulsion and no law. It is boundless freedom.

. . . .

Now the question arises, what necessarily resulted from that state of things? But the only sane answer is that where freedom was boundless nothing in particular necessarily resulted.

. . . .

I say that nothing *necessarily* resulted from the Nothing of boundless freedom. That is, nothing according to deductive logic. But such is not the logic of freedom or possibility. The logic of freedom, or potentiality, is that it shall annul itself. For if it does not annul itself, it remains a completely idle and do-nothing potentiality; and a completely idle potentiality is annulled by its complete idleness. (CP 6.215–19)

The principle that the logic of the universe is at least as sophisticated as our own—that it therefore includes retroduction, the spontaneous form of inference that initiates a stream of inference—leads us to an account of the first stirrings of determination in the utter indeterminacy of Nothing. This is the first appearance of a mode of positive possibility, different from the mere absence of determination that characterizes the initial zero-state.

I do not mean that potentiality immediately results in actuality. Mediately perhaps it does; but what immediately resulted was that unbounded potentiality became potentiality of this or that sort—that is, of some *quality*.
Thus the zero of bare possibility, by evolutionary logic, leapt into the *unit* of some quality. This was hypothetic inference. (CP 6.220)

The potentiality of a quality, in Peirce's metaphysics, is analogous to the Platonic Form or Idea. It is an eternal, self-subsisting possibility that serves as the metaphysical ground of the world of actual existence. "The evolutionary process is, therefore, not a mere evolution of the *existing universe,* but rather a process by which the very Platonic forms themselves have become or are becoming developed" (CP 6.194).

The very earliest stages of cosmological evolution, like the early stages of every process of evolution, are characterized by extreme vagueness of form (CP 6.191). Our hypothetical single, spontaneously emerging qualitative possibility is not sharp-edged; the process of determination as yet consists only in a lone arbitrary determination within the zero-state. This is the possibility of *a* quality, indeed, but a quality that is not distinct from any other qualities. It thus brings a whole unordered universe of immediately connected possible qualities into being. The process has to unfold further before qualities can meaningfully be considered distinct.

> [W]e must not assume that the qualities arose separate and came into relation afterward. It was just the reverse. The general indefinite potentiality became limited and heterogeneous. (CP 6.199)
> The evolution of forms begins or, at any rate, has for an early stage of it, a vague potentiality; and that either is or is followed by a continuum of forms having a multitude of dimensions too great for the individual dimensions to be distinct. It must be by a contraction of the vagueness of that potentiality of everything in general, but of nothing in particular, that the world of forms comes about. (CP 6.196)

The emergence of the continuum of positive possibility establishes the first of the three "universes of experience," the Universe of Ideas or Possibility (CP 6.455).

Note that all three of the metaphysical principles appear in this universe. Firstness predominates, because the universe consists of ideas, mere "airy nothings" whose "Being consists in mere capability of getting thought" (CP 6.455). The doctrine that there is a mode of being, potentiality, that is dominated by the element of Firstness is called *Tychism*. There is, however, an element of Secondness in the emergence of a universe of forms where there was only indefinite nothingness before, and an element of Thirdness in the connectedness and eternal subsistence of those forms.

As the evolution continues, Secondness comes to the fore. Nascent relations of identity and difference emerge in and among parts of the universe of forms, and qualities thereby come to be differentiated. So far we have considered the transition from an initial "zero-state" to the first element, the "unit" of the first quality.

> The *second* element we have to assume is that there could be accidental reactions between those qualities. The qualities themselves are mere eternal possibilities. But these reactions we must think of as *events*. Not that *Time* was. But still, they had all the here-and-nowness of events. I really do not see how the metaphysician can explain either of these elements as results, further than this, that it may be said that the accidental reaction was, at first, one of the special determinations that came about by pure spontaneity or chance. (CP 6.200)

The next milestone in the evolution of the cosmos is the appearance of enduring existence, the Universe of Brute Actuality of things and facts (CP 6.455). The evolutionary shift from the first universe to the second, however, is not abrupt. Peirce describes a continuous process of beginning. The designation of the different universes only indicates stages in the process. As the development of relations progresses, through several stages of evolution by chance occurrence, time and space emerge.

> Out of the womb of indeterminacy we must say that there would have come something, by the principle of Firstness, which we may call a flash. Then by the principle of habit there would have been a second flash. Though time would not yet have been, this second flash was in some sense after the first, because resulting from it. Then there would have come other successions ever more and more closely connected, the habits and the tendency to take them ever strengthening themselves, until the events would have been bound together into something like a continuous flow. (CP 1.412)

This continuous "quasi-flow" represents the headwaters of an almost perfectly continuous temporal stream.

> The quasi-flow which would result would, however, differ essentially from time in this respect, that it would not necessarily be in a single stream. Different flashes might start different streams, between which there should be no relations of contemporaneity or succession. So one stream might branch into two, or two might coalesce. But the further result of habit would inevitably be to separate utterly those that were long separated, and to make those which presented frequent common points coalesce into perfect union. Those that were completely separated would be so many different worlds which would know nothing of one another; so that the effect would be just what we actually observe. (CP 1.412)

Space develops in a similar fashion, through the spontaneous occurrence of pairs of events that tend to become ever more regular under the influence of the principle of habit.

> Secondness is of two types. Consequently besides flashes genuinely second to others, so as to come after them, there will be pairs of flashes, or, since time is now supposed to be developed, we had better say pairs of states, which are reciprocally

second, each member of the pair to the other. This is the first germ of spatial extension. (CP 1.413)

As pairs of states continue to emerge, relations develop among them. The effect of habit is to establish certain relations as pathways for change among the states.

> Those states to which a state will immediately pass will be adjacent to it; and thus habits will be formed which constitute a spatial continuum, but differing from our space by being very irregular in its connections, having one number of dimensions in one place and another number in another place, and being different for one moving state from what it is for another. (CP 1.413)

Time thus develops out of the occurrence of pairs of events, bound in a genuine dyadic relation such that the "second" event is what it is only relative to the "first," and vice versa. This elementary ordering relation begets continuous temporal succession. Space develops out of relations among various pairs of states, in which pairs the "first" and "second" states are bound by a degenerate dyadic relation. Each state in such a relation would be what it is independent of the other's existence, but they do occur together.

Substance, the distinguishing feature of an enduring thing, develops out of the establishment of habits within such degenerate pairings.

> Pairs of states will also begin to take habits, and thus each state having different habits with reference to the different other states will give rise to bundles of habits, which will be substances. Some of these states will chance to take habits of persistency, and will get to be less and less liable to disappear; while those that fail to take such habits will fall out of existence. Thus, substances will get to be permanent. (CP 1.414)

In the nascent time and space, then, organized bundles of habits come to embody particular qualities that are distinguishable from other bundles of habits embodying other qualities. Those bundles of habits that tend to persist, which happen to acquire the habit of enduring, come to dominate the universe in the form of existing things or actualities. Thus the cosmos develops into a state where Secondness predominates: the Universe of Actuality (CP 6.455).

Actuality is comprised of enduring entities or "individuals." Two-valued logic supposes that it is possible to determine, with respect to any quality, whether a given individual possesses that quality. In short, the principles of contradiction and excluded middle apply to logical individuals. This is perfectly acceptable and even necessary for most logical operations. Peirce insisted, however, that the notion of the individual is misleading for metaphysics.[18] In metaphysics we must distinguish between the idea of "the absolutely indivisible and that which is one in number from a particular point of view," between *individual* (**το 'ἄτομον**) and *singular* (**τὸ καθ' ἕκαστον**) (CP 3.93). An absolute individual would be completely determinate in all respects, but there is no such entity in the Universe of Actuality. "There is but one *individual*, or completely determinate, state of things, namely, the all of reality" (CP 5.549). This is the hypothetical and unreachable dynamical object of all representation.

As the account of substance shows, what we designate in metaphysics as an individual is anything "whose identity consists in a continuity of reactions," any bundle of habits that exhibits the property of resistance against an other (CP 3.613). It is only with respect to particular purposes, however, and hence from particular points of view, that things emerge as individuals. Metaphysically, we should suppose that these purportedly individual things are united in a continuous system.

> [I]ndividual existence depends upon the circumstance that not all that is possible is possible in conjunction. But existence is continuous as far as the nature of the case admits. At every point of it, it reunites all qualities each in some degree. (MS 942, pp. 13–14)

> The absolute individual . . . cannot exist, properly speaking. For whatever lasts for any time, however short, is capable of logical division, because in that time it will undergo some change in its relations. But what does not exist for any time, however short, does not exist at all. (CP 3.93n.1)

As with the Universe of Ideas, all three metaphysical principles are in evidence in the Universe of Actuality, the realm of existence. That there should *be* substances, which can endure and enter into existence, is a completely arbitrary fact. Peirce adopts Duns Scotus's term *haecceity* to designate the arbitrary here-and-nowness of existence, and like Scotus, he accepts *haecceity* as an independent and uncaused principle of being.[19] *Haecceity*, arising by chance, functions to originate the Universe of Actuality. Habit-taking, as we have seen, is also crucial to this universe: it is the tendency of the different pairs of states to instantiate different qualities, and to persist in those instantiations, which gives rise to permanent substances.

Peirce describes the principle of habit-taking, and its most dramatic effect on the evolving cosmos, in the following terms:

all things have a tendency to take habits. . . . [For] every conceivable real object, there is a greater probability of acting as on a former like occasion than otherwise. This tendency itself constitutes a regularity, and is continually on the increase. . . . It is a generalizing tendency; it causes actions in the future to follow some generalization of past actions; and this tendency itself is something capable of similar generalizations; and thus, it is self-generative. (CP 1.409)

The principle of habit-taking, operative in the first two stages of cosmic evolution, begins to come to prominence once actuality is well established. Actuality is characterized by reactions among enduring things. The character of such things, and consequently the relations and modes of interaction among them, would be extremely irregular at first. The principle of habit-taking has the effect of making events in the Universe of Actuality more stable and regular. It underlies the emergence of permanent substances, as we have seen. Beyond this, it has the effect of stabilizing the kinds of reaction that tend to occur among different substances. Nothing *forces* a tendency toward regularity in the Universe of Actuality, for the notion of force implies necessity, an advanced variety of the regularity we are trying to explain (CP 1.407). Regularity, like possibility and particularity, must appear in the evolving cosmos by chance. But just as we have seen the tendency to take habits operate on Firstness to establish the Universe of Ideas and on Secondness to establish the universe of Actuality, so does it operate on Thirdness, on itself, to establish a universe dominated by Thirdness, lawfulness, order, and reasonableness.

The element of habit-taking has a peculiarity about it. it is the only possibility that, once occurring, "can grow by its own virtue" (CP 6.101). Thus it operates in the respective universes with increasing efficiency. In the Universe of Actuality it serves to establish regularity in the various substances, both in their internal nature and in their external relations to one another. It gives rise, in short, to the regularities we recognize as the laws of nature. According to Peirce's cosmology, "each law of nature would consist in some permanence, such as the permanence of mass, momentum, and energy. In this respect, the theory suits the facts admirably" (CP 1.415). As the principle of habit-taking operates to promulgate its own influence, events in the actual world become more regular, more predictable. *Necessity*—as embodied, for example, in the idea of necessary connection that Hume rightly said is absent from the observable realm of existent things—emerges in the form of laws that govern events. Necessity is the support of actuality by reason, the generalization of the particular events in the Universe of Actuality (MS 277, p. 123).

As law takes hold, the evolving cosmos can be seen wending its way toward a Universe of Necessity, in which law would be perfect. This

Universe is the completely reasonable state of things that is identified in esthetics as an ideal. This universe is, on the one hand, unrealizable in principle, because it would imply the complete eclipse of Possibility and Haecceity, which are as fundamental as Necessity; on the other hand, it is the regulative ideal toward which self-controlled thought and action aim. The increase of reasonable thought and action, in the context of all three universes, is accordingly the summum bonum in Peirce's philosophy.

Peirce's cosmology gives us a picture, then, of continuous evolution from an absolutely indeterminate zero-state toward a universe of absolute order. Of course, this process is and can never be anywhere near complete. In its current state, the Universe of Necessity "comprises everything whose being consists in active power to establish connections between different objects, especially between objects in different Universes" (CP 6.455). We have seen this passage before: the only things that possess this "active power" to unite objects from different universes are symbols, most familiar to us as the medium of thought. The complete symbol unites elements of quality (qualisigns), reaction (indices), and law (legisigns) in the irreducibly triadic representation relation. Though many of the writings on cosmology that serve as the basis for the present discussion pre-date Peirce's detailed work on semeiotic, his cosmology and metaphysics are ultimately best understood as semiotic systems. This connection is crucial for understanding the details of his metaphysics. The next sections suggest a few broad implications of this connection for Peirce's metaphysics.

COSMOLOGICAL IMPLICATIONS OF SEMEIOTIC

The first thing to be noted is that semiosis is an infinite process. The genuine sign is an essentially triadic relation among object, sign, and interpretant. Any genuine sign therefore presupposes both an object that is its antecedent and an interpretant that is its consequent. Semiosis can in principle have no absolute beginning or end. The cosmological process of evolution, which paradoxically *begins before time,* is the metaphysical analogue to the process of beginning that gives rise to the hypothetical first representation, or, in psychology, to the "first impression of sense" in the perceptual judgment. Likewise, semiosis can have no absolute end. The account of the *entelechy* in **καινὰ στοιχεῖα** as the perfect sign that would represent absolute truth (NEM 4:239–40) ought to be read alongside Peirce's account of the origin of the Universes. The description of the *entelechy* is in fact the conclusion to Peirce's speculative cosmology. This absolute end of the universe is real in the same metaphorical or analogical sense that the postulated initial zero-state is real. These are limits to the infinite process and hence are not attainable points.

The second thing to be noted is the relation of Peirce's notion of evolutionary love to semiosis. Recall that symbols are teleological entities. The hypothesis that reality ought to be conceived in semiotic terms indicates that the cosmos, too, is teleological. The teleology of semiosis is manifest in Peirce's metaphysical concept of evolution. Peirce identified three different theories of evolution that ought to be considered as possible accounts of the increasing specialization and diversification that characterize the development of the cosmos (CP 6.296-302).[20] The first, which he calls "tychastic evolution" or simply *tychasm*, is evolution by fortuitous variation, exemplified in Darwin's theory. The second, which he calls "anancastic evolution" or *anancasm*, is evolution according to mechanical necessity. Under this head Peirce included not only those theories, which hold that the transformations leading to speciation occur due to a not-yet-understood internal principle that requires them, but also those that attribute the variation of species to external causes such as cataclysmic changes in the environment that affect one or a few generations. The third, "agapastic evolution" or *agapasm*, is evolution by creative love. "The doctrines which represent these as severally of principal importance we may term *tychasticism, anancasticism*, and *agapasticism*" (CP 6.302). While Peirce saw much in the first two of these theories, he argued that both describe cosmic evolution inadequately.

Anancasticism is on the right track with its suggestion that events as a whole are tending toward "a foreordained perfection" (CP 6.305). Its flaws are two, however. First, "living freedom is practically omitted" from this account (CP 6.305). As noted previously, Peirce insisted that experience simply does not sanction the idea that the logic of events adheres to mechanical determination. A second objection not articulated by Peirce might be that the versions of anancasticism that attribute variation to rigid internal principles have simply been unable to discover any such principles. To the extent that mechanical causation operates in heredity, it apparently only operates between successive generations. There is no good evidence of what might be called "emergent mechanical causes," whose effects are indiscernible between successive generations, but which become evident over the course of several or many generations as one type of organism develops into another. To posit such causes is to admit all the effects of fortuitous variation, but to insist that the variation is necessary rather than fortuitous. Yet something like emergent mechanical causes must be introduced if mechanism is to explain anything except direct transmission of traits. To say simply that such emergent mechanical causes are not explainable would, of course, be unacceptable for Peirce.

Peirce had no similar scientific objection to tychasticism; the idea of fortuitous variation is prominent in his own theory of agapasticism. His objection is to its ethical implications. Tychasm posits that variation is due to chance mutations, but this alone is inadequate to ensure that the advantageous changes will be preserved in subsequent generations. Darwin therefore introduced natural selection, "the crowding out of the weak" or less fortunate, as the principle that allows fortuitous variations to take hold (CP 6.296). If adopted as a metaphysical hypothesis, the theory would seem to imply that the good, the summum bonum, is advanced through a combination of fortunate birth and a willingness to ruthlessly crush one's neighbors underfoot. It makes the individual the primary agent of change, and moreover, it appears to endorse a particularly brutal brand of individualism. The supreme importance of the individual in this theory does not accord well with the metaphysics of continuity. Its inadequacy becomes especially clear when we conceive synechism on the model of semeiotic, where the notion of the singular sign (the "individual") logically presupposes the whole semiotic continuum.

Tychasm cannot be rejected out of hand, then, and anancasm is at least on the right track in neutralizing the radical individualism of tychasm. Peirce's theory of agapastic evolution represents an attempt to preserve *both* the element of chance posited in tychasm *and* the teleological element posited in anancasm, while negating the individualism of the former and the determinism of the latter.

Peirce suggested that our conception of cosmic evolution be modeled on the evolutionary theory of Lamarck:

> According to his view, all that distinguishes the highest organic forms from the most rudimentary has been brought about by little hypertrophies or atrophies which have affected individuals early in their lives, and have been transmitted to their offspring. Such a transmission of acquired characters is of the general nature of habit-taking. . . . The Lamarckians further suppose that, although some of the modifications of form so transmitted were originally due to mechanical causes, yet the chief factors of their first production were the straining of endeavor and the overgrowth superinduced by exercise, together with the opposite actions. Now, endeavor, since it is directed toward an end, is essentially psychical, even though it be sometimes unconscious. . . . (CP 6.299)

Thus in Peirce's understanding of the Lamarckian theory, fortuitous deviation from the norm remains a crucial element in evolution. These deviations occur in individuals, and even when they arise not by pure chance but as the result of external or internal circumstances, the nature of the resulting deviation is largely tychastic. In the face of similar demands, different individuals will develop very different and often novel adaptive responses.

In Darwin's tychastic evolution, successful adaptations persist primarily because those individuals who possess them crowd out those who possess other adaptations. In Lamarckian evolution, adaptations persist primarily because of what can be described as a generalizing tendency. What was once peculiar to a single individual begins to spread, until it becomes a trait of the species. Although this is perhaps not as plausible an account of biological evolution as Darwinian theory, it precisely describes the way symbols evolve. With each generation of an interpretant there is the possibility (perhaps even an inevitability) that a small hypertrophy or atrophy of information will occur and be embodied in the new symbol. This occurs, as we saw in chapter 6, because the process of semiosis itself continually remakes its dynamical object by depositing new features into it. Today's novel interpretant becomes part of tomorrow's settled fact, a potential object of subsequent representation.

Peirce also saw a teleological aspect to Lamarckian evolution. Although the specific nature of a given deviation is open to chance, the fact that there is a deviation is usually the result of some unusual exertion or endeavor on the individual's part. The deviation arises when the individual exerts itself in the pursuit of some end. Broadly speaking, then, exertion is seen as a form of expression of love for this end. In Peirce's semeiotic-based metaphysics, the end of ends toward which all things strive is the summum bonum. Signs strive to express absolute truth; singular parts of the cosmos strive to express or bring about absolute reality.

Carl Hausman notes that this love for an end might take either of two forms: "Eros is love that is expressed by what seeks something more perfect, or more fulfilling, than what is possessed by the lover in the absence of union with the beloved. . . . Agape, on the other hand, is love expressed by an agent already fulfilled in its own terms, and it is directed not as a seeking but as a concern for the beloved."[21] Both forms of love operate in Peircean evolution. In so far as the end of the process appears as a determinate and perfect goal, that end operates through eros and "lures" the process toward it. The semiotic ideal of perfect representation in the *entelechy*, and the metaphysical ideal of perfect order in the Universe of Necessity, both appear to any singular part of the respective processes as perfections of themselves. But neither of these ideals are or ever can be fully determinate goals. Their details are waiting to be filled out by the very processes they motivate. Hausman points out that in these circumstances, the end becomes more determinate through the spontaneous and creative action of the singular "subjects" of the process: "the subject must be concerned for a future creature which will or would exemplify an excellence in an end to be realized if the process is or were completed."[22] The love guiding both semeiotic and metaphysical evolution is agape, directed at the always unrealized end. The greatest good, the summum bonum, then is the cherishing act of bringing this end into being.

Peirce suggested that the "propositions that absolute chance, mechanical necessity, and the law of love are severally operative in the cosmos may receive the names of *tychism*, *anancism*, and *agapism*" (CP 6.302). For reasons noted earlier, however, Peirce tended to emphasize the notion of continuity in the Universe of Actuality rather than the notion of mechanical reaction. Accordingly, his three metaphysical principles, each of them operative in all of being, are *tychism, synechism,* and *agapism.*

THE PROBLEM OF EXTRA-SEMIOTIC ENTITIES

There is one particular problem that the semiotic conception of the universe raises, and which deserves special treatment here. It concerns the ontological status of existent entities, of the individual things that common sense insists are "out there," external to all thought. The question may be put in the following terms: If all of reality is to be conceived in terms of semeiotic, as governed by the law of mind, does all of reality then have ontological status only as it enters into sign-action? One answer to this question has been proposed in the assertion by David Savan that Peirce was a "semiotic idealist."[23] I contend that, whatever merit the theory of semiotic idealism may have, Savan is mistaken in attributing a version of it to Peirce.

First of all, our account of the internal structure of a complete symbol indicates that there must be elements of the universe that are not merely semiotic. Because a complete symbol requires indices and sinsigns, which are defined as individual existent things involved in dyadic relations to other existents, the answer to the question whether Peirce was a semiotic idealist is in one respect relatively simple. Although everything there is may *potentially* be a sign, not everything that has being is *only* a sign.[24] There are non-semiotic aspects to the universe, so it seems that Savan is right to say that Peirce rejected "strong" semiotic idealism: he did *not* maintain that "the very existence of any thing depends upon the system of signs, representations, and interpretations which purport to refer to it."[25] The catch is that a thing is a constituent part of reality only in so far as it would become an element of the complete symbol Peirce called the *entelechy.*

Savan characterizes Peirce as a "mild" semiotic idealist. This position maintains that "any properties, attributes, or characteristics of whatever exists depend upon the system of signs, representations, or interpretations through which they are signified."[26] The mild semiotic idealist accepts that there are independently existing things, but insists that their *properties* are determined by the sign-system in which they function (in Peirce's case, that system is the process of evolution toward the perfectly real sign). Peirce did not adhere to strong semiotic idealism, which makes the extra-semiotic entities' very existence depend upon the sign system. Savan finds the anti-"semiotic idealist" position he calls "extreme realism" unacceptable, as well, and argues that Peirce likewise rejected it. Savan says that this position (let us call it *extreme semiotic realism*) "is of no interest to anyone who is in pursuit of understanding. For such a realist, whatever [apparent] knowledge and understanding human inquiry may attain, the truth may quite possibly be otherwise. Such a possibility can not be the goal or presupposition of science."[27] I argue that, as unsettling as the position may be, Peirce's logical realism implies just this form of extreme semiotic realism.

Peirce held that there are existent things, characterized predominantly by Secondness, independent of semiosis. This position is rooted in logic, which according to Peirce must hope (among other things) "that any given question is susceptible of a true answer, and that this answer is discoverable, that *being* and *being represented* are different, that there is a reality, and that the real world is governed by ideas" (NEM 4:20). Here we see the joint assertion that there is objective truth and that metaphysics must suppose the world to be governed by the law of mind. Peirce's assertion in this passage that *being* and *being represented* are different can be understood to mean that existent things have ontological status independently of semiosis.

Note that both mild semiotic idealism and extreme semiotic realism presume the existence of extra-semiotic individuals. This is necessary, as Savan points out, in order to account for the fact of surprising and compelling elements in experience.[28] Peirce's theory of perceptual judgment requires the hypothesis of an independent external world. Perception, for Peirce, is a representation of some object by one's present self to one's future self, which interprets the object as a perceived event: "In a perceptual judgment the mind professes to tell the mind's future self what the character of the present percept is" (CP 7.630). Now what gets represented in a perceptual judgment often comes without any warning, and enters the stream of cognition contrary to all expectation. I flip a light switch and experience a loud pop and darkness rather than the expected bright light. I have no control over the process by which I represent these phenomena to myself, but the process is indeed describable in semiotic terms.

If we ask what the object of the perceptual judgment is, we come into murky waters. We can identify no prior cognition that would have the perception of a loud pop and darkness as its proper interpretant. The only prior cognition of which we *may* have been aware would have had a representation of bright, room-filling light as its interpretant. The novel cognition must have come from somewhere, though, and all we can do is to suggest a hypothesis about what kind of object would generate this kind of surprising sign. Thus we embrace the metaphysical hypothesis that there is indeed a system of individual enduring things, connected through dyadic reactions, which exist independently of semiosis. These extra-semiotic individuals are the dynamical object of my perceptual judgment, and make their presence known in unexpected intrusions into the semiotic flow of cognition.

Independent existence, then, is hypothesized as the dynamical object of certain representations. Because existence is proposed as an object of representation, and because (following Peirce) we have rejected nominalism in favor of logical realism, we must suppose there is some determinate truth about it which would be revealed as the final interpretant of a perfect representation of that object. Here is where I part company with Savan. He argues that Peirce's alleged "mild semiotic idealism" makes the characters (though not the existence) of the extra-semiotic world depend on the sign-system. If it makes any sense to speak of truth in connection with the object of perceptual judgments, though, that truth must be objective in the sense that it does *not* depend upon our particular perceptions of it. The definition of truth deriving from Peirce's logical realism makes truth independent of what any finite inquiry, or any finite process of semiosis, may happen to lead us to believe. A true interpretant would never be revised, because it would accord in all respects with the objectively determinate character of the object. There is an independent world of dyadic existence, we must suppose, and some parts of this world *may* not be incorporated into any sign until the end of semiosis. Their characters would not be known until that mythical moment, but they must be *something* independent of their representation: existence has the special characteristic "of being absolutely determinate" (CP 6.439). Until the end of semiosis and the realization of a perfect symbol, our knowledge of these characters very well might be radically mistaken.

In "How to Make Our Ideas Clear," Peirce introduced his notorious example of the diamond that materializes and is utterly destroyed without ever having been perceived or tested for hardness. In that article, Peirce wrote that there would be "no *falsity*" in saying that the diamond is soft. Such modes of speech "would involve a modification of our present usage of speech with regard to the words hard and soft, but not of their meanings. For they represent no fact to be different than what it is; only they involve arrangements of facts which would be exceedingly maladroit" (CP 5.403). This might be taken to suggest that the existent thing that never enters the semiotic sphere does not *have* a determinate property of hardness, and is thus neither hard nor soft. As an inoculation against this interpretation, Peirce wrote in the 1905 "Issues of Pragmaticism": "Remember that this diamond's condition is not an isolated fact. There is no such thing; and an isolated fact could hardly be real. It is an unsevered, though presciss part of the unitary fact of nature" (CP 5.457). If it is anything but a pure logical fiction, even in its relatively isolated state the diamond must enter into some dyadic relations with some other part of the world. There are, again, no *absolutely* isolated individuals or facts about individuals. The diamond's existence must surely have some effect on its surroundings, and either its hardness or other properties associated with its hardness will leave a mark on the one determinate dynamical object that is the existent world. Though this effect, and hence the diamond's hardness may remain unknown until the end of inquiry, Peirce insisted that *at* the end of inquiry, all information about the world would be represented in the perfect and all-encompassing *entelechy*. Short of that perfect state of information, though, we may well be ignorant or mistaken about any given character of existence.

Savan claims, again, that this extreme semiotic realism is of "no inter-est to anyone who is in pursuit of understanding," because it allows that the truth "may quite possibly be otherwise" than what inquiry suggests. Savan is correct to say that this ontology leaves the door wide open for all our present readings of the book of nature to be exposed as mistaken. Though *quite* unlikely, it is just possible that we will discover there are no such things as fossils after all, but only bone-shaped rocks. This is hardly a position of "no interest" to one who pursues understanding, however: it is a direct consequence of the principle of fallibilism. Peirce balanced this skeptical strain with the affirmation that, after all, whenever we engage in rational thought we tacitly suppose that our thought is leading toward the truth in the long run, and that if there is indeed such a thing as truth, then all we need do is to persist in the methods of science to get close to it (SS 75).

The Development of Reason

Peirce's metaphysics provides us with a complex picture of the universe as a vast semiotic process, evolving under the gentle guidance of agapism toward greater rationality and order.

> The very being of the General, of Reason, *consists* in its govern-ing individual events. So, then, the essence of Reason is such that its being never can have been completely perfected. It always must be in a state of incipiency, of growth. . . . This development of Reason consists, you will observe, in embodi-ment, that is, in manifestation. The creation of the universe, which did not take place during a certain busy week, in the year 4004 B.C., but is going on today and never will be done, is this very developement [sic] of Reason. (CP 1.615)

A metaphysical theory must ultimately offer us something humanly signifi-cant, a measure of comprehension of the universe in which we find our-selves. If we are extremely fortunate, the metaphysical guesses we advance are not entirely wrong and offer some approximate representation of the truth about our place in the universe. According to Peirce, though, truth is not something that we come to possess by merely looking at the world as spectators and which, once we have it, is merely to be asserted in true propositions. It is rather something discovered, internalized, and expressed in the course of active inquiry.

The most important feature of Peirce's synechism is the notion that we are constitutive parts of the cosmic development of reason, and that our various inquiries, conducted well or badly, contribute to the evolution of reason. Metaphysical knowledge, like any knowledge, must directly or indirectly feed back into our actions or else be meaningless and dead. Peirce's metaphysics, in short, makes it an ideal of conduct to continue the process of self-controlled inquiry of which, on his account, we are but infinitesimal parts.

> I do not see how one can have a more satisfying ideal of the admirable than the development of Reason so understood. The one thing whose admirableness is not due to an ulterior reason is Reason itself comprehended in all its fullness, so far as we can comprehend it. Under this conception, the ideal of conduct will be to execute our little function in the operation of the creation by giving a hand toward rendering the world more reasonable whenever, as the slang is, it is "up to us" to do so. (CP 1.615)

The fulfillment of this ideal requires us to submit all our thoughts and actions to criticism, constantly to evaluate them in terms of what they contribute to the summum bonum. Philosophy is the self-conscious, critical attempt to describe and employ the most effective means of transforming ideas so as to contribute to the growth of reasonableness in the cosmos.

Testing Metaphysical Hypotheses

The demand that philosophical thought (including metaphysical speculation) be subject to criticism and revision may strike us as admirable but hopeless. We must consider the question of the testability of synechism. We begin by looking at some of the specific ideas that it generates, and then close by raising the Peircean question of questions: Is the hypothesis of synechism itself in any sense subject to confirmation or falsification?

The salient claim of synechism is that there is something very close to true continuity in the world. Several consequences can be deduced from this hypothesis, and these consequences ought to be subject to some degree of verification if the general hypothesis is true. One such consequence of the continuity hypothesis is that the notion of the infinitesimal ought to be a logically consistent mathematical notion. As noted in chapter 4, this result was proven by Robinson, whose system of "non-standard analysis" depends on the logical admissibility of infinitesimals.

Peirce claims more for continuity than mere logical consistency, however. He claims that continuity is manifest to some degree in the actual universe. This would imply, for one thing, that there are real infinitesimal quantities in nature. Robinson vigorously denied that his infinitesimals correspond to anything in nature, but the founder of a theory is seldom able to foresee all of its implications. Engineers and physicists have long gone about their work just *as if* infinitesimal quantities really existed.[29] With the theory of non-standard analysis established, that practice does seem to have received a common-sense vindication. More significant evidence of real infinitesimals may come in the future. To give meaning to the notion of "real infinitesimals," a situation would have to arise where we must work with phenomena involving infinitesimal quantities that cannot be dealt with in the standard Weierstrassian system, but which can be handled consistently using non-standard techniques. To my knowledge, no such phenomena have yet been identified. Based on the general observations that mathematical tools tend to beget their own unique applications, and that the human mind is quite often inept at noticing phenomena that it lacks the ability to explain, it seems worth speculating that, with non-standard analysis now available, we may at some point encounter "real infinitesimals."

Another consequence of synechism is that there are real generals in nature. A general property "surrenders to the interpreter the right of completing the determination for himself" (CP 5.505). As Edward C. Moore observes, a real general would then be objectively indeterminate in respect to some property.[30] Moore cites several examples from the sciences that at least suggest objective indeterminacy in some phenomena. Most prominent among these is the Einsteinian principle that an object's length, mass, and time are relative to the velocity of the observer. Moore comments,

> Now, if the temporal and spatial dimensions of objects are general, and if the mass measurements show mass to be a general property, what remains that is particular in the physicalistic sense? It would seem to me that what we have are general objects, not particular objects. The physicist may not wish to draw this conclusion, but what better can a metaphysician do?[31]

Moore cites the "Copenhagen interpretation" of quantum theory as another case in point. The principle of indeterminacy here requires that in describing the state of an electron, we must think of it as having either a generalized location or a generalized velocity. *In principle* only one of these variables is determinate in any given case.[32]

In chapter 3 I discussed the main implication of continuity for logic, which Peirce himself identified: that we can introduce into our deductive systems a third truth value, the "Limit" between "Truth" and "Falsity." This approach, along with various forms of modal logic, have been suggested as strategies for coping with what appears to be indeterminacy at the quantum level.

These instances of apparent agreement with some of the more intriguing consequences of synechism do not, of course, come near to confirming the metaphysical theory. They do suggest that Peirce was at least a sufficiently good student of late nineteenth-century science to be able to detect the general drift of its ideas, and to foresee that indeterminacy was likely to become a concept of great importance in our understanding of physical phenomena. If indeterminacy and genuine possibility are conceptual problems for science, then Peirce would urge scientists to take whatever they can from his metaphysics and put it to work to resolve those problems. Only in that way will we discover the merits of these hypotheses.

The most comprehensive assertion of synechism is not one that can be corroborated by the findings of physics or any other particular science, however. The central hypothesis of synechism is that logical thought necessarily involves the conception of reality, where reality is conceived as the object of truth represented in the semiotic continuum. Peirce's philosophy stands or falls with this hypothesis. We want to hold Peirce to his word when he insists that his metaphysics be subjected to the same criticism and criteria of testability as any other scientific theory. So we ask: Is the hypothesis of synechism itself in any sense subject to confirmation or falsification?

First, we must clarify what it means to have a testable hypothesis. An account of valid hypothesis-formation appears in the entry "Probable Inference" that Peirce wrote for Baldwin's *Dictionary*: "The presumptive conclusion is accepted only problematically, that is to say, as meriting an inductive examination. The principal rule of presumption is that its conclusion should be such that definite consequences can be plentifully deduced from it of a kind which can be checked by observation" (CP 2.786). Here the indication is that a hypothesis should produce fruitful implications that admit of practical tests.

Clearly this is appropriate when the hypothesis concerns matters of experimental inquiry, as in physics, chemistry, or psychology. Some inquiries allow for more convenient tests than others, though. It seems that in general, the more powerful the synthesis a hypothesis effects in our thought, the less stringent we are in requiring practical testability. The physical sciences, for example, suppose that *all* matter and energy in the cosmos behaves in approximately the same ways under similar circumstances. This hypothesis is extremely powerful for inquiry, but it is not practically testable. It *is* testable in principle, however. Given an unlimited community of inquirers with unlimited observational capacities and resources, it could be verified or refuted. That it never fully *will* be is of little concern to the physicist.

The most fundamental hypotheses seem usually to be of this sort. This is especially true of philosophical hypotheses: "The best that can be done is to supply a hypothesis, not devoid of all likelihood, in the general line of growth of scientific ideas, and capable of being verified or refuted by future observers" (CP 1.7). Some hypotheses are simply untestable; others are easily testable; still others are testable only in principle. The latter kind could be confirmed or rejected *only* by a community of inquirers "without definite limits, and capable of an indefinite increase of knowledge" (W 2:239). The hypothesis expressed in the principle of synechism—that logical thought necessarily involves the conception of reality—is only testable in principle, in the infinitely long run.

The validity of this hypothesis, as of any other, hinges on its synthesizing power and on its capacity for being implemented and tested. Its synthesizing power cannot be denied. If we suppose logic to be the study of objectively real forms that would emerge fully determinate at the end of inquiry, then the ubiquity and reliability of the basic logical forms so far described can be explained. If we deny this hypothesis, as the nominalist does, rational thought forever remains a contingent affair, merely a useful tool for dealing with the situations we encounter locally. The security that Peirce's alternative offers is certainly attractive: It assures us that the Quest for Certainty will have its grail at the end of inquiry. To accept this hypothesis on the basis of our natural preference for the more secure position would be illegitimate, however. If we choose the hypothesis, it must be because it is *valid,* and this means it must be testable, at least in principle.

Is synechism testable in principle? The answer is "yes or no." Yes, synechism is testable in principle—*if* we accept the hypothesis that inquiry gradually approaches a state of complete truth and reality. The test would be complete only at that limit-point. And No, synechism is not testable even in principle—*if* we deny that inquiry would ever realize the fully unified and determinate situation of an ultimate judgment. In this case, the test could never be carried out. Synechism is a valid hypothesis, if synechism is correct, but synechism is an invalid hypothesis, if synechism is incorrect. The truth of synechism is, in short, undecidable within the framework of logic. In Peirce's three-valued logic, such an undecidable proposition is assigned the value *L*, indicating that its truth-value is as the limit between Truth and Falsity.

Peirce is right in at least one respect: "[T]he assumption that man or the community (which may be wider than man) shall ever arrive at a state of information greater than some definite finite information, is entirely unsupported by reasons" (W 2:271). We cannot decide which alternative is correct through ratiocination, because what is in *question* is whether logical discourse tells us anything about a rational order of reality. For the nominalist, the rational order is an illusion; for Peirce, it is indeterminate but capable of becoming more reasonable all the time. Nor does induction allow us to conclude much on this matter, because our sample of experiments is too small in relation to the infinite universe that the question concerns. We are finally thrown back to the question whether synechism is a valid hypothesis. The nominalist insists it is not; Peirce, following the principle itself, is led to say it is. In deciding about this ultimate logical principle, logic is of no help.

Faced with two viable but contradictory alternatives concerning the fundamental nature of logic, we are led to raise *the* pragmatic question: What difference does it make? Meaning is a matter of experienceable differences. What we face in the dispute over synechism is the question of the value of rational thought. John McDermott has described humans as mere "recombinant organisms in a cosmic DNA chain."[33] The point of his statement is that human beings, rational and truth-loving though we may be, have no exalted status, no privileged place in the cosmos. Peirce, the philosopher of cosmic evolution, would applaud McDermott's image but not his point. Even at the biological level, Peirce saw final causes directing evolution—though typically not describable by us, they could be discerned (CP 1.204). Though humans are exceedingly important vehicles of controlled reason, we are after all but a tiny part of the cosmos, and not its culmination and crowning achievement. For us to venture more than a *guess* at the riddle of the universe would be an act of great presumption. On the other hand, we must not underrate the potential of the human mind to further the cosmic ideal of "concrete reasonableness." In Peirce's view, rational thought *is* the cosmic DNA, of which we are parts. Its constant transmissions of information, as well as its constant mutations, are all directed toward an ideal state of perfection: a self-consistent, law-governed universe. The infinite community would be finally united, contemplating itself in a perfectly harmonious activity, eternally complete. This ideal guides rational thought, though Peirce stresses that it will always remain unrealized.

For Peirce, the ultimate meaning of rationality involves the ideal one would will for the whole universe (recall Kant's decisive influence on Peirce). The rational life, for Peirce, is a kind of religious life. It requires that we bind ourselves in spirit to the unfolding of the cosmos, and devote our energies to the improvement of all, in the extremely long run.[34] The realization of meaning transcends the finite human time frame, and literally reaches cosmic proportions in Peirce's view. To embrace synechism is to wager that we are indeed but infinitesimal parts of something infinitely greater.

The philosophy of synechism thus affects our conduct. What is important for Peirce is not and cannot be that we attain absolute truth. Rather, it is that we devote our efforts to the increase of reasonableness, to the advancement of inquiry and knowledge, to the controlled and critical direction of our energies so as to contribute to the betterment of the universe where we are. In short, we must endeavor to think, act, and feel *as if* synechism were true. We can have no assurance that synechism is true. To embrace the hypothesis is to accept a wager, perhaps with miserable odds. But Peirce urges us to see that our one hope of knowing anything, of bettering the world, is to embrace the philosophy of synechism, to give ourselves over to agapism, the cherishing love of truth, and to trust the contingent belief that the odds in this wager are destined to improve if we will only put more into the game. "Such contingent belief, which yet forms the ground for the actual employment of means to certain actions," wrote Kant in the chapter which led Peirce to rethink philosophy, "I entitle *pragmatic belief*."[35]

Notes
Works Cited
Index

Notes

INTRODUCTION

1. Immanuel Kant, *Critique of Pure Reason*, trans. Norman Kemp Smith (New York: St. Martin's Press, 1965), A 832, B 860.

2. Peirce adopted the name Santiago (St. James) late in life, though precisely when and why is uncertain. According to André De Tienne, the earliest apparent "Santiago" signature is on the manuscript of the last of the 1903 Harvard Pragmatism Lectures, MS 316a, dated 15 May 1903. However, a bibliographic entry reading "Peirce, Charles S(antiago)" appears in Ernst Schroeder, *Vorlesungen ueber die Algebra der Logik*, vol. 1 (Leipzig: Teubner, 1890), 710. The 1890 date opens the possibility that the James being honored was not William, but rather William's father Henry James, Sr. It is also possible that the Schroeder entry was simply a mistake, but was inspirational for Peirce. (André De Tienne, communication posted to the Peirce-L electronic discussion list, 16 May 1995.)

3. Max H. Fisch, Kenneth L. Ketner, and Christian J. W. Kloesel, "The New Tools of Peirce Scholarship, with Particular Reference to Semiotic," in *Studies in Peirce's Semiotic*, Peirce Studies, no. 1 (Lubbock, Texas: Institute for Studies in Pragmaticism, Texas Tech Universtiy, 1979), 3–4.

4. The notion that Peirce is an interesting failure is not exactly false, of course, but it is sufficiently far from being true that it will not do as a basis for interpreting his philosophy. See Fisch, Ketner, and Kloesel, "New Tools," 15, for a discussion of this notion. The thesis that a fundamental conflict in Peirce's temperament caused his philosophy to split into two irreconcilable strains is advanced in Thomas A. Goudge, *The Thought of C. S. Peirce* (Toronto: University of Toronto Press, 1950).

5. The reader will note that the spelling of the name for the theory of signs varies according to context in this study. Peirce himself used *semeiotic, semeiotics, semiotic,* and *semeotic* in various places. In all references to Peirce's theory of signs, I adopt the spelling *semeiotic.* This spelling most closely reflects the etymology of the word, which derives from the Greek σημεῖον. Although Peirce apparently never used the variant *semiotics,* it has become common among those working in the theory of signs today. I accordingly employ this spelling only when discussing theories other than Peirce's. See Max H. Fisch, "Peirce's General Theory of Signs" in *Peirce, Semeiotic, and Pragmatism*, ed. Kenneth Laine Ketner and Christian J. W. Kloesel (Bloomington: Indiana University Press, 1986), 321–22, for an account of Peirce's spelling and pronunciation of *semeiotic* and related terms.

Murray G. Murphey, *The Development of Peirce's Philosophy* (Cambridge: Harvard University Press, 1961; reprinted with new preface and appendix, Indianapolis: Hackett Publishing, 1993) is by far the best available survey of Peirce's philosophy as a whole, but Murphey seriously underestimates the importance of semeiotic for Peirce. The work is also unsympathetic to Peirce's religious concerns, which are now coming to be recognized as being perhaps as philosophically important as his well-known scientific concerns.

I discuss the religious aspect of Peirce's thought in "C. S. Peirce and the Philosophy of Religion," *Southern Journal of Philosophy* 28 (1990): 193-213. Two longer works treating this topic have also recently appeared: Donna M. Orange, *Peirce's Conception of God*, Peirce Studies No. 2 (Lubbock, Texas: Institute for Studies in Pragmaticism, Texas Tech University, 1984), and Michael L. Raposa, *Peirce's Philosophy of Religion*, Peirce Studies No. 5 (Bloomington: Indiana University Press, 1989).

6. Murphey, 218.

7. Peirce is a dialectical thinker, and his conception of the system of philosophical sciences reflects Hegel's: "The whole of philosophy in this way resembles a circle of circles. The Idea appears in each single circle, but, at the same time, the whole Idea is constituted by the system of these peculiar phases, and each is a necessary member of the organization." G. W. F. Hegel, *Hegel's Logic: Being Part One of the "Encyclopaedia of the Philosophical Sciences,"* trans. W. Wallace (Oxford: Clarendon Press, 1975), section 15. Though his references to Hegel are often quite critical, Peirce does once refer to him as being "in some respects the greatest philosopher that ever lived" (CP 1.524).

8. Peirce writes: "No responsibility could be much more grave in my opinion than that of being charged to imbue a considerable number of young men with ideas of logic. For as I understand logic, the practical issues of it are momentous. Nevertheless, there is no sacrifice which I could make, consistently with duty, that I would not gladly make to have that opportunity of usefulness." The letter is quoted in Kenneth Laine Ketner and Hilary Putnam, "Introduction: Consequences of Mathematics," *Reasoning and the Logic of Things: The Cambridge Conferences Lectures of 1898*, ed. Kenneth Laine Ketner (Cambridge, Mass.: Harvard University Press, 1992), 16.

9. Parts of the application, one of the most valuable records of how Peirce envisioned his mature system, appear in NEM 4:13–73. A more complete edition is available as *Manuscript L 75: Application to the Carnegie Institution*, ed. Joseph Ransdell, online electronic text (Peirce Telecommunity Project, 1993). The fascinating and tragic story of the Carnegie Institution's rejection of the application is related in Joseph Brent, *Charles Sanders Peirce: A Life* (Bloomington and Indianapolis: Indiana University Press, 1993), 277–89.

CHAPTER 1

1. These terms are anticipated as early as 1865 (W 1:174). Peirce does not develop his mature definitions of the categories until 1885, however, and he does not commonly use the terms Firstness, Secondness, and Thirdness until the mid-1890s. Accordingly, I will not apply these well-known names to Peirce's earlier descriptions of the categories.

With respect to the three categories, Peirce observes "My philosophy resuscitates Hegel, though in a strange costume" (CP 1.42). The similarity between Peirce's philosophy and Hegel's is so striking that the question of Hegel's influence on Peirce must be addressed. Peirce told a Harvard audience in 1903: "In regard to [the three universal categories], it appears to me that Hegel is so nearly right that my own doctrine might very well be taken for a variety of Hegelianism, although in point of fact it was determined in my mind by considerations entirely foreign to Hegel, at a time when my attitude toward Hegelianism was one of contempt. There was no influence upon me from Hegel unless it was of so occult a kind as to entirely escape my ken; and if there was such an occult influence, it strikes me as about as good an argument for the essential truth of the doctrine, as is the coincidence that Hegel and I arrived in quite independent ways substantially to the same result" (CP 5.38).

The present study accepts Peirce's claims about his inspirations. The similarity between the two systems is unmistakable, but can be explained if we accept that Peirce's basic conceptions, like Hegel's, "grew originally out of the study of the table of Kant" (CP 1.300).

2. Murphey, 412. This passage is from MS 720, the second of four drafts of "On a New List" reproduced in the appendix to Murphey's book.

3. Ibid., 412 (MS 720).

4. Kant, *Critique of Pure Reason*, A50, B74; A68, B93.

5. Ibid., A68, B93.

6. Ibid., B163.

7. Ibid., A64, B89.

8. Ibid., A67, B92.

9. Ibid., A69, B93–94.

10. At least it must have appeared easy to Kant, who neglected to explain precisely how he got the particular categories he did from the table of judgments.

11. Kant, *Critique of Pure Reason*, B viii.

12. Murphey, 412 (MS 720).

13. Peirce heeded this lesson in his own search for the categories. His claim that the forms of relation can be known a priori contains a fallibilistic hedge. Although a priori knowledge does not appeal to the evidence of experience for its validity, neither is it created ex nihilo, and it is not absolutely true. "All our thought begins with experience, the mind furnishes no material for thought whatever" (W 1:246). Once provided with material, however, the mind may discover things that it would be pointless to confirm by observation. But it would be absurd to claim that we possess complete a priori knowledge at any time, because new information may accrue even to a priori ideas. A priori knowledge can be incomplete, and hence incorrect. The a priori principles of logic are "satisfactory," or manifestly true in the current state of information.

14. CP 4.2; see also W 1:280, W 1:505–514, and W 2:23–48.

15. Kant, *Critique of Pure Reason*, A108–109.

16. Peirce argues that *all* mental action, including sensation and emotion, is reducible to these forms (W 2:214–17, 228–29). He further argues that the existence of fallacious reasoning is not an exception, as the mistake in reasoning never concerns the procedure of the mind, but lies rather in the falsity of premises or the confusion of propositions (W 2:221–23).

17. Peirce's apparent allusion to other forms of inference in some passages is a recognition that most inferences are more complex, comprehending the results of more than one simple inference. Such complex inferences can, however, be broken down into their component deductive, inductive, and retroductive parts.

18. Formulas for induction and hypothesis are based on W 2:47.

19. Peirce could give no account of why there should be three particular principles and three elementary forms of inference until he discovered the logic of relatives, which allowed him to describe possible kinds of relation a priori. In his early works Peirce relied on introspection far more than he would have liked.

20. The present section provides a brief sketch of Peirce's early theory of representation. Chapters 6 and 7 are devoted to his mature philosophy of representation, the general theory of semeiotic.

21. Except where noted, material in the present paragraph is drawn from W 2:51–55.

22. James Jakób Liszka, "Peirce's Interpretant," *Transactions* 26 (Winter 1990): 27.

23. There are no appropriate examples for the first two possibilities. A chaotic succession of abstract qualities, or a universe of enduring abstract quality without concrete embodiment, can only be conceived as occurring in a realm of ideas. In fact, Peirce suggests that if we think of Plato's realm of ideas at all, we must think that the orderly realm of ideas has evolved from a chaos of feeling. The forms "have become or are becoming developed" (CP 6.194).

24. Hanna Buczyńska-Garewicz, "Sign and Continuity," *ars semeiotica* 2 (1978): 7.

25. Murphey, 55–56, 58.

26. Ibid., 126–28. For a more extensive account of Peirce's relation to Duns Scotus, see John F. Boler, *Charles Peirce and Scholastic Realism* (Seattle: University of Washington Press, 1963).

27. Boler, 50, 62–63.

28. In a fascinating passage from the 1866 Lowell Lectures, Peirce identifies this all-embracing interpreter and interpretant with God (W 1:502–503).

29. This is a modification of the medieval definition of the real, which he relates as "that which is not whatever we happen to think it, but is unaffected by what we may think of it" (W 2:467).

30. In a discussion of his form of realism in 1873, Peirce attributes the kernel of this theory to Kant, though it is doubtful that Kant would have recognized it: "It was the essence of his philosophy to regard the real object as determined by the mind. . . . In short, it was to regard the reality as the normal product of mental action, and not as the incognizable cause of it" (W 2:470–71).

31. Peirce notes this phenomenon at CP 6.316–17, in a paper published in 1893. He refuses to place much weight on the observation, but exclaims "what an argument for the continuity of mind" this would be!

32. In 1905, after William James and F. C. S. Schiller had popularized the word pragmatism, and cited this passage as the first statement of their principles, Peirce renamed his philosophy: "So, then, the writer, finding his bantling 'pragmatism' so promoted, feels that it is time to kiss his child good-by and relinquish it to its higher destiny; while to serve the precise purpose of expressing the original definition, he begs to announce the birth of the new word 'pragmaticism,' which is ugly enough to be safe from kidnappers" (CP 5.414). The 1898 lecture in which James "kidnapped" the word, together with his later reflections on it, is given in "Philosophical Conceptions and Practical Results," in *The Writings of William James,* ed. John J. McDermott (Chicago: University of Chicago Press, 1977), 345–62.

33. André De Tienne, "Peirce's Early Method of Finding the Categories," *Transactions* 25 (1989): 405.

34. See chapter 7 for further discussion of the role of each variety of inference in inquiry.

35. Murphey, 108.

36. David Hume, *An Enquiry Concerning Human Understanding,* ed. Antony Flew (LaSalle, Illinois: Open Court, 1988), 64.

37. This phrase is Peirce's, and appears in a manuscript, "Appendix. No. 2" (MS 740), quoted in Murphey, 70–71.

38. Peirce greatly refines this account of the origins of cognition in 1902, when he develops his theory of the perceptual judgment. The view that the sensation or percep-

tion is a hypothesis that is not subject to criticism or control, however, remains central to the later account. See chapter 6.

39. Murphey, 119–20.

40. The development is traced in Vincent G. Potter and Paul B. Shields, "Peirce's Definitions of Continuity," *Transactions* 13 (1977): 20–34, and in Wayne C. Myrvold, "Peirce on Cantor's Paradox and the Continuum," *Transactions* 31 (1995): 508–41.

41. Murphey says that "In Peirce's system, the infinite future plays the part of the philosopher's stone" (Murphey, 169). I would add that the principle of continuity is his alchemist's vessel, in which the continuum spawns the concepts of infinite community and infinitesimal cognition.

42. Charles S. Peirce, ed., *Studies in Logic by Members of the Johns Hopkins University (1883)*, reprinted in Foundations of Semiotics, vol. 1, Achim Eisbach, gen. ed. (Philadelphia: John Benjamins Publishing Company, 1983).

43. "On the Algebra of Logic: A Contribution to the Philosophy of Notation" (CP 3.359–403M), the "Review of Royce" (CP 8.39–54), and the series of "One, Two, Three" MSS (W 5: 235–47, 292–308).

44. Presented 23 April 1860, published in *Transactions of the Cambridge Philosophical Society*, 10 (1864): 428–87. The date of Peirce's acquaintance with the paper is established by his reference to it in "Grounds of Validity." See Daniel D. Merrill, "Introduction," W 3:xliv.

45. "Description of a Notation for the Logic of Relatives, resulting from an Amplification of the Conceptions of Boole's Calculus of Logic," originally published in *Memoirs of the American Academy of Arts and Sciences* in 1873; W 2:359–429.

46. Murphey, 152–53.

47. The editors of the *Collected Papers* date this fragment (MS 904) ca. 1875, but it is testimony to the difficult conditions under which they worked that they overlooked the 1882 watermark on the manuscript, which Robin notes in his catalog. The editors of the Peirce Edition include this fragment with the group of "One, Two, Three" MSS and date it Summer-Fall 1886.

48. Bernhard Riemann, "On the Hypotheses which Lie at the Basis of Geometry," trans. W. K. Clifford, *Nature* 8 (May 1873): 37. Quoted in Murphey, 222.

49. Murphey, 298.

50. See chapter 4, note 3, for those of Cantor's works that apparently influenced Peirce.

51. Chapter 4 presents a much more thorough discussion of Cantor's theories and of Peirce's reception of them.

52. Robert R. Stoll, *Set Theory and Logic* (San Francisco: W. H. Freeman, 1963).

CHAPTER 2

1. MS 909; parts published as CP 1.354–68, 1.373–75, and 1.379–416. The editors of the Peirce Edition have revised the CP dating of ca. 1890. "A Guess at the Riddle" developed out of the 1885–1886 "One, Two, Three" project mentioned in the previous chapter, in which Peirce revised his categories extensively.

2. Murphey, 330–31.

3. Peirce published a similar classification in 1889, in the *Century Dictionary*. He referred to it favorably in "The Regenerated Logic," published in the *Monist* in 1896 (CP

3.427). It shows mathematics as the basic science, followed by philosophy, which is divided into logic and metaphysics. Though this classification more closely resembles his later views than it does his earlier (such as the classification published at W 1:487, from 1866), there is yet no hint of the impending revolution in his thought, which would introduce phenomenology and the normative sciences into the scheme.

4. Peirce says that the truths of the inward and outward world are alike known "by experimentation only." The difference is that "Over the Inward, I have considerable control, over the Outward very little. It is a question of degree only." The difference of degree, however, "is certainly very, very great, with a remarkable absence of intermediate phenomena" (CP 4.87).

5. See "First Impressions" in chapter 1.

6. The details of this distinction are discussed later in the section titled "Mathematics and Logic."

7. See Max H. Fisch, "Peirce as Scientist, Mathematician, Historian, Logician, and Philosopher," in *Peirce, Semeiotic, and Pragmatism* (Bloomington: Indiana University Press, 1986), 376–400.

8. The two lecture series from 1865 and 1866 are published in W 1:162–302 and W 1:358–504. The "Illustrations" series was published in *Popular Science Monthly,* and appears in W 3:242–338. It consists of six essays, including Peirce's best-known writings: "The Fixation of Belief" and "How to Make our Ideas Clear."

9. Alasdair MacIntyre, *Three Rival Versions of Moral Enquiry: Encyclopaedia, Genealogy, and Tradition* (Notre Dame: University of Notre Dame Press, 1990), 18.

10. Ibid., 19.

11. Peirce's evolutionism here conflicted not only with Platonism but also with his beloved Scotism, which must be "torn away from its medievalism" and informed by conceptions "drawn from the history of science and from mathematics" (CP 1.6). As was noted in chapter 1, Duns Scotus maintained that universals are objectively real in the sense that they are independent of the mind, but are nonetheless inseparable from particulars. Peirce's theory of natural classes transforms this position concerning universals in two ways: First, it associates universals less with particulars and more with the laws governing production of particulars, and second, it makes these laws (and hence "the very Platonic forms themselves") subject to evolutionary development (CP 6.194).

12. In what follows, I will be discussing the classification of *objects.* In order to forestall confusion, however, I want to stress that, though they are not *physical* objects, the sciences are objects *of the science of classification* in the same way that birds or lamps would be.

13. The chart reconstructs Peirce's classification, based on the Carnegie Application (NEM 4:17, dated 1902), *A Syllabus of Certain Topics of Logic* (CP 1.180–202, dated 1903), a more detailed classification (CP 1.203–283, dated 1902), and "Reason's Conscience" (NEM 4:185–215, undated). Beverley Kent, *Charles S. Peirce: Logic and the Classification of the Sciences* (Montreal: McGill-Queen's University Press, 1987) gives an exhaustive account of the development of Peirce's classifications. The present outline largely agrees with her reconstruction of Peirce's detailed "Perennial Classification," 134–35.

14. In many of his classifications, Peirce makes the sciences of review a subbranch of the sciences of discovery. Figure 2.1 follows Peirce's indication in a late

manuscript that they ought to be a distinct branch (MS 675, p.10, ca. 1911).

15. What we might normally consider the philosophy of science is the subject of methodeutic, which appears under the heading of theoretical sciences rather than the sciences of review. Methodeutic is a normative discipline; its aim is to tell how an inquiry into truth ought to proceed. It is the general theory of inquiry. I suggest that when Peirce said that "the endeavor to form a philosophy of science" belongs to the sciences of review, he was referring to the philosophy of science as a descriptive theory of the organization of existing sciences.

16. Peirce often used Jeremy Bentham's terms *coenoscopy*, a synonym for philosophy (the observation of common experience) and *idioscopy*, a synonym for the special sciences. Bentham is cited in the notes to CP 1.241 and 1.242.

17. Cantor's and Peirce's accounts of the grades of infinity are discussed in more detail in chapter 4.

18. Thompson notes that "[d]ichotomic mathematics. . . provides the formal structure for ordinary syllogistic, just as trichotomic mathematics performs a similar service for the logic of relatives." Manley Thompson, *The Pragmatic Philosophy of C. S. Peirce* (Chicago: University of Chicago Press, 1953), 161.

19. Carolyn Eisele, *Studies in the Scientific and Mathematical Philosophy of Charles S. Peirce* (New York: Mouton Publishers, 1979), 213.

20. Ibid.

21. See Max Fisch and Atwell Turquette, "Peirce's Triadic Logic," *Transactions* 2 (1966): 71–85.

22. William James, "The Moral Philosopher and the Moral Life," in *The Will to Believe and Other Essays in Popular Philosophy* (Cambridge: Harvard University Press, 1979), 156.

23. Vincent G. Potter, *Charles S. Peirce on Norms and Ideals* (Amherst: University of Massachusetts Press, 1967), 40.

24. Ibid., 46.

25. Immanuel Kant, *Grounding for the Metaphysics of Morals,* trans. James W. Ellington (Indianapolis: Hackett Publishing Co., 1981), 42. (Menzer edition, Berlin, 1911, 437).

26. Ibid., (Menzer ed., 436).

27. The esthetic dimension of this ideal is hinted at in the Socratic κόσμον καλοῦσιν (Plato, *Gorgias,* 508a).

28. Potter, 32.

29. Ibid., 19.

30. Ibid., 19.

31. A cursory look at issues of *Transactions of the Charles S. Peirce Society* between 1970 and the time of this writing reveals no fewer than sixteen articles directly concerned with realism and idealism in Peirce's metaphysics.

32. Murphey, 379.

33. I differ from Kent's characterization of religious metaphysics as concerning "the universe in relation to human spiritual interests" (Kent, 134). Given Peirce's characterization of *mind,* it seems incorrect to restrict the scope of religion to the human sphere.

34. Ibid., 136–39.

35. Ibid., 137.

CHAPTER 3

1. Hans G. Herzberger, "Peirce's Remarkable Theorem," in *Pragmatism and Purpose*, eds. L. W. Sumner, John G. Slater, and Fred Wilson (Toronto: University of Toronto Press, 1981), 41–58, and Kenneth L. Ketner, "Peirce's 'Most Lucid and Interesting Paper'" provide the best available introductions to Peirce's "valency theory" of mathematical relations and its importance for his system, which is the concern of this chapter.

2. Kant, *Critique of Pure Reason*, A 839, B 867.

3. MS 901, dated 1885. Parts published as CP 1.369–72, 1.376–78.

4. Augustus De Morgan, "On the Syllogism IV, and the Logic of Relations," *Cambridge Philosophical Transactions*, vol. 10 (1859): 331–58.

5. Murphey, 303.

6. The results of this work were published in the essays by Peirce, Christine Ladd, and O. H. Mitchell in the 1883 *Studies in Logic*.

7. Murphey, 300.

8. The term "singulary" is suggested by Quine as an alternative to "unary" or "unitary" for describing a relative with valence of one. The series continues with "binary," "ternary," "quaternary," and, of course, "quinary." Willard V. O. Quine, *Mathematical Logic* (Cambridge: Harvard University Press, 1947), 13, note 1.

9. Felicia Kruse, "Genuineness and Degeneracy in Peirce's Categories," *Transactions* 27 (1991): 272. Peirce discussed the geometrical meaning of these terms in MS 304, pp. 35–36.

10. Note that in the case of degenerate dyads, the relation among objects exists "internally" in a mind, not in the existent state of affairs. In the case of a genuine triad, the opposite is the case: Mind is present as an element in the "external" existent state of affairs.

11. This identification of mind as the third element in a genuine triad will have metaphysical implications. If there are real laws that govern natural events, they are instances of Thirdness and must in some sense represent the action of mind in the natural world.

12. The general medium is classified in Peirce's general theory of signs as the symbolic legisign. See chapter 7.

13. Alfred North Whitehead and Bertrand Russell, *Principia Mathematica* (Cambridge: Cambridge University Press, 1910–1913).

14. Old peep-show viewing machines worked this way, but were not commonly used to show the mind in action.

15. Don D. Roberts, *The Existential Graphs of Charles S. Peirce* (The Hague: Mouton, 1973), Appendix 4, 139–51.

16. See John Sowa, "Matching Logical Structure to Linguistic Structure," in *Studies in the Logic of Charles Sanders Peirce*, ed. N. Houser, D. Roberts, and J. Van Evra (Bloomington: Indiana University Press, 1997), 418–44.

17. This graphical argument is very similar in structure to the argument offered in "One, Two, Three: Fundamental Categories of Thought and of Nature" in 1885 (MS 901, pp. 16–17). There he used the image of a roadway to illustrate his point.

18. Peirce was led by these considerations to characterize the branching symbol as "an emblem of fertility in comparison with which the holy phallus of religion's youth is a poor stick indeed" (CP 4.310).

19. Quine, 201.

20. On Peirce's reduction thesis, see Herzberger, "Peirce's Remarkable Theorem"; Ketner, "Peirce's 'Most Lucid and Interesting Paper'"; and Robert W. Burch, *A Peircean Reduction Thesis: The Foundations of Topological Logic,* Philosophical Inquiries No. 1 (Lubbock: Texas Tech University Press, 1991).

21. Any logical statement can be considered as the expression of a thought. In Peirce's view, logic "is quite indifferent whether it be regarded as having to do with thought or with language, the wrapping of thought, since thought, like an onion, is composed of nothing but wrappings" (MS 675, p. 17).

22. Fisch and Turquette, "Peirce's Triadic Logic," 78–82.

23. Vol. 7, no. 2 (1885): 180–202, 23.

24. The relevant pages from the notebook are reproduced as plates 1–3 in Fisch and Turquette, "Peirce's Triadic Logic," 73–75. Quotations are taken from these plates. Turquette has published two other articles concerning these fragments: "Peirce's *Phi* and *Psi* Operators for Triadic Logic," *Transactions* 3 (1967): 66–73, and "Peirce's Complete System of Triadic Logic," *Transactions* 5 (1969): 199–210.

25. Fisch and Turquette, "Peirce's Triadic Logic," 77.

26. Fisch and Turquette, "Peirce's Triadic Logic," plate 3, p. 75.

27. Fisch and Turquette, "Peirce's Triadic Logic," 80, offer two examples (which Peirce could not have known) as cases where L may be needed: Hans Reichenbach's analysis of indeterminate statements in quantum mechanics, and the formally undecidable sentences identified by Kurt Gödel.

28. Though Peirce often argued against Descartes, his chief objections were directed against Cartesians. Descartes himself did require a third sort of substance besides mind and body: God, the infinite substance. Though Descartes' concepts of infinity and continuity were precisely the *wrong* concepts for Peirce's category of Thirdness, Descartes himself was at any rate closer to Peirce's view than those who construe Descartes as a mere dualist.

29. Michael L. Raposa has aptly called Peirce's religious philosophy "theosemiotic" in *Peirce's Philosophy of Religion.* See also Parker, "C.S. Peirce and the Philosophy of Religion."

CHAPTER 4

1. In the 1903 Pragmatism Lectures, Peirce says: "All philosophers must in future study the mathematicological doctrine of multitude. We now have no difficulty in reasoning with mathematical exactitude about infinity. I regret that I cannot include it in these lectures, but I should be happy if any of you could find the time for them, to give two or three lectures on that subject" (MS 309, p. 23 verso).

2. See, for example, Peirce's comments in NEM 3:101.

3. Peirce knew Cantor's work from three publications: "Grundlagen einer allgemeinen Mannichfaltigkeitslehre" (Leipzig, 1883), "Mitteilungen zur Lehre vom Transfiniten," *Zeitschrift für Philos. und philos. Kritik* 91 (1887), 92 (1888), and "Beiträge zur Begründung der transfiniten Mengenlehre," *Mathematische Annalen,* 46 (1895), 49 (1897), [trans. Philip E. B. Jourdain, *Contributions to the Founding of the Theory of Transfinite Numbers* (New York: Dover, 1952)]. Peirce read most of the first work in its French publication [*Acta Mathematica* 2 (1883)], some parts of the second work, and the part of the third that was published in 1897. On the basis of Peirce's apparent mis-

understanding of the theory of ordinals, Murphey suggests that Peirce read these materials selectively (Murphey, 240–41).

4. Abraham A. Fraenkel, *Abstract Set Theory*, second, completely revised edition, Studies in Logic and the Foundations of Mathematics, ed. L. E. J. Brouwer et al. (Amsterdam: North-Holland Publishing, 1961); Robert R. Stoll, *Set Theory and Logic* (San Francisco: W. H. Freeman, 1963); A. W. Moore, *The Infinite*, The Problems of Philosophy: Their Past and Present, gen. ed. Ted Honderich (New York: Routledge, 1990).

5. Fraenkel, 9, from Cantor, "Beiträge zur Begründung der transfiniten Mengenlehre," 1895.

6. Ibid., 59.

7. Ibid., 24, 60.

8. Ibid., 28.

9. Ibid., 29.

10. Ibid., 13.

11. Ibid., 33.

12. See Moore, 118–20, for a standard statement of the "diagonal method" proof of this result. Peirce's proof appears at CP 3.548 (Myrvold, 510–11).

13. Fraenkel, 112.

14. Ibid., 70–72; Myrvold, 509.

15. Ibid., 50–53; Moore, 118–120. The name "diagonal method" comes from the graphical arrangement of numbers in the presentation of this kind of proof. A series of successive decimal fractions are written in rows, and a new number not occurring in the series is constructed by changing a numeral from each decimal listed. The numerals that are changed trace out a diagonal on the original matrix.

16. Moore, 154.

17. For this reason, among others, Peirce disagreed with Cantor's identification of the continuum with the set of reals. Indeed the reals can be used to describe any point on a continuum, but Peirce refused to identify the reals *as* the continuum.

18. The proofs for these two results are given in Fraenkel, 112–13.

19. Ibid., 128.

20. Ibid., 134.

21. Ibid., 138.

22. Ibid., 175.

23. Ibid., 187.

24. "Shape" is a descriptive term, with no technical definition in set theory. It is borrowed from Moore, 124.

25. Ibid., 125–27; Fraenkel, 207–8.

26. Fraenkel, 217.

27. Ibid.

28. Ibid., 218.

29. The "generalized continuum hypothesis" states that, for a given ordinal a, $2^{\aleph_a} = \aleph_{a+1}$. Ibid., 229.

30. On the history of the idea of infinity, see Norman Kretzman, ed., *Infinity and Continuity in Ancient and Medieval Thought* (Ithaca: Cornell University Press, 1982); John E. Murdoch, "Infinity and Continuity" in *The Cambridge History of Later Medieval Philosophy*, ed. Norman Kretzman et al. (New York: Cambridge University Press, 1982); and Moore, *The Infinite*.

31. Murphey, 255.

32. It took Peirce many years to arrive at this position. Vincent G. Potter and Paul B. Shields trace Peirce's progress through four stages in "Peirce's Definitions of Continuity." The four stages are: (1) pre-Cantorean, until 1884, (2) Cantorean, 1884–1894, (3) Kantistic, 1894–1908, and (4) post-Cantorean, 1908–1911. The divisions are useful, except that they do not recognize Peirce's concern with continuity in the last two years of his life. See MS S3, p. 72 and MS 1575a for evidence of this continued interest. I focus on Peirce's last period of thought on continuity.

33. Murphey, 266–74.

34. Murphey misreads Peirce on this point, saying that Peirce thinks the proposition that there is no greatest multitude leads to an absurdity (Murphey, 260–62). Potter and Shields (27–29) argue that Murphey misreads Peirce because he fails to distinguish Peirce's terms "multitude" and "multiplicity." *Multitude* refers only to discrete collections; *multiplicity* refers both to discrete and continuous collections (CP 4.175).

35. Murphey, 266–74.

36. In a passage written in 1911, Peirce says "this ridiculous little catch presents no difficulty at all to a mind adequately trained in mathematics and in logic" (CP 6.177). Elsewhere, he refers to the Achilles paradox as "a contemptible catch" (CP 6.467).

37. "In short, the principle of excluded middle, or that of contradiction, ought to be regarded as violated here; or there is a limitation here to the applicability of the relation of negation which those principles define" (NEM 3:747).

38. Peirce uses the term "analytic continuity" with reference to this system in his notes for the 1903 Lowell Lectures (NEM 3:391). He more often refers to the analytic continuum as a "pseudo-continuum." There are actually an infinite number of possible "pseudo-continua," however, each with a number of elements corresponding to a transfinite cardinal. The analytic continuum is postulated for analytic geometry. Peirce uniformly refers to his own concept as the "true continuum."

39. For example, if $f(v)=(\frac{1}{v-2})+1$, then we might plug in 0 as the value for v and get 1/2 as t_1.

40. This was done by both Newton and Leibniz, who at least implicitly accepted infinitesimals. It is also the usual practice of engineers, physicists, and others who merely need calculations to *work,* and are not disturbed by the theoretical problems which mathematicians have identified. The Marquis de l'Hospital, a pupil of Leibniz, explicitly asserted the reality of infinitesimals. For the history of the debate over infinitesimals, see Martin Davis and Reuben Hersh, "Nonstandard Analysis," *Scientific American* 226 (June 1972): 81–82, and Abraham Robinson, "The Metaphysics of the Calculus," *Selected Papers of Abraham Robinson,* vol. 2, ed. H. J. Keisler et al. (New Haven: Yale University Press, 1979), 540–43.

41. The method just outlined applies only to a Cantorean continuum, but Peirce suggests that an analogous method could be developed for pseudo-continua of larger multitudes than the primipostnumeral (NEM 3:746).

42. Peirce also notes that the success of the doctrine of limits does not preclude the legitimacy of infinitesimals, though it may render them unnecessary for most purposes. "[A]ttempts have been made to apply the method of limits to show the absurdity of the idea of infinitesimals. Is it not a strange logical procedure to deduce as a consequence of one hypothesis that a conflicting hypothesis is untrue? Of course, it is untrue if the first one remains true; but how is a mere hypothesis to decide that it cannot itself be set aside?" (NEM 3:120).

43. Topology has developed without encountering the problems Peirce envisioned. The method of limits has been adapted and applied to topology so as to avoid raising paradoxical questions such as Peirce presents here. Nonetheless, it is possible that Peirce's alternative would work as well or better than the Cantorean concept of continuity that now holds sway, and that such paradoxes as Peirce identifies could be answered rather than merely avoided.

44. Potter and Shields, 27.

45. The reference in Kant is *Critique of Pure Reason,* A 169, B 211. For the evolution of Peirce's reading of this definition, see the series of papers published in CP 6.164–68.

46. Bernhard Riemann addressed the problem of determining whether the manifoldness that is studied in geometry is continuous or discrete in an 1854 lecture at Göttingen ("On the Hypotheses Which Lie at the Basis of Geometry," trans. W. K. Clifford, *Nature* 7 (May 1873): 14–17, 36f). In that lecture he said "in a discrete manifoldness, the ground of its metric relations is given in the notion of it, while in a continuous manifoldness, this ground must come from outside. Either therefore the reality which underlies space must form a discrete manifoldness, or we must seek the ground of its metric relations outside it, in binding forces which act upon it." Murphey notes that Riemann left the answer to this question to physics—mathematics is incapable of deciding whether the manifoldness is discrete or continuous (Murphey, 222). As was pointed out in chapter 1, Peirce knew Riemann's work, and opted for the view that the manifoldness is continuous. The spatial continuum, in Peirce's view, is a continuum of possible determinations, wherein any number of points may be imposed from outside by the "binding force" of an action of mind.

47. For Peirce, time is the most excellent kind of continuum, but is not perfectly continuous. Bertrand P. Helm, "The Nature and Modes of Time" *Monist* 63 (1980): 375–85, and see CP 1.412 and NEM 4:344–45.

48. In particular, we should note that the analytic continuum consists of material parts (points) whose mode of connection is co-being on a line.

49. Benson Mates, *The Philosophy of Leibniz: Metaphysics and Language* (New York: Oxford University Press, 1986), 123.

50. For Leibniz, empirically undiscoverable differences are not decisive. If there is a difference between A and B that is not discoverable to us, but would be apparent only to God, then it *is* a difference and A and B are consequently not identical (Mates, 132–36).

51. NEM 4:342–43. The lectures are reprinted in full in *Reasoning and the Logic of Things,* ed. Kenneth Laine Ketner and Hilary Putnam. Part IV of the editors' introduction includes a lengthy discussion of this example, which brought it to my attention.

52. This is based on the triadic relation Peirce defines in a slightly different context in NEM 3:108.

53. Though we have here focused on a "point" being divided into *two* ordered parts, it might have been divided into many more parts: "The end of a line might burst into any discrete multitude of points whatever, and they would all have been one point before the explosion. Points might fly off, in multitude and order like all the real irrational quantities from 0 to 1; and they might all have had that order of succession in the line and yet all have been at one point" (NEM 4:343). This possibility follows from Peirce's assertion that all parts of a continuum have the same dimensionality as the whole.

54. Peirce's favorite metaphor for the relation of parts in a continuum is that the separate parts are welded, a fusion that cannot be accounted for by infinite divisibility: "Breaking grains of sand more and more will only make the sand more broken. It will

not weld the grains into unbroken continuity" (CP 6.168). The metaphor is apt: In weld-
ing, pieces of metal are liquified and physically intermingled so as to form a joint. At
their joint they are no longer entirely distinct, but away from the joint the original pieces
are still recognizably distinct.

55. Eisele writes that Peirce "never relinquished his belief in the need for the
infinitesimal concept in a context where points clustered about limits and piled up in
density so as to merge at last, making of the limit a general" (NEM 3:xvii). See CP 5.436.

56. That is, they elude dyadically structured thought. Continuity and combination
are essentially triadic according to Peirce.

57. Fraenkel, 121.

58. Ibid.

59. Ibid., 96.

60. Ibid. The same objection holds if we attempt to define infinitesimals using
transfinite ordinals, because ordinals describe the size and shape of sets.

61. John W. Lango, "Whitehead's Actual Occasions and the New Infinitesimals"
Transactions 25 (1989): 31–32, appears to use just this conception of the ordinal to
describe the infinitesimal.

62. This is true of his mature position, at any rate. Prior to 1908 he did often try to
locate the true continuum relative to the power-set series of cardinals. See CP 4.218,
where he says "In fact writing Exp. n for 2^n, (Exp.)$\aleph^\aleph$ is evidently so great that . . . it represents a collection no longer discrete." In *Development*, 260–62, Murphey observes that
this multiplicity fails to meet the condition that its power-set is equivalent to itself, which
he supposes is the defining characteristic of Peirce's true continuum. Potter and Shields,
in "Peirce's Definitions of Continuity," 28–29, show that this is irrelevant to Peirce's conception: Peirce here merely offers an example of *a* continuous multiplicity. This
approach failed, however, and he came to consider the mode of connection among parts
the crucial characteristic of a continuum. With this, the questions of *size* became relatively unimportant. As to the size question, Peirce says that even in a denumerable collection
one finds "symptoms of incipient cohesiveness" among the members, a premonition of
continuity (NEM 3:87). True continuity emerges *somewhere* in the power set series, after
the primipostnumeral multitude. "It is, however, of secondary importance at what particular place in the series of multitudes this phenomenon occurs. It must occur somewhere"
(NEM 3:121n.1).

63. With respect to the passage in MS 908 (which deals explicitly with combination
in thought) it is pertinent to recall that a continuum may be a continuum of ideas,
though mathematics usually treats it as a continuum of quantity or of space (CP 6.174).

64. J. Jay Zeman, "Peirce's Graphs—the Continuity Interpretation" *Transactions* 4
(1968): 148.

65. Notice that excluded middle is suspended in the case of a *general,* but the principle of contradiction is observed. The answer here cannot be that the ball is both in
motion and not in motion. The principle of contradiction might not apply to *vague*
terms, however, "For it is false neither that an animal (in a vague sense) is male, nor that
an animal is female" (CP 5.505).

66. That any such system could be imposed on the true continuum is made clear by
the following statement: "[W]hat I mean by a truly continuous line is a line upon which
there is room for any multitude of points whatsoever. Then the multitude or what corresponds to multitude of possible points,—exceeds all multitude. These points are pure
possibilities" (NEM 3:388).

67. "On a continuous line there are not really any points at all. Two lines which intersect, intersect in a point. That is true for the intersection breaks the continuity and makes a point where there was none before the intersection" (NEM 3:388); see also CP 3.568.

68. Peirce follows the confident assertion just quoted by saying "Of course, I cannot carry you through that demonstration. But it is no matter of *opinion*" (NEM 4:343).

69. Fraenkel, 121–22.

70. This challenge is stated outright in the 1898 Cambridge Conferences Lectures: "Men will say this is self-contradictory. It is not so. If it be so prove it" (NEM 4:343).

71. The following account of Robinson's work is taken from Abraham Robinson, "The Metaphysics of the Calculus," in *Selected Papers of Abraham Robinson*, vol. 2, 537–49; and Davis and Hersh, "Nonstandard Analysis." See also Abraham Robinson, *Non-Standard Analysis* (London: North-Holland Publishing, 1966).

72. Robinson, "The Metaphysics of the Calculus," 542–43.

73. Davis and Hersh, 86; George B. Seligman, "Biography of Abraham Robinson," in *Selected Papers of Abraham Robinson*, vol. 2, xxvii.

74. Scholars would do well to take seriously Peirce's claim to have a proof, given his integrity concerning such matters and given the significance of what the proof may contain.

75. The completeness theorem was published by Kurt Gödel in 1930, and the finiteness principle (or compactness theorem) was published by A. I. Malcev in 1936. Abraham Robinson, "Model Theory," in *Selected Papers of Abraham Robinson*, vol. 2, 524–36.

76. It must be emphasized that Robinson's work solves the *mathematical* problem of infinitesimals, but not the *metaphysical* question of their reality. Robinson's philosophy of mathematics was shaped mainly by Leibniz, Kant, David Hilbert's formalism, and by the rejection of Gödel's Platonism and of logical positivism. He maintains a variety of mathematical formalism: "My position concerning the foundations of Mathematics is based on the following two main points or principles.

(i) Infinite totalities do not exist in any sense of the word (i.e., either really or ideally). More precisely, any mention, or purported mention, of infinite totalities is, literally, *meaningless.*

(ii) Nevertheless, we should continue the business of Mathematics 'as usual,' i.e., we should act *as if* infinite totalities really existed" (Robinson, "Formalism 64," in *Selected Papers,* vol. 2, 507). In the last paragraph of *Non-Standard Analysis,* Robinson asserts that "what we have done is to introduce *new deductive procedures* rather than new mathematical entities."

Peirce would probably object to this formalistic fence-sitting. The Peircean mathematician, of course, need not be concerned with metaphysics, but the Peircean physical scientist must embrace some metaphysical framework. Peirce says that for the scientist, "the infinitesimals must be actual real distances, and not the mere mathematical conceptions, like $\sqrt{-1}$" (CP 3.570).

CHAPTER 5

1. William James, *A Pluralistic Universe* (Cambridge: Harvard University Press, 1977), 154. See also Sandra Rosenthal, *Speculative Pragmatism* (La Salle, Illinois: Open Court, 1986), 140.

2. In the Carnegie Application, dated July 15, 1902, the place later occupied by phenomenology in the classification of sciences is labeled "Categorics" (NEM 4:17).

3. The passage cited is highlighted in Nathan Houser, "La Structure de l'expérience selon Peirce," *Études Phénoménologiques* 5 (1989): 77–111. I have consulted the author's unpublished English text.

4. Peirce's comment that "A Phenomenology which does not reckon with pure mathematics . . . will be the same pitiful club-footed affair that Hegel produced" (CP 5.40) drives this point home.

Ketner notes that "As a telescope is used in astronomy, so mathematics is the 'scope' of phaneroscopy, and the means whereby mind can be scientifically observed and studied." Ketner, "Peirce's 'Most Lucid and Interesting Paper,'" 391.

5. In 1894 Peirce wrote that the *list of categories* "is a table of conceptions drawn from the logical analysis of thought and regarded as applicable to being" (CP 1.300). According to the present interpretation of Peirce's system, the categories are first analyzed as formal conceptions, then described in experience phenomenologically, and then elaborated in terms of semeiotic. Only in the last stage of philosophy are they considered as applicable to *being,* as metaphysical categories.

6. To my knowledge, no commentator has examined Peirce's writings to extract even a provisional list of the particular categories. These would be of more importance for the special sciences than for philosophy.

7. The distinguishing feature of the philosophical sciences, as opposed to the special sciences, is that no special equipment is needed to carry out investigations. The reader who wishes to replicate Peirce's investigations need not obtain a phaneroscope, but only learn a bit of the "simplest mathematics."

8. Rosenthal, 105. The reference is to CP 1.525–26.

9. I did not say "in an instant," for reasons that will become clear.

10. William James, "Does 'Consciousness' Exist?" *Essays in Radical Empiricism* (Cambridge: Harvard University Press, 1976), 6–7.

11. Our analysis from this point onward will follow the lines of Peirce's account of perception, so as to introduce his terminology and his findings.

12. It is probably not accurate to say that *I* am aware of the snap at the moment of its occurrence. At this level, we say only "there is awareness of the snapping."

13. It should be noted that these elements are present in any phenomenon, regardless whether that phenomenon turns out to be "real," "imagined," "dreamed," "hallucinatory," or simply misunderstood. These distinctions are certainly important, but they are not part of the immediate percipuum. Such classifications concern the relative success of rational predictions about the perception, of what relations it has or will have to other perceptions (CP 7.644). This is the basis for the pragmatic definition of truth. The true understanding of a phenomenon is the one that best harmonizes with subsequent experience.

14. In doing so, we move away from phenomenological investigation of a particular event (the pencil lead snapping) to consider another phenomenon that is likewise present to the mind: the general experience of time as such.

15. I will not undertake to present a thorough phenomenology of time here. As Peirce says, "Fully to unfold all the implications of the deliverance of the percipuum would require a small treatise, if written in the English style, or three stout octavos in German" (CP 7.650). The German phenomenologist Edmund Husserl and his followers have of course devoted many more than *three* volumes to the subject.

16. We could also consider the second sense of presence, which would involve an examination of the continuity of experienced *space*. The results of such an examination would duplicate and reinforce what is revealed in the consideration of time that follows. Peirce himself concentrates on the experience of time, however, and I follow his lead here.

17. Rosenthal, 113. In "The Law of Mind," Peirce refers to time as "the universal form of change." *Process* does not appear as a category because it is, generally speaking, what Peirce wants his categorial system to explain.

18. The question of the relation between process, time, and consciousness might be raised at this point. However, the question of which of these, if any, is in some sense primary can only be a metaphysical question. In experienced time, all are aspects of the same phenomena. Our present concern is to investigate the features of those phenomena; metaphysics is still a long way off.

19. Time is "the form under which logic presents itself to objective intuition" (CP 6.87).

20. We should note that it is not oxygen but carbon (atomic weight 12) that today serves as the standard. Peirce's point is unaffected, however; *any* abundant and stable element might be chosen as the standard.

21. Helm, 378.

22. Heraclitus, Fragment 12, in G.S. Kirk, J. E. Raven, and M. Schofield, *The Presocratic Philosophers*, 2nd ed. (New York: Cambridge University Press, 1983), 194–95.

23. Heraclitus, Fragment 67, Ibid., 190.

24. This is an example of "the generalizing power of the mathematician," which Peirce mentions as essential to phenomenology in CP 5.42.

25. Raposa, 21.

26. Rosenthal, 39.

27. Raposa, 44–45.

28. Rosenthal, 124.

29. Ibid., 63–64.

30. It could be argued, as well, that some persons not from Western technological cultures might well find the psychological notion of "individual consciousness" odd, if not incomprehensible.

31. "Does 'Consciousness' Exist?" originally appeared in the *Journal of Philosophy, Psychology and Scientific Methods,* Vol. 1, No. 18, September 1, 1904.

32. In this brief statement, "idea" could be substituted for "phaneron" to name what is present to the mind during an infinitesimal moment. Peirce avoided speaking of "ideas," however, in an effort to avoid the psychological connotations that philosophers such as John Locke had attached to the term.

33. William James, *Principles of Psychology* (Cambridge: Harvard University Press, 1983), 219.

34. In fact, it is the fundamental continuity of inference, and the generality of the rules governing inference, that accounts for the continuity of time. Time is generated from the continuum of possibility that governs the process of representation, and functions as "the form under which logic presents itself to objective intuition" (CP 6.87).

CHAPTER 6

1. Potter, 40.

2. This passage, published in the *Monist* in 1893, is a none too subtle reference to

Andrew Carnegie's popular essay "The Gospel of Wealth," which originally appeared under the title "Wealth" in the *North American Review,* June 1889. The *Pall Mall Gazette* republished the essay in England at Gladstone's request, under the new title.

3. This way of presenting the relation among the categories is not exclusive of other characterizations, as all categories are present in some degree in any phenomenon. We might for other purposes say that Secondness, existence, is the bridge between the merely possible and what ought to be, or that Firstness is the limitless fund of mere possibility that enables the actual to evolve into the potential. In CP 1.362, for example, Peirce characterizes existence as the mediating element; in CP 5.433 he indicates that Thirdness mediates evolution.

4. In semeiotic, this notion is expressed in the assertion that *symbols* are living, growing things.

5. The phrase "eternal order of things" is the language of stasis, but the conception of continuity always implies, for Peirce, a continuity of process.

6. Likewise, ethics pertains to the operation of Secondness or existential action and esthetics concerns Firstness or quality of feeling.

7. Max H. Fisch observes that "there are, or may be, idioscopic studies of signs as various as the idioscopic sciences themselves." The "internal logics" mentioned in the previous paragraph are cases of *idioscopic* semeiotic, in the terminology Peirce borrowed from Bentham. Peirce sought to describe the general theory of sign-action which would be applicable to all such special inquiries—a *coenoscopic* semeiotic. Fisch, 339.

8. Felicia Kruse, "Nature and Semiosis," *Transactions* 26 (1990): 211–24, and "Is Cosmic Evolution Semiosis?" in *From Time and Chance to Consciousness,* ed. Edward C. Moore and Richard S. Robin (Providence, R.I.: Berg Publishers, 1994), 87–98.

9. David Savan, "Toward a Refutation of Semiotic Idealism," *RS/SI: Recherches Sémiotiques/Semiotic Inquiry* 3 (1983): 1–8.

10. See figure 7.3 and the accompanying discussion of the internal structure of a complete symbol.

11. Peirce adopted the terms 'speculative grammar' and 'speculative rhetoric' from medieval logic. "Speculative" is from the Latin translation of the Greek "theoretical." The medieval work on speculative grammar that apparently influenced Peirce the most was *De modis significandi, sive grammatica speculativa.* When Peirce wrote, this work was thought to be by Duns Scotus, but has since been attributed to Thomas of Erfurt. See Christian J. W. Kloesel, "Speculative Grammar: From Duns Scotus to Charles Peirce" in *Proceedings of the C. S. Peirce Bicentennial International Congress,* ed. Kenneth L. Ketner et al., Graduate Studies No. 23 (Lubbock: Texas Tech Press, 1981), 127–33.

12. Fisch identifies twenty-five stages in the development of Peirce's thought about semeiotic and the logic of mathematics. Many of these developments affect the basic conception of semeiotic, but the two I outline later are crucial. See Fisch, 330–37.

13. Peirce quotes from Locke (*An Essay Concerning Human Understanding,* Book iii, Ch. 2, Sections 4–7) in explicating the operation of a symbol. Peirce derived the notion that symbols are governed by "innate" principles of the association of ideas directly from Locke. Like Locke, Peirce was an empiricist, but Peirce's account of the origin of these principles is given in the mathematical and phenomenological account of the categories. There they are shown to have the a priori validity of any mathematical thought. Like all mathematical knowledge, though, they are discovered through a certain kind of observation or experience.

14. Nelson Goodman, *Languages of Art* (Indianapolis: Hackett, 1976) proposes just

this approach to artistic expression, though his effort does not draw explicitly on Peirce's philosophy.

15. Stechiology, and the variant Stecheotic, appear occasionally in place of Speculative Grammar as the name of the first division of semeiotic throughout the third period. See CP 4.9 and NEM 4:235–63 for this usage. The latter selection is a manuscript entitled καινά στοιχεῖα, "New Elements." In his lectures and publications, Peirce retained the name Speculative Grammar, although the conception of the first division of semeiotic had shifted.

16. Fisch, 339.

17. Of course, the broad features of the special subject-matter must already be familiar to the inquirer. Otherwise, careful inquiry would never be initiated.

18. Charles Morris, Thomas Sebeok, Umberto Eco, and David Savan are semioticians of particular note. Additionally, institutions such as the International Association for Semiotic Studies and journals such as *Semiotica* and *ars semeiotica* encourage the development of semiotics as a discipline.

19. Peirce sometimes calls this the *dynamic* or *dynamoid object*; he also refers to it as the *Real Object*.

20. Wittgenstein begins the *Tractatus Logico-Philosophicus* with the statement that "The world is all that is the case." Peirce's equivalent formulation would be that the complete dynamical object is all that is the case.

21. Buczyńska-Garewicz, "Sign and Continuity," 7.

22. See chapter 1, "First Impressions."

23. This is analogous to the problem of the origin of language, which proved so intractable that one society of linguists reportedly banned its discussion at their meetings in the early part of this century.

24. See chapter 5, figure 5.1.

25. Eco notes that the possibility of representation also allows the possibility of *mis*representation, of lying. The semiotic process involved in a lie is the same as that involved in an attempt to represent the truth. In the case of lying, the aim is to generate an interpretant that adequately represents a deceptive immediate object, one that is deliberately manipulated so as to distort the nature of the truth in the course of abstraction. He suggests that semiotics, as the theory of signs, be defined as "the discipline studying everything which can be used to lie." Umberto Eco, *A Theory of Semiotics* (Bloomington: Indiana University Press, 1976), 7.

26. In a letter to Lady Welby dated 14 December 1908, Peirce identified the three interpretants as the Destinate, Effective, and Explicit Interpretants. This letter appears to be a draft of the letter published as CP 8.342–79, however, where he uses the terminology adopted previously.

27. Note that the *ultimate* interpretant is different from the *final* (or *normal*) interpretant. The former has to do with the meaning of a sign, the latter with the truth of the sign. See the discussion in Short, 107.

28. Hanna Buczyńska-Garewicz, "The Idea of Object of Knowledge in Peirce's Theory of Signs" in *Proceedings of the C. S. Peirce Bicentennial International Congress*, ed. Kenneth L. Ketner et al., Graduate Studies No. 23 (Lubbock: Texas Tech Press, 1981), 42.

29. Fitzgerald lists Paul Weiss, Arthur Burks, Thomas Goudge, James Feibleman, Justice Buchler, and Manley Thompson among those who made this assumption. John J.

Fitzgerald, *Peirce's Theory of Signs as Foundation for Pragmatism,* Studies in Philosophy, No. 11 (The Hague: Mouton & Co., 1966), 78.

30. Ibid., 78–83.

31. Thomas L. Short, "Life among the Legisigns," in *Frontiers in Semiotics,* ed. John Deely, Brooke Williams, and Felicia Kruse (Bloomington: Indiana University Press, 1986), 107. Short also notes, however, that "everything I have said about interpretants . . . is contradicted at one place or another" in Peirce's writings.

32. Milton stated his intention at the beginning of Book I:

That to the highth of this great argument
I may assert Eternal Providence,
And justify the ways of God to men.

33. Short, 108.

34. NEM 4:248; Buczyńska-Garewicz, "Sign and Continuity," 6.

CHAPTER 7

1. The first classification appears in a manuscript extension of the 1903 "Syllabus," published in CP 2.233–68. The same classification also appears in SS 35–36. The second classification is presented in CP 8.343–76 and again in SS 83–85.

2. This summary of the two classifications is based on Irwin C. Lieb's account of the classifications in "Appendix B" of SS; Gary Sanders, "Peirce's Sixty-Six Signs?" *Transactions* 6 (1970): 3–16; T. L. Short, "Life Among the Legisigns," 107; and Richard J. Parmentier, "Peirce Divested for Non-Intimates," *RS/SI:Recherches Sémiotiques/Semiotic Inquiry* 7 (1987): 31–33. Sanders's article points out systematic errors in previous interpretations of the second classification, including Lieb's. Neither Sanders nor any other commentator I have encountered, however, has proposed an account of how the longer classification ought to be understood once these errors are taken into consideration.

3. Short, 109; CP 2.235–37; SS 84.

4. Indeed, anything there is will resemble anything else there is in *some* respect, and hence could conceivably function as an icon. Iconicity is such a loose connection that there are even icons of nonexistent objects, such as paintings of unicorns.

5. Robert Marty, "C. S. Peirce's Phaneroscopy and Semiotics," *Semiotica* 41 (1982): 176.

6. As such, the classes of signs also serve as a starting point for a systematic theory of what there is: Metaphysics builds upon semeiotic.

7. These passages from Locke and Reid are cited under "consciousness" in the *Compact Edition of the Oxford English Dictionary* (New York: Oxford University Press, 1971).

8. Even in the human sphere, we can identify any number of habits that are not preceded by the *conscious* formulation of a rule: accents, gestures, and patterns of neurotic behavior are a few examples.

9. Cf. CP 2.302.

10. The whole letter might be described as "A Short Introduction to C.S. Peirce"— he was introducing himself to Kehler in the letter. Fisch describes this letter as "the nearest thing to a retrospective summing up" of Peirce's thought on logic (Fisch, 337).

11. See chapter 1. The names in parentheses are variants. Peirce was never quite content with his terminology in this matter, although his conception of the three forms of inference stood virtually unchanged during almost fifty years of work in logic. The letter to Kehler includes a discussion of the origin of the term *induction,* which he traces to Cicero's Latinization of Socrates' ἐπαγωγή. Peirce suggested that a better translation would have been *adduction,* based on Aristotle's use of the word in the last chapter of the first book of the Topics (NEM 3:183, 190, 193). He accordingly uses "adduction" in parts of this letter and elsewhere. Peirce also comments that *retroduction* is "a poor name"—though he apparently had come to prefer it over *abduction* (NEM 3:206).

12. *Manuscript L 75,* Draft E, 164-65.

13. Peirce insisted that "it is quite a mistake to suppose that, for the purposes of the doctrine of chances, it suffices to suppose that the events in question are subject to unknown laws" (NEM 4:24, cf. 4:59–60). Induction cannot appeal to uniformities in nature governed by such unknown laws. The validity of induction must be established prior to the postulation of such laws, since it is only by inferring from limited samples to a general tendency that we could come to know of such uniformities in the first place. The supposition that there are unknown laws is a *result* of induction, not a condition for its success (NEM 3:203).

14. "We must accept the Deductive conclusion because we have already assented to it [in accepting the premisses], and consistency requires it. We accept the Adductive conclusion because though it may not be accurate, yet persistence in the same method of reasoning will diminish the error, if there be one, until it indefinitely approaches exactitude" (NEM 3:203).

15. Nicholas Rescher, *Peirce's Philosophy of Science* (Notre Dame: University of Notre Dame Press, 1978), 2–3 and throughout.

16. The last three of the whole series, Numbers 34 through 36, will not be discussed here. They were to illustrate how methodeutic applies to inquiry concerning the uniformity of nature, metaphysics, and the reality of time and space (NEM 3:31–32).

17. Peirce's writings on the economy of research are published in CP 7.139–61 and W 4:72–78. The ideas there presented are explicated and compared with some contemporary work in Rescher, chapter 4.

18. Ricardo published his major contribution, *Principles of Political Economy and Taxation,* in 1817. Peirce commented that the "chief fault" of economic analysis is that "no coefficient of average stupidity is introduced and no coefficient of average sentimentality, which could have been introduced into the formulae. Of course, their values would have to be determined for each class of society" (NEM 4:62). This appears in a discarded draft of the Carnegie Application; it is not clear whether Peirce was joking, or simply decided the world was not yet ready for this particular idea.

19. Karl R. Popper, *The Logic of Scientific Discovery* (New York: Harper and Row, 1968). Popper expresses his admiration for Peirce's work in *Of Clouds and Clocks: An Approach to the Problem of Rationality and the Freedom of Man,* The Arthur Holly Compton Memorial Lecture, Washington University, 1965 (St. Louis: Washington University, 1966), 5.

20. He was also unsure about how to arrange these three memoirs. In alternative drafts, "On the Course of Research" appears as the last of the three to be considered, rather than the first.

21. Thomas S. Kuhn, *The Structure of Scientific Revolutions,* 2nd enlarged ed., International Encyclopedia of Unified Science, vol. 2, no. 2 (Chicago: University of Chicago Press, 1970).

22. Rescher, 26. Alfred North Whitehead also proposed a similar view, asserting that over time scientific knowledge makes an asymptotical approach to the truth.

23. This is not to be confused with Popper's *falsifiability,* which has to do with the testability of a theory.

24. Fitzgerald, 154.

25. Note that in each case, the ongoing inquiry builds up our knowledge toward truth; but in neither case does the ongoing inquiry *create* truth. The adoption of the objectivity of truth as a metaphysical principle makes Peirce a realist, and he believed this realism decisively separated his "pragmaticism" from the "pragmatism" of James and Dewey.

26. For more on the role of sentiment in Peirce's philosophy, see John K. Sheriff, *Charles Peirce's Guess at the Riddle* (Bloomington: Indiana University Press, 1994), chapter 6.

CHAPTER 8

1. See, for example, Michael Raposa, *Peirce's Philosophy of Religion;* Joseph Esposito, *Evolutionary Metaphysics* (Athens, Ohio: Ohio University Press, 1980); and Carl R. Hausman, *Charles S. Peirce's Evolutionary Philosophy* (New York: Cambridge University Press, 1993).

2. Peirce saw the actual *practice* of modern science as involving the metaphysics of realism (CP 4.1). His concern was to remove the nominalism *ostensively* associated with science, so as to improve the state of metaphysics and to free science from the narrow conception of its own underpinnings that had been imposed upon it by philosophers.

3. See chapter 6, "Logical Critic."

4. Esposito, 127.

5. Peirce rendered the principle in these words: "Try the theory of fewest elements first; and only complicate it as such complication proves indispensable for the ascertainment of truth" (CP 4.35).

6. The following historical account appears in SS 114–16, CP 1.17–19, and is discussed in Boler, 19–20.

7. There are, of course, other reasons that could be offered to explain the persistence of nominalism. Politically, the nominalistic insistence upon the observation of particular facts is an antidote to the conservative force of tradition; and philosophically, some later Scotists undoubtedly did indulge in the kind of empty logical hair-splitting for which they were ridiculed.

8. Peirce sometimes distinguished cosmology from metaphysics proper: "So, instead of merely jeering at metaphysics . . . the pragmaticist extracts from it a precious essence, which will serve to give life and light to cosmology and physics" (CP 5.423). Because cosmology has to do with the origin of law itself, however, it seems more appropriate to consider this study as part of general metaphysics.

9. The matter of the testability and explanatory success of Peirce's metaphysics is considered later.

10. For Peirce, "The world does not consist of two mutually exclusive kinds of things, signs and non-signs. . . . The fundamental distinction is not between things that are signs and things that are not, but between triadic or sign-*action* and dynamic or dyadical *action.*" Fisch, 329–30.

11. For the connection between abduction and indeterminism, see the discussion of the emergence of pure possibility from the initial "zero-state" of Nothing in the section on "Speculative Cosmology," later in this chapter.

12. Likewise, if we characterize Peirce's metaphysics as panpsychist, we must also insist that it is panmaterialist. Though he adopted the language of the materialism-idealism debates, and embraced idealism, Peirce used this language to express a theory that is neither strictly materialistic nor strictly idealistic.

13. Hartshorne argues that "Peirce's greatest single mistake . . . was his 'Synechism', which consisted in trying to make continuity the key principle to every relationship, both of actuality and possibility." He writes: "Peirce looked upon time as the embodiment of this continuity. There is, he held, a real continuity of becoming, so that in the fraction of a second in which we see one color follow upon another we pass through all possible intermediate hues or tints." Charles Hartshorne, "Charles Peirce's 'One Contribution to Philosophy' and His Most Serious Mistake," *Studies in the Philosophy of Charles Sanders Peirce, Second Series,* ed. E. C. Moore and R. Robin (Amherst: University of Massachusetts Press, 1964), 467.

To claim that actuality is perfectly continuous would indeed be a serious mistake for Peirce; he claimed only that possibility is continuous (as Hartshorne notes), and that necessity or lawfulness, in so far as it obtains in the experienced world, is also continuous. We have seen already that he denied the perfect continuity of time; as we shall see later, in "The Problem of Extra-Semiotic Entities," the fact that perceptual judgments often *are* discontinuous with antecedent cognitions is a primary reason why Peirce posited an extra-semiotic mode of being, *existence.*

14. Cosmological speculation, like geometry, merely describes the consequences that follow from given hypotheses. In this aspect it is a priori, though it does not possess a formal deductive procedure as rigorous as that of geometry. The cosmologist does have recourse to experience to check the suitability of a system, as does the mathematician who, possessing a variety of alternative geometries, proceeds to ask the cosmological question "which one best describes reality?"

15. Nonetheless, because it is in principle not possible for science to explain or predict a *spontaneous* deviation from laws, "no phenomena ever have resulted which we are forced to attribute to such chance concentrations of heat, or which anybody, wise or foolish, has ever dreamed of accounting for in that manner" (CP 6.47).

16. Although Peirce discussed indeterminacy in physical events at the atomic and molecular level, his theory suggests that it should appear at other levels of physical organization as well. We should, however, be careful not to read too much into his insistence upon indeterminism. As Ketner and Putnam point out, Peirce in no way supposed that indeterminacy is *ubiquitous* at the subatomic level, as modern physics suggests. Ketner and Putnam, "Some Comments on the Lectures," Lecture Seven, *Reasoning and the Logic of Things.*

17. At William James's urging, Peirce abandoned these drafts for the more popularly oriented lectures on *Reasoning and the Logic of Things.*

18. Peirce's three-valued logic, as we have seen, provides a way to deal with the concern that this notion of the individual is not absolutely valid for all of logic. Thus while the practical applications of the three-valued system may be limited, the triadic logic serves as the basis for Peirce's metaphysics.

19. Boler, 51.

20. I wish to acknowledge a considerable debt, in what follows, to the discussion of the forms of evolution presented in Raposa, 72–82.

21. Carl R. Hausman, "Eros and Agape in Creative Evolution: A Peircean Insight" *Process Studies* 4 (1974): 15.

22. Ibid., 17.

23. Savan defines *semiotic idealism* in general by defining its "strong" and "mild" forms, which are discussed below. If we want a general definition, we may accept Jeremiah McCarthy's: semiotic idealism is "a form of idealism according to which all real things are signs." Jeremiah McCarthy, Semiotic Idealism, unpublished typescript, 1.

24. Fisch, 330.

25. Savan, 1.

26. Ibid., 1, 7.

27. Ibid., 7.

28. Ibid., 6.

29. Calculations are simpler without the apparatus which allows us to avoid using the paradoxical infinitesimal quantities. See Davis and Hersh, 81.

30. Edward C. Moore, "On an Alleged Incompatibility between Peirce's Metaphysics and His Pragmatism," *Proceedings of the C. S. Peirce Bicentennial International Congress,* ed. K. Ketner et al. (Lubbock: Texas Tech University Press, 1981), 169.

31. Ibid., 170–71.

32. Ibid., 171. Moore also discusses the notion of indeterminacy in biology and the social sciences, but these examples from physics are the most compelling.

33. John McDermott, "The Aesthetic Drama of the Ordinary," in *Streams of Experience* (Amherst: University of Massachusetts Press, 1986), 134.

34. See CP 1.673 and the discussion of this theme in Parker, "Peirce's Philosophy of Religion."

35. Kant, *Critique of Pure Reason,* A824, B852.

Works Cited

BIBLIOGRAPHIES OF PEIRCE'S WRITINGS

Ketner, Kenneth L. *A Comprehensive Bibliography of the Published Works of Charles Sanders Peirce with a Bibliography of Secondary Studies.* 2d edition, revised. Bowling Green, Ohio: Philosophy Documentation Center, 1986.
Robin, Richard S. *Annotated Catalogue of the Papers of Charles S. Peirce.* Amherst: University of Massachusetts Press, 1967.
———. "The Peirce Papers: A Supplementary Catalogue." *Transactions* 7 (1971): 37–57.

WRITINGS BY CHARLES S. PEIRCE

The Charles S. Peirce Papers. Originals housed in the Houghton Library, Harvard University, Cambridge, Massachusetts. Copies housed in the offices of the Peirce Edition Project, Indiana University–Purdue University at Indianapolis, Indiana.
Collected Papers of Charles Sanders Peirce. 8 vols. Vols. 1–6 edited by Charles Hartshorne and Paul Weiss. Vols. 7–8 edited by Arthur Burks. Cambridge: Harvard University Press, 1931–35, 1958.
Manuscript L 75: Application to the Carnegie Institution. Edited by Joseph Ransdell. Online electronic text. Peirce Telecommunity Project, 1993.
The New Elements of Mathematics. 4 vols. Edited by Carolyn Eisele. The Hague: Mouton Publishers, 1976.
Reasoning and the Logic of Things: The Cambridge Conferences Lectures of 1898. Edited by Kenneth L. Ketner. Cambridge: Harvard University Press, 1992.
Semiotic and Significs: The Correspondence between Charles S. Peirce and Victoria Lady Welby. Edited by Charles Hardwick. Bloomington: Indiana University Press, 1977.
Studies in Logic by Members of the Johns Hopkins University (1883). Edited by Charles S. Peirce. Reprinted in Foundations of Semiotics, vol. 1. Achim Eisbach, general editor. Philadelphia: John Benjamins Publishing, 1983.
Writings Of Charles S. Peirce: A Chronological Edition. 5 vols. to date. Edited by Edward Moore, Christian J. W. Kloesel, et al. Bloomington: Indiana University Press, 1982–.

WRITINGS BY OTHER AUTHORS

Boler, John F. *Charles Peirce and Scholastic Realism.* Seattle: University of Washington Press, 1963.
Brent, Joseph. *Charles Sanders Perice: A Life.* Bloomington: Indiana University Press, 1993.
Buczyńska-Garewicz, Hanna. "The Idea of Object of Knowledge in Peirce's Theory of

Signs." *Proceedings of the C. S. Peirce Bicentennial International Congress*. Edited by Kenneth L. Ketner et al. Graduate Studies No. 23. Lubbock: Texas Tech Press, 1981, 35–43.

———. "Sign and Continuity." *ars semeiotica* 2 (1978): 3–15.

Burch, Robert W. *A Peircean Reduction Thesis: The Foundations of Topological Logic*. Philosophical Inquiries No. 1. Lubbock: Texas Tech University Press, 1991.

Cantor, Georg. "Beiträge zur Begründung der transfiniten Mengenlehre," *Mathematische Annalen* 46 (1895), 49 (1897). Translated by Philip E. B. Jourdain, in *Contributions to the Founding of the Theory of Transfinite Numbers*. New York: Dover, 1952.

———. "Grundlagen einer allgemeinen Mannichfaltigkeitslehre." Leipzig, 1883.

———. "Mitteilungen zur Lehre vom Transfiniten." *Zeitschrift für Philos. und philos. Kritik* 91 (1887), 92 (1888).

Davis, Martin and Reuben Hersh. "Nonstandard Analysis." *Scientific American* 226 (June 1972): 78–86.

De Morgan, Augustus. "On the Syllogism IV, and the Logic of Relations." *Cambridge Philosophical Transactions* 10 (1859): 331–58.

De Tienne, André. "Peirce's Early Method of Finding the Categories." *Transactions* 25 (1989): 385–406.

Eco, Umberto. *A Theory of Semiotics*. Bloomington: Indiana University Press, 1976.

Eisele, Carolyn. *Studies in the Scientific and Mathematical Philosophy of Charles S. Peirce*. New York: Mouton Publishers, 1979.

Esposito, Joseph. *Evolutionary Metaphysics*. Athens, Ohio: Ohio University Press, 1980.

Fisch, Max H. "Peirce's General Theory of Signs," in *Peirce, Semeiotic, and Pragmatism*. Edited by Kenneth L. Ketner and Christian J. W. Kloesel. Bloomington: Indiana University Press, 1986.

———. "Peirce as Scientist, Mathemetician, Historian, Logician, and Philosopher, in *Peirce, Semeiotic, and Pragmatism*. Edited by Kenneth L. Ketner and Christian J. W. Kloesel. Bloomington: Indiana University Press, 1986, 376–400.

Fisch, Max H., Kenneth L. Ketner, and Christian J. W. Kloesel. "The New Tools of Peirce Scholarship, with Particular Reference to Semiotic." *Studies in Peirce's Semiotic*. Peirce Studies No. 1. Lubbock, Texas: Institute for Studies in Pragmaticism, Texas Tech University, 1979, 1–17.

Fisch, Max H. and Atwell Turquette. "Peirce's Triadic Logic." *Transactions* 2 (1966): 71–85.

Fitzgerald, John J. *Peirce's Theory of Signs as Foundation for Pragmatism*. Studies in Philosophy No. 11. The Hague: Mouton, 1966.

Fraenkel, Abraham A. *Abstract Set Theory*. 2nd edition, revised. Studies in Logic and the Foundations of Mathematics. Edited by L. E. J. Brouwer et al. Amsterdam: North-Holland Publishing, 1961.

Goodman, Nelson. *Languages of Art*. Indianapolis: Hackett Publishing, 1976.

Goudge, Thomas A. *The Thought of C. S. Peirce*. Toronto: University of Toronto Press, 1950.

Hartshorne, Charles. "Charles Peirce's 'One Contribution to Philosophy' and His Most Serious Mistake." *Studies in the Philosophy of Charles Sanders Peirce*, 2nd series. Edited by E. C. Moore and R. Robin. Amherst: University of Massachusetts Press, 1964, 455–474.

Hausman, Carl R. *Charles S. Peirce's Evolutionary Philosophy.* New York: Cambridge University Press, 1993.

———. "Eros and Agape in Creative Evolution: A Peircean Insight." *Process Studies* 4 (1974): 11–25.

Hegel, G. W. F. *Hegel's Logic: Being Part One of the "Encyclopaedia of the Philosophical Sciences".* Trans. W. Wallace. Oxford: Clarendon Press, 1975.

Helm, Bertrand P. "The Nature and Modes of Time." *Monist* 63 (1980): 375–85.

Herzberger, Hans G. "Peirce's Remarkable Theorem." *Pragmatism and Purpose.* Edited by L. W. Sumner, John G. Slater, and Fred Wilson. Toronto: University of Toronto Press, 1981, 41–58.

Houser, Nathan. "La Structure formelle de l'expérience selon Peirce." *Études Phénoménologiques* 5 (1989): 77–111.

Hume, David. *An Enquiry Concerning Human Understanding.* Edited by Antony Flew. LaSalle, Illinois: Open Court, 1988.

James, William. "Does 'Consciousness' Exist?" *Essays in Radical Empiricism.* Cambridge: Harvard University Press, 1976, 3–19.

———. "The Moral Philosopher and the Moral Life." *The Will to Believe and Other Essays in Popular Philosophy.* Cambridge: Harvard University Press, 1979, 141–62.

———. *A Pluralistic Universe.* Cambridge: Harvard University Press, 1977.

———. *Principles of Psychology.* Cambridge: Harvard University Press, 1983.

———. *The Writings of William James.* Edited by John J. McDermott. Chicago: University of Chicago Press, 1977.

Kant, Immanuel. *Critique of Pure Reason.* Translated by Norman Kemp Smith. New York: St. Martin's Press, 1965.

———. *Grounding for the Metaphysics of Morals.* Translated by James W. Ellington. Indianapolis: Hackett Publishing, 1981.

Kent, Beverley. *Charles S. Peirce: Logic and the Classification of the Sciences.* Montreal: McGill-Queen's University Press, 1987.

Ketner, Kenneth L. "Peirce's 'Most Lucid and Interesting Paper': An Introduction to Cenopythagoreanism." *International Philosophical Quarterly* 26 (1986): 375–92.

Ketner, Kenneth L. and Hilary Putnam. "Introduction: Consequences of Mathematics." *Reasoning and the Logic of Things: The 1898 Cambridge Conferences Lectures.* Edited by Kenneth L. Ketner. Cambridge: Harvard University Press, 1992.

Kirk, G. S., J. E. Raven, and M. Schofield. *The Presocratic Philosophers.* 2nd edition. New York: Cambridge University Press, 1983.

Kloesel, Christian J. W. "Speculative Grammar: From Duns Scotus to Charles Peirce." *Proceedings of the C. S. Peirce Bicentennial International Congress.* Edited by Kenneth L. Ketner et al. Graduate Studies No. 23. Lubbock: Texas Tech Press, 1981, 127–33.

Kretzman, Norman, editor. *Infinity and Continuity in Ancient and Medieval Thought.* Ithaca: Cornell University Press, 1982.

Kruse, Felicia. "Genuineness and Degeneracy in Peirce's Categories." *Transactions* 27 (1991): 267–98.

———. "Is Cosmic Evolution Semiosis?" In *From Time and Chance to Consciousness.* Edited by Edward C. Moore and Richard S. Robin. Providence, R.I.: Berg Publishers, 1994, 87–98.

———. "Nature and Semiosis." *Transactions* 26 (1990): 211–24.

Kuhn, Thomas S. *The Structure of Scientific Revolutions.* 2nd enlarged edition.

International Encyclopedia of Unified Science, Vol. 2, No. 2. Chicago: University of Chicago Press, 1970.

Lango, John W. "Whitehead's Actual Occasions and the New Infinitesimals." *Transactions* 25 (1989): 29–39.

Liszka, James Jakób. "Peirce's Interpretant." *Transactions* 26 (1990): 17–62.

MacIntyre, Alasdair. *Three Rival Versions of Moral Enquiry: Encyclopaedia,Genealogy, and Tradition.* Notre Dame: University of Notre Dame Press, 1990.

Marty, Robert. "C. S. Peirce's Phaneroscopy and Semiotics." *Semiotica* 41 (1982): 169–81.

Mates, Benson. *The Philosophy of Leibniz: Metaphysics and Language.* New York: Oxford University Press, 1986.

McCarthy, Jeremiah E. Semiotic Idealism. Unpublished typescript. Revision of "Semiotic Idealism." *Transactions* 20 (1984): 395–433.

McDermott, John J. "The Aesthetic Drama of the Ordinary." *Streams of Experience.* Amherst: University of Massachusetts Press, 1986, 129–40.

Moore, A. W. *The Infinite.* The Problems of Philosophy: Their Past and Present. Ted Honderich, general editor. New York: Routledge, 1990.

Moore, Edward C. "On an Alleged Incompatibility between Peirce's Metaphysics and His Pragmatism." *Proceedings of the C. S. Peirce Bicentennial International Congress.* Edited by Kenneth L. Ketner et al. Graduate Studies No. 23. Lubbock: Texas Tech Press, 1981, 169–78.

Murdoch, John E. "Infinity and Continuity." *The Cambridge History of Later Medieval Philosophy.* Edited by Norman Kretzman et al. New York: Cambridge University Press, 1982.

Murphey, Murray G. *The Development of Peirce's Philosophy.* Cambridge: Harvard University Press, 1961. Reprinted with new preface and appendix. Indianapolis: Hackett Publishing, 1993.

Myrvold, Wayne C. "Peirce on Cantor's Paradox and the Continuum." *Transactions* 31 (1995): 508–41.

Noble, N. A. Brian. "Peirce's Definitions of Continuity and the Concept of Possibility." *Transactions* 25 (1989): 149–74.

Orange, Donna M. *Peirce's Conception of God.* Peirce Studies No. 2. Lubbock, Texas: Institute for Studies in Pragmaticism, Texas Tech University, 1984.

Parker, Kelly. "C. S. Peirce and the Philosophy of Religion." *Southern Journal of Philosophy* 28 (1990): 193–213.

———. "Peirce's Semeiotic and Ontology." *Transactions* 30 (1994): 51–75.

Parmentier, Richard J. "Peirce Divested for Non-Intimates." *RS/SI: Recherches Sémiotiques/Semiotic Inquiry* 7 (1987): 19–39.

Plato. *Gorgias.* Translated by Donald J. Zeyl. Indianapolis: Hackett Publishing, 1987.

Popper, Karl R. *The Logic of Scientific Discovery.* New York: Harper and Row, 1968.

———. *Of Clouds and Clocks: An Approach to the Problem of Rationality and the Freedom of Man.* The Arthur Holly Compton Memorial Lecture, Washington University, 1965. St. Louis: Washington University, 1966.

Potter, Vincent G. *Charles S. Peirce on Norms and Ideals.* Amherst: University of Massachusetts Press, 1967.

Potter, Vincent G., and Paul B. Shields. "Peirce's Definitions of Continuity." *Transactions* 13 (1977): 20–34.

Quine, Willard V. O. *Mathematical Logic.* Cambridge: Harvard University Press, 1947.

Raposa, Michael L. *Peirce's Philosophy of Religion.* Peirce Studies No. 5. Bloomington: Indiana University Press, 1989.

Rescher, Nicholas. *Peirce's Philosophy of Science.* Notre Dame: University of Notre Dame Press, 1978.

Riemann, Bernhard. "On the Hypotheses Which Lie at the Basis of Geometry." Translated by W. K. Clifford. *Nature* 7 (May 1873): 14–17, 36, 37.

Roberts, Don D. *The Existential Graphs of Charles S. Peirce.* The Hague: Mouton, 1973.

Robinson, Abraham. *Non-Standard Analysis.* London: North-Holland Publishing, 1966.

———. *Selected Papers of Abraham Robinson,* vol. 2. Edited by H. J. Keisler et al. New Haven: Yale University Press, 1979.

Rosenthal, Sandra. *Speculative Pragmatism.* La Salle, Illinois: Open Court, 1986.

Sanders, Gary. "Peirce's Sixty-Six Signs?" *Transactions* 6 (1970): 3–16.

Savan, David. "Toward a Refutation of Semiotic Idealism." *RS/SI: Recherches Sémiotiques/Semiotic Inquiry* 3 (1983): 1–8.

Schroeder, Ernst. *Vorlesungen ueber die Algebra der Logik,* vol. 1. Leipzig: Teubner, 1890.

Seligman, George B. "Biography of Abraham Robinson." *Selected Papers of Abraham Robinson,* vol. 2. Edited by H. J. Keisler et al. New Haven: Yale University Press, 1979.

Sheriff, John K. *Charles Peirce's Guess at the Riddle.* Bloomington: Indiana University Press, 1994.

Short, Thomas L. "Life among the Legisigns." *Frontiers in Semiotics.* Edited by John Deely, Brooke Williams, and Felicia Kruse. Bloomington: Indiana University Press, 1986, 105–19.

Sowa, John. "Matching Logical Structure to Linguistic Structure." *Studies in the Logic of Charles Sanders Peirce.* Edited by N. Houser, D. Roberts, and J. Van Evra, 418–44. Bloomington: Indiana University Press, 1997.

Stoll, Robert R. *Set Theory and Logic.* San Francisco: W. H. Freeman, 1963.

Thompson, Manley. *The Pragmatic Philosophy of C. S. Peirce.* Chicago: University of Chicago Press, 1953.

Turquette, Atwell R. "Peirce's Complete System of Triadic Logic." *Transactions* 5 (1969): 199–210.

———. "Peirce's *Phi* and *Psi* Operators for Triadic Logic." *Transactions* 3 (1967): 66–73.

Whitehead, Alfred North, and Bertrand Russell. *Principia Mathematica.* Cambridge: Cambridge University Press, 1910–1913.

Wittgenstein, Ludwig. *Philosophical Investigations.* 3rd Edition. Translated by G. E. M. Anscombe. New York: Macmillan, 1958.

———. *Tractatus Logico-Philosophicus.* Translated by C. K. Ogden. New York: Routledge, 1922.

Zeman, J. Jay. "Peirce's Graphs—the Continuity Interpretation." *Transactions* 4 (1968): 144–54.

Index

abduction. *See* retroduction

abstraction, 120–21; in representation of object, 146, 148–49

Achilles paradox, 11, 21–22. *See also* Zeno of Elea

action, 53; dyadic, 197, 199; and ethics, 130–31, 133; and semiosis, 151; sign, 251n.10; and thought, 52; triadic, 133, 134, 197, 199

actuality: in phenomena, 113; and possibility, 119, 120–21; universe of, 211–14. *See also* Secondness

adduction. *See* induction

agapism: in evolutionary theory, 16, 216–19; and inquiry, 228

Agassiz, Louis, 33, 180

analytic, 141. *See also* stecheotic

anancasticism. *See* necessity in evolution

Arabian Nights, 64

architectonic philosophy, xi, xii–xiii, 2–27; and classification of sciences, 57–58; development of, 60–61, 141; fallibilism in, 29; hypotheses in, 87

argument, 168–69; as class of sign, 157, 158 table 7.3, 159, 162–63; as conclusion to inference, 166; leading principles of, 5–6, 118, 169; as symbol, 161; universe as, 204. *See also* critic; inference, forms of

Arisbe, xi

Aristotle, 11; categories of, 2, 105, 197; on causation, 115, 183; and entelechy, 152–53, 203

arithmetic, 43

art, 160–61

Baynes, Thomas Spencer, 33

beauty, 185; and esthetics, 50

Being, 60

belief, pragmatic, 228

Bentham, Jeremy, 237n.16

Berkeley, George, 13

Boole, George, 24

Buddhism, 132–33

Buczyńska-Garewicz, Hanna, 148

calculus: in classification of sciences, 44; and infinitesimals, 97

Cantor, Georg, 17; and analytic continuum, 84–85, 97; on infinitesimals, 92–93; and "pseudo-continua," 44; theory of infinite sets, 75–86, 101. *See also* continuum hypothesis

Cantor's Theorem, 27, 76, 80

cardinality, 44, 93; defined, 76; Peirce on, 79, 81

Carnegie, Andrew, 246n.2

Carnegie Institution, xv, 232n.9

categories: and architectonic philosophy, xiii; and cosmology, 210, 213–14; interrelations among, 120–22; in Kant, 2–4, 28–29, 60; and logic, 2–4, 7, 9, 17–19, 30, 61–63; and metaphysics, 39, 196–97, 200, 202, 207; nomenclature for, 232n.1; and normative science, 131, 133; particular, 105–06; phenomenological, 105, 112–16; and relations, 63; and semeiotic, 154, 162; universal, 48, 105–6, 108. *See also* Firstness; reduction thesis; Secondness; Thirdness

cause, 134, 183–84; in evolution, 216. *See also* efficient cause; final cause

chance. *See* tychism

change, 111

chemistry, 63

Christianity, 132–33

circularity: in definition of continuity, 116–18; in derivation of categories, 18, 68

class, natural. *See* natural class

classification, principles of, 35–36, 179. *See also* signs, classification of; sciences, classification of

Coast Survey. *See* U. S. Coast and Geodetic Survey

259

INDEX

reference, 140–42, 161
regress, infinite: in origin of cognition, 11–12, 17, 21; in semiosis, 149, 215. *See also* Zeno of Elea
regularity: and law, 115
Reid, Thomas, 164
relations: continuous, 69, 71, 95; in experience, 105; forms of, 42; genuine and degenerate, 63–65; and iconic representation, 139; infinite, 71; necessary number of, 66–68, 121; of reason, 64
relations, logic of, 44; and categories, 61–62; chemical model for, 63; development, 24; and mathematics of logic, 39, 42, 45, 141; notation, 65–66; and phenomenology, 121; and proof of infinitesimals, 97, 98–99
relativity, theory of, 224
religion, 227, 231n.5
replica: of legisign, 156–57; in mathematics, 65; and sign, 153–54
representamen, 137, 145, 147; and non-human interpreter, 165; and object, 156–57; as replica or token, 153–54, 155–56
representation: and being, 197, 215; defined, 9; phenomena as, 5, 19, 126; philosophy of, 136
Rescher, Nicholas, 175, 179
retroduction, 6, 9, 176; in cosmology, 209; in nature, 184, 199–200; and normative logic, 45; and perception, 32; and qualitative induction, 175
rheme, 157–58, 162–63; examples of, 159
Ricardo, David, 177
Riemann, Bernhard, 25, 242n.46
right, 183, 185
Robinson, Abraham, 98–99, 223–24
Rosenthal, Sandra, 106, 123
Russell, Bertrand, 65

sampling, 172–74, 180, 226
Santayana, George, 115
Savan, David, 135, 219–22
Schiller, F. C. S., 234n.32
science, 34, 36, 37 figure 2.1, 38, 231n.5; encyclopedic conception, 33; and

faith, 186; forensic, 160; and instinct, 129; of metaphysics, 189–97; normal, 179–80; philosophy of, 33, 177, 179–81. *See also* sciences
sciences, xiv, 30, 57, 143–44; classification of, 28–58, 37 figure 2.1, 179, 190
Secondness: as existence, 112–13, 119; and habit, 166, 183; and normative science, 131; in phenomena, 48, 54, 108; and physicalism, xii, xiii, 200; and quantification, 62; and semiosis, 151; in signs, 155–58, 163, 167; and summum bonum, 129. *See also* categories
self, 122–27
self-control, 49, 131, 170, 176, 184–85; in development of universe, 215, 223, 227
semeiotic, 100, 134–54, 155–87, 189, 231n.5; conception of self, 122, 123; divisions of, 136–43; and logic, 134; and metaphysics, 55, 135–36, 197–200, 202–4, 198–200; normative, 53, 54; as science, 143–44, 153; variant spellings, 231n.5
semiosis, 134–36; as continuum, 149; and cosmology, 215–18; end of, 221; in non-human systems, 165–67; reality as, 202, 222
semiotic. *See* semeiotic
sentiment, 187
set theory: definitions in, 75–79; development of transfinite, 26–27. *See also* Cantor's theorem; continuum
Shields, Paul B., 86
Short, Thomas L., 152
sign: defined, 136–37, 144–45; and replica, 153–54; self as, 122; universe as, 203–4. *See also* semeiotic; semiosis; signs, classification of
sign vehicle. *See* representamen
significance. *See* meaning
signs, classification of: early, 7, 8; mature, 153, 155–63, 158 table 7.3; and metaphysics, 199
singular, 213
sinsign, 156, 158 table 7.3, 162–63; examples of, 159; and ontology, 202–3

social sciences. *See* psychical sciences
Socrates, 46
space, 112, 211–12, 246n.16; and potentiality, 122
special sciences. *See* idioscopy
speculative grammar, 140–41. *See also*
  stecheotic
speculative rhetoric, 140–41. *See also*
  methodeutic
Spencer, Herbert, 15
statistical syllogism, 171, 173
stecheotic, 143–54; in classification of sciences, 53; and metaphysics, 57, 197.
  See also semeiotic, divisions of
stechiology, 141
Stoll, Robert B., 75
subject, 107, 111–12, 190
substance, 60, 119, 212–14
summum bonum, 50–52, 129–33; and
  evolution, 216–17; and inquiry,
  176–77, 185, 223; and metaphysics,
  196, 203, 215, 218; and semiosis,
  150, 152–53, 168. *See also* good, ultimate
surprise, 106, 220
symbol, 158 table 7.3, 162; defined, 157;
  in early classification, 8, 10, 137–39;
  examples of, 159; general as, 198;
  internal structure of, 163 figure 7.1;
  and ontology, 203, 215; perfect, 221
syllogistic forms: and cognition, 22; non-
  reducibility of, 4. *See also* inference,
  forms of
symbolic logic. *See* deduction; relations,
  logic of
synechism, xv, 186, 200; and continuity,
  16; and evolution, 217–19; and existential graphs, 95; as hypothesis, 205,
  223–28; and reason, 57, 204,
  222–23; and synectics, xiii; and time,
  110
synectics, xiii, 44
systematic philosophy. *See* architectonic
  philosophy

teleology: in evolutionary theory, 15,
  216–18; in metaphysics, 200, 215; in
  phenomena, 115–16; in representa-

tion, 127, 150–53, 168, 198. *See also*
  final cause
term, 63. *See also* rheme
Thirdness: and continuity, xiii, 62–63,
  117, 149; and habit, 166, 183, 200;
  and idealism, xiii; as interpretant,
  151; as lawfulness, 112, 115; and
  logic of relations, 25; and normative
  science, 131–32, 142; and personality, 126; in phenomena, 48, 54; as
  possibility, 114–15; in signs, 155–58,
  163, 168; and summum bonum, 129,
  133. *See also* categories
Thomas of Erfurt, 247n.11
thought: as action, 52; continuum of, 23,
  54, 122–27, 131, 243n.63; in Hegel,
  183; and language, 239n.21; in non-
  human systems, 167; as semiosis,
  142, 149; value of, 227. *See also* mind
time: continuity of, 85, 88, 110–12; origin
  of, 210–11; as phenomenon, 109,
  116; and potentiality, 122; and reality, 129, 215
token: as symbol, 139; and type, 153–54
topical geometry, 86, 94. *See also* synectics
transcendental deduction: impossibility of,
  17–19, 29, 68
transcendental object, 4, 19–21
transfinite sets, 17, 26–27; and cardinal
  numbers, 76; and infinitesimals,
  92–93; and ordinal numbers, 78–79;
  Peirce's nomenclature for, 81. *See also*
  infinity; continuity; continuum
triad, 64–65, 99; necessity of, 66–67; as
  primitive, 69, 70, 94, 99; sign as,
  153, 159–60, 215; and Thirdness, 63
truth: absolute, 14, 198, 203, 215, 218,
  227; and being, 146, 183; and fallibilism, 180; and induction, 172; and
  logic, 45, 53, 142; as object of argument, 169; as postulate for inquiry,
  186; pragmatic definition of, 192,
  245n.13; and purpose of inquiry,
  176, 185, 228; and realism, 191–92,
  219–22; and semiosis, 150–53, 168
tychism, 200, 207, 210; in evolutionary
  theory, 16, 216–17, 219; and qualisign, 202; and three-valued logic, 73

KELLY A. PARKER is assistant professor of philosophy at Grand Valley State University, in Allendale, Michigan. His research and publications focus primarily on American pragmatism and environmental philosophy.

THE CONTINUITY OF PEIRCE'S THOUGHT

was composed electronically using
Berkeley Book typefaces, with displays in
Berkeley, Berkeley Black, Berkeley Bold, and Futura Bold.
The book was printed on 60# Natural Smooth acid-free paper,
and was Smyth sewn and cased in Pearl Linen
by BookCrafters.
The dust jacket was printed in three colors by
Vanderbilt University Printing Services.
Book and dust jacket designs are the work of Deborah Hightower.
Published by Vanderbilt University Press
Nashville, Tennessee 37235